Civil War Boston

~ ~ ~ ~ ~ ~ ~

"Home from the War," Harper's Weekly, *June 13, 1863*

Civil War Boston
Home Front and Battlefield

~ ~ ~ ~ ~ ~ ~

Thomas H. O'Connor

Northeastern University Press

BOSTON

Library of Congress Cataloging-in-Publication Data
O'Connor, Thomas H., 1922–
Civil War Boston : home front and battlefield / Thomas H.
O'Connor
p. cm.
Includes bibliographical references and index.
ISBN 1-55553-318-3 (acid-free paper)
1. Boston (Mass.)—History—Civil War, 1861–1865. 2. Boston
(Mass.)—History—Civil War, 1861–1865—Social Aspects. I. Title
F73.44.O25 1997
974.4'6103—dc21 97-15747

Designed by Joyce C. Weston

Composed in Sabon by Graphic Composition, Inc., Athens, Georgia.
Printed and bound by Edwards Brothers, Inc., Ann Arbor, Michigan.
The paper is Glatfelter Offset, an acid-free stock.

MANUFACTURED IN THE UNITED STATES OF AMERICA
01 00 99 98 97 5 4 3 2 1

~ ~ ~ ~ ~ ~ ~

TO MARY
with love, always

Contents

~ ~ ~ ~ ~ ~ ~

Illustrations

~ ~ ~ ~ ~ ~ ~

~ ~ ~ ~ ~ ~ ~

Bow down, dear Land, for thou hast found release!
Thy God, in these distempered days,
Hath taught thee sure wisdom of His ways,

And through thine enemies hath wrought thy peace!
Bow down in prayer and praise!

No poorest in thy borders but may now
Lift to the juster skies a man's enfranchised brow.
O Beautiful! my Country! ours once more!

—James Russell Lowell
Ode Recited at the Harvard
Commemoration, July 21, 1865

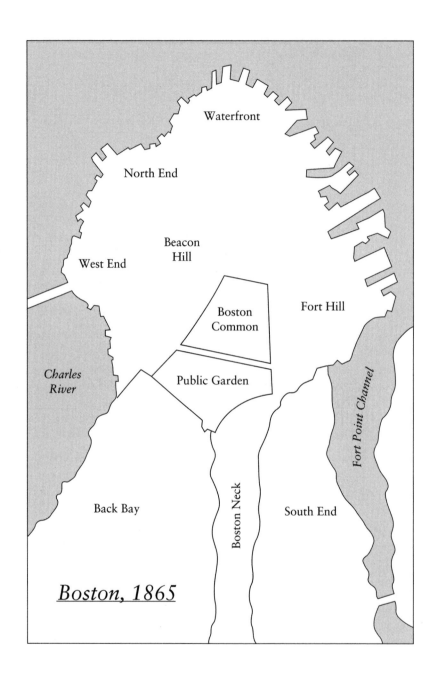

Waterfront

North End

Beacon
Hill

West End

Boston
Common

Fort Hill

Charles
River

Public Garden

Fort Point Channel

Back Bay

Boston Neck

South End

Boston, 1865

Introduction

~ ~ ~ ~ ~ ~ ~

The origins of this work go back more than thirty years, to the mid-1960s, when, as a young assistant professor of history, I was appointed to the Massachusetts Civil War Centennial Commission. Engaging in community events and activities commemorating the hundredth anniversary of the Civil War, I was impressed by the incredible number of books that had been written about the military history of the war—the late Bruce Catton was perhaps the most prolific and popular author at that time—and the numerous specialized studies that had been done about the Bay State's part in the slavery controversy and the abolition movement. I did not, however, find many works about the unique part that Boston and Bostonians had in the war or, more to the point, about overall effects the war itself might have had on the Boston community. And here, too, I found that not a great deal had been done on identifying and assessing the groups that made up the Boston community during the Civil War years, or on providing an understandable synthesis of those elements as a whole instead of focusing on the separate parts.

Certainly over the years specialized studies have analyzed the history of individual groups in the Boston community. Oscar Handlin's study, *Boston's Immigrants* (Cambridge, 1941), is a classic and invaluable study of the early years of Boston's Irish population to which all scholars are deeply indebted. James and Lois Horton published a pioneering study, *Black Bostonians* (New York, 1979), which traces the city's African-American population from the early history of the Republic to the Civil War. Richard H. Abbott, in his *Cotton and Capital* (Amherst, 1991), has more recently expanded the study of Boston's businessmen beyond the antebellum influence of the Cotton Whigs I described in my own *Lords of the Loom* (New York, 1968) to cover the more complex activities of the city's financial leaders during the Civil War and Reconstruction. And women writers like Nancy Cott, with her *Bonds of Womanhood* (New Haven, 1977), and Catherine Clinton and Nina Silber, with their

Divided Houses: Gender and the Civil War (New York, 1992), are currently opening up new and exciting vistas on women's changing role in the mid-nineteenth century. Stimulating and significant works such as these have kept the idea of a historical synthesis alive in the back of my mind all these years, but different interests and other commitments kept it from coming to the fore-front—until recently.

The stimulus that finally forced the idea into the open came when I read Doris Kearns Goodwin's Pulitzer Prize–winning book, *No Ordinary Time* (New York, 1994). Because the period about which she wrote was definitely "my" time—those critical wartime years during which I moved from adolescence to maturity—I was absorbed by the work and fascinated by the perceptive ideas with which it was filled. Although Goodwin mainly focused upon the complex relationship between Franklin and Eleanor Roosevelt, she also described the many ways in which the climactic events in World War II changed forever the lives of many ordinary Americans on the home front—especially African Americans and American women.

I vividly recall the many changes those four years of war brought to my family, my friends, my city—indeed, to my whole generation—fifty years ago. Fathers and uncles, cousins and nephews were suddenly gone from the scene; members of the "old gang" disappeared, and many of them never returned. Mothers left home in the darkness early on winter mornings to work in the shipyards; daughters went out at twilight to their jobs on the special "Victory Shift" at the local manufacturing plant. Younger brothers and sisters who stayed at home worked out the intricacies of ration books to obtain scarce portions of sugar, coffee, butter, and cheese for family dinners. The daily routine on the home front was no longer the same, with scrap-metal drives and victory gardens during the day, and air-raid drills and enforced blackouts at night. Small red-white-and-blue service flags hung in the windows of homes, reminding friends and neighbors how many family members were serving in the armed forces. A blue star was for everyone on active service; a gold star was for someone who had been killed in action. In so many ways, World War II marked the end of one distinctive era in Boston's social, cultural, and economic history, and ushered in another era that was dramatically different. The world was never the same.

Reviewing my recollections of these less than "ordinary" times, I could not help wondering if the four years of the Civil War had produced similar effects upon various elements in the Boston community a century and a half ago. Did the Civil War exert the same influence upon the general population on the home front, or did they feel only a momentary interruption in normal daily life? Were the lives of ordinary people changed during the four years of

conflict, or did things go on pretty much as before? Did the turmoil and excitement of war end with the surrender at Appomattox, or did the Civil War produce changes that had transforming effects upon the general population during
the postwar era? What *was* Boston's population like before the Civil War burst
on the scene? Could one identify observable and definable groups in the city
and examine them to answer these questions?

Looking over the history of antebellum Boston, I seemed to find at least
four identifiable groups who were significant in the city's life, and with whom
I could effectively deal: (1) the business community, (2) the Irish-Catholic community, (3) the African-American community, and (4) the city's female
community. Each of these groups appeared to have clear physical attri-
butes, distinctive social characteristics, a fairly well-defined and recognizable
living space in the city, and coherent values and beliefs that ordered their
personal and professional lives. When I later described what I was doing in a
conversation with a friend, a sociologist, he immediately brightened up and
announced: "Aha! You're writing about class, ethnicity, race, and gender."
I hadn't really thought about it in that way, but I guess that adds one more
argument to justify my choice of these four elements in Boston's prewar community.

Although my main focus in this study is the City of Boston, its uniqueness
as both the largest city and the capital city in the Commonwealth of Massachusetts occasionally makes it necessary to touch upon events and personali-
ties beyond the city proper. Rather than diminishing the influence of Boston
during such a historic conflict, however, I feel that including from time to time
developments in other parts of the Commonwealth helps reinforce Boston's
importance as the focus of events during those trying years.

The Civil War itself is, of course, essential to this story, and forms a constant and integral part of the narrative. Throughout the four years of conflict
the civilian population is constantly reading about every aspect of the war in
their daily newspapers, following the details of every battle, poring over the
list of casualties, hoping against hope that they will not find the name of a
father, a son, a relative, a loved one, or a friend. But I emphasize that this is
not intended to be a military history of the Civil War, and I have done nothing
to question or alter the major accounts and interpretations of military events
provided by such leading historians as James M. McPherson, William C.
Davis, Shelby Foote, and Bruce Catton. My main interest in this study is not
so much in the military events of the war itself, therefore, but about how the
battlefield events touched the lives of people on the home front—how they
changed their lives, disrupted their homes, altered their work habits, reshaped
their political allegiances, transformed their ideas during the time the poet

James Russell Lowell, in the "Ode" he recited at the Harvard Commemoration on July 21, 1865, called "these distempered days."

~ ~ ~

I EXPRESS my gratitude to those who have helped me in preparing this text and seeing it through to publication. For their friendly advice and professional assistance in locating appropriate photographs and illustrations, I wish to thank Douglas Southard, Librarian of The Bostonian Society; Chris Steele, Curator of Photographs at the Massachusetts Historical Society; Eugene Zsep of the Department of Rare Books and Manuscripts and Aaron Schmidt of the Print Department of the Boston Public Library.

I am grateful to William Frohlich, director at Northeastern University Press, for his continued friendship, support, and encouragement; I am indebted to John Weingartner, senior editor, for his sound editorial advice as well as his highly informed guidance; and I am greatly appreciative of the unfailing good taste and excellent judgment of Ann Twombly in her role as production director at Northeastern University Press.

Chestnut Hill, Massachusetts
February 12, 1997

Civil War Boston

~ ~ ~ ~ ~ ~ ~

Park Street, looking toward Tremont Street, ca. 1858. The Amory-Ticknor House is at the far left at the corner of Beacon and Park Streets. Next door on Park Street is the residence of Abbott Lawrence, which in 1863 became the Union Club. This is the view that Governor John Andrew saw when he stood on the steps of the State House and presented the colors to the Massachusetts regiments as they went off to war. (The Bostonian Society)

I   The Rising Storm
~ ~ ~ ~ ~ ~ ~

Jefferson Davis was in town.

    In summer 1858, the fifty-year-old senator from Mississippi had taken his family to Maine, following his doctor's insistence that he have absolute rest. Tensions from work and politics had sent the former Secretary of War to bed with a bad case of neuralgia and such painful eye problems that he was forced to spend weeks in a totally darkened room. Traveling to Portland by packet boat, Senator and Mrs. Davis, together with their children, Maggie and the baby Jeff, enjoyed several pleasant months among the hospitable people of Maine. The quiet life in the country, the refreshing mountain air, the lively clambakes and outdoor picnics, all helped restore the senator's health and ready him for his return to Mississippi. On their way home, however, the Davis family was forced to put in at Boston and take rooms at the Tremont Hotel when little Jeff came down with a violent croup that almost proved fatal. Never had Boston extended a more generous welcome to an out-of-town guest. Mrs. Harrison Gray Otis, widow of that "urbane federalist" who had served as the city's third mayor, came over to the hotel to nurse the infant through the night so that poor Varina Davis could get some much-needed rest.[1]

The Davis family found themselves in a city that was still slowly transforming itself from a parochial colonial seaport to a modern commercial metropolis. In a quarter of a century, Boston's population had more than doubled, going from 58,277 in 1825 to 136,881 in 1850, forcing authorities to find more living space to accommodate even more people who wanted to live in the city. Working-class laborers and truckmen, along with middle-class merchants and clerks, continued to make their homes in the crowded old part of town east of Tremont Street, the main thoroughfare on which Senator Davis's hotel was located. More recently, and especially after the terrible Potato Famine that ravaged Ireland in the mid-1840s, lodgings along the waterfront from

Fort Hill to the North End had been taken over by Irish immigrants. In 1850, about 35,000 Irish were reported to be domiciled in the city; by 1855 it had 50,000—almost all natives of the southern and western counties in Ireland. Considering that the city's population in 1855 had gone up to about 160,000, the Irish were already almost one-third of Boston's population.[2] The older part of the city was also experiencing other changes. Just off Washington Street, down from the historic Old South Meeting House, Bulfinch's handsome Tontine Crescent and Franklin Place were being demolished to make way for blocks of stone stores and granite warehouses. Horse cars belonging to the Metropolitan Railroad had already begun to operate from Scollay Square across the narrow neck of the peninsula through the South End to Roxbury.[3] On the west side of Tremont Street, behind the senator's temporary lodgings, were more fashionable areas where well-to-do Bostonians had moved when the old part of town had become too densely populated and badly run-down. Descendants of the old mercantile aristocracy and post-Revolutionary shipping families—the Otises, the Amories, the Searses, the Masons, the Higginsons—remained settled in the Federal townhouses that had been erected on the land created by cutting down Beacon Hill. Members of the newer industrial and financial leadership—Robert Bennet Forbes, Robert C. Winthrop, Amos A. Lawrence, John Amory Lowell, Joseph Coolidge—had moved into elegant residences nearby, after Pemberton Hill had been reduced to manageable size.[4]

Along with other urban centers in the Northeast, Boston was only now beginning to rise from the dismal aftereffects of the Panic of 1857. Overspeculation had caused an inflated economy to completely collapse late in summer 1857, producing its severest effects in the commercial and financial centers in the Northeast.[5] By the end of September, every bank in Philadelphia had failed; by mid-October the New York City banks too had shut down. Boston suffered greatly as the crisis forced businesses into bankruptcy and factories into collapse. "Our manufacturing interest is for the present completely broken down and discredited," complained Amos A. Lawrence, one of the city's leading textile magnates.[6] In a desperate effort to rebuild their economy, Boston businessmen found it both advisable and necessary to renew old friendships and cultivate new ones among their associates in the South upon whom they depended for the cotton to feed their factories, load their ships, and sustain their banks. Northerners had become increasingly apprehensive about warnings from the South that unless they adopted a less antagonistic approach toward southern issues, the cotton states would boycott all merchandise "purchased directly or indirectly in any of the Northern States."[7] "What would happen if no cotton was furnished for three years?" asked Senator James Hammond of South Carolina, conjuring up the frightful specter of empty spindles and idle mills.[8] In haste—indeed, in panic—the North's business interests adopted a much more tolerant attitude toward the South in general and the slavery issue in particular. During winter and spring in 1857–1858, conservatives through-out the Northeast reassured their "Southern brethren" about their support and their good intentions.

The unexpected arrival of Jefferson Davis in fall 1858 provided Boston conservatives with a heaven-sent opportunity to display their warmest regards to the southern senator. A committee of prominent officials prepared a gala reception, and invited Senator Davis to speak at Faneuil Hall. On the evening of October 11, 1858, the "Cradle of Liberty" was packed, and on the platform sat men like Edward Everett, former governor, U.S. senator, Secretary of State, and president of Harvard College; Robert C. Winthrop, former Whig con-gressman and one-time Speaker of the House; and Caleb Cushing, former commissioner to China, state senator, congressman, and attorney general in Franklin Pierce's Cabinet. The toastmaster introduced the guest as the personi-fication of "intellectual cultivation and of eloquence, with the practical quali-ties of a statesman and a general." As Davis stepped forward to the rostrum the audience, mostly conservative Bostonians, rose to give the southern states-man a deafening ovation, according to the *Boston Morning Post*. Addressing his assembled hosts as "Countrymen, brethren, and Democrats," Davis pro-ceeded to speak out in the very stronghold of abolitionism about the ways in which American history, the Constitution, and the Bible supported the institu-tion of slavery in the United States. He closed with a moving plea that the original ties that had bound the American colonies in the early days of their greatest trials should not be broken now over an issue that was best left to the states and to the people. It was the last time, recalled one listener, that "a great slaveholder" stood on the historic Faneuil Hall platform and "talked out of his heart to the people of Boston."[9]

From all accounts, Jefferson Davis captivated his Boston audience that night with a seemingly rational explanation of individual liberties and a patri-otic appeal for national unity. For those inclined to see the event as positive, Davis's emotional speech was evidence that the worst of the sectional crisis was now over, that spokesmen with reason and intelligence were taking over from advocates of hatred and fear, and that a new period of mutual under-standing and tolerance was about to begin.

For nearly twenty-five years the slavery issue had been driving a wedge between North and South, and Puritan Boston was the most prominent and disturbing example of everything the Cotton Kingdom despised and rejected. With his public demand for totally and immediately emancipating slaves, Wil-liam Lloyd Garrison and his abolition movement in 1831 had declared slavery a moral evil that had to be wholly eradicated. Defiant Southerners, in response, insisted that their "peculiar institution" was nothing less than a positive moral good, supported by the Bible and sanctioned by the Constitution. After 1831, proslavery and antislavery arguments so solidified that they influenced not only the Union's current status but also conditions in the western territories that would be added during the 1840s in the full flush of Manifest Destiny.

New England's social and cultural traditions of course clashed with those of the South in many other ways. Most Southerners, for example, were repelled by the growing industrialism in the Northeast, where communities such as Lowell and Lawrence had transformed acres of green fields and pleasant streams into ugly clusters of mill towns. The daily parades of faceless wage-workers to and from their rows of wooden boardinghouses to the redbrick textile factories made the South's peculiar institution look positively benefi-cent. This was certainly not an economic direction that Southerners wanted to follow as they praised the natural beauty of their rolling fields, the pleasant geometry followed by their familiar plantations, and the noble yeoman farm-er's simple agrarian traditions.

Southerners were also at a loss to understand the remarkable wave of lib-eral social reforms that swept through the Boston area during the 1830s and 1840s, advocating such idealistic goals as temperance, prison reform, universal peace, women's rights, and abolition of slavery. Most Southerners viewed the notions that citizens should refrain from alcohol, coddle convicted prisoners, surrender their weapons, allow their wives to leave the kitchen, and set Afri-cans loose on the community as nothing less than a perversion of the entire natural order put forward by a pack of liberal radicals and professional do-gooders—"long-haired men and short-haired women," they scoffed—who were out of touch with reality and would weaken the nation's moral fabric.[10] The New England brand of Puritan righteousness was both a real and a fright-ening threat, writes historian Joel Silbey. According to a southern newspaper, the Boston area abounded with reformers, "people [who] imagine that nothing exists that may not be improved . . . and that they are divinely commissioned agents to accomplish this favorable change." Southerners saw their differences with New England Puritanism as rooted not only in slavery, but also in differ-ences of "manner, habits, and social life, and different notions about politics, morals, and religion."[11] Furthermore, ideas expressed by such Boston reform-ers as Horace Mann, Samuel Gridley Howe, and Dorothea Lynde Dix, call-ing for government funds to be used to promote public education, to help the disabled, and to assist the mentally ill, were antithetical to such deep-rooted southern principles as limited government and restricted public expen-diture. The ideas Bostonians were proposing certainly did not provide a vision of future American society that was acceptable or appealing to the average Southerner.

Southerners found it particularly difficult to understand why so many northern women were turning away from hearth and home, the natural and time-honored family traditions, and going into the working world to involve themselves in activities that were clearly men's exclusive domain. During colonial times, when most people lived on farms in rural areas where traditional ways of life persisted, women generally worked alongside men as part of the family labor force. Early in nineteenth-century America, however, industrialization, along with a changing market economy, significantly changed the accepted patterns of gender relations—especially in Boston and other Northeast urban areas. While the income-earning husband went off to work outside the home—to an office, a shop, a store, a business, or a profession—the middle-class wife remained at home, extending her influence over an independent realm of her own. Once home manufacturing shifted to the workplace and the factory, women exercised authority over the "domestic sphere" and assumed primary responsibility for housekeeping, child rearing, and directing the family's moral and religious life. "Domestic life," historian Nancy Woloch writes, "was now under female control." [12]

Outside the home and beyond the family, religion was one of the few activities in which middle-class women could participate without abandoning their "proper" domestic sphere or compromising their respectability. Many women therefore were caught up in the passionate revivalism of the Second Great Awakening early in the 1800s, and soon formed the bulk of religious congregations. These provided not only vital security and self-esteem for the members themselves, but also the base for an expanding network of voluntary religious societies and associations. Along with their active participation as "auxiliaries" in such organizations as the American Bible Society, the Tract Society, the Home Missionary Society, and the Sunday-School Union, local women also banded together in the Boston Female Society for Missionary Purposes to sew clothing and to knit goods for all kinds of religious causes. [13]

By the 1830s, northern women had begun to form associations for pious and benevolent purposes and for much broader charitable and humanitarian causes. In their efforts to participate in early reform activities dealing with issues said to be distinctly related to men, such as intemperate drinking and imprisonment for crime, women found that such movements were dominated by men in general, and ministers in particular. In such movements, women were purely "auxiliaries" and were not allowed either to attend conventions or to run for office. One female temperance spokesperson from New York, Elizabeth Cady Stanton, made the shocking proposal that drunkenness should be cause for divorce. [14] When women applied their organizing talent to areas more directly related to women's problems and needs, however, they were much more successful. In 1835, seventy women formed the Boston Female

Moral Reform Society, which gradually expanded to an influential national association. A number of "respectable ladies" organized the Boston Society for Widows and Orphans, and in 1833, Sarah Hale formed the Seaman's Aid Society to help the wives, widows, and orphans of Boston sailors who had gone to sea and never returned. Hale, a widow herself, became a commentator on women's fashions, and her short-lived *Ladies Magazine* merged into the more successful and influential *Godey's Lady's Book*. Staffed mainly by women, in the editorial offices as well as the pressrooms, in 1852 *Godey's* began to carry a section headed "Employment for Women," recording the latest entrances by females into the commercial workforce.[15]

Other Boston women turned to charitable programs that would rescue prostitutes and lift up "fallen women" by establishing a Home for Unprotected Girls, a Refuge for Migrant Women, and an Asylum for the Repentant. These women also set up agencies to help rehabilitated women find gainful employment, and created day nurseries where employed mothers could leave their children during working hours. For the most part, the conservative Boston establishment looked favorably upon these early activities by female organizations. Most such associations were seen as still somehow related to the woman's sphere: they demonstrated a generally pious or religious purpose; they were charitable and compassionate because they assisted the unfortunate victims of society's ills without trying to reform the ills themselves; and they were "safe" because they were exclusively women who associated with other women and not the other sex.[16]

It was only a matter of time, however, before the habit of forming voluntary associations to assist the deprived and the depraved brought some of these same respectable, middle-class women into other movements seeking reforms that were much further from home and church, and much more radical and controversial. The first was the abolition movement, started in Boston in 1831 by William Lloyd Garrison, calling for total, immediate, and uncompensated emancipation of slaves. Within a year, women had joined the movement and formed the Boston Female Antislavery Society. Maria Weston Chapman was influential in Massachusetts; Susan B. Anthony from New York and Lucretia Mott from Philadelphia added their strong voices to the cause; and in 1837, Sarah and Angelina Grimké came up from South Carolina to lecture on behalf of abolition. In the following year, Angelina scandalized the community at Beacon Hill by addressing the male members of the Commonwealth's House of Representatives.[17]

As women worked tirelessly in an auxiliary capacity for abolition, keeping minutes, circulating petitions, writing letters, sending out forms, signing up new members, they quickly gained self-confidence, a sense of autonomy, and a deeper political consciousness that soon flared up into a rebellion of their own. It was one thing for women abolitionists to face social ostracism, public ridicule, and even physical harassment from those in their own conservative community who could not countenance freedom for slaves and who saw the abolition movement as violating social standards and moral orthodoxy. It was quite another thing, however, for women to find themselves continually marginalized within the abolition movement itself, and also excluded from the platform at abolition meetings. And when, in 1840, a group of American female delegates were refused admission to sessions at the World's Anti-Slavery Convention in London just because they were women, it had become clear that women too needed to be emancipated. Lucretia Mott and Elizabeth Cady Stanton called for a Women's Rights Convention at Seneca Falls, New York, to set in motion a movement for women's rights that would be based on the assertion that "all men and women are created equal." [18]

Bringing with them the experiences, strategies, and techniques they had developed in the abolition movement, as well as in such associated activities as temperance, rehabilitation, and prison reform, women such as Elizabeth Cady Stanton, Susan B. Anthony, Maria Weston Chapman, Lucy Stone, Abby Kelley, Lucretia Mott, Amelia Jenks Bloomer, and the Grimké sisters plunged into a movement to secure for American women the civil, political, and economic rights that had been denied them for centuries. In a relatively short time, a remarkable number of intelligent and highly motivated women had moved far beyond the generally accepted "bonds of femininity" in quest of a new social order for America and a new fulfillment for themselves. If these women had their way, no longer would a "sphere" separate men and women. Women would be able to attend college, teach school, become doctors as Elizabeth Blackwell had, operate hospitals, and travel the country like Dorothea Lynde Dix to improve conditions for the mentally ill. Women would work in offices, lecture to "mixed" audiences as Angelina Grimké did in Boston, turn out books and novels, follow Sarah Hale's example with her ladies' magazine, write for newspapers as Cornelia Wells Walter did for the *Boston Transcript* and as Margaret Fuller was doing for the *New York Tribune*. There was no limit to where a woman could go or what she could do. [19]

Many of these women were not from New England, but most gravitated toward Boston, which at that time was seen as the "Cradle of Liberty," the "Athens of America," the one place where free expression of ideas was possible and social-reform ideas were everywhere. As a result, people outside New England, especially residents of the South, identified the "Yankee Women," the "Bloomer Women," the "Boston Women," as a cohesive force, a powerful phalanx, working together as a force that historian Henry Steele Commager referred to as an "interlocking directorate of reformers." They became, in effect, a community within a community. Strong, determined, and positively indefatigable, many from old Boston families, they knew one another, met regularly, networked effectively, and planned imaginatively to change the nation's traditional social structure. But all this was too much for most Southerners, who could not fathom why women would want to do such things, and why they would want to fly in the face of natural law as well as the injunctions in the Holy Bible. Thought to be little more than a ridiculous dreamer and frustrated spinster, the Yankee Woman was often held up as a prime example of why the plantation South wanted to remain separate from the North's so-called progressive and modern tendencies.[20]

Apart from political rivalries, economic controversies, and gender differences, however, the discussion always came back to slavery. On this issue most Southerners continued to believe that it was among the members of Boston's conservative business community that they had their friendliest source of rational support and social understanding. Forty years earlier, during the War of 1812, British embargoes and wartime blockades had caused Yankee mercantilists to divert their idle capital into textile manufacturing. Although the profitable enterprise was originally intended as a temporary expedient, the entrepreneurs decided to continue it after the war had ended. In 1813, a number of Boston merchants, led by Francis Cabot Lowell, Patrick Tracy Jackson, and Nathan Appleton, organized the Boston Manufacturing Company and set up textile operations in Waltham. Nine years later they opened new plants along the Merrimack River in Lowell. In the 1830s, they were joined by Amos and Abbott Lawrence, who established the factory town that bears their family name. By 1845, about eighty of these prominent Bostonians made up an elite group known as the Boston Associates. They had interests in thirty-one companies and already controlled 20 percent of the nation's textile industry. This group further solidified its economic dominance in Massachusetts by investments in both railroading and banking. In 1848, seventeen of these men served as directors of banks that controlled more than 40 percent of Boston's banking capital. Eleven men served on the boards of five New England railroads; the Boston Associates also held directorships in major insurance companies. By the mid-1840s, the Boston entrepreneurs and their families dominated Boston's cultural, economic, and political life.

By the standards of nineteenth-century America, most of the Boston Associates were clearly racist at a time when the French visitor Alexis de Tocqueville observed that racial prejudice appeared even stronger in the North than in the South. The entrepreneurs were generally willing to tolerate the peculiar institution where it already existed under state sanction, but most were especially reluctant to see it expand beyond the 36°30' line that had been worked out in the Missouri Compromise of 1820. Many businessmen were concerned about the injurious effects of slavery, however, and people such as Amos Lawrence signed up with the American Colonization Society to purchase freedom for African-American slaves and send them back to Africa. Lawrence predicted that the Liberian experiment would make "a greater change in the condition of the blacks than any other event since the Christian era." His son, Amos A. Lawrence, also worked for colonization, and reported that on several occasions free blacks came to his downtown office seeking money to take themselves and their families to Africa.[21]

These same businessmen, however, totally rejected the militant and immediatist approach of William Lloyd Garrison, who ran off the first issue of a newspaper called *The Liberator* on January 1, 1831, declaring slavery to be a moral evil and a crime against humanity. The colonization movement was nothing less than "White-Manism," charged Garrison, and he refused to accept any resolution of the slavery question that did not call for total and immediate emancipation for every slave.

Boston businessmen rejected both the Biblical basis of the abolitionist argument and the confrontational techniques that Garrison and his followers advocated. Despite rejecting what they saw as simpleminded idealism among the abolitionist agitators, however, most members of the business community still refused to see themselves as supporting the institution of slavery. Their aversion to slavery grew especially strong during the 1840s, when it became evident that acquiring additional territories in the West meant the institution's inevitable expansion. This spread of slavery was something Boston businessmen did not want; they would try to prevent it within the limits of the law. Their motives were not generally based on either religious grounds or moral principles. More often than not, they followed principles that they regarded as political standards: inalienable rights and the democratic theories of equal opportunities, as well as the financial realities that constituted an efficient labor force. For the most part they welcomed the end of slavery not so much for any benefits it would bring to the slaves, but for the long-range practical benefits it would bring to white Americans and the expanding industrial system.[22]

The Boston businessmen were, in effect, men on a tightrope—desperate to maintain a precarious balance between proslavery forces on the one side, and antislavery forces on the other. Without doubt, many of their personal fortunes were tied up in southern cotton production, upon which they depended to keep their textile mills running, their cargo ships sailing, and their bank profits rising. They also had strong personal attachments to many individuals in the South with whom they had formed not only extensive commercial ties but also warm personal friendships. Most northern businessmen found it extremely difficult, if not impossible, to reconcile the charming and gracious Southerners with whom they regularly associated with the sadistic monsters and heartless villains portrayed by Garrison and the abolitionists.[23]

At the time of the Civil War, the corner of Winter, Washington, and Summer Streets in downtown Boston was the center of business activity. A variety of shops and businesses attracted men and women from all parts of the city. The greater portion of this part of the business district, looking down Washington Street toward the Old South Meeting House, was almost completely destroyed by the Great Fire of 1872. (Courtesy of the Boston Public Library, Print Department)

And still, as time went on, though they obviously did not want to precipitate a crisis or do anything to disturb their warm relationships with people they referred to as their "southern brethren," the New England industrialists increasingly feared that the expansion of slavery would endanger future freedom in the new western lands. That was certainly the attitude expressed by northern businessmen when in 1845 Congress began debating whether Texas should be admitted to the Union. Senator Daniel Webster of Massachusetts openly condemned slavery as a "great moral, social, and political evil," and strongly opposed annexing a "new, vastly extensive, slaveholding country." Boston's Whig congressman, Robert Winthrop, opposed annexing Texas because it involved "an extension of domestic slavery." "I am uncompromisingly opposed," he said, "to the addition of another *inch* of slaveholding Territory to this Nation." [24] Abbott Lawrence agreed with his colleague, and said he considered the Texas issue "the most important matter we have had to deal with since the Independence of this country." [25] And Charles Francis Adams expressed de-

light that, in an anti-Texas convention at Faneuil Hall in June, many conservative Whigs publicly supported an anti-Texas, antislavery resolution.[26]

Even now, however, conservative businessmen tried hard to avoid an open
break with their slaveholder friends in the South, despite attempts by young
liberals such as Charles Francis Adams and Charles Sumner, who wanted to
use the Texas issue to force the Whig party to take a stand against slavery. In
holding the line against these so-called Conscience Whigs, most of whom were
lawyers and politicians who had few contacts with the business community,
Amos A. Lawrence, Edward Atkinson, John Murray Forbes, and other leaders
in the dominant Cotton Whig faction refused to budge. They did not feel that
in keeping slavery out of politics they were sanctioning the institution. They
believed they were merely preventing it from becoming a divisive *political* issue
that could split the Whig party and divide the Union, just as it was already
separating the states.[27]

But the controversy over Texas late in the 1840s proved to be only a side-
show compared with the explosive reaction in 1854 when Stephen A. Douglas
of Illinois introduced his Kansas-Nebraska Bill that would allow slavery to
spread northward into the unorganized territories above the 36°30' line. With
a stroke of the pen, the provisions in the old Compromise of 1820 were erased,
the spirit of the recent Compromise of 1850 was annulled, and slavery was
back in national politics with a vengeance. With Kansas Territory as the rallying point, the proslavery and antislavery forces drew up their lines and prepared for battle.[28]

Once again it was Boston that took the lead in opposing Douglas and
denouncing his "nefarious" Nebraska bill. As expected, Garrison and his abolitionist supporters leaped to the attack, accusing Douglas and the "slavocracy" of allowing slavery to expand even further. This time, however,
conservative businessmen departed from their customary neutrality, and for
the first time joined in the struggle to keep the peculiar institution south of its
boundaries. They saw that Douglas's proposal allowing slavery to expand
north of the 36°30' line would effectively cut off the industrial Northeast from
the vast future free markets in the West. "What it all came down to," writes
the historian Eric Foner, "was whether the western social order would resem-
ble that of the South or of the North."[29] For the first time, the gentlemen of
property and standing in Boston took a positive stand against further expansion of slavery. "The commercial class of the city have [*sic*] taken a new position on the great question of the day," observed the Boston *Times*.[30] "You may
rely on it," textile magnate Amos A. Lawrence told a friend, "that the sentiment at this time among the powerful and conservative class of men is the
same as it is in the country towns throughout New England."[31]

The Boston businessmen joined financial leaders in other northern cities in organizing emigrant-aid societies that would send waves of Free-Soil volunteers to populate Kansas and vote against the introduction of slavery. Opposition proslavery forces, however, especially settlers in next-door Missouri who crossed into Kansas and voted in a proslavery territorial legislature, created two conflicting governments. Each insisted it was the rightful authority in the territory and regarded the other as fraudulent.[32] Even as tensions in Kansas became more violent, Bostonians displayed ever-greater determination to keep slavery out of the Northwest, and sent hundreds of the new Sharps repeating rifles to the Free-Soil settlers to defend themselves and save the territory. "When farmers turn soldiers," Amos Lawrence wrote to Dr. Thomas Webb, "they must have *arms*," and justified this position to his friend in the White House, President Franklin Pierce of New Hampshire.[33]

The changed attitude in Boston's business community was as sudden as it was profound. "We went to bed one night, old-fashioned, conservative, compromise Union Whigs," recalled Amos A. Lawrence, "and we waked up stark mad Abolitionists." Actually, Lawrence and his business associates had *not* become abolitionists by any stretch of the imagination. Most industrialists insisted that they had nothing in common with Garrison, his radical theories, or his militant tactics. They still refused to regard their southern brethren as evil or immoral people; they still were not prepared to touch slavery where it already existed in the states; they still would not interfere with slavery in the territories—except when it threatened to intrude upon their own free lands and their own system of free competition. It was a thin line, to be sure, a dangerous tightrope, but conservative business interests continued to make every effort to maintain the delicate balance between recognizing the South's slaveholding interests and supporting the North's competitive free-soil ideals.[34]

Maintaining that thin line became more and more difficult, however, as the crisis in Kansas caused deep divisions and violent reactions everywhere. In Washington, D.C., Senator Charles Sumner delivered an impassioned address titled "The Crime Against Kansas," in which he denounced the slavocracy of the South and ridiculed the disabilities of Senator Andrew Pickens of South Carolina. Two days later, on May 21, 1854, Sumner was attacked with a cane by Representative Preston Brooks of South Carolina, who left the Massachusetts senator bleeding and unconscious on the Senate floor. At just about the same time, out in Kansas, a proslavery posse sacked the "Boston abolition town" of Lawrence, and arrested several Free-Soil leaders. Several days later, on the evening of May 24, a settler named John Brown, his sons, and several followers brutally hacked to death five proslavery settlers in retaliation. It was now an eye for an eye and a tooth for a tooth, as the Kansas plains became one of the bloodiest battlegrounds in American history. Northern businessmen watched the national scene with increasing apprehension, wondering how long they could avoid making the final commitment that would place them solidly on one side or the other.[35]

If Boston's business community was still indecisive about its principles and unsure about its goals, in other communities in the city slavery and racism evoked reactions that were much more volatile and much more clearly defined. Most members of the city's white business and financial community lived in the elegant residences and fashionable townhouses on the forward slope of Beacon Hill overlooking historic Boston Common. Just a few steps away, on the other side of the crest of Beacon Hill, sloping down from the Bulfinch state house to Cambridge Street, lived Boston's African-American community. Many were descendants of the few African Americans who had been brought to the town as early as the seventeenth century to work as domestic slaves in the homes of wealthy Yankee families. After the Revolution, Boston's black residents were emancipated and settled down as a permanent community that varied slightly between 1,800 and 2,000 people. Although some blacks lived in other parts of the city, often in small quarters in the white households where they worked, a good two-thirds of the city's black population lived in boarding houses and two-story brick dwellings on the back slope of Beacon Hill, popularly known as "Nigger Hill."

The black community's extent and influence were not confined to the backside of Beacon Hill, however, nor did they end abruptly at the bottom, along Cambridge Street. During the Revolutionary period, the largest black district in town had been off to the northeast, near the congested waterfront wharves where black residents had located their places of business. James W. Stewart, for example, who had served in the U.S. Navy during the War of 1812, had established a shop on Broad Street, where he outfitted whaling and fishing vessels that sailed out of Boston. Thomas Cole was a hairdresser who operated a shop nearby on Congress Street before moving his business to Atkinson Street. He was active in church and fraternal organizations as well as antislavery activities, and upon his death in 1847 left an estate valued at just under $3,000. In Dock Square, David Walker, a free black immigrant from North Carolina, first set up a successful clothing store before moving his enterprise to Brattle Street. By early in the 1830s, however, more and more Irish immigrants had arrived in Boston, and were moving along the waterfront, occupying lodgings in Broad Street and Ann Street, and edging blacks out of the menial jobs they once held on the wharves and the piers.[36] "Every hour sees us elbowed out of some employment," Frederick Douglass later complained, expressing the frustration felt by many native-born African Americans, "to make room perhaps for some newly arrived immigrants, whose hunger and color are thought to give them title to a special favor." Doctor John Rock spoke about this development on the anniversary of Boston's black patriot, Crispus

Attucks. The black workers were losing their places, he said, because the Irish were able to live on less than other Americans. Once upon a time many blacks had worked as stevedores along the Boston waterfront, but now hardly any were left.[37] As ships brought ashore additional European immigrants, the town's black population moved away from the waterfront and edged farther to the northwest, into Ward 5, a district called the West End. In these streets were gradually located many of the stores, shops, and markets of a small but active black business community that served both black and white patrons.

With neither the time nor the opportunity to accumulate the capital necessary to establish large business enterprises or to gain the apprenticeship experience to qualify as skilled artisans, most African Americans around Boston worked at low-level jobs requiring little certified preparation or formal education. Several men, however, had achieved remarkable success in their personal and professional lives and stood out as models for their community. Robert Morris, for example, grandson of a slave brought to Ipswich during the colonial period, was one of the city's few black lawyers. As a boy, Robert had worked for a wealthy Boston family before becoming a law clerk for Ellis Gray Loring, a distinguished Boston lawyer and antislavery advocate. After passing the Massachusetts bar examination in 1847, Morris was actively involved in the city's black community affairs, became a member of the Boston Vigilance Committee, and provided important legal services to the black underground railroad.[38] Another leading professional figure was John Swett Rock, a native of New Jersey, who had studied medicine before turning to dentistry. Doctor, historian, lecturer, temperance advocate, and militant antislavery activist, Rock came to Boston in 1853, where he promoted abolition and various forms of black capitalism to dramatize black people's talents and abilities.[39] Only a few years earlier Lewis Hayden, who had escaped from slavery with his family, arrived in Boston and opened a successful clothing store on Phillips Street. A man of forceful personality and great energy, Hayden was an active abolitionist who hosted meetings of prominent antislavery leaders in his home and later supported John Brown's actions.[40]

William Cooper Nell was the son of William G. Nell, a well-known founder of the Massachusetts General Colored Association, and was a native of Boston, born on Beacon Hill in 1817. As a boy, Nell had attended the all-black Smith School in the basement of the African Meeting House off Belknap (later Joy) Street, and later became a leader in the movement to integrate schools, churches, and other public facilities in Boston.[41] Charles Lenox Remond, too, was a native of Boston whose father had become a naturalized citizen of Massachusetts in 1811. Remond became one of the first paid, full-time, professional antislavery speakers in the area. He toured extensively during the 1830s for the American Anti-Slavery Society, and in 1840 traveled to London as a black American dele-

*Charles L. Remond was a native of Boston, a member of the Massachusetts
Anti-Slavery Society, and one of the most eloquent black abolitionists in Boston.
He was appointed an American delegate to the World Anti-Slavery Convention in
London in 1840. In 1842 he was the first of his race to address the Massachusetts
House of Representatives, protesting segregation in public facilities
and railroad accommodations in the Bay State. (Courtesy of the Boston
Public Library, Rare Book Department).*

gate to the World Anti-Slavery Convention. On his return to America, Remond brought with him the "Great Irish Address"—a communication signed by 60,000 Irishmen urging their Irish countrymen in the United States to support the cause of abolition and black equality.[42]

Although such men as Morris, Rock, Hayden, Nell, and Remond served as inspirational models for their people throughout the antebellum period because of their prominence in both professional affairs and community activities, they were exceptions to the rule. According to city directories and tax records, more than 68 percent of black workers held unskilled and semiskilled occupations. Typically, most of these people were day laborers, unskilled workers, domestic servants, or seamen whose employment was usually sporadic and often insecure. A number of semiskilled workers, however, served their community as carpenters, shoemakers, brickmasons, and blacksmiths— the kinds of jobs that often carried over from slavery. Even more black men and women specialized in service jobs as cleaners, launderers, cooks, caterers, waiters, musicians, hairdressers, and barbers. A clothing dealership too was a profitable black enterprise, in which owners sold new and used clothing to barbers, hairdressers, waiters, salesmen, and transients moving through Boston to other parts of the country. Particularly successful was the "slop shop" operated by David Walker at his place at 24 Brattle Street, where sailors on leave sold all sorts of clothing and equipment to get quick cash for shore-leave entertainment. Such shops usually repaired and reconditioned these items and later sold them at a profit to other sailors about to leave port. As time went on, clothing dealers like John Manley, James Scott, Lewis Hayden, and John Taylor used their facilities to give shelter to fugitive slaves from the South, often exchanging their dilapidated slave garments for clothing that was less incriminating and better suited to their appearance as free persons.[43]

"The history of black Americans is closely bound up with the history of the black church," write the historians James and Lois Horton. Certainly this description was true of the African-American experience in Boston, where the black church exercised one of the earliest and most pervasive influences in providing the black community with a spirit of common purpose as well as a sense of moral direction. During the colonial period, black people, many of them slaves, had attended religious services in various white churches, where they were discreetly hidden away in "Negro Pews."[44] When the Bay State emancipated slaves after the Revolution, most blacks withdrew from white churches and experimented with their own forms of worship until finally, in August 1805, black leaders persuaded the white membership of the First and Second Baptist Churches to recognize formation of the African Baptist Church. In the following year a meetinghouse was constructed on Smith Court, near Belknap (Joy) Street where, on December 4, 1806, the Reverend

Thomas Paul was installed as pastor. The African Baptist Church functioned as the sole black Baptist church in Boston until 1840, when a group of dissident members, led by the Reverend George Black, broke away to form the Twelfth Baptist Church. In the meantime, several other black denominations had appeared in Boston, including the African Methodist Episcopal Church in 1818, and the African Methodist Episcopal Zion Church in 1838. By 1860, at least six churches were serving the black community, including the Free Church, later called Tremont Temple, which was established in 1836 as a fully integrated Christian church in protest against the practice of segregated seating that continued in many of Boston's white churches. The black church's primary mission was to hold services, read the Bible, preach the Christian message, and inspire their congregations to high moral standards. They particularly emphasized the Old Testament, the Hebrew people's prolonged suffering under ancient Egypt's oppressive slavery, and their eventual liberation by Moses, who led them out of bondage into the promised land.[45]

As it carried out its obvious religious functions, the black church also filled several other vital slots in the African-American community. It served as an active social center where members could meet, make social contacts, engage in economic arrangements, and participate in church suppers, where newcomers to the city could get to know residents. The church was also a cultural center that organized choirs and bands, sponsored musical concerts and dramatic productions, and encouraged literary societies and debating clubs. Needless to say, these same churches and their ministers, who were invariably influential and respected natural leaders, campaigned against slavery and spoke out against all forms of racial injustice. Perhaps the city's best-known activist black minister was Rev. Leonard A. Grimes, who had come up from Virginia to New Bedford before arriving in Boston in 1848 to become minister to the Twelfth Baptist Church. In a remarkably short time, Rev. Grimes transformed a twenty-three-member church members into an active congregation with 250 members, whose church became a center for abolition protest and an important station on the underground railroad.[46]

Clearly, the terrible scourge that was human slavery was uppermost in the hearts and minds of the city's African-American community, and the members worked constantly not just to abolish the institution in the South, but to remove its insidious side effects, racism and segregation, in the North. Using the various black churches as well as the African Masonic Lodge and other benevolent and fraternal associations, the movement in Boston to abolish slavery dated back to the eighteenth century, according to James and Lois Horton. By 1826, black residents had formed the Massachusetts General Colored Association, regarded as the most significant pre-Garrisonian abolitionist group in Boston. The city's black community responded enthusiastically to the fiery appeal expressed by one of their own, the local clothing dealer David Walker. In his famed antislavery tract, *Walker's Appeal,* published in 1829, Walker captured his people's imagination by exhorting the slaves in the South to recover their manhood and rise up against their white masters.[47] The black abolitionists' goals found even greater impetus among members of Boston's white community only two years later, in 1831, when William Lloyd Garrison came out with his antislavery newspaper, *The Liberator,* demanding total and immediate emancipation for slaves. Although Garrison and his newspaper were despised in the South and rejected in most of the North, black Bostonians not only provided moral encouragement and financial support, but furnished black apprentices such as Thomas Paul, Jr., and William C. Nell, who helped print the paper and promote its circulation. Throughout the 1830s and into the 1840s, such prominent professional men as Dr. John Rock and lawyer Robert Morris, leading ministers including Thomas Paul and Samuel Snowden, and successful businessmen such as Lewis Hayden, Thomas Cole, and Walker Lewis provided funds and facilities to support Garrison and his abolition movement and to stimulate interest among their own people for expanded civil rights and greater educational opportunities. During this increase in antislavery agitation, women in the city's black community had a substantial part, not only in raising much-needed funds through church socials, colorful bazaars, and community fairs, but in more direct and individual activities. Susan Paul, for example, daughter of Rev. Thomas Paul of the Twelfth Baptist Church, was a life member of the Massachusetts Anti-Slavery Society and a member of the prestigious Boston Female Anti-Slavery Society. Isabella and Holmes Snowden, daughters of Rev. Samuel Snowden of the African Methodist Episcopal Church, actually took fugitive slaves into their homes, providing them with food and clothing. Sarah Parker Remond and Caroline Remond Putnam, wife and daughter of Charles Lenox Remond, were active in organized abolition groups and particularly in protesting against segregation in the city's public institutions.[48]

Increased educational opportunities were greatly desired by Boston's African-American community, and this wish grew even stronger as the abolition movement gained strength and membership during the 1840s. Back in 1789, when they could get no educational assistance from the town fathers, black citizens in Boston had set up a school of their own in the home of Prince Hall, founder of Boston's African Masonic Lodge. In 1806, the school was transferred to the African Meeting House until a new school could be constructed in 1835 with a legacy from Abiel Smith, a wealthy merchant and admirer of Prince Sanders, a black schoolmaster. The Smith School eventually came under the jurisdiction of the Boston Primary School Board, which recognized it as a separate primary school exclusively for black children. Starting in

1844, however, a group of Boston black citizens began petitioning the Boston School Board to abolish the Smith School and allow black children to enroll in the city's other public schools. In this effort they were encouraged by William Lloyd Garrison and the local abolitionists as well as the Massachusetts Anti-Slavery Society, which informed all black people of their legal rights and offered them all possible aid in securing "the full and equal enjoyment of the public schools." Although a majority of the school board consistently voted against the black petitioners—arguing that it was the board's responsibility to keep apart the two races that "the All-Wise Creator had seen fit to establish"— the black citizens and their white supporters kept up the fight through community organizations, public petition, and legal action.[49]

In fall 1849, Benjamin Roberts, a local black printer, brought suit against the city of Boston on behalf of his five-year-old daughter, Sarah, who had been denied admission to a nearby white school solely because of her color. The famous case was argued before the Supreme Court of Massachusetts, with Charles Sumner, then a prominent abolitionist attorney, representing Sarah Roberts, and Robert Morris, only black member of the Massachusetts bar, serving as assistant counsel. Despite Sumner's eloquent appeal for "equality before the law," and his arguments that both black children and white children suffer from attending segregated schools, Chief Justice Lemuel Shaw decided against the plaintiff. Even though they lost the Sarah Roberts case, black and white abolitionists renewed their efforts for integrated education in Boston. Switching their attacks from the judicial chamber to the political arena, they were able to bring enough public pressure to bear to persuade the state legislature to repudiate the court's decision. On April 28, 1854, the General Court of Massachusetts passed a law stating that no child, on account of "race, color, or religious opinions" could be excluded from any public school in the Commonwealth. Following passage of this statute, some boys from the all-white Phillips School were transferred to the all-black Smith School, and a corresponding number of black boys from the Smith School were sent over to the Phillips School. Although in many ways it was a small victory, nevertheless, to members of the city's African-American community, passage of the school legislation seemed a symbol of the coming day when slavery would be a thing of the past and racial equality a thing of the future.[50]

The city's black community may have been content with its vision of a more promising future, but another part of the Boston community was far from satisfied that abolition of slavery was to be welcomed or that racial equality was to be desired. In the half-century from 1810 to 1860, Boston's Irish Catholic community had grown from a small, inconsequential handful of immigrants to nearly one-third of the city's population.

Throughout the colonial period, thanks to strong Anglo-Saxon animosity

against the Irish, as well as violent Protestant revulsion against the Roman
Catholic religion, the only Irish people who dared settle in the Boston area
were Presbyterians from Northern Ireland, who found reluctant acceptance in
the Puritan colony's stern and hardworking atmosphere. Only during the later
stages in the Revolutionary War, as the American rebels adopted friendly relations with France, did a few Catholic families feel safe enough to come out of
hiding and form themselves into a small congregation that soon began to increase. After the abortive insurrection by the Society of United Irishmen in
1789, Britain's oppressive Penal Laws so subjugated the Irish people that emigration to America seemed the only alternative. During the 1820s and 1830s,
increasing numbers of Catholics from Ireland's southern counties came to Boston, settling along the waterfront district in cellars, shacks, and hovels. In the
years that followed, they suffered hunger, devastating tuberculosis and cholera,
and general contempt from the city's predominantly Anglo-Saxon, Protestant
establishment. To make matters worse, local capital dispersed into textile enterprises in such outlying areas as Lowell and Lawrence, leaving the city of
Boston without industrial centers capable of supplying work to unskilled laborers.[51] Most immigrant families were forced to rely upon whatever mothers,
wives, sisters, and daughters could earn as domestic servants in nearby private
homes and hotels, while the men scraped up temporary jobs as day laborers—
sweeping streets, tending horses, cleaning stables, unloading ships, and cutting
fish. Looked upon as lazy, shiftless, and violent people who could never be
assimilated into the American culture, the Irish became the objects of bigotry,
discrimination, and outright violence. By the mid-1820s, attacks against persons and property were common in Ann Street, Broad Street, and other sections near the waterfront where the Irish lived. The mayor and the board of
aldermen finally agreed to station six constables in the Irish district from 10:00
at night until daybreak in an attempt to keep the peace.[52]

As they settled into their new American environment and attempted to
adjust to Boston's distinctive social and economic conditions, the Irish also
sought to conform to their adopted country's constitutional ideals. Thanks in
great part to the two Catholic bishops who presided over the diocese of Boston
during the four decades from 1825 to 1866, the newcomers transferred their
political loyalties wholeheartedly to the government of the United States.
Bishop Benedict J. Fenwick was a Maryland-born Jesuit who succeeded Boston's popular first bishop, Jean Lefebvre de Cheverus, in 1825; Bishop John B.
Fitzpatrick, who succeeded Fenwick in 1846, was born in Boston and graduated from Boston Latin School before going off to study for the priesthood.
That both these prelates were born in the United States and were devoted to
the principles of the Constitution did much to influence immigrant attitudes
in pre–Civil War Boston. They urged the Irish to become naturalized citizens

as soon as possible, to exercise their right to vote on every occasion, and to avoid public violence in favor of legal recourse. Confrontations were inevitable, of course, between desperate Irish immigrants and angry Yankee workmen who feared that hungry newcomers would take their jobs. A group of day laborers, such as bricklayers and "truckmen"—those brawny men who drove the big horse-drawn teams—burned down the small Ursuline convent in Charlestown in 1834. Nevertheless, ethnic and religious conflict in Boston never grew as violent as similar conflicts in other American cities at the time. In 1842, and again in 1844, violent street riots between natives and Irish immigrants rocked the city of New York; rioting in St. Louis was responsible for at least one death; bloodshed erupted in Cincinnati in 1842; during summer 1844, clashes over Bible reading in the suburb of Kensington, just outside Philadelphia, produced a three-day battle in which thirteen people were killed and fifty wounded. Although the Irish in Boston continued to experience harassment and discrimination, cooler heads usually prevailed and bloodshed was always avoided.[53]

As the Irish took stock of the conflicting issues on the American scene during the 1830s and 1840s, inevitably they confronted the growing controversy between those who believed that slavery was a moral evil that should be abolished, and those who viewed it as an established social institution that should be left alone. For the most part, Irish Catholics were not inclined to get involved in an institution that appeared to be old and historic, and in which they had never played a part. As a generally conservative people, members of a church that emphasized tradition, precedent, and good order, the Irish appeared satisfied with the status quo.[54] The institution of slavery had existed in the South for nearly two hundred years, and it had been formally sanctioned by the U.S. Constitution. Preoccupied with their own immediate circumstances as strangers in a new and often hostile environment, most immigrants gave little thought to the country's "peculiar institution." Although they gave no indication of wanting such an institution for themselves, they conceded that citizens in other parts of the country had the right to hold slave property until some means could eventually be found to eliminate the institution peacefully and gradually.[55]

Most Irish residents had no objection to the white Bostonians whose humanitarian motives supported the American Colonization Society and contributed funds to send slaves back to Liberia. This seemed like a sensible solution to the problem. The Irish took strong exception, however, to the militant rhetoric and radical demands of William Lloyd Garrison and his liberal supporters, who called for total and immediate emancipation for African-American slaves, giving no compensation to the slave owners. The laws of the various states "identify the negro with property," declared the *United States Catholic Intelli-*

gencer, forerunner of *The Boston Pilot,* and so any such attempt by abolitionists to "alienate property" in this manner, declared the paper, was tantamount either to "flagrant injustice" or to "commercial theft."[56] If slavery were such a "blot on the escutcheon of American freedom," asked the paper, then why didn't the Founding Fathers wipe it out completely in 1787 when they drew up the Constitution? They deliberately left that institution "undisturbed," the paper responded, so that "no injury could fall upon the public from the colored population." This reference undoubtedly applied to recent reports that slaves had been found plotting violence and insurrection. On August 20, 1831, the paper published an item describing the discovery of nearly 11,000 weapons and 15,000 rounds of ammunition in a field near Jacksonville, Florida. "Negroes intended to rise as soon as the sickly season began," charged the *Intelligencer,* telling its readers that the slaves planned to "obtain possession of the city," kill the planters, and massacre the whole "white population."[57] And on October 1, 1831, the newspaper published the news of Nat Turner's bloody rebellion in Southampton, Virginia, which took the lives of sixty whites and ended with the death of Turner himself along with more than a hundred of his black followers.[58] Confronting such alarming violence, the Catholic paper suggested that Garrison and his followers would do more good by going out, purchasing the freedom of slaves as the Colonization Society proposed, and shipping them back to Africa. This would not only be a "practicable" solution, but it would also be "benevolent" and "wisely calculated." It would slow the coming of that "awful catastrophe" (emancipation) that would some day bring total and "promiscuous ruin" to every aspect of American life and society.[59]

From the very day on which Garrison's *Liberator* was published, the city's immigrant community came out forcefully and consistently against both objectives and methods suggested by those who proposed to emancipate the slaves. In taking the position they did, supporting the institution and opposing the abolitionists' demands, the Irish attitude was greatly strengthened, either consciously or unconsciously, by at least three major considerations.

First, for reasons that still are not entirely clear, the Irish seem to have arrived in America with a distinctly negative and openly racist attitude toward the black race in general and African-American slaves in particular.[60] "Of all the ethnic antagonisms that have arisen in the turbulence of American social development," wrote the late Dennis Clark, "few have such a distinctly rancorous history as that between the Irish and the Black."[61] Without question, the Irish shared a form of racism common to most white Americans early in the nineteenth century that viewed black people as members of an inferior race—ignorant, savage, and brutish—given to uncontrollable emotional impulses and destructive animal passions integral to the African personality. In the minds of such white people, slavery was the only practical and sensible means by which civilized society could safeguard itself from these passions. If once the "maddening spirit of revolution" were let loose from "the prison of the African heart," with all its "brute, ferocious force," warned the *Intelligencer*, it would present to the eyes of the astonished world "a more bloody spectacle than St. Domingo ever displayed." The supreme irony, of course, was that in many parts of Boston the Irish and the African Americans were considered comparable in both general appearance and social behavior. In the twentieth century, social scientists correctly insist that the Irish should be categorized as an ethnic group. In the nineteenth century, however, the Irish regarded themselves as a separate race; some not only maintained that the Irish were a "separate caste," but even suggested that they came from a "dark race"—possibly African in origin.[62] Native white Bostonians agreed that members of both groups were "violent prone by nature," and complained that neither had any feelings for "law and order." Says David Roediger, Irish behavior was frequently associated with that of the blacks, and it was common for rowdy, undisciplined behavior to be referred to as "acting Irish."[63] Indeed, the two groups were regarded as so similar that song-and-dance men in the minstrel shows easily made the transition from their blackface parodies to "mockeries of the Irish."[64] Recalling a visit he made to Ireland during the 1840s, the noted black spokesman Frederick Douglass observed the many ways in which blinding poverty and heavy manual labor had produced remarkable physical similarities between the typical Irish farmer and his fellow African-American slave:

> The open, uneducated mouth—the long, gaunt arm—the badly formed foot and ankles—the shuffling gait—the retreating forehead and vacant expression—all reminded me of the plantation and my own cruelly abused people.

Douglass also mentions how both the Irish and the blacks engaged in "petty quarrels and fights," and shared in a "wailing and longing to be back home."[65]

The Irish, however, failed to discern any similarities between themselves as white people and African-Americans as black people. They refused to accept the idea that slaves should be emancipated, or that the actual condition of Negro slaves was as bad as the abolitionists painted it. *The Boston Pilot*, for example, reminded its readers that England had imposed a "worse slavery" upon the "noble and intelligent" people of Ireland than slaveholders had imposed upon Negroes in America. Admittedly, it conceded, many aspects of slavery were "gross" and "horrible," such as separating husbands from wives, or taking children from their parents. Nevertheless, most of these abuses were not widespread, it maintained, nor was the material condition of slaves as "degrading" as the abolitionists reported. Indeed, continued *The Pilot*, taking up where the *Intelligencer* left off, many Irish immigrants found on their arrival in America that those very slaves, about whom the newcomers had heard so many "pathetic appeals," were a far sight better clothed, better housed, and less burdened than the immigrants themselves had been back in Ireland. Therefore, it concluded, the few instances of abuse against a minority that it referred to as "not particularly ill-used" did not warrant jeopardizing the country's unity and harmony by supporting the irresponsible abolitionists, who were demanding immediate freedom for the slaves.[66] "There are one thousand Stowes weeping over the woes of an imaginary Uncle Tom," wrote *The Pilot's* editor in a caustic response to the popular *Uncle Tom's Cabin,* "[compared] to the one which looked after the real Uncle Tom."[67]

The Pilot's increasingly sharp tone and confrontational style were due in great part to the paper's new publisher, Patrick Donahoe. Born in 1811 in County Cavan, Ireland, Donahoe had emigrated to Boston with his laborer father at age ten. He started out working as a printer's devil for the *Columbian Centinel,* and then worked his way up the ladder with diligence and determination until he had saved enough money to purchase the tottering Irish-Catholic weekly, which he proceeded to transform into the most popular Catholic publication in the country. Donahoe seemed to enjoy taking a contentious approach toward the city's Protestant establishment, and vigorously opposed the idea of Catholics becoming assimilated into the prevailing Anglo-Saxon culture. Deliberately dramatizing the extraordinarily high Irish birthrate, he taunted the local Brahmins by pointing out that although the immigrants composed only 20 percent of the population, they already accounted for 40 percent of the marriages—a statistic he gleefully predicted would produce an eventual Catholic majority in the Bay State.[68]

That Irish immigrants viewed the leaders of Boston's abolitionist movement with fierce and unremitting animosity only added to the stubbornness with which they opposed emancipation for the slaves. Except for Garrison himself, who started out as a humble printer in Newburyport, a seaport on Boston's North Shore, most abolition movement leaders came from established Boston families and were members of an elite upper class that strongly resembled the haughty English establishment that had stolen their lands and oppressed their people. The Irish saw these antislavery reformers as barefaced bigots and hypocrites who cared no more for the black people they supposedly championed "than they cared for the fifth wheel of an omnibus." The only reason the white liberals took up the slavery question at all, said *The Pilot,* was that it was the "safest way of pushing their insane radicalism."[69] Garrison and his followers went about preaching liberty and equality for black people, at the same time working hard to deprive white immigrants of their hard-earned civil and political rights. Their hearts were as "soft as butter" toward the oppressed black laborer in the South, charged *The Pilot,* but they were "hard as flint" toward the white laborer in the North.[70]

Then too, most Irish immigrants were absolutely convinced that the abolitionist leaders' fiery rhetoric and dramatic posturing were an affront to the U.S. government. As newcomers who had transferred their allegiance to the representative government and constitutional principles of their adopted country, the immigrants were appalled to learn that Garrison had publicly labeled the U.S. Constitution a "covenant with death and an agreement with hell" because it had sanctioned the institution of slavery. Something called a "higher law" was inconceivable to a people who believed that individuals must subordinate their own views to those in lawful authority—in matters of state as well as religion. Immigrants had little respect for people supposedly highly educated who believed that a citizen was required to obey the country's laws only as far "as they agree with his or her individual notions of right or wrong." When such people believe that slavery is morally wrong, and find that it is maintained by government and laws, observed *The Pilot* in obvious disapproval, "they bravely avow that neither the government nor the laws are to be obeyed."[71] The relativist notion that individuals should obey only the laws with which they happen to agree was abhorrent to the immigrant mind and contrary to their communitarian spirit. Catholics were convinced that the abolitionists' militant rhetoric and confrontational tactics were designed to promote civic disorder and public violence. Even when the abolitionist spokesman Edmund Quincy wrote to *The Pilot* to assure Catholic readers that his people employed only "Peaceful Agitation," and did not advocate violence in any form, it was obvious that most Catholics were not convinced. It would be better for the black man to remain in "nominal bondage," concluded *The Pilot,* than attempt to win his freedom by physical force, reminding its readers about the sentiments of the great Irish patriot Daniel O'Connell, that "the greatest political advantages are not worth one drop of human blood."[72]

Certainly another major reason for the fierce antagonism that most Irish Catholics displayed toward Boston abolitionism was their conviction that it was essentially a pro-English plot masquerading as a humanitarian crusade. *The Pilot* insinuated that England was one of the hidden forces behind the agitation about "Southern Slavery" that had suddenly seized the country and awakened the most "alarming apprehensions" in the minds of "every true lover of the American Constitution."[73] Ever since England had set itself up as the "champion of the Black" and finally abolished slavery in 1839, observed the local paper, it had been seeking to win others over to the English way of thinking. With "revolting hypocrisy," England pretended an "enthusiastic interest" in the condition of the black population in the American South, but all the time continued to trample, "with the iron hoof of oppression," upon the millions of its own subjects across the sea in Ireland. The Irish were more convinced than ever about the validity of this English conspiracy when they heard that William Lloyd Garrison had proclaimed that England and the English people were, "in the sight of the Almighty," a people who had truly worked His will. "We in America look to you as to Him for our emancipation."

The Pilot was quick to point out that the abolition movement was playing directly into English hands, and warned its readers not to let their age-old hatred for Great Britain be diluted by any well-intentioned compassion for the black people. Irish leaders feared their followers might be swayed if abolitionists were able to link the fight for freedom in Ireland with the fight for emancipation in the United States. This fear was heightened in 1842 when the black orator Charles Lenox Remond returned from the World Anti-Slavery Convention in London with the "Great Irish Address," signed by Irish patriot Daniel O'Connell along with 60,000 other Irishmen, urging Irish-Americans to "treat the Negroes as friends and to make common cause among the abolitionists." O'Connell confessed he was at a loss to explain the lack of sympathy among the American Irish for the slave's plight. "It was not in Ireland that you learned this cruelty," he wrote sadly. "How then can you have become so depraved? How can your souls have become stained with a darkness blacker than a Negro's skin?"[74] He encouraged his countrymen in America to continue their work on behalf of the Repeal movement, but he also appealed to them to begin using their influence in "prostrating the institution of Black Slavery." The address fell on deaf ears in America, however, and *The Pilot* immediately leaped to the attack before such an eloquent appeal could gain momentum. Irish Americans were certainly at liberty to sympathize with the "enslaved Negro" as an individual, conceded the paper, but under no circumstances should they associate themselves as part of the Irish Repeal Movement with any other causes—especially with one that "so seriously engenders bitterness and disunion as Abolitionism." The Irish must not encourage a group such as the abolitionists, whose agitations would push the United States toward the "precipice down which England is plotting her fall."[75]

In many ways, the unexpected Kansas-Nebraska Act in 1854 was a dramatic turning point in the long and bitter controversy over slavery. At a single blow it brought slavery back into politics, nullified the Compromise of 1850, reinvigorated the abolitionists, aroused black antislavery leaders, destroyed the Whig party, and forced the northern business community to finally draw the line delimiting slavery's westward expansion.[76] But the Boston Irish still refused to budge.[77] In contrast to the angry businessmen who raged against Senator Stephen A. Douglas and his "nefarious" Nebraska bill, spokesmen for the Catholic community urged their people to remain steadfast in their traditional views. Slavery was still protected by the Constitution; southern citizens still had the right to take their personal property with them wherever they went; and slavery was still the only effective safeguard protecting white civilization from an inferior race's pent-up passions. Furthermore, the Yankee abolitionists were still bigoted hypocrites who were now showing their true colors by supporting the newly organized American party—popularly known as the Know-Nothing party—a flagrant attack on foreigners in general and Roman Catholics in particular.[78] Any chance that immigrants would take Daniel O'Connell's advice and make common cause with abolitionists was out of the question during the mid-1850s, when the boorish so-called Nunnery Committee scandalized local Catholics with their heavy-footed "inspections" of convents and parochial schools.[79]

Nothing, perhaps, better demonstrated the distance that separated the Irish attitude from Boston's changing social consciousness than an incident in June 1854 associated with returning a runaway slave named Anthony Burns. Apprehended in Boston under the Fugitive Slave Act, Burns was marched down State Street to a waiting vessel through a cordon of 2,000 uniformed troops assembled to guard against any rescue attempt by the enraged populace that lined the street. Conspicuous among the troops assigned to enforce Burns's return was the Columbian Artillery, almost entirely local Irish Catholics commanded by Captain Thomas Cass.[80] Townspeople saw the Irish troops as simply one more instance of Catholic collaboration with the forces of "slavocracy." One critic accused the city's Catholics of using "the shallow pretext of upholding the law" as a device to force black people back into slavery, especially after reading statements in *The Pilot* denouncing the local protesters as "anarchists," approving of returning Burns to his "rightful owner," and referring approvingly to the court's ruling as "a perfect triumph of law and order."[81]

Despite pressure and recrimination, the Irish persisted in their position on slavery, and considered their consistency more than justified when, in March 1857, Chief Justice Roger B. Taney, himself a Catholic, handed down the Dred Scott decision, declaring black people to be "beings of an inferior order, and altogether unfit to associate with the white race." According to Taney, Negroes possessed "no rights which the white man was bound to respect," and insisted that they had never been included under the term "citizen" as defined by the Constitution. Reinforced in their racial attitudes, and rededicated to the Democratic party's states'-rights principles, the Irish made it clear that they would support President James Buchanan, follow Senator Douglas's Kansas-Nebraska Act, accept the Fugitive Slave Act, and acknowledge the Dred Scott decision. This segment of the Boston community was still determined not to accept the rest of the city's apparently general and growing consensus about emancipating the slaves.[82]

With the highest court in the land openly preaching proslavery doctrine, African Americans were now convinced that it would take nothing less than a most drastic political or social revolution to bring an end to slavery. Despite the "monstrous" character of Taney's decision, Frederick Douglass urged his people to respond to it in a "cheerful spirit," and see in this attempt to "blot out forever the hopes of an enslaved people" just one more necessary link in the chain of events that would lead inevitably to "the complete overthrow of the whole slave system."[83] The Court's decision that blacks were an inferior race, that black people had no rights that white people were bound to respect, and that African-Americans had never been recognized as American citizens, was hardly cause for a "cheerful spirit" among Boston's black community. Living in the shadow of Faneuil Hall, Old North Church, and Bunker Hill monument, a number of black families could trace their Boston ancestry back to the colonial era; others had conducted business and financial enterprises in the town for years, had fought in the Revolutionary War, had sailed with the American navy in the War of 1812, and were furious at this preposterous and degrading pronouncement. They wanted some action that would demonstrate their patriotism as American citizens and also dramatize their pride as a race and their courage as a people. Using the first annual Crispus Attucks Day in March 1858 on the anniversary of the Boston Massacre, Boston blacks gathered to commemorate the heroism shown by "the first Boston martyr," and display their unity in pursuing human freedom. After a parade and speeches, William Cooper Nell denounced despotism in America, suppression of free speech in the South, and "annihilation of the citizenship of Colored Americans by the Dred Scott decision." The most rousing speech was given by thirty-three-year-old Dr. John Rock, whose failing health made it necessary to shorten his remarks, but perhaps made their effect on the audience all the more memorable. Striking out at the black-submission myth, he appealed to history to illustrate the courage of African heroes such as Crispus Attucks, and suggested that American slaves might soon have the opportunity to strike a blow for their own freedom. "Sooner or later," declared Rock prophetically, "the clashing of arms will be heard in this country, and the black man's service will be needed: 150,000 freemen capable of bearing arms, and not all cowards and fools, and three quarters of a million slaves, wild with the enthusiasm caused by the dawn of the glorious opportunity of being able to strike a genuine blow for freedom, will be a power."[84]

Angry reaction to the Dred Scott decision, swelling racial pride, and consciousness about the black courage exemplified by Crispus Attucks stimulated

Boston's African-American community leaders to establish an independent black military unit. As early as 1852, Robert Morris, the black attorney, together with Charles Lenox Remond, had petitioned the state legislature for permission to establish a black military company. Turned down, they resubmitted the petition to the legislature in 1853, as Morris cited an old Massachusetts law that, during colonial days, had required blacks aged sixteen years and older to enroll in a militia company under pain of a 20-shilling fine. Pleading eloquently, Morris asked the legislature to establish this military company as a symbol of black pride and a response to the hunger among the city's black citizens for "propriety and advancement." Once again, however, the legislature rejected the request, on the grounds that establishing a black military company would conflict with the Constitution and the Supreme Court's decisions.[85]

Disappointed but not discouraged by the state authorities' negative response, black citizens pursued their objective on their own. Morris and Remond's initial efforts were now supported by others in the black neighborhood. Community leaders including William C. Nell and Lewis Hayden; clothing-shop owners John P. Coburn and John Wright; hairdresser and salon operator Benjamin P. Barrett; waiters like Thomas Brown and L. W. Thacker; laborers such as J. J. Fatal and George Washington, all contributed time and money to the cause. With this support, in 1854 Boston residents organized a black military company of their own, called the "Massasoit Guards," without state sponsorship.[86] Indeed, a year later, when the Guards applied to the state legislature for assistance in purchasing arms and equipment, the request was denied. Any equipment the black militiamen received was provided by private efforts and community contributions.[87]

Until a war seemed possible that might change circumstances drastically, the black community's efforts to become part of the state militia were constantly and brusquely denied. But the efforts themselves were important to the black people in Boston, expressing unity and solidarity in the face of political assault, asserting potency amid judicial denial. "The positive, visible, and even inspirational presence of disciplined, organized, and armed community members," according to James and Lois Horton, discouraged slave catchers who hunted for fugitive slaves and also helped bolster courage among the men, women, and children in an isolated community that felt itself under siege.[88]

In 1806 free blacks in Boston's small African-American community raised $7,700 to enable black craftsmen and laborers to build the African Meeting House on Joy Street on Beacon Hill. Until 1898 the Meeting House served as the home of the First African Baptist Church, was the social and cultural center of the black community, and provided a base for antislavery activity. During the Civil War church members raised funds for black troops. (Massachusetts Historical Society)

2 ～～～～～～ The Call to Arms

John Brown was dead.

If the Kansas-Nebraska Act of 1854 gave the United States the initial push that sent it sliding down the slippery slope toward civil war, John Brown's ill-fated but historic raid at Harpers Ferry added plenty of grease to the skids. On October 16, 1859, Brown and a small band of followers set out from a farmhouse in southern Maryland, crossed the Potomac River, and launched an attack against the town of Harpers Ferry, Virginia, where a small federal arsenal was located. Although the poorly organized raid was quickly put down and the leaders taken into custody, the startling event produced dramatic repercussions on both sides of the Mason-Dixon line—but especially in Boston, where the antislavery fever still burned bright.

Reports that a "disturbance" had taken place at Harpers Ferry came in as sketchy and incomplete telegraphic dispatches. Wild rumors and exaggerations ran the gamut from an "insurrection" involving hundreds of blacks and whites to a minor labor dispute, a "magnified row," with only a handful of disgruntled workers.[1] Gradually, a more accurate picture began to form about the unexpected attack on the arsenal across the Potomac River and John Brown's part in it. To those in Boston who had known Brown from his exploits in Kansas, but who had not been privy to his latest plans to take the crusade against slavery into the South, the early Harpers Ferry reports produced both surprise and some annoyance. William Lloyd Garrison, although he was sure the raid was "well intended," concluded that it was "misguided, wild, and apparently insane." Anticipating the upcoming presidential contest of 1860, Senator Henry Wilson, long an opponent of slavery, was disturbed about how John Brown's raid might affect his plans to strengthen the state's Republican party. "If we are defeated next year," he wrote in obvious frustration, "we owe it to that foolish and insane movement of Brown's."[2] The *Worcester Spy*, a well-known antislavery newspaper, agreed that the raid was "one of the rashest and maddest enterprises ever."[3]

John Brown was found guilty of treason against the state of Virginia, and on December 2, 1859, he was led out of his cell, marched to the gallows, and hanged. Some rejoiced that John Brown was dead; others mourned his passing. Southerners were convinced that the "Old Man" symbolized the entire North's hatred, and were more determined than ever that the "Black Republicans" must not take over the presidency. Northerners, on the other hand, began to hail Brown as a heroic figure. Samuel Bowles's *Springfield Republican,* which in October had dismissed Brown as a madman, was now calling him "a true man and a Christian," whose spirit would live on to inspire the North and whose influence would always be present in every planter's mansion and every Negro hut in all Virginia.[4] Although most white antislavery leaders were pacifists, they approved of Brown's willingness to face death for the cause of freedom. From his sickbed in Italy, where he was dying of consumption, Rev. Theodore Parker declared that Brown was "not only a martyr . . . but also a SAINT," and Ralph Waldo Emerson told his audiences that the old warrior's death would "make the gallows as glorious as the cross." In offering "A Plea for Captain John Brown," which he read to sympathetic audiences in Concord, Worcester, and Boston, Henry David Thoreau described Brown as a "crucified hero," and showed no remorse about the violence at Harpers Ferry. Indeed, he insisted that for once the Sharps rifle had been used in a righteous cause—not for shooting Indians or hunting down helpless fugitive slaves.[5] The young William Dean Howells, who was writing a campaign biography of Abraham Lincoln, suggested that Brown was no longer simply a person, but had actually become "an idea"—an idea that was "a thousand times purer and better and loftier than the Republican idea."[6] William Lloyd Garrison struggled to reconcile Brown's use of violence at Harpers Ferry with his own lifelong devotion to pacifism and nonviolence. Although in the October 28 issue of the *The Liberator* he restated his commitment to peace and repeated his judgment that the raid was "misguided," he also attacked the hypocrisy of Brown's enemies, who always praised the heroes of Concord, Lexington, and Bunker Hill. If early American patriots were justified in resorting to violence over something as trivial as a three-penny tax on tea, Garrison asked, then how much more so were those who, bound in chains, saw their children marching off to the auction block? Slavery itself was a form of violence, he argued; one must choose between the spirit of Bunker Hill and the servility of the slave plantation.[7]

On December 2, 1859, the day of Brown's execution, Boston witnessed a tremendous outpouring of emotion. Church bells tolled, minute guns fired solemn salutes; ministers preached sermons of commemoration; thousands bowed in silent reverence for the martyr of liberty. "I have seen nothing like it," recalled Charles Eliot Norton of Harvard, who was not easily impressed.[8] Although members of Boston's black community generally admitted that Brown had acted rashly and prematurely, they also hailed him as a martyr to the cause of black freedom. In his trips to Boston, Brown had become acquainted with many prominent black citizens, and on at least one occasion he and his sons had been house guests of Lewis Hayden and his family. "It is extremely likely that Hayden, Rock, and other Boston blacks aided Brown directly or indirectly," write James and Lois Horton, "by donating money to his venture or by helping to recruit volunteers for his band.[9] Convinced that his venture would launch African Americans into a guerrilla struggle for their own freedom, Brown had tried to attract more black recruits. He made a special attempt to persuade Frederick Douglass to join him as a sort of liaison officer to the slaves he expected would join the uprising. Douglass could not be persuaded, however. Seeing that Harpers Ferry was situated on a peninsula formed by the confluence of the Potomac and the Shenandoah rivers, the black leader immediately spotted it as a "perfect steel trap," that would be indefensible against a counterattack. You will "never get out alive," he warned Brown. Douglass was convinced that Brown was embarking on a suicidal mission, "an attack on the federal government" that would "array the whole country against us." The old Kansas warrior was disappointed at Douglass's refusal, but went ahead with his plans anyway, certain that the slaves would rise spontaneously to the cause of freedom. Although the attack proved to be the tactical failure Douglass had predicted, black Bostonians loudly praised the Old Man's courage. On the day of Brown's execution, black businessmen closed their doors and draped their shops in mourning; individuals wore black crêpe armbands—the antiabolitionist *Boston Post* reporting snidely that it was impossible to get a haircut or to have one's shoes blacked all day long.[10] Religious groups organized two-day vigils at the Twelfth Baptist Church and at integrated meetings in Tremont Temple, where prominent black speakers addressed the assemblages, and where both "the eloquent and the unlettered" offered heartfelt prayers for the soul of John Brown. Those in attendance at both locations sang antislavery anthems and protest songs well into the night.[11]

Some black leaders experienced self-doubt following the raid. Charles L. Remond, the well-known black abolitionist spokesman from Salem, expressed deep disappointment that no general uprising of slaves had occurred in Virginia. Convinced that blacks would have to fight for their own freedom, he warned the ministers that prayers alone would never be enough to break the chains.[12] The Reverend John Sella Martin, however, minister of the Black Baptist Church and a former slave himself, presented the position of the slaves in the Harpers Ferry region in a different light, claiming that because Brown had not been willing to shed the white owners' blood, he was unable to gain the slaves' trust. The slaves were not cowards in declining to rally to Brown, he argued; they were merely showing the distrust for white people they had learned through generations of bondage and treachery. But Martin, too, expressed the hope that the day would come when a black John Brown would appear.[13]

While antislavery supporters, white and black, were commemorating John Brown's deeds, Boston's Irish community refused to join in any such endorsement. Even with the shocking news about the raid, the Irish refused to be stampeded into changing their views on slavery. They saw John Brown's act of terrorism as one more example of the totally irresponsible Harvard-educated liberals' willingness to break the law and flout the U.S. Constitution in favor of some ill-defined "higher law." The incident at Harpers Ferry was simply one more foolhardy adventure that would go down as a footnote in the history of lost causes, and posterity would regard John Brown himself as nothing more than a bloodthirsty sociopath. In its first accounts of the raid, the weekly *Boston Pilot* labeled Brown a "radical insurrectionist" who planned violence against innocent people and the government itself. It told readers that one of the first acts by this so-called defender of black people was to kill a black railroad porter named Hayward, and leave his body "naked in the streets." Surely, commented the editor caustically, this was not the act of a humane and truly caring abolitionist.[14] Indeed, the paper went on to applaud officers and "gentlemen" such as Lieutenant J. E. B. Stuart for putting down the madman's raid.[15] *The Pilot* took particular pride in telling its readers that no "shadow of an Irish name" would be found among the insurrectionists. "Not one single Irishman, thank God, appears to be implicated directly or indirectly, in this disgraceful affair," the paper announced proudly, also pointing out that the first man to die in the fighting was an Irishman named Barney, and "the gallant Sgt. Quinn" was the first U.S. Marine to "patriotically charge the engine house" where Brown and his men had taken shelter.[16] Indeed, Brown and his cohorts were all clearly of Puritan ancestry, enemies of the Catholic Church, and men who had helped turn New England into "a moral and political bedlam," said *The Pilot*. Brown represented the ultimate Protestant, reincarnating a Puritan Roundhead (shades of Oliver Cromwell) who defended his fanaticism with heretical principles derived from private interpretation of the Scriptures. The Irish weekly argued that Brown was but a tool in an English plot that was designed to impair its greatest commercial rival—the United States of America.[17] In subsequent issues, *The Pilot* deplored the ways in which abolitionists and Republicans had reacted to Brown's terrible deed. "Our expectation that the Republicans and abolitionists would treat John Brown as a martyr has been verified to an extent far beyond out expectations," it wrote, expressing disgust that the "Black Republicans" would hold public meetings in the city "to get sympathy for Brown." [18] For Boston's Irish Democrats, Brown's raid confirmed their opinion that the Republican party would produce only division, disunion, and civil war. The Republican nominee, John Andrew, was a candidate of the fanatical "John Brown clique of Republicans," wrote *The Pilot,* who would "eliminate the slaves by fire and sword." [19]

The Democrats, on the other hand, were the only ones who could find common ground between North and South—especially under the enlightened and rational leadership of Senator Stephen A. Douglas of Illinois. The "Little Giant" had already made his views clear during the previous year's well-publicized senatorial campaign debates with his Republican opponent, Abraham Lincoln, when he continued to support the popular-sovereignty doctrine, upheld white supremacy, and emphasized the people's sovereignty in deciding whether or not slavery would be allowed in a state or a territory. Without question, the Democratic party platform, not that of the Republicans, would save the Union and prevent civil war. Upon hearing that the Democratic party had officially nominated Douglas as its presidential candidate for 1860, Patrick Donahoe of *The Pilot* joined Irish colleagues in arranging for a one-hundred-gun salute on Boston Common. And when the Illinois senator came to Boston on a campaign tour in October 1860, thousands of Irish Catholics lined the streets to catch a glimpse of their hero and to attend a massive rally at Fort Hill. [20]

In opposing the Republican party, the Irish were motivated by traditional party loyalties and also by deep religious convictions. Immigrant voters in Boston put most Republican leaders in the same category as Anglo-Saxon, Protestant abolitionists, who preached liberty and equality for black people while doing nothing to improve white immigrants' deplorable social and economic condition. Indeed, even the *Springfield Republican* was forced to admit that at times the Republicans were "as much a vehicle for anti-Catholic and anti-foreign sentiment as for anti-slavery." [21] And that so many former members of the anti-Catholic American (Know-Nothing) party had become Republicans after the party collapsed in 1856 was further proof for the Irish that the Republican party had become "the pernicious successor to the Know Nothings." [22] Emphasizing the Republicans' political image as the "nigger party" that would endanger their economic future by eventually working toward full Negro equality in America, the Democrats and the Irish entered into the state that David Roediger calls a "lasting marriage," stressing commonality of "whiteness" and solidarity of state sovereignty. [23]

Although the Irish community was unified in its political allegiance, the city's conservative business community was by no means clear about where to put its political faith. Of all the groups in town, they were probably the most confused and apprehensive about long-range repercussions from John Brown's invading the South. For more than a quarter of a century they had worked hard to convince their southern brethren that the abolitionist troublemakers were only an insignificant minority in the North. They certainly did not represent the conservative views of those "gentlemen of property and standing" who controlled the region's financial interests. But in an instant, John Brown's raid had destroyed all that. Now the distinction between "good" and "bad" Northerners was irrelevant; Southerners were convinced that *all* Northerners were alike. They were all abolitionists at heart; they were all intent on destroying slavery and the southern way of life.[24] The North has "sanctioned and applauded theft, murder, treason," cried *De Bow's Review,* in accusatory tones, and one Baltimore newspaper asked how the South could any longer afford "to live under a government, the majority of whose subjects or citizens regard John Brown as a martyr and a Christian hero?"[25] It was not so much that Brown had taken up arms against the federal government, or even that he had invaded Virginia, that created such hysterical demands for his death. It was that he had actually tried to incite a slave revolt. All their lives, Southerners had lived in mortal fear of slave uprisings; and now a Northern man, a white man, had threatened to make that nightmare a reality. An apprehensive South was put on a war footing, rigid curfews were established, and increased appropriations were demanded for tighter local-defense measures. Southerners blamed the entire North for encouraging such an attack, and called for a full-scale investigation to discover exactly how John Brown, a person without visible sources of income, had managed to get the money and the weapons for his outrageous invasion. The Senate subsequently appointed a special investigating committee, headed by Senator James Mason of Virginia and Senator Jefferson Davis of Mississippi, to uncover the "higher and wickeder" villains in the nefarious scheme and to make them share in John Brown's punishment.[26]

Although more than 400 miles lay between Harpers Ferry, Virginia, and Boston, Massachusetts, John Brown's raid made that distance seem much shorter. A number of prominent Boston men had been associated with John Brown over the past three or four years, and now it looked as though they were implicated in a criminal conspiracy. It was well known that industrialists such as Amos A. Lawrence, William Appleton, and Edward Atkinson had sent both money and guns to "Captain" Brown during his military exploits in Kansas. George Luther Stearns, a wealthy Boston businessman, had made unlimited funds available to Brown and was later found to be one of the "Secret Six" who had conspired to assist Brown in his newest undertaking. Dr. Samuel Gridley Howe, prominent physician and reformer, had become one of Brown's closest associates in the East; preachers such as the Unitarian Thomas Wentworth Higginson and the Transcendentalist Theodore Parker had also become

ardent Brown supporters; Wendell Phillips, the "golden trumpet" for Garrison's abolition movement, spoke out on his behalf; and young Franklin B.
Sanborn, a Concord schoolteacher just recently out of Harvard, was a disciple
of the Old Man from Kansas. Suddenly Senator Jefferson Davis, the Mississippi statesman who had been wined and dined in Boston only a year earlier,
became nemesis of the North, avenger of the South. Some of Brown's supporters remained steadfast in supporting their hero during the Senate's investiga-
tions. Theodore Parker was still in Europe, but wrote back his approval of
what Brown done; Thomas Wentworth Higginson dared the southern senators
to call him to the witness stand. But many more feared losing their good
names, their businesses, and quite possibly their freedom. Franklin Sanborn,
Dr. Samuel Gridley Howe, George Luther Stearns, and several other Boston
residents suddenly decided it was time to pay a visit to Canada "for reasons
of health."[27]

Conservatives throughout Boston were appalled by the aftereffects from
John Brown's raid. Mournfully, Edward Everett warned his friend Robert C.
Winthrop that this event would surely pave the way for "final catastrophe."[28]
For some local businessmen, now that the Whig party had disappeared and
the short-lived American party had collapsed, the Republican party seemed
the only political mechanism by which they could prevent the westward expansion of slavery without actually threatening the existence of slavery itself. The
risk, of course, was to promote division of the country along geographic lines;
but they were ready to accept that risk as a temporary condition they were
sure would gradually break down as modern technology made slavery a relic
of the past that would inevitably "wither on the vine."

Some of the city's leading businessmen had already decided to become
Republicans. John Murray Forbes was one of the earliest to support the new
antislavery party, although he continued to clearly distinguish between his own
political views on slavery and the moral positions taken by leaders of the abolitionist movement. The extension of slavery had to be resisted, he insisted, not
for the slave's sake but for "the safety of the North and the Union." He proposed to use the Republican party's political mechanism to prevent adding
more slave states to the Union, and in this way prevent the southern states
from dominating Congress.[29] Soon other conservatives followed Forbes's lead.
Former members of the New England Emigrant Aid Company, including John
M. S. Williams, Edward Atkinson, and John Lowell joined the Republicans.
In the 1856 presidential election, George Luther Stearns had supported the
Republican candidate, John C. Frémont, and now he was backing forty-one-
year-old John Albion Andrew as the state's Republican gubernatorial candidate.[30] An antislavery lawyer who had been a Conscience Whig, a Free-Soiler,
and a member of the Emigrant Aid Company, Andrew was a Republican party

organizer in Massachusetts and staunchly supported Abraham Lincoln after the Chicago convention nominated the Illinois railsplitter as their presidential candidate in May 1860.[31] Despite their preference for New York governor William Seward, many of the so-called Radicals in the Republican party believed that Lincoln's strong antislavery sentiments were very similar to their own.[32] Gerrit Smith of New York, one of the nation's leading abolitionists, expressed confidence that Lincoln was, "in his heart an abolitionist."[33] The new Bay State Republican governor, John A. Andrew, and William Schouler, soon to be Andrew's wartime adjutant-general, both expressed their satisfaction with Lincoln's election.[34] And the *Springfield Republican* looked forward to an administration "whose influence shall be positively and effectively on the side of human freedom."[35] Local Garrisonians were especially delighted by John Andrew's gubernatorial nomination and called upon all abolitionists to vote for Andrew and the entire Republican ticket.[36]

But others in Boston's conservative business community still refused to believe that a confrontation between two distinctly regional parties was the best way to hold the Union together. The most influential figure in the Emigrant Aid Company, Amos A. Lawrence, still would not join the Republican party. He maintained that because most financial support for the effort in Kansas had been provided by the conservative "old Hunkers," he did not want to lose their support.[37] Lawrence feared that the Republican party, with its openly sectional appeal, would further alienate the South and endanger the Union. Realizing that the Whig party was gone forever, his only hope was to form a new conservative coalition that could attract old-time Whigs, former Know-Nothings, and lukewarm Democrats.[38] On December 8, 1859, therefore, less than a week after John Brown was hanged, Amos A. Lawrence called together local conservative leaders at Boston's Faneuil Hall to organize such a party, made up of men "who honor and cherish the Union—who mean to maintain the Constitution of the United States and faithfully carry out all its requirements and obligations."[39] Lawrence himself, William Appleton, Edward Everett, Edward S. Tobey (prosperous banker and businessman), George C. Richardson (prominent dry-goods merchant), and some old-time Cotton Whigs passed resolutions deploring the Brown raid and expressing sympathy for Virginia's white people. They proceeded to officially organize the Constitutional Union party. Taking no public position on the slavery question, and promising to support the Constitution, they set out to create a completely neutral political party, a party "knowing no North and no South," which would appeal to conservatives in all sections of the country.[40] Although they had hoped to persuade Senator John J. Crittenden of Kentucky to be their standard-bearer, they had to settle for the less-familiar John Bell, a Unionist senator from Tennessee, along with their own Edward Everett of Massachusetts, to dramatize the new party's interregional character. The party's distinctly Boston makeup was so conspicuous, however, that one Republican poked fun at the Brahmin organizers as men who believed that "the sun rises in Chelsea, comes up over State Street, hovers above the State House, and sinks into the waters of the Back Bay." The *Springfield Republican* also ridiculed the Bell-Everett ticket's elitist cast, saying that it was "worthy to be printed on gilt-edged satin paper and laid away in a box."[41]

The 1860 presidential election was a four-cornered race, with each of the candidates—Lincoln for the Republicans, Douglas for the mainline Democrats, John C. Breckinridge for the secessionist Democrats, and Bell for the Constitutional Union party—claiming to be the person who would preserve the Union and prevent civil war. Although Douglas campaigned through New England, the West, and the South in a vigorous one-man crusade, the split over slavery within the Democratic party proved insurmountable. With such advantages as a unified organization, a wealthy treasury, and an enthusiastic following, the Republicans piled up electoral votes for their candidate in the more heavily populated northern states. When the votes were counted, Abraham Lincoln of Illinois had taken all but one of the northern states, had carried the electoral college, and was president of the United States. In Massachusetts, Lincoln received 106,533 votes (about 63 percent of the ballots cast), Douglas trailed with 34,370 votes (the Irish remained loyal), and John Bell received only 22,232 votes (13 percent), which came mostly from the former Whig business community in Boston. Not only did the Republicans enjoy a national landslide, but their gubernatorial candidate, John Andrew, won the state office by a similar margin.[42]

About the only satisfaction Republican opponents could enjoy was the victory by the Democratic candidate, Joseph Wightman, in the Boston mayoral contest a month later. A manufacturer of scientific equipment, Wightman was the Democratic chairman of the city's Board of Aldermen, and in this year found himself supported by the Irish Democrats and by a local business leaders' group known as the "Parker House Clique," who admired his calm managerial style. The *Boston Post* declared that a vote for Wightman would keep Boston from becoming "the headquarters of Negro meetings, a Negro militia, and the advocates of John Brown's raid."[43] On December 10, Wightman won handily over his Republican opponent, Moses Kimball, and other Bay State cities such as Worcester, Springfield, New Bedford, Lynn, and Newburyport also elected non-Republican mayors, although each of these cities had given Abraham Lincoln a sizable majority.[44] In spite of their dismal showing in the presidential race, however, the city's Cotton Whigs were not entirely discouraged by Lincoln's election, hoping that his long history as a Whig would help moderate the Republican party's abolitionist tendencies. "It is too early, as yet, to judge the result," remarked Robert C. Winthrop to a local businessman, "but as Mr. Lincoln is a much more moderate person than any of the leaders of his party, I hope for the best."[45]

But if some Americans were willing to accept Lincoln as a suitable president, others clearly were not. On December 20, 1860, delegates to a state convention in South Carolina voted to take that state out of the Union. By February 1, 1861, six more southern states had joined South Carolina, and were busily engaged in establishing a new nation—the Confederate States of America. Amos Lawrence's worst fears were now realized: the Union to which he was so dedicated had been dissolved. The fact of secession, the prospect of disunion, and the possibility of civil war threw Boston into fear, panic, and disorder during the 1860–1861 winter.[46]

On at least three occasions during December and January, mob violence threatened the community's peace and its citizens' lives. On December 3, 1860, one year after John Brown's death, Boston abolitionists, black and white, held gatherings to commemorate the anniversary of his execution. One of these was held in Tremont Temple, where white abolitionists such as Frank Sanborn, James Redpath, and Parker Pillsbury sat alongside about a hundred African Americans, including Frederick Douglass and Rev. John Sella Martin. Also in attendance, however, were many who despised the abolitionists and opposed praising a terrorist like John Brown. Wealthy businessmen (Amos A. Lawrence was there), clerks, bookkeepers, "broadcloth rowdies," Irish laborers—people eager to let the South know that the abolitionists did not speak for Boston—were a majority in the audience. Apparently well organized, the antiabolitionists ("mainly Irish," said the *Boston Evening Transcript,* hired by "commercial interests") gave three cheers for Virginia's Governor Henry Wise, who had sent Brown to the gallows, and waited for the proceedings to begin.[47] When Rev. Martin called the meeting to order and invited Frank Sanborn to assume the chair, the meeting erupted. Antiabolitionists leaped to their feet, announced that Richard S. Fay, a businessman from Lynn, would be the chairman, and hoisted their man to the stage. Leaning over the podium, Fay lashed out at the abolitionists, expressed sympathy for the South, and then pointed his finger at the blacks in the audience, declaring that if the present crisis continued, white residents would "hang these gentlemen as high as Haman." Asserting that Boston had allowed abolitionist agitators to disturb the city's peace for too long, to the cheers of his supporters in the audience he promised that that "particular nuisance" would be "summarily abated" in the interest of self-defense. Frederick Douglass angrily elbowed his way to the podium and tried to speak. "I know your masters," he shouted at the antiabolitionists; "I have served the same masters as yourselves!" Telling the audience that a counting-house clerk in the front row had just called him a "nigger," Douglass

This engraving from Harper's Weekly *shows a white mob breaking up a memorial service for John Brown on December 15, 1860. Brown had been executed one year earlier for leading his insurrection at Harpers Ferry, Virginia. Black residents and white abolitionist sympathizers had organized the service in Brown's honor, but were forced out of the hall by white opponents who were shocked by Brown's actions and fearful of a possible civil war. (Courtesy of the Boston Public Library, Print Department)*

retorted: "If I were a slave-driver and got hold of that man for five minutes, I would let more light through his skin than ever got there before." Then violence exploded in the hall, fistfights broke out, and Douglass was pulled off the stage, attacked, and thrown down the main staircase.[48] Wendell Phillips, the white abolitionist orator who had also taken part in the meeting, had to be escorted to his home on Essex Street by forty volunteers to protect him from the rampaging mob.[49]

Refusing to be silenced, the abolitionists organized a second meeting later in that same afternoon at the black Baptist Church on Joy Street, where Douglass, Phillips, John Brown, Jr., and John Sella Martin, the church's minister, joined others in eulogizing Brown. Phillips remarked how fitting it was that they should find sanctuary in a black church. He denounced the city government for failing to provide protection, but observed that "we abolitionists are accustomed to live without government." Once again another group of about a thousand hostile antiabolitionists gathered outside the church, some drunk and throwing bricks, others harassing and beating passing black people; still others were urging that the church be burned to the ground. This time, however, the city police stepped in to prevent the meeting from being disrupted.[50]

Two weeks later, Wendell Phillips once again had to seek police protection after another mob interrupted an address he was giving to an abolitionist audience at the Music Hall, during which he had lashed out at the "broadcloth mob" that had disrupted the Tremont Temple meeting. An angry crowd followed him all the way home, and one member was heard to shout: "Damn him! He has depreciated stocks three million dollars by his slang!" Despite these attacks, local abolitionists looked upon the Tremont Temple riot as a great victory because of the publicity it gave to their cause. "The storm seems to howl more fearfully than ever," wrote Maria Weston Chapman, long an abolitionist and staunch supporter of William Lloyd Garrison, "but it is a comfort to have it raging where the North can see and understand."[51] *The Liberator* sarcastically thanked the hostile rioters for demonstrating so clearly "the incompatibility of the slaveholding spirit, as well in the North as in the South, with the freedom of speech and Republican institutions."[52] The rioting gave Wendell Phillips the opportunity to make perhaps one of his most eloquent comments on the nature of a free government: "Government exists to protect the rights of minorities," he declared. "The loved and the rich need no protection. . . . The community which dares not protect the humblest and most hated member in the free utterance of his opinions . . . is only a gang of slaves."[53]

Conservative and antiabolitionist groups in the city clearly were frustrated by the public demonstrations praising John Brown and obviously bothered by reactions among their southern brethren. According to the *Boston Post,* the *Richmond Enquirer* had expressed surprise that Boston businessmen had not come out publicly to denounce Brown's raid and to uphold the slaveholding states' constitutional rights. A short time later, handbills were circulated throughout the city calling upon all those who "honor and cherish the Constitution" to come to a "Union" meeting at Faneuil Hall. In the evening on December 8, 1860, the Cradle of Liberty was packed with prosperous businessmen and conservative political leaders eager to rehabilitate the Bay State's reputation by showing that Massachusetts had been "falsely exhibited in the eyes of the nation." The distinguished Edward Everett set the tone for the proceedings. Governor of Massachusetts, president of Harvard College, Secretary of State, minister to Great Britain, U.S. senator, Everett employed all his celebrated oratorical skills in dramatizing the crisis of the moment. The Republicans had exploited the South's emotional response to John Brown's raid for their own political advantage, he charged, and had pushed the country to the brink of a "final catastrophe." Before long, he prophesied, the nation would be in a state where houses would be attacked, their occupants mobbed, statues knocked over, and other "lawless outrages" would become "the order of the day." He cautioned his audience not to be complacent just because business was prosperous and industry operating as usual, pointing out that the Paris theaters had been packed during the Reign of Terror, and that French stocks had been at an all-time high just before the Revolution of 1848. The great "social machine" might continue to move, the old statesman warned, but it might well conceal an inner cancer. Playing on his listeners' racial fears, Everett asked them to recall the horrors in the black Haiti uprising as the century began—the midnight burnings, the merciless tortures, the white babies impaled on pikes, and "other abominations not to be named by Christian lips." And yet John Brown had tried to turn the South into another Haiti, charged Everett, by placing New England pikes in the hands of "an ignorant subject race"—even though the white people of the South are "our compatriots," who attend the same churches and read the same Bible as the people in the North.[54]

Evidence that tensions were still running high could be seen a few weeks later when the Massachusetts Anti-Slavery Society made plans to hold its annual January meeting in Boston's Tremont Temple. The new Democratic mayor, Joseph Wightman, issued a virtual invitation to the city's antiabolitionists to attack the meeting by refusing to grant the abolitionists' request for police protection and by informing the superintendent of the Temple that he and the officers of the Anti-Slavery Society would be held responsible for any disturbances. As a result, a motley group assembled on January 24, 1861: abolitionists and secessionists, African Americans and Irish Americans, ministers and rum sellers, stockholders and truckmen, pickpockets and state officials, shopkeepers and ladies who had been spirited into the hall through a private passageway. As soon as a well-known abolitionist, Francis Jackson, stepped forward to begin the proceedings, the hall erupted with hoots and catcalls from the "broadcloth rowdies," who shouted "Down with the Nigger!" and gave three cheers for South Carolina. Notable figures such as Ralph Waldo Emerson and James Freeman Clark tried to make their voices heard over the tumult, but with little success. "I guess the Irish boys here will earn their holiday pretty well," snarled Edmund Quincy. "Perhaps they are glad to be excused from sweeping out their masters' shops." Only Wendell Phillips was able to complete his prepared address, adopting the professional speaker's device of gradually lowering his voice until even his opponents had to stop yelling to hear what he had to say. As soon as he finished, however, the mob again silenced any speaker who came to the podium. After he had spoken, Phillips and several others slipped out the back door to ask Governor Andrew to send in the militia to control the troublemakers, but Andrew explained that by law he could not use the militia without a formal request from the mayor, which Mayor Wightman refused to do.[55] As the afternoon wore on, the scene in Tremont Temple had degenerated into an ugly disturbance that threatened to spill into the streets. Mayor Wightman himself then walked into the chamber and loudly ordered the hall cleared. When the Anti-Slavery Society organizers later returned, they found the doors locked and guarded by policemen. Citing an anonymous threat to murder Wendell Phillips, the mayor had declared that there would be no further antislavery meeting that day.[56]

Along with disorder in the streets, Boston experienced a general business depression after Lincoln's election and the subsequent news about Southern secession. Charles Eliot Norton commented on the "universal alarm, general financial pressure, and great commercial embarrassment" that resulted from numerous business failures and factory shutdowns.[57] "Men with plenty of money held on to the money bags," reported the *Boston Herald,* "as if no more was ever coming in."[58] Some factories had already cut back on their production, one Boston citizen told a friend in South Carolina, "either by dismissing a part of their hands or working them on short time."[59] During January alone, sixty firms in Massachusetts had failed, and the state's unemployment spiraled upward accordingly, causing the *Boston Courier* to report that the "Boston streets today are full of discharged workmen."[60] According to the *Herald,* the Overseers of the Poor received more applications for relief "than they can possibly provide for."[61] An associate of Governor Andrew informed him late in that month about "a terrific rush of manufacturers, merchants, business men and politicians . . . urging and insisting upon some sort of compromise to save the Union!"[62] John Murray Forbes confirmed this panic atmosphere when he told Charles Sumner two days after South Carolina seceded that "our money people here have been badly frightened," predicting that conservatives were ready to support any kind of compromise that would "patch up our difficulties and their pockets."[63]

And Forbes was right. Some Bostonians were already taking steps to demonstrate to their southern brethren that Boston had not become hospitable to radical antislavery views. As early as December 10, Amos A. Lawrence had met with prominent Whig leaders and businessmen such as Edward Everett, Robert C. Winthrop, Edward S. Tobey, and James Beebe to develop proposals for halting the secession movement by some sort of compromise. They settled on three major points of agreement: (1) to back Kentucky Senator John J. Crittenden's compromise on the question of slavery in the territories that would extend the 36°30' line all the way to the Pacific; (2) to seek to amend or repeal the so-called personal-liberty laws passed by Massachusetts that obstructed the federal Fugitive Slave Law by guaranteeing fugitive slaves the writ of habeas corpus and trial by jury; and (3) to work for the success of a Peace

Convention that had been called by Virginia to assemble in Washington.[64] Lawrence and his band of Boston "Union-Savers" enthusiastically endorsed the Crittenden proposals, and early in February 1861 had collected 22,313 signatures in Massachusetts for a petition favoring the slavery compromise. A group of delegates, including Lawrence, Everett, Winthrop, and Tobey then carried the petition (more than 100 yards long) to Congress and asked Massachusetts representatives to present it to their colleagues. Lawrence tried to get Charles Sumner to approve it, but the abolitionist senator only scoffed at the petition, dismissing it as "all wind."[65]

John Murray Forbes and other Bay State Republicans strongly opposed the Crittenden proposal, and felt that the Bay State should do nothing to support any form of compromise. Governor John Andrew, however, believed that Massachusetts could not afford to go unrepresented at the Washington Peace Convention and risk later recriminations that the Bay State had not done its best to avoid civil war. He decided, however, that he would not send any conservative Hunkers such as Amos Lawrence or Edward Everett—only "able, firm men" who would uphold Republican party principles; and so he selected Forbes, along with other reliable Republicans.[66] Throughout the endless conference meetings, it was impossible for the delegates to arrive at satisfactory grounds for compromise. Every attempt to bring up the Crittenden proposals was fought down by Northerners as outright "surrender," and the Southern representatives were absolutely determined to accept nothing less.[67] During the proceedings, Forbes was taken aside at a dinner by W. H. Aspinwall, an influential New York businessman who wanted the Bostonian's help in buying a ship or two to relieve the threatened federal garrison at Fort Sumter. He explained that the idea came from an "able and experienced naval officer," Gustavus V. Fox, from Saugus, Massachusetts, who offered to lead the expedition himself. Although Forbes took to the plan right away, it was quickly vetoed by high-ranking army and navy personnel, especially by Buchanan's obstinate Secretary of the Navy, Isaac Toucey, former Democratic governor of Connecticut, "whose loyalty was more than doubtful," snapped Forbes.[68] In the meantime, the Peace Convention "was slowly talking against time, and coming to no conclusions," Forbes observed with some satisfaction.[69] Just before March 4, 1861, the ineffectual delegates concluded their sessions, packed their bags, and returned to their homes, making it perfectly evident to everyone that all hope of arriving at a peaceful solution had disappeared.

While all the discussions on compromise and concession had been going on, Boston's black community expressed fear that white Bay State political leaders, pressured by local financial interests, would back down and come to terms with the South. Reacting to early reports indicating that the Crittenden proposals were getting a favorable reception, African Americans were worried not only that slavery would be allowed to expand across the continent, but also that northern states would repeal their personal-liberty laws and then deny black citizens the right to vote. Boston blacks gathered at the Joy Street Church to consider their response if the compromise proposals were accepted. George T. Downing, a well-to-do caterer, warned his listeners that any such compromise would be a prelude to an organized effort to deport all free blacks. The North, he predicted, "would sacrifice the whole race of colored people to save the Union." Joshua B. Smith, a former fugitive slave now known locally as the "Prince of Caterers," continued the evening's depressing tone and cautioned his associates not to rely on white people to see them safely through the crisis; they should get themselves ready for their own defense. Those attending the meeting petitioned the state legislature to reject the Crittenden proposals and to grant blacks "the most absolute equality in every respect." They concluded their appeal with a cry of defiance: "We will never be driven from the United States by any compulsion!"[70]

Up on Beacon Hill, the new governor was also watching national events with growing anxiety. His own visits to Washington, his talks with Southern leaders, and his correspondence with associates had led Governor John Andrew long ago to make up his mind that compromise was impossible and that civil war was only a matter of time.[71] He had been in office only a week in January 1861, when he ordered a one-hundred-gun salute on Boston Common to commemorate Andrew Jackson's victory in New Orleans. When frightened residents woke up on January 8 to the sounds of crashing guns, the governor explained that the time had come for everyone "to get accustomed to the smell of gunpowder."[72] Having begun to condition the civilians to the sounds of war, the dynamic forty-three-year-old governor went to work on readying his troops. With his General Order Number 4, Andrew ordered the state militia to take immediate steps to overhaul its organization. Men unable to serve on active duty were to be removed from their posts and replaced with men who could respond to an emergency alert at a moment's notice.[73] Finding that the men in his militia brigade had no overcoats, General Benjamin F. Butler went to Governor Andrew and persuaded him to obtain from the state legislature a $100,000 military appropriation, and to place an order immediately for 2,000 woolen overcoats for the Massachusetts militia. With advice from a special war council, the governor also used the funds to purchase additional blankets and knapsacks. If called upon to show their mettle in the near future, Massachusetts troops were going to be well trained and well equipped.[74] Governor Andrew felt more reassured than ever that he had been wise to undertake these military preparations when word arrived late in February that the Peace Convention was a dismal failure and that Washington, D.C., was in the grip of despair.

The first days in March were dark, bleak, and raw, as Massachusetts, along with the rest of the nation, anxiously awaited the new Republican president's inauguration. Against a background of secession, disunion, plots, rumors, and threats of assassination, Abraham Lincoln solemnly took the oath of office on March 4, 1861. In strong, measured tones, the new president emphasized his duty to maintain the Union and to uphold the federal government's authority. There would be no conflict, he pointed out, unless the South provoked it. For him, the Union was permanent and indivisible. He would continue to act just as any president would in all matters affecting the government and the Union. For all its eloquence and pathos, Lincoln's inaugural address left the national situation exactly as he found it in March 1861—tense, uncertain, and explosive.

Already the events had been set in motion that would cause that situation to explode into violence. Word came to Washington from Major Robert Anderson in Fort Sumter, in Charleston Harbor, South Carolina, that the federal garrison under his command must either be supplied with provisions by April 15, or be withdrawn. What would Lincoln do? If he did not exercise his regular functions as commander-in-chief, he would be acknowledging that the Confederate states had, in fact, actually broken from the Union. If, on the other hand, he did send supplies, against South Carolina's wishes, he would be committing an act of aggression that would undoubtedly touch off a dreaded civil war. Lincoln weighed his deep and deadly problem with great care.[75]

While the nation waited for President Lincoln's fateful decision, seventy-five-year-old William Appleton, a wealthy Bostonian and a close friend of Amos Lawrence, was sailing out of New York Harbor, aboard the steamer *Nashville,* bound for Charleston, South Carolina. The old man insisted that his trip to the South was for "reasons of health," but many of his Bay State neighbors suspected that the old Whig, who was still a member of the U.S. Congress, was going to try to make a last-minute attempt at some kind of compromise.[76] On Thursday evening, April 11, 1861, the *Nashville* lay off the Bar, just outside Charleston Harbor, waiting for the morning tide to turn while its passengers slept soundly. About 4:00 A.M., the air was split by thunderous roar of cannon fire. The startled passengers tumbled out of their bunks and rushed from their cabins in their nightclothes to see what was happening. Standing along the railings, they peered into the predawn darkness and watched the Fort Johnson shore batteries firing upon Fort Sumter. "Every flash we could see," wrote Mr. Appleton, shaking and breathless with excitement. "Then the smoke; then followed the report; the bombshells we saw ascend and would anxiously watch whether they fell in Fort Sumter."[77] As soon as he could get ashore, the old gentleman gingerly elbowed his way through the cheering crowds in Charleston and telegraphed the electrifying news to his friends back in Boston. President Lincoln had decided to send provisions to Fort Sumter, and South Carolina had taken the president's announcement as an act of war and ordered the Confederate guns to open fire. As Mr. Appleton had seen with his own eyes that April morning, the war was on.[78] For the moment, however, the old Yankee seemed to take things in stride. After a leisurely visit with friends and associates in the countryside, he got permission from General Beauregard to visit Fort Sumter, which he found to be "an awful wreck." For several more days he continued visiting friends and inspecting plantations, with no mention in his diary of any warlike preparations, and then eventually made his way home to Boston on May 15, "right glad to see my dear children and others I much love."[79]

Events in Boston had been taking place at a feverish pace. Once the attack on Fort Sumter became known, citizens sprang to their muskets, their bank accounts, and their pulpits to defend the Union cause. Men of all parties proclaimed their determination to suppress the rebellion as soon as possible. They were ready to inflict harsh punishment on those who had instigated the conflict, not merely for firing on one fort, but for a long train of abuses extending back for decades. The deepseated hostility against the alien slave society turned to anger, with some Bible-thumping Yankees talking of turning South Carolina into a desert and sowing its barren fields with salt. Confident of their own superiority in numbers and resources, Bay Staters believed the task would be completed before summer's end. But if most people received the war news with a sense of inevitability, some saw the future with deep foreboding. "Mr. Lincoln has plunged us into war," wrote Charles Francis Adams, grandson of John Adams, the country's second president and son of John Quincy Adams, the nation's sixth president, who had recently been appointed by the Lincoln administration U.S. ambassador to Great Britain. Expressing doubts about the president's ability to lead, and worried about his own sons' fate, he could not help reflecting on mistakes in the past. "We, the children of the third and fourth generations," he mused, "are doomed to pay the penalties of the compromises made by the first."[80] His friend Senator Charles Sumner was no less appalled by the prospect of war, and expressed regret that the nation had not chosen the road of amicable separation. "Alas!" he wrote to the poet Henry Wadsworth Longfellow, "that I, loving peace, should be called to take such a great responsibility in a dreadful ghastly civil war."[81]

Many other Bostonians, however, responded more enthusiastically to the opening hostilities, and saw the advantages in the South's having fired the first shots. Nothing could have been more "fortunate," wrote Charles Eliot Norton, than a rebellious state's bombarding the fort and lowering the national flag. "The whole Northern people was heartily united," he observed, "and there was but one feeling and one will among them."[82] The *Boston Recorder* agreed with Norton's assessment, and publicly thanked God for allowing the North to begin the struggle with a clear conscience. Boston abolitionists, always known for their devotion to nonviolence, were especially grateful that they could view the conflict as a rebellion rather than a war. Despite the terrible prospects of bloodshed, William Lloyd Garrison cautioned his supporters to hold back on criticizing the Lincoln administration for not being forceful enough in pushing for emancipation lest public opinion turn against them. "There must be no needless turning of popular violence upon ourselves," he warned, and urged his fellow abolitionists to practice circumspection to avoid creating harmful divisions among Northerners. The abolitionist leader was confident that the war—which the administration insisted was being fought only to save the Union—would eventually turn into a war to free the slaves.[83] His friend and colleague Wendell Phillips, who on April 9 had urged Massachusetts to avoid using war as a way of keeping the slave states in the Union, changed his mind after the attack on Fort Sumter forced him to undergo "an agony of indecision." For the first time in his life, he told a massive crowd, he was proud to stand beneath the national government's emblem. "Today the slave asks but a sight of this banner, and calls it the twilight of his redemption; today it represents sovereignty and justice."[84]

Black citizens were no less enthusiastic in their support for the administration. They crowded into a Boston Baptist church to pledge 50,000 troops to fight for the Union if only the color bar on enlistment were lifted. Clearly they wanted to participate actively in the coming struggle. Over the two previous decades, Massachusetts had removed laws that condoned segregation in schools and in public transportation, as well as those forbidding marriage between the races. And on October 19, 1859, shortly after John Brown's attack on Harpers Ferry, the state legislature finally proposed to repeal the law that prohibited blacks from becoming part of the state militia.[85]

Although this opportunity brought great pleasure to blacks as well as to white abolitionists in the city, it produced a different reaction in the Democratic party and particularly its Irish supporters. Benjamin F. Butler, a controversial lawyer-politician from Lowell who had already accused Republicans of claiming to be the slaves' friend while ignoring poor immigrant textile workers' needs, objected strenuously to serving alongside "the blackest Negro that came out of Guinea."[86] As a general in the state militia, Butler warned that his men's morale would suffer if this forced integration were passed into law. Anyone who did not agree with him, he said, "had better exhibit his taste in that line by taking himself a black wife." According to the Democratic *Post,* there could be only one purpose in enrolling blacks in the state militia at this time— to help future John Browns to burn and pillage. Bay State Republicans, argued the Democrats, would never use black militiamen to curb internal disorder, for

*William Lloyd Garrison came to Boston from Newburyport, and on
January 1, 1831, published the first issue of* The Liberator, *in which he called for
the total and immediate emancipation of all slaves. Viewing slavery as a moral evil,
Garrison founded the American Anti-Slavery Society in 1833 and began a lifelong
campaign to bring about the end of slavery. Despite his opposition to violence,
Garrison became a strong supporter of Abraham Lincoln and the Civil War,
pressing constantly for the Emancipation Proclamation and the eventual
Thirteenth Amendment. (The Bostonian Society)*

any law they enforced would become so odious it could never be maintained. Democrats expressed the hope that the "Negroes-with-guns" image would be enough to bring about a sharp reaction against the Republicans at the polls in the next election.[87]

In an interesting reaction to these Democratic assaults, the *Springfield Republican* ridiculed Ben Butler for opposing admission of blacks into the state militia, recalling that it was Butler himself who earlier had supported allowing the Irish into the same militia. Most people in Massachusetts, remarked the *Republican* with an anti-Catholic bigotry typical of the period, would sooner trust their lives and property to Negroes than to Irishmen.[88] Although the outgoing governor, Nathaniel P. Banks, vetoed the militia bill, the election in 1860 of the Republican abolitionist governor, John A. Andrew, gave new hope that military necessity would eventually force repeal of state militia laws and, indeed, all federal laws that continued to exclude blacks from military service.[89]

By this time, even local conservatives were ready to prosecute the war. Edward Everett, most recently vice-presidential candidate for the Constitutional Union party, appeared at a flag-raising ceremony in Boston's Chester Square and conceded that defeating the rebels was now the only way to save the country from "general anarchy and confusion." We must forget that we ever had been "partisans," he announced, and remember only that "we are Americans and that our country is in peril."[90] In a patriotic spirit, the *Boston Post* called upon businessmen to put aside thoughts of making money until the war was over. "We may not make money for a season—perhaps we have thought too much of money in the past," the paper philosophized, "but we are united . . . it [the war] is to be pursued until treason is rooted out and crushed."[91] Although the *Boston Courier* continued to blame Lincoln for bringing on the war, the paper's motto was "Our Country, Right or Wrong" as it called upon every Boston citizen to support the federal government. The commercial community was eager to prove its loyalty. Boston's banks loaned $3,500,000 to the state treasury and gave substantial aid toward mobilizing Massachusetts troops. Railroad and steamship-line operators offered to transport troops; counting houses promised to continue their clerks' salaries while they were away at war. Some merchants actually seemed relieved that the period of ambiguity was finally over. "Anything like certainty, even with an unfavorable result," explained the *Commercial Bulletin,* "is better than a period of suspense." "We must stand by our country," John Whitin, a successful manufacturer of textile machinery, told one of his customers forcefully.[92] Robert C. Winthrop, former Whig congressman, agreed that he could see no alternative but "to support the powers that be . . . in their measures for defending the Capital and upholding the Flag of the Country."[93]

Ten days after the attack on Fort Sumter one hundred Boston businessmen met in the Board of Trade rooms and organized a Massachusetts Soldiers' Fund to solicit contributions for supporting families of men recruited into the army. John Murray Forbes, already a staunch supporter of the Republican administration, urged President Lincoln to use the Union navy to blockade Southern ports, and then went off to Washington to pressure the authorities into putting "overpowering forces" in the field to bring the war to a rapid conclusion. Governor John Andrew almost immediately appointed Forbes to his war council, where he helped the governor make initial arrangements for transporting Massachusetts troops to Washington by water and by rail in case they were needed.[94] In close contact with railroad associates such as S. M. Felton, president of the Philadelphia, Wilmington, and Baltimore Railroad, it was Forbes who first suggested sending Massachusetts troops by water, thus bypassing any attempts to sabotage the railroad lines to Washington. Against instructions by General Winfield Scott, Forbes made plans to send troops to Fortress Monroe by chartered steamer—an idea that General Benjamin F. Butler later claimed as his own, causing Forbes to despise the "political General" ever after.[95] Throughout the war's early weeks and months, Forbes was busy buying steamers for transports, securing cannons from the Navy Yard to arm them, and engaging officers and sailors to man them.[96]

Forbes's friend Amos A. Lawrence, recent organizer of the now-defunct Constitutional Union party, had also become a vigorous administration supporter. Having given up all thought of further compromise, Lawrence assured his colleague William Appleton, who was still in Charleston, South Carolina, that in the North there was now "a unanimity of sentiment about sustaining the government." He said he could see no difficulty in obtaining the necessary number of troops "if the means of supply and transportation are at hand," and promptly went off to offer his own services to the Commonwealth. Turning his resources over to the federal government, Lawrence devoted all his extra time to instructing young Harvard undergraduates in the manual of arms. The prosperous manufacturer now became as enthusiastic in the cause of winning the war as he had been in working to preserve the peace—indeed, he expressed disappointment when, on April 15, President Lincoln called for only 75,000 volunteers. Five hundred thousand would be more like it, he told William Appleton.[97] A short time later he offered his services to Secretary of the Treasury Salmon P. Chase, who wanted to work out a plan to move southern staple products to northern markets. Reminding Chase about his years of experience as a large buyer in southern markets for manufacturing purposes, Lawrence offered to serve the government without pay "at any personal inconvenience and risk on any part of the Atlantic coast."[98] Even abolitionist Wendell Phillips had to confess that he was both surprised and impressed at this outburst of patriotic unity from State Street businessmen, and admitted that he might have been mistaken in assuming that Massachusetts was "wholly choked with cotton dust and cankered with gold."[99]

Throughout winter and spring of 1860 and 1861, the Democratic party in Massachusetts had loudly criticized the Republican party for agitating the slavery issue and for so provoking the Southern states that they had seceded from the Union. With the attack on Fort Sumter in April 1861, however, most Bay State Democrats pulled in their horns and voiced their enthusiastic support for the Northern war effort. Anything short of bipartisanship now, they feared, might sound like downright disloyalty. Too many prominent Democrats had already defected to the Republican party—Salmon P. Chase, Hannibal Hamlin, Lyman Trumbull, Gideon Welles, and Montgomery and Frank Blair. Others, such as Edwin Stanton and Andrew Johnson, would also join the Lincoln administration once the war was under way.[100] The Democratic party's first duty, therefore, was to hunker down and stay alive until the first wave of patriotic fervor had run its course and people were in a sufficiently sober mood to appreciate the benefits in a healthy two-party system.[101] Then too, though they were still generally sympathetic to the South on slavery, few Northern Democrats believed the Southern states were justified in resorting to outright rebellion. George S. Hillard, for example, long a Boston Democrat and editor of the *Boston Courier,* spoke at a public meeting about the need for all Northern citizens, whether Democrat or Republican, to support and defend the Union. The *Boston Post,* the city's leading Democratic newspaper, which had come out six months earlier supporting Breckinridge for president, now headed its lead editorial with the United States flag and the stirring caption "Stand by the Flag."[102] Caleb Cushing, staunch Massachusetts Democrat and editor of the *Post,* called for subordinating politics to preserve the Union. "Whatever may have been our antecedents, there is no uncertainty as to the duty of every citizen of the United States," he said in an informal conference with other Democrats on Cape Cod. "Party now is but the dust in the balance, the foam on the wave in comparison with Union and liberty."[103] Benjamin F. Hallet, a respected Bay State Democrat and member of the Massachusetts delegation that had nominated secessionist John C. Breckinridge at the Richmond convention, also voiced his support for the Union cause and called for an end to all partisan politics until the threat to the Union had been resolved. "Let Massachusetts be a unit in supporting the Union," he said, "and let there be no division as to men in this election."[104] Indeed, so powerful was the Democrats' support for preserving the Union that even Charles Sumner, the radical Republican senator, was suitably impressed. Although he never thought the North would be truly divided once the war came, he admitted he had never expected to witness the "ferocious unity" and the "high strung determination" that was now taking place.[105]

Even the Irish community fell into line once hostilities had begun. When the first seven southern states seceded from the Union during December and January, the Irish had been confronted with an awkward dilemma. On the one hand, for at least thirty years they had denounced the abolitionists, promoted white supremacy, defended slavery, and sympathized with the southern point of view. On the other hand, as loyal and patriotic citizens in their newly adopted country, they had announced their unquestioning devotion to the Constitution and pledged their unswerving loyalty to the Union.[106] The act of secession had brought these two positions into dramatic conflict. For a short time the Boston Irish tried to resolve their dilemma by sympathizing with the South while pleading for some practical solution to ease national tensions. With the attack on Fort Sumter on April 12, 1861, however, it was perfectly clear where the Irish stood. Indeed, about two weeks later, on the morning of April 27, word spread through the North End that a ship from Savannah, Georgia, had pulled into Boston Harbor flying the Confederacy's "rattle-snake" flag. Several hundred angry people, most of them Irish immigrants, assembled on Gray's Wharf where the vessel was tied up and demanded that the captain "lower the treasonable colors" and replace the flag with the Stars and Stripes. Although the captain and crew initially shouted defiance at the crowd and threatened to open up with the ship's guns, the pressure finally became so great that the captain was "intimidated" into complying and ordered the offending flag lowered. Not content with this concession, the crowd demanded "custody" of the banner, and when the ship's crew reluctantly flung it ashore, the Irish residents angrily tore it into small pieces, which they then paraded through the city streets.[107] *The Pilot* supported this display of patriotic enthusiasm with editorials assuring the city that "the Irish adopted citizens are true, to a man, to the Constitution" and would fight to preserve the Union. Still expressing sympathy for everything the South had suffered at the hands of "northern fanatics," *The Pilot* nevertheless insisted that nothing could justify secession and civil war. "We have hoisted the American Stars and Stripes over THE PILOT Establishment," wrote the editor, "and there they shall wave till the 'star of peace' returns."[108] At Boston's Jackson Democratic Club on Hanover Street, in a "full and enthusiastic" meeting, "adopted citizens of Boston" passed resolutions declaring it to be the "solemn duty of every man" to put aside all partisan issues and to "defend the national government and put down secession and treason wherever they may occur."[109]

On April 15, 1861, three days after Fort Sumter fell, President Abraham Lincoln had issued a proclamation calling forth "the militia of the several States of the Union" to suppress the rebellion, and later that day Secretary of War Simon Cameron sent word to Governor Andrew asking that Massachusetts send forward 1,500 men to defend Washington.[110] Lincoln's call for state militia units caused Northern states' governors to issue their own calls for enough troops to bring their state militias up to their assigned quotas. Mass meetings were held to attract local volunteers, and as soon as companies were filled they were assembled into regiments and sent along to the national government. Company commanders were invariably selected by the men themselves, and regimental officers were usually selected by the governor. In a short time more than enough troops were available, but weapons, ammunition, and military equipment were totally inadequate. Uniforms were scarce and varied, officers were inexperienced, and most recruits were without the slightest knowledge about military training and discipline.

The military situation in Massachusetts was much better than that in most other Northern states, for the well-trained and well-equipped Bay State militia was among the first to respond to Lincoln's call to arms. As soon as he was officially contacted by the Secretary of War, Governor John Andrew called upon four Massachusetts regiments, just over 3,000 men, to report for active duty.[111] The response was speedy and efficient, a tribute to Andrew's commitment to the Union cause and testimony to the work and dedication he had put into creating an organized and disciplined militia force for the Commonwealth.

Like volunteer militia units in other states in the decades before the Civil War, when there were no international dangers and few domestic perils, Massachusetts units had low enrollments and little public support. In 1851, however, things began to change when Governor George Boutwell appointed Ebenezer W. Stone as the state's adjutant general. A fifty-year-old Boston clothing merchant who had served in the state militia before becoming commander of the prestigious Ancient and Honorable Artillery Company of Massachusetts, Stone was determined to turn the militia into a first-class reserve force.[112] Working with tireless energy, he traveled around the state inspecting local militia companies, certifying muster rolls, updating regulations and training manuals, and replacing old flintlock muskets with the new percussion rifles. When John A. Andrew became governor in January 1861, he appointed William Schouler, a former Whig newspaper editor turned Republican, as his adjutant general, and the two men continued to upgrade the state militia at the very time the rebellious states were meeting in Montgomery, Alabama, to form the Confederate States of America.[113] Together they stimulated recruitment, inspected armories, let out contracts for uniforms and blankets, and worked out details for transporting troops by land and by sea. By the time war finally came in April, therefore, Governor Andrew found himself able to respond immediately to President Lincoln's call for volunteers with a well-trained, well-equipped, and well-organized militia force that one modern writer describes as "a vindication of the devotion and determination of scores of forgotten men who had labored faithfully over the years for just that moment."[114]

When the call went out from Governor Andrew on April 15, Massachusetts responded with remarkable speed. Before darkness fell that day, Adjutant General Schouler dispatched "Order No. 14" to the Massachusetts militia, ordering Colonel Edward F. Jones of the 6th Regiment, Colonel Abner B. Packard of the 4th Regiment, Colonel David W. Wardrop of the 3rd Regiment, and Lt. Colonel Timothy Monroe of the 8th Regiment to muster their commands, in uniform, on Boston Common *forthwith*.[115] In the meantime, General Benjamin F. Butler telegraphed his friend Senator Henry Wilson in Washington, requesting him to make known the need for a Brigadier to accompany the troops. Governor Andrew signed the necessary papers for the appointment, and Butler set up temporary headquarters in the State House.[116] Next day, three companies of the Massachusetts 8th Regiment, from Marblehead, pulled into Boston. With flags flying and fife and drum playing "Yankee Doodle," they marched from the trains to Faneuil Hall in the teeth of a howling storm.[117] Here the men were issued new gray overcoats that had just arrived, and many of them exchanged old smoothbore muskets for new rifles. On the following morning, April 17, the 6th Regiment, also equipped with new rifles, arrived in Boston. Shortly after noon, the two regiments marched up onto Beacon Street and halted smartly before the broad State House steps. Standing stiffly at attention, they watched proudly as Governor Andrew walked down the steps and presented their regimental colors to Colonel Edward F. Jones. Company commanders barked out their commands, rifles came up sharply, and the men of Massachusetts stepped forward into history while crowds of onlookers cheered them on their way.[118]

Although Governor Andrew had already made arrangements with John Murray Forbes to have the Massachusetts troops leave for Washington by water, Secretary of War Cameron wired that he considered that the forces would arrive more quickly if they came by railroad by way of Baltimore. The 6th Regiment plans were changed accordingly, and on April 17 the 800 men boarded the train heading south.[119] Next morning, after breakfasting in New York hotels, the Massachusetts militia marched proudly down Broadway as throngs of cheering spectators, lined along the route to the Hudson Ferry, waved flags, banners, and handkerchiefs. The New York diarist George Templeton Strong was deeply moved as he watched the men of the 6th Regiment marching through the city. "Immense crowd; immense cheering," he wrote. "My eyes filled with tears, and I was half-choked in sympathy with the contagious excitement." Strong found the feeling of unity far beyond anything he had hoped for: "If it only lasts, we are safe."[120] Next day, shortly before noon on April 19, the men of the 6th arrived at the President Street station in Baltimore and boarded the horse-drawn railroad cars that took them across town to the Camden Street station.[121] In this manner seven companies of the 6th were taken across with city without incident—when suddenly violence erupted.

Maryland was one of the states that lay between the North and the South, one of the "border states" whose loyalties would remain divided all through the war. Ever since Sumter had been fired upon, Baltimore had been in turmoil. One moment Southern sympathizers would be singing "Dixie" or tearing down the Stars and Stripes; the next moment Union sympathizers would be chanting the "Star Spangled Banner" or burning Rebel banners in the streets. As the last three Massachusetts companies were being drawn across the city, an excited mob of Confederate sympathizers quickly gathered, hooted and jeered, and then began pelting the soldiers with rocks and stones. Pistol shots rang out, one of the soldiers crumpled to the ground, and then the troops fired into the crowd and cleared a path with their bayonets. Rejoining the rest of their regiment on the other side of the city, the 6th Massachusetts Regiment continued its determined journey toward the nation's capital.[122]

In the meantime, reports had reached Washington about the clash between the Baltimore mob and the Massachusetts troops. After the troops' bloody passage, angry Confederate sympathizers had shut down the President Street station, destroyed all the railroad bridges into the capital, and cut down all the telegraph lines. It was now impossible for any more Union troops to reach Washington by way of Baltimore. With rioting Maryland on one side, and Confederate troops under General Beauregard on the other, official Washington was desperate to know the whereabouts of the men from the Massachusetts 6th. Shortly after 5:00 that evening, a special train came puffing into the Washington station. A great cheer went up as the Washington citizens recognized the men in the dark gray overcoats as the 6th Massachusetts Regiment. These were the first armed volunteers to come to defend the nation's capital, and the residents rushed to take care of those who had been wounded in the violent march through Baltimore. The remaining members of the regiment wearily made their way to the Senate Chambers, where they dropped to the floor, wrapped themselves in their blankets, and took any rest they could, preparing for an uncertain morrow. At a time when everything seemed lost, President Abraham Lincoln appreciated this gesture by Massachusetts more than words could tell, he said when he walked over to the Senate building to speak with the soldiers from Massachusetts. "I don't believe there is any North," said the president in obvious distress. "The Seventh Regiment is a myth. Rhode Island is not known in our geography any longer. *You* are the only Northern realities." The men who had paraded through the streets of Boston only a few days earlier were now the only Union regiment on hand that could have met a Confederate attack upon the capital during its six days of complete isolation.[123]

But the Confederates did not come, and on April 25 the citizens heard a welcome sound. With drums crashing out a lively cadence, the New York 7th Regiment marched into Washington, smartly dressed in their new gray uniforms with white crossbelts. Next came the 1st Rhode Island, clad in gray pants and dark blue shirts, with rolled scarlet blankets slung across their shoulders. Then the Massachusetts 6th let out a cheer, for into the capital marched their Bay State comrades, the 8th Massachusetts Regiment. When General Butler and his regiment had arrived in Philadelphia on April 20, he learned that the direct route to Washington by way of Baltimore had been closed. With instant resourcefulness, he took his troops by rail to Chesapeake Bay, put them on a boat, and steamed down to Annapolis, ignoring Governor Thomas Hicks's protests against this uninvited landing on Maryland soil.[124] At Annapolis, the Massachusetts troops repaired the railroad lines, laid new track, and put the railroad locomotives in working condition. Looking tired and worn, their uniforms already badly torn by their labors, the men of the 8th were a welcome sight.[125] Handshaking and backslapping were the order of the day when the newly arrived troops were finally dismissed and broke ranks to greet their friends who had fought their way through the Baltimore mobs. Then all drifted over to the Capitol, where the 8th was quartered in the huge Rotunda, next to their comrades in the 6th. For days the hallowed halls and marble chambers resounded to the tramping and laughing and cheering of the men who had last seen one another ten days earlier in Boston.[126]

Back in Massachusetts, the citizens were of one mind and one spirit, mobilized first by the attack on Fort Sumter, and then solidly united by the news that their own boys had been fired upon by hostile rebels—and that on the anniversary of the battles of Lexington and Concord, eighty-six years earlier. Local statesmen, newspapers, clergymen, and other molders of public opinion quickly pointed out the parallels between "the shot heard 'round the world" and the shots fired during the bloody attack in Baltimore. The news that the Massachusetts minutemen were once again fighting and dying for freedom caused party differences to be put aside and old enmities to be forgotten, as the Bay State gave its undivided allegiance to President Lincoln and Governor Andrew. Demands that Baltimore be razed coincided with praise for the Massachusetts troops. "Everybody in Massachusetts seems to be congratulating himself that he is a citizen of such a state," wrote the well-known columnist, "Warrington."[127]

Along with people in the other Northern states, most Massachusetts citizens looked forward to a short military confrontation, certainly not more than three months long ("Peace in Ninety Days" was the popular slogan), during which they would show the rebellious Southerners that federal right and might should not be challenged. Young men rushed to join the colors; older men offered their money and services to the cause; women hastened to aid the sick and wounded. Governor Andrew, thrilled with his state's patriotic response, vowed that he would never forget "that great week in April when Massa-chusetts rose up at the sound of the cannonade of Sumter and her Militia Bri-gade, springing to arms, appeared on Boston Common." Those were the days, he added gravely and somewhat prophetically, which would never again be matched in the war's history.[128]

The "great and necessary struggle" had begun. No one in the Bay State could possibly know how long the war would last. No one could look into the future and see what the coming months and years would bring. But one thing the Commonwealth's people were sure of—one thing they were most proud of—Massachusetts had kept faith with the Union.

HARPER'S WEEKLY

A JOURNAL OF CIVILIZATION

VOL. VI.—No. 262.]   NEW YORK, SATURDAY, JANUARY 4, 1862.   [SINGLE COPIES SIX CENTS. $2 50 PER YEAR IN ADVANCE.

Entered according to Act of Congress, in the Year 1861, by Harper & Brothers, in the Clerk's Office of the District Court for the Southern District of New York.

Christmas Boxes in Camp—Christmas, 1861.

This scene from the January 4, 1862, edition of Harper's Weekly *shows Union troops enjoying the festivities of their first Christmas away from home. Boxes of food and clothing have obviously just arrived, and the troops are taking advantage of winter's inactivity to share in the spoils and enjoy themselves before the spring offensive takes them back to war's harsh realities. (Massachusetts Historical Society)*

3 Baptism of Fire
~~~~~~~

*T*he Brothers' War had begun.

During the week following the attack on Fort Sumter, people in the United States found their attitude toward the reality of civil war drastically changed. Those who supported the Union cause believed firing on the fort was a deliberate attack on federal authority by a subordinate element in the federal Union. It was the fuse that started the flames of defiance blazing all through the South, and most Massachusetts citizens agreed that the rebellion should be suppressed at once.

Just as the 6th and 8th Massachusetts regiments had marched off to relieve Washington in the fighting's first days, other militia units had responded promptly to the call to arms. In the morning on April 16, the 3rd Regiment had arrived in Boston, and the 4th Regiment arrived later in the same day. Next afternoon, the 4th left for Fall River, where the nine companies (one each from Stoughton-Canton, Easton, Braintree, Randolph, Abington, Foxboro, Taunton, Quincy, and Hingham) embarked on the steamer *State of Maine* for Fortress Monroe, Virginia. Arriving at the fort early on April 20, these Bay State units were the first Union Army troops to set foot in a seceded state. The men of the 4th Regiment were assigned garrison duty at the fort, and were later transferred to Newport News, where they were stationed for the rest of their tour of duty. A few hours later the 3rd Regiment, mostly companies from Bristol and Plymouth counties, arrived at Fortress Monroe. Shortly after their landing, the troops were shifted to the *Pawnee,* a U.S. sloop of war, and assigned the task of destroying the Navy Yard at Gosport. When they had completed that assignment, they too were assigned to garrison duty at Fortress Monroe. The 5th Massachusetts Regiment was called to duty on April 19, and as requested by Brigadier General Benjamin F. Butler of Lowell, the 5th Regiment and the Boston Light Artillery embarked for Washington two days later.

Back in Boston, Governor John Andrew set about the complicated business of getting the Bay State ready for a full-scale war. He had to supply some of the first troops for federal service, and also look to the state's coastal defenses. In the chaotic days following the Fort Sumter attack, state authorities were shocked to discover that the military garrison on Castle Island had disappeared—not just from the island but from the records. "Fort Independence has forty-three guns mounted, and is supplied with ammunition, while only two men are there to defend it," reported the *Boston Post*. "A small privateer, with a few men, might easily run in and take possession, destroy a large portion of the city and escape, all in one night," it informed its readers.[1] Obviously disturbed by the prospect of a surprise enemy raid, Governor Andrew sent the New England Guards, also known as the 4th Battalion, Massachusetts Volunteer Militia, to occupy Fort Independence as an emergency measure. The Guards had many young volunteers from Boston's wealthiest families, and some were still undergraduates in Harvard College. Young Charles Francis Adams, serving as a private with the battalion, later referred to his experience on the island as a "military kindergarten."[2] Eventually, troops from the 11th Infantry, U.S. Army, arrived with 14 officers and 87 men, as a permanent garrison for the fort.[3] Assisted by a large sum of money subscribed by the city's businessmen, Governor Andrew made additional repairs on Fort Independence and Fort Warren, to billet regiments waiting to be mustered into federal service, and to imprison some Confederate officers later in the war.[4]

Across the harbor on George's Island, Governor Andrew found conditions at Fort Warren even more discouraging. Constructed of heavy Quincy granite, with high parapets and walls eight feet thick, the fort presented an imposing appearance; in fact, however, it had no guns and was worthless for defensive purposes. On April 29, the governor sent in four companies of the 2nd Infantry, known as the Tiger Battalion, to occupy the site, clear the overgrown parade grounds, and put the fortress in proper shape. During their generally distasteful labors, the young Tigers took to singing an old gospel hymn, to which they put the words of "John Brown's Body," so that after Fletcher Webster's 12th Massachusetts Regiment arrived at Fort Warren the whole regiment was soon marching to the new melody. On July 18, when the Webster Regiment came to Boston to take part in a grand review, its band struck up "John Brown's Body," the soldiers all joined in the chorus, and soon the new song was a popular sensation.[5]

Although it was quickly seen that Fort Warren was ineffective as a defense against naval attack, authorities agreed that its spacious rooms could be used to accommodate Confederate prisoners of war. After the attack on Massachusetts troops in Baltimore only a few weeks earlier, George Proctor Kane, the Baltimore chief of police, and a number of local Confederate sympathizers were arrested, taken to Fort Lafayette, and then shipped to Fort Warren. Law-rence Sangstrom, a former member of the Maryland legislature, was agreeably surprised that the Yankees fed the prisoners extremely well and treated them with "none of the rudeness and insolence we had to encounter daily at Fort Lafayette."[6]

Problems with coastal defense were complicated by difficult finances that required immediate attention by state authorities. Massachusetts troops had to be paid out of state funds from the first day they reported until the day they were formally mustered into federal service. Because the state legislature was not in session to vote these funds, the governor, with his council's consent, expended money and issued contracts that he expected the legislature (the General Court) to ratify when it eventually convened.[7] The banks in Boston, realizing that Andrew was in effect pledging the state's credit, offered more than $3.5 million as a voluntary loan to meet the state's obligations. Other banks throughout the state also pledged a part of their funds, with the under-standing that the sums would be repaid when the legislature assembled.[8] On May 14, 1861, Governor Andrew called the General Court into special ses-sion, and informed the legislators about the action he had taken during the emergency. In a short time the legislature passed laws confirming all the war expenditures and contracts made by the governor and the council in the previ-ous month, and authorizing the governor to take any measures necessary for maintaining "the integrity and the authority of the government of the United States." The legislature also voted other regulations designed to make recruit-ing troops easier for the governor to accomplish. Andrew was empowered to name a quartermaster general, for example, as well as a commissary general and a surgeon general to assist him in his work.[9] The legislature also passed an act "in aid of the families of volunteers, and for other purposes," providing that towns and cities might use tax funds to give aid to a volunteer's wife, children, or other dependent relatives. It also pledged that the state would reimburse a town up to $12 a month for each volunteer who received such an allotment. Towns themselves were forbidden to pay bounties to volunteers at this time. Finally, money was voted, scrip was issued, bonds were offered, and the credit of the Commonwealth of Massachusetts was pledged for up to thirty years so that Massachusetts would meet its obligations. These measures ac-complished, the legislature adjourned after a brief but momentous session.[10]

Besides the official steps the Commonwealth took to assist the soldier and his family, citizens throughout the Commonwealth's cities and towns took more immediate measures to support the fighting man. Soldiers' Relief Socie-ties were organized all over the state almost at once "to hold communication with the families of the soldiers" and provide them with "sympathy, counsel, and aid." Massachusetts troops now in the field "demand and deserve our anxious care," Governor Andrew wrote to Dr. Samuel Gridley Howe of Boston, about their "sanitary conditions" and matters involving "the departments of the commissary and the quartermaster."[11] Public funds were voted in several cities and towns to support this work, and these grants were matched by large private donations. Plans were formulated, too, for bringing home wounded soldiers for hospitalization and care, thus relieving the strain on the overburdened hospitals and medical facilities around Washington that would shortly be caring for battlefield casualties from the disastrous northern Virginia campaigns.

When the war broke out, the U.S. government was woefully unprepared either to handle the massive number of war casualties in the field or to transport them swiftly from battlefield to hospitals. In 1861, the Union Medical Department was understaffed and without general hospitals in Washington, and only a few in scattered locations around the country.[12] Furthermore, the Quartermaster General was reluctant to build more hospitals, for that would divert money from much-needed military equipment. "Men need guns, not beds," he growled, voicing an opinion that was fairly common in military circles.[13] Contemporary newspapers, however, called for the public's assistance to fight the war and also to alleviate the Union soldier's suffering. Throughout 1862, the *Boston Daily Evening Traveller* and the *Boston Daily Advertiser* ran advertisements in every issue seeking medical personnel to serve in volunteer regiments. These notices were written under the official seal of the Commonwealth of Massachusetts, in the official language of William J. Dale, Surgeon General. Ironically, many of the men who received appointments as surgeons were subsequently shown to have had little, if any, formal medical education. The only requirements mentioned in the notices were the vaguely worded "evidence of a regular medical education," along with the expectation that they would have "strictly temperate habits and good moral character." Unfortunately, many of the men who became surgeons proved to be little more than incompetent butchers. The *Springfield Republican* for November 11, 1862, complained that many surgeons were "incompetent as operators," and also incapable of judging "when operations are required, and at what time and under what conditions of the system they can be safely performed." Many of these doctors, charged the newspaper, labored under the delusion that "the main business of the surgeon is to perform operations, instead of preventing them."[14] Trying to improve conditions, Massachusetts General Hospital officials made their facilities available for the wartime emergency, and planned to temporarily expand their buildings to meet the needs of the disabled once the war was over. Individual physicians in several cities and towns pledged their services without charge to servicemen's families. Local medical societies voted to provide the same free service, and before long the Massachusetts Homeopathic Medical Society and the Boston Obstetrical Society pledged their memberships to the same end.

Clearly, greatly improved medical care would have to be addressed more intensively as the war expanded and the casualties mounted. The pressing need at the moment, however, was for fighting men to serve at the front. On May 3, 1861, President Lincoln issued a proclamation calling for 42,034 volunteers to serve for three years in the infantry and cavalry, and for 18,000 seamen for duty with the U.S. Navy. Two weeks later, Secretary of War Cameron indicated to Governor Andrew that the quota for Massachusetts was six infantry regiments, and he made a point of instructing the enthusiastic young governor not to supply more troops than requested.[15] The president would inform Congress in July that "one of the greatest complexities of this government is to avoid receiving troops faster than it can provide for them." Andrew immediately designated the 1st, 2nd, 7th, 9th, 10th, and 11th Regiments to meet the latest call.

Now that war had become a reality, Boston's black community hoped that the time had finally come for them to shoulder a musket and fight for their own freedom. Although in 1859 Governor Banks had vetoed a bill that would allow blacks to serve in the state militia, John A. Andrew's election gave new hope that state laws would be changed to allow blacks to serve in the military. The laws were not changed, however, and much to their anger and chagrin, African Americans were not accepted into military service. In spring 1861, at a Twelfth Baptist Church meeting, Boston's black residents called for repeal of laws against black military service. Robert Morris, the highly respected black lawyer, expressed his friends' and colleagues' eagerness to take an active part in the fight for freedom. "If the Government would only take away the disability," he pleaded, "there was not a man who would not leap for his knapsack and musket, and they would make it intolerable [sic] hot for old Virginia."[16] Deciding to take matters into their own hands, on April 29, 1861, black residents organized their own black drill society in Boston.[17] At the same time, as "recognized citizens of Massachusetts," they forwarded new petitions to the state legislature asking that the word "white" be removed from the militia law of the Commonwealth and that they be allowed into the state militia system.[18] The legislature took no action on the petition, however, and once again African Americans were unsuccessful in trying to end this form of racial discrimination.[19]

Now that the nation was at war, the Massachusetts regiments were reorganized to conform to U.S. Army standards. Each new regiment had ten companies, and each company had a captain, two lieutenants, and ninety-eight enlisted men. The regimental field officers were the colonel, who commanded the regiment; a lieutenant colonel; and a major. Staff officers were the adjutant, quartermaster, chaplain, surgeon and assistant surgeon, sergeant major, quartermaster sergeant, hospital steward, and two principal musicians, for each regiment also had a twenty-four-piece band in the war's first year.[20] Throughout the state almost 200 companies had already been formed, and thousands of young men volunteered to begin active duty. Under the Secretary of War's plan, only about 20 percent of the men would actually be called up. In their eagerness to serve, 3,000 men from Massachusetts enlisted in other states (six companies in New York state alone), but still the supply of men who desired to enlist was greater than the demand in spring 1861. Governor Andrew offered Simon Cameron ten additional regiments and, aided by Horace Greeley of the *New York Tribune* and General Walbridge of New York, he badgered the Secretary of War into calling for the additional regiments from Massachusetts by mid-June. Within two weeks, the 12th Regiment, commanded by Colonel Fletcher Webster, son of the illustrious Daniel, was mustered into service, and by early September, the 11th, 12th, 13th, 14th, 15th, 16th, 17th, 18th, 19th, 20th, and 21st Regiments were brought into federal service.[21] In summer 1861, Congress authorized the president to call up to 500,000 volunteers, and Massachusetts continued to exceed its quota. Under the new authorization, state governors were empowered to commission all field, staff, and company officers; but the president retained the power to appoint major generals and brigadier generals.[22]

Massachusetts was almost unique among the states in the Union in that it had few units that wore elaborate or outlandish uniforms: two Zouave companies, but no Turkish or Swiss Guards, or Mozart Regiments (a New York unit with several Massachusetts companies). Some companies had fine uniforms left over from their prewar days and wore them proudly. Many regiments, despite their drab attire, were still colorful in the types of men who served and the quality of their leadership.[23] When a company was organized, it was customary for the young women in the town or city to make some simple item of uniform or equipment for the men. Some ladies' groups made the regimental flags, which called for impressive ceremonies at which to officially present and accept the colorful standards. Some drilling and training were followed by regimental parades and reviews for issuing orders, appointments, and promotions, and next usually came a collation and romantic promenade. When all the preliminaries were completed and the local unit was ready to go to the front, the company would parade down the town's main street, escorted by a band and a collection of local dignitaries, and be given a gala sendoff at the railroad depot as they boarded the train for Boston.[24]

Prominent Massachusetts citizens helped organize regiments and recruit the men to fill them. Fletcher Webster had already raised the 12th Regiment and served as its commander. Senator Henry Wilson organized the 22nd Regiment and served as its colonel for six weeks in fall 1861. James Buffinton, first

mayor of Fall River and Civil War congressman, enlisted as a private in the
7th Regiment at age forty-five and served until mustered out by order of the
Secretary of War.[25] In the beginning, at least, this was a young man's war. Few
enlisted men in the Massachusetts regiments were older than twenty-five, and
very few officers were more than thirty-five. Throughout New England, college
enrollments declined significantly as young men left the classrooms and went
off to war in large numbers. Enrollment at Harvard declined from 443 to 385;
Yale from 521 to 438; Williams from 238 to 182; Amherst from 220 to 212.[26]
Harvard sent 56 percent of those who graduated in spring 1861 to serve in the
Union army, Yale sent 42 percent, Dartmouth 35 percent, and Brown 50 percent. More than 24 percent of Harvard graduates from 1841 to 1861 served
in Lincoln's armies, and Yale sent almost 23 percent, proportions far larger
than in the overall Northern population. The old-line Boston establishment
took great pride in its young men's courage and heroism, and Thomas Wentworth Higginson observed how large was the proportion among those of "Puritan and Revolutionary descent." "There is no class of men in this republic,"
he added, "from whom the response of patriotism comes more promptly and
surely than from its most educated class."[27] Young lawyers and businessmen
applied for commissions, and if these were not available they frequently enlisted as privates. Illustrious Massachusetts names such as Church, Winslow,
Bradford, Revere, Cabot, Frothingham, Adams, Holmes, Higginson, Quincy,
Webster, and Amory appear on the Adjutant General's rolls for this period;
but so too did such new names as Eppendorp, Potvin, Maggi, Wesselhoeft,
Jorgensen, Schnepp, Schaefer, Ferrero, Screibener, Eishmann, Cailloux,
Schnell, Krasinkia, and Marz. Nothing indicated more clearly than these varied names that the "melting pot" was slowly becoming a reality in the Bay
State. The army proved to be a remarkable "mixer" and a good leveler.[28] Men
who might never have met socially as civilians now became close friends in the
army, and many of these friendships continued long after the war had ended.
On the home front, too, social distinctions broke down when the mothers,
wives, and sweethearts of soldiers with various ranks and assignments met at
relief meetings and donation parties and shared an interest in the welfare of
their boys in blue.

Anticipating rapid and unprecedented growth in the armed forces, during
April and May 1861 the Union army reorganized the military system and created two new army departments: the Department of Pennsylvania and the
Department of Northeastern Virginia. Major General Robert Patterson
commanded the Department of Pennsylvania (taking in Pennsylvania, Delaware, and Maryland, exclusive of Washington and Annapolis), to which the
2nd Massachusetts Infantry was assigned as part of the 6th Brigade. In the
Department of Northeastern Virginia, commanded by Brigadier General Irvin

McDowell, the 1st Massachusetts Regiment became part of the 4th Brigade, 1st Division, commanded by Brigadier General Daniel Tyler, and the 5th and 11th Regiments formed part of the 1st Brigade, 3rd Division, commanded by Colonel W. B. Franklin.

Several regiments in the Union army have claimed credit for being first to participate actively in the Civil War. Early in June, two midwesterners were wounded in a skirmish at Philippi in western Virginia. About a week later, a Massachusetts volunteer was killed—probably the first battle death in the war. On the night of June 9, 1861, five companies of the 4th Massachusetts Regiment (a three-months regiment) had joined New York and Vermont troops in an expedition against Big Bethel, Virginia, under ten miles from Fortress Monroe. During an unsuccessful attack upon the fortification on June 10, one man in the 4th Regiment was killed and two were wounded in the first combat engagement by volunteer troops in the Civil War.[29] On July 15, 1861, the 4th Regiment was returned to Boston and on July 23, their three months of service having come to an end, the men were mustered out.

Although Winfield Scott, general-in-chief of the U.S. Army, urged the nation to prepare for a protracted war, most Northerners cavalierly assumed that a quick march upon the enemy capital at Richmond, Virginia, would cause the Confederacy to collapse immediately. Yielding to public pressure, on June 29, 1861, President Lincoln assigned the task to General Irvin McDowell—and it was "On to Richmond!" On July 16, McDowell's army moved out of Washington, crossed the bridges across the Potomac, and headed for the railroad junction at Manassas. Waiting for the Federals was Confederate General P. T. G. Beauregard, with almost the same number of troops, equally unseasoned, settled on the southern side of a little stream called Bull Run. On the morning of July 21, the two armies were lined up and ready to go at each other. McDowell confidently drove his columns against the Confederate left flank in a maneuver that seemed sure to sweep the Southerners from the field by noontime. A "stonewall" defense by General Thomas Jackson, however, stalled the Federal assault long enough for the Confederates to bring up their reserves and for General Joseph E. Johnston to come driving in from the west. McDowell's decision to pull his troops back to safer positions in the rear caused panic among the inexperienced troops, and the result was a headlong flight back to Washington.[30] The Massachusetts 5th and 11th Regiments had taken an active part in the battle of Bull Run, and had suffered heavy casualties. Nine men in the 5th were killed and two were wounded; in the 11th, casualties were even higher, with twenty-one men killed and thirty wounded. An added blow to the families at home was the news that at least fifty men from Massachusetts, including several high-ranking officers, had been captured and taken off to Confederate prisons. Seven of the wounded captives eventually died in prison, and most of the prisoners were not exchanged for many months.[31]

Because early telegraphic reports had predicted a decisive Union victory at Bull Run, the people in Boston and other Northern cities were stunned by later reports about a Union defeat. They had fully expected the war to be over in one glorious victory, and now had to swallow a bitter fact—it was an ignominious thrashing. But the disaster at Bull Run did accomplish one result: it convinced the leaders, in both North and South, that the war would be no summer picnic, no "peace in ninety days," no mere quelling of a minor insurrection. It would be a long, tedious, costly, and tragic affair in which all other interests would have to become secondary to the main goal: winning the war. "We who have so long been eager in the pursuit and accumulation of riches," said Charles Eliot Norton of Harvard, "are now to show more generous energies in the free-spending of our means to gain the valuable object for which we have gone to war."[32] Furthermore, it would not be a war that would be won by amateurs and volunteers, no matter how enthusiastic and well-meaning; it was a conflict that would require professional training and military discipline. "Enthusiasm" will no longer take the place of discipline, insisted Norton, emphasizing that the one thing most needed at this moment was the professional military attitude—the conviction that "the first duty of a soldier is obedience."[33] Even in the weeks after Bull Run, it was noticeable to civilian observers that military units were already beginning to function with much better spirit and decidedly more discipline. Rules and regulations were being rigorously enforced, reported Frederick Law Olmsted, and were producing "the most beneficial results" among older regiments as well as among newer units.[34]

Even this early in the fighting, Boston, like so many other towns and villages throughout the country, was bitterly mourning over many a soldier who would not return. When, only a few months later, a Massachusetts poet named George Frederick Root wrote "The Vacant Chair," a sadly sentimental song, many wives, mothers, and sweethearts must have felt that the words applied to them as they sang:

> We shall meet, but we shall miss him,
> There will be one vacant chair,
> We shall linger to caress him,
> When we breathe our evening prayer.[35]

Fortunately for those at home, however, Massachusetts units saw little action during this month, although a small group did take part in another "first"—initially capturing Confederate-held territory in North Carolina. The Confederates had built two forts at Cape Hatteras Inlet, Fort Hatteras and Fort Clark, which were designed to protect the North Carolina coast. Late in

August, General Butler of Massachusetts, then commanding Fortress Monroe, took troops away from three New York regiments and a U.S. Army artillery battery to undertake a move against these Confederate outposts.[36] Accompanied by a naval force under Commodore Silas Stringham, Butler's forces captured the forts without much opposition, and left a garrison behind to establish a strategic foothold on the Confederate coast. In the expedition were troops from the Union Coast Guard, soon to be named the 99th New York Regiment, in which more than 300 Massachusetts soldiers had enlisted.[37] Except for this limited action, very little combat activity went on in the Eastern theater of operations during the rest of the spring.[38] The three-months regiments returned home and were mustered out. The 3rd, which had spent most of its tour of duty at Hampton and Fortress Monroe, and the 4th, which had participated in the attack on Big Bethel, arrived in Boston just before the Battle of Bull Run, and were mustered out on the following day. The 6th, the regiment that had withstood the Baltimore attack, and the 8th, which had gotten the railroad into Washington working again, had done most of their subsequent duty in the Baltimore and Washington areas. The 5th, now a veteran unit that had lost men in battle, had also completed its three months of service and returned home a week later. All three regiments were mustered out on August 1, 1861.[39] But Massachusetts still had ten regiments to raise, and many veterans from these first five regiments reenlisted in the new regiments—this time for three years. New regiments and artillery batteries were formed, drilled, mustered in, and sent off to war.

Among the new units headed for the front were some regiments with men from Boston's Irish community who were eager to take part in the war to restore the Union and who had come out to support the Lincoln administration once the shooting had begun. On the day the Massachusetts 6th Regiment was attacked in Baltimore, leading Irish Americans in the city sponsored a public meeting at which they asserted their allegiance to the government and offered their service to preserve the Union. Thomas Cass, former commander of the Columbian Artillery, the Irish militia unit that had been forced to disband in 1855 by Know-Nothing hysteria, now offered his services to Governor Andrew and proposed to organize a regiment of Irishmen.[40] Born in 1821 in the town of Farmley, Queen's County, Ireland, Cass had been brought to Boston by his parents when he was only nine months old. After marrying at twenty-one, Cass became an owner of vessels trading with the Azores Islands and a stockholder in a Boston towboat company. He became active in local political affairs, and when the war broke out was serving on the Board of the School Committee.[41] Now, with the governor's enthusiastic permission and an authorized rank of colonel, during April and May 1861, Cass used the nucleus from the old Columbian Artillery to recruit the 9th Regiment, Massachusetts Volunteer Infantry. Recruiting commenced at the Columbian Association armory on Sudbury Street, where companies from Boston were augmented by companies of Irishmen coming in from Salem, Milford, Marlboro, and Stoughton. The new regiment was made up of ten companies in whose ranks were men from the old Columbian Guard and former members of the disbanded Emmett, Shields, Sarsfield, and Jackson Guards.[42]

Beyond small clusters of wartime letters that occasionally come to light—such as those recently discovered from a twenty-two-year-old printer, Michael H. Leary of Company B, to his sweetheart Ellen ("Nellie") back in Boston, describing the regiment's movements and assuring her that the Rebels would get "what Paddy gave the drum, that is a fine beating"—original sources to document the day-to-day activities of the men who fought in the 9th Regiment are painfully lacking.[43] Fortunately, however, the unit had two brothers from Boston who joined it on the same day (June 11, 1861), saw two years' active service, and were mustered out together on the same day (June 21, 1863). Both wrote histories of the Irish regiment. Michael MacNamara, twenty-four years old, the older of the two brothers, became a first lieutenant in Company E, but was court-martialed and discharged in November 1861. Nonplussed at this unfortunate turn of events, Michael reenlisted as a private the following summer, and eventually became quartermaster-sergeant. Daniel MacNamara, twenty-one years old, had been a bookkeeper when he enlisted, and in September 1862 was commissioned second lieutenant. Michael wrote his mainly anecdotal history of the regiment in 1867, shortly after the war ended; Daniel wrote his history in 1899, thirty-two years later, when more plentiful records and documents were an advantage.[44]

Initially, 9th Regiment companies were drilled in any open buildings that were available, usually without uniforms or weapons. Morale suffered greatly in these conditions, and company commanders complained that their recruits were drifting away. To combat desertion, the regiment was marched to Faneuil Hall to train as a group, and regular guard duty was instituted to stanch the flow of stragglers.[45] Meanwhile, to help pay for raising such a regiment, Patrick Donahoe, publisher of *The Boston Pilot*, enlisted the weekly newspaper in the Union cause, although he continued to emphasize that Irish Catholics were fighting only to save the Union—not to free the slaves. If emancipation were to become the war's military objective, wrote Donahoe, then the result would be "the spreading of Negroes over every part of the country." "The white men of the free states do not wish to labor side by side with the Negro," he announced. "Not one volunteer in a hundred has gone forth . . . to liberate slaves."[46] Despite his obvious racist reservations, however, Donahoe took a very active part in recruiting Irish volunteers for Cass's 9th Regiment and agreed to serve as treasurer of a citizens' committee to raise funds for equipping the Irish regiment when it was finally formed.[47]

The new Irish regiment filled up quickly, and on May 12, 1862, after Governor Andrew had commissioned the officers, the regiment boarded the steamer *Nellie Baker* for a short trip to a camp on Long Island, in Boston Harbor. Named Camp Wightman to honor the mayor of Boston, it had "green fields, pure salt air, and a bright sky." With pickets on sentry duty along the shore and tents pitched across the sprawling fields, Long Island looked like a true military encampment. Equipped with new .69 caliber muskets, the soldiers engaged in company drills, guard mountings, and dress parades under Cass's strict supervision. On Sundays, training was suspended and the men were allowed to roam freely about the island with family members and visitors who had brought food, refreshments, and other items for their loved ones.[48] Although he was obviously pleased with his success in launching an all-Irish regiment, Governor Andrew was disturbed by persistent rumors about inappropriate behavior among the Irish troops training at Long Island. To obtain information unofficially, he sent a Brahmin friend and Harvard Law School graduate, George D. Welles. In a confidential report to the governor, Welles expressed horror at the "disgraceful" conditions he found among the Irish troops, and offered the opinion that the unit might well turn out to be a calamity for the state. Too many officers, he reported, were ignorant, vicious, and vile; too many enlisted men were drunkards, misfits, and jailbirds. Discipline was lax, the men tippled with their own officers, and nobody cared anything about military authority. Andrew was upset by this dispatch and by similar reports, but he apparently decided to take no immediate action, hoping that Colonel Cass's notoriously strict discipline and the troops' slowly progressing military training would gradually iron out most of the worst problems. Perhaps, too, he felt that his friend Welles was overreacting to idiosyncrasies among an exuberant people he did not really know or fully understand.[49]

On Tuesday, June 25, one month after arriving at Long Island, the Irish troops again boarded the *Nellie Baker*, returned to Boston to receive their flags from the governor, and were greeted at Long Wharf by an immense crowd. Headed by Gilmore's Band and Mooney's Juvenile Drum Corps and escorted by local Irish societies, the 9th Regiment, with Colonel Thomas Cass in the lead, marched proudly up State Street toward the State House. "The crowd in the street was immense," said *The Pilot* proudly, "The windows of the banking houses and insurance offices were crowded."[50] Both sides of the street were lined with men, women, and children, cheering loudly, waving handkerchiefs, and applauding the soldiers all the way. "The appearance of the men was remarkably fine and imposing," reported the *Boston Herald*, "and gave promise

*A photograph attributed to Matthew Brady showing Irish troops of the New York
69th Regiment attending a mass in the field. Not too many hours after this was
taken, 133 members of the regiment lay dead on the battlefield at Bull Run. Boston's
Bishop John Fitzpatrick encouraged the recruitment of Irish troops, but he also insisted
that Catholic soldiers have their own chaplains and the opportunity to attend their own
religious services. (Courtesy of the Boston Public Library, Print Department)*

of an efficiency in the field which will redound to the honor of the State." [51]
Halting in front of the State House, the men stood at attention as Governor
Andrew, his staff officers, and state officials walked down the steps toward
them. Thanking Colonel Cass for raising "this splendid regiment," Andrew
presented him with a flag bearing the Bay State emblem. The United States
knows no distinction "between its native-born citizens and those born in other
countries," said Andrew, and promised that future generations would remember the patriotism being demonstrated by Boston's "adopted citizens." Along
with the national and state flags, Andrew presented to the regiment a green
silk Irish flag inscribed on one side: "Thy Sons by Adoption; Thy Firm Supporters and Defenders from Duty, Affection and Choice." At the center was
the American coat of arms, eagle, and shield. Beneath it, in gold letters, was
inscribed: "Presented to Colonel Thomas Cass, Ninth Regiment Massachu-

setts Irish Volunteers." On the reverse was the Irish harp, surmounted by thirty-four stars and surrounded by a wreath of shamrocks.[52]

After the formal ceremonies at the State House, the regiment marched down Beacon Street to Boston Common, where Mayor Joseph Wightman and several members of the city government reviewed the regiment, after which Colonel Cass made a short speech that was received with cheers. According to *The Pilot*, the troops were "well received" all along the route, and many times "the Irish 'hurrah' filled the ears of the volunteers," but at least one angry voice was heard to mutter, "There goes a load of Irish rubbish out of the city."[53] Later the regiment was presented another Irish flag of green silk, donated by Mrs. Harrison Gray Otis. Next day, Wednesday, June 26, the Irish 9th boarded three government transports and headed out of Boston, bound for the seat of war. But appreciation for the Irish service to the Union cause continued even after the men had departed, and the city gave a tangible sign of gratitude and recognition by raising an Irish flag on the Fourth of July, 1861, among the flags of all nations on Boston Common. Thus the city authorities publicly honored the Irish flag for the first time, and also ordered that the Irish national anthem be performed, along with those of other nations.[54]

Once he had raised new Bay State regiments, including the first Irish regiment, Governor Andrew was eager to do more. After a discussion with the local Catholic bishop, John Fitzpatrick, *The Pilot* publisher, Patrick Donahoe, and other prominent representatives of the Irish community, the governor wrote to President Lincoln in July 1861, asking permission to raise additional regiments in the Bay State—including another Irish regiment. After some delay Lincoln authorized ten additional regiments from Massachusetts, and late in September the governor informed Donahoe that he could right away begin recruiting a second Irish regiment. Undoubtedly bothered by criticism of poor discipline among some regimental commanders and unruly behavior by many Irish soldiers in their training camps, Andrew urged Donahoe to get "*good* captains." "We stand splendidly in the army now," he wrote, "and I know you will be proud to keep the standards high."[55] A short time later, *The Pilot* announced that recruiting had begun for a new regiment to be commanded by Colonel Thomas Murphy of the New York Montgomery Guards. This regiment would be attached to General Benjamin F. Butler's brigade. He had long been a Democrat and was a favorite among the Irish because of his factory-reform legislation and his defense of Catholic rights. *The Pilot* pointed out that pay and rations would begin upon enlistment, that the state would provide for families, and that each volunteer would receive a hundred-dollar bounty when the campaign was over. A big benefit in joining the new Irish unit, the paper pointed out, was that a Catholic chaplain would accompany the regiment. Here was another opportunity for the Irish to show their sympathy for "the country of their adoption" and for the "safety and protection of the Union."

Recruiting for the second Irish unit—now designated the 28th Regiment—moved to completion toward the end of 1861, and Patrick Donahoe continued prominent in raising funds and suggesting names for regimental positions. Indeed, Governor Andrew was so impressed with Donahoe's judgment in such matters that he accepted his personal recommendations and appointed William Monteith colonel of the regiment, McClelland Moore lieutenant colonel, and George W. Cartwright major. Donahoe's efforts for the Irish regiment were so well known that Captain William Mitchel, commander of Company A, informed the publisher that the men in his company had voted to have themselves known as "The Donahoe Guard." [56] The 28th Regiment was finally sworn into U.S. service on December 13, 1861, with Colonel Monteith in command. On January 11, 1862, at Camp Cameron in Cambridge, just before its departure for New York, Boston presented to the regiment an emerald-green banner bearing the Gaelic slogan *Fag au Bealac* (Clear the Road). Mayor Wightman and Boston City Council members attended the departure ceremonies along with Governor Andrew and other state officials, who presented the national and state flags to the regiment. The sentiments expressed in the governor's and the mayor's addresses as they presented the banners to Colonel Monteith were reminiscent of those heard seven months earlier when the "Fighting Ninth," as it was now called, was praised for its courage and patriotism.

The 28th Regiment presumably went off to New York, where it was to become one of the five regiments that made up the Irish Brigade—the 63rd, 69th, and 88th from New York, the 166th from Pennsylvania, and the 28th from Massachusetts. The Irish Brigade was mostly created by Thomas Francis Meagher, an Irish revolutionary originally sentenced to death by the British government but later banished to Tasmania. Meagher escaped his confinement in 1852, landed in New York, married a rich New York merchant's daughter, practiced law, and edited a newspaper. As captain of a Zouave company in the 69th New York State Militia, Meagher fought valiantly at the Battle of Bull Run, set about recruiting an all-Irish brigade, and in February 1862 was appointed brigadier general to command it. [57] When General Meagher and his New York staff came to welcome the newly arrived Massachusetts regiment, to their great surprise they found not the Irish 28th, but the thoroughly Yankee 29th, composed of men with names like Barnes, Chipman, Brown, and Cogswell, and a Protestant chaplain, Henry Hempstead. With consummate tact, Meagher quickly changed his planned welcoming speech, eliminating references to the glories of Old Erin and inserting fulsome praises for the part Massachusetts had played in the American Revolution. In a remarkably short time the Irishmen in the brigade's other regiments overcame their traditional dislike for the Yankees with their biblical names and their nasal twang; the Yankees, in turn, became proud of their association with a hard-fighting brigade whose green flags were always in the forefront of battle. Indeed, the men of the 29th showed such courage that the Irishmen in the three New York regiments gave the "Yankee" regiment a green banner like their own—embroidered with Old Ireland's gold harp. This was the banner the 29th carried in battles for almost a year, until military orders were finally straightened out and the Irish 28th Regiment arrived in November 1862 to take the place it had originally been assigned in Meagher's Irish Brigade.[58] The Yankee 9th Regiment, in turn, was reassigned to join General Grant's forces, which were engaged in the siege of Vicksburg. Near Frederick, Maryland, thirty-two-year-old Peter Welsh of Boston caught up with his Irish comrades. Born in Prince Edward Island, Peter had come to Boston and settled in Charlestown, where in 1857 he married Margaret Prendergast of County Kildare. On September 3, 1862, after a wild drinking spree, Peter enlisted in Company K of the 28th Massachusetts Volunteer Infantry and was promptly shipped off to the front. The letters Welsh wrote to his wife Margaret in Boston from the camps and battlefields are a valuable glimpse into an Irishman's growing pride in the loyalty of his comrades, the faith of his Church, and the integrity of the Union for which he was willing to lay down his life.[59]

The impressive patriotism displayed by the Boston Catholics, their heroism on the battlefield, the financial contributions from men like Patrick Donahoe and Andrew Carney, and the pro-Union stand held by *The Boston Pilot* inspired a wave of tolerance throughout the city and brought unusual honors for Bishop John Fitzpatrick, tangibly expressing the city's gratitude. In July 1861, Harvard President Cornelius Conway Felton informed Fitzpatrick that the college trustees had voted to confer upon him an honorary doctor of divinity degree "as an expression of their respect for your character and learning." "This is probably the first time it [an honorary degree] was ever bestowed on a Roman Catholic Ecclesiastic at Cambridge," wrote the businessman Amos A. Lawrence, a member of the Harvard Corporation and a personal friend of the bishop; "and this would not have been done," he conceded, "were it not for the loyalty shown by him and by the Irish who have offered themselves freely for the army."[60] Another concession offered to the city's Catholic community responded to a vexing question: whether Catholic children would continue to be forced to read the Protestant version of the Bible in the public schools. Trying to appease the Catholics' feelings, both houses in the state legislature agreed on a compromise bill to have the school committees require that some portion of the Bible be read daily, but "without written note or oral comment." The bill further stipulated that students could not be required to read from any version of the Bible that went against their parents' or guardians' "conscientious scruples." This piece of legislation, observed *The Pilot* with obvious satisfaction, was a "long stride" from the Know-Nothing spirit of the mid-1850s, and clearly acknowledged the loyalty being displayed by "the adopted citizens in this hour of national trial."[61]

As he worked closely with Governor Andrew in recruiting volunteers for the Irish regiments, Bishop Fitzpatrick was careful to see that Catholic troops were given the means and opportunities to practice their religion, and that Catholic chaplains were immediately provided for the newly formed 9th and 28th regiments.[62] The bishop was also eager to have the government provide more Catholic chaplains throughout the armed forces. In a July issue of *The Pilot,* publisher Patrick Donahoe reported that more than 100,000 Roman Catholics were in the U.S. Army—about one-fifth of that body. Although 400 chaplains had been appointed to serve the Northern troops, only 12 were Catholic priests, he wrote, commenting that "the prudence of the thing is equally contestable with its justice."[63] To keep his readers well informed about Irish feats of bravery on the battlefield, Donahoe initiated a feature series in *The Pilot* titled "Records of Irish American Patriotism" to demonstrate that even though the Celts were only half American in name, they were 100 percent American in deed. The weekly newspaper took pride in reporting courageous actions by Celtic soldiers, and often reminded the nation about its good fortune to be supported by such a noble race. Ever on the alert for any slight against Catholics or signs of complacency among the Irish themselves, however, Donahoe warned his readers that in many quarters the Irish were still looked upon as "only good for powder," and that just because an Irishman might have lost an arm, an eye, or a leg in the service of his country, he should not expect "he will be treated decently hereafter."[64]

Meanwhile, of course, politics went on as usual. In the nineteenth century, Massachusetts held elections every year for state officials. Now that the war was on, some thought it might be a good idea to convert the Republican party into a wartime "People's" party by nominating for office on the Republican ticket some loyal Democrats or former Whigs. Some credence was given to this idea when city leaders with different political affiliations held a pro-Union meeting in Faneuil Hall on September 9, 1861. George S. Boutwell, former Democratic governor who had turned Republican organizer; Robert C. Winthrop, prominent Whig statesman; and Josiah Abbott, long a city Democrat, were among those who organized the meeting that promoted party harmony during the crisis. "No matter who carries the flag," they announced, "we follow the stars and stripes."[65] Despite some good intentions, however, the plan fizzled, and politics continued to prevail along strictly partisan lines. Massachusetts Democrats ignored suggestions for a People's party and held their own convention, at which they nominated Isaac Davis for governor along with a full Democratic ticket. Although they continued to voice their general approval for Lincoln's conduct of the war so far, as long as it was accompanied by "the most liberal proffers of peace," they also expressed their unease with the Lincoln administration's apparent policy of trampling on individual liberties.[66] They especially cited Lincoln's actions in Maryland, where he suspended habeas corpus and imprisoned rebel leaders without a trial. Initiating a theme that would expand as the war continued, the Massachusetts Democrats called upon the Lincoln administration to show greater respect for individual rights protected by the U.S. Constitution.[67]

Taking an equally strong stand, the Republicans, at their state convention in Worcester on October 1, supported vigorous prosecution of the war, but also demanded that all citizens support the constitutional authorities "without reservation" to restore to the Constitution and the Laws their sway "over every portion of the country."[68] Despite an emotional speech by Charles Sumner urging the delegates to endorse using the war to destroy the institution of slavery, more-conservative members of the Republican party carefully shied away from Sumner's "holy crusade" and pushed through a war platform supporting Abraham Lincoln and emphasizing that the war was being fought to subdue a rebellion and to reunite the nation.[69] "The Republican party in Massachusetts was not yet ready to stand for emancipation as a military measure," writes the political historian Edith Ware; "in fact, the proposition was considered to be ill-timed and out of place."[70] In a gesture they assumed would be one of good faith, Republican leaders nominated Edward Dickinson, a former Bell-Everett supporter, for lieutenant governor, and Josiah Abbott, a well-known Democrat, for attorney general. Both Dickinson and Abbott declined the nominations, however, indicating that if they had been offered by a People's party they might have been interested. Coming from a Republican party that had refused to give up its party label, however, they preferred to remain independent.[71] Because no provision had been made for absentee soldiers to vote in the 1861 elections, an issue that would become important in other states, the vote in Massachusetts that year was unusually small—fewer than 100,000. Governor John Andrew was reelected by a more than two-to-one vote—gathering 65,261 votes to Davis's 31,264—gratifying his supporters and pleasing President Lincoln, who looked upon the young antislavery governor as a tower of strength and reliability in New England.[72] The majority in the state legislature remained with Andrew's party, and even the political minority was strongly pro-Union. All in all, the state vote in 1861 showed confidence in Andrew and the Lincoln administration.

During the summer months in 1861, Massachusetts regiments had a few skirmishes with the enemy, but the results were unimportant and the losses comparatively light. Most troops spent the summer in garrison duty, on picket duty, and in the drilling and training that the Bull Run disaster showed the green volunteers badly needed. These were long, idle days and sad, boring nights, reflected in such songs as "Tenting Tonight," "Tramp, Tramp, Tramp, the Boys Are Marching," and especially in the picket's song that men on both sides knew so well:

> All quiet along the Potomac tonight
> Except here and there a stray picket
> Is shot, as he walks to his beat to and fro,
> By a rifleman hid in the thicket.[73]

Activity began to pick up after July 25, 1861, when the Department of Washington and the Department of Northeastern Virginia were combined to form the Army of the Potomac, and placed under thirty-four-year-old Major General George B. McClellan. Young, dynamic, and brilliant (he was often compared to Napoleon Bonaparte), "Little Mac" restored morale among both the troops and the general public as he vowed to build one of the greatest fighting machines in history.[74] Lincoln's appointment of McClellan, however, produced consternation among the Bay State's more radical Republicans because the young general was known to be a Democrat. For some time many of the Radicals had been unhappy with the president's insistence on bringing prominent Democrats like Montgomery Blair and Gideon Welles into his administration, and antislavery leaders complained that when the war broke out he did not demand that such high-ranking Democratic generals as McClellan, Henry W. Halleck, and Don Carlos Buell resign. "No emancipation policy is of any value," said Wendell Phillips bluntly before a large Boston audience, "unless its earnest and downright friends are put at the head of affairs."[75] McClellan's appointment as commander of all Union forces after the defeat at Bull Run was especially difficult to swallow. Bay State Radicals protested against his initial appointment and continued to voice their disapproval when he failed to move speedily against the enemy and secure a quick victory over the South. In congressional sessions and in subsequent meetings of the Joint Congressional Committee on the Conduct of the War, Massachusetts Radicals took the lead in demanding that President Lincoln either remove McClellan from command or order him to move against Richmond. We are paying millions of dollars, complained Wendell Phillips, for having a "timid, ignorant President," and one Radical congressman remarked sarcastically that "Mr. Lincoln seems to have a theory of carrying on the war without hurting the enemy."[76]

A skillful organizer, McClellan refused to move in force against the enemy until his forces were large enough to ensure victory, and until his men were totally prepared for the task. Many congressmen were fascinated by the sight of what one historian calls "an emerging military colossus," and took regular excursions out to the drill fields in their carriages to observe the exciting spectacle of thousands of men maneuvering with remarkable precision.[77] Several Massachusetts regiments were immediately assigned to this new army and became part of the growing force of nearly 190,000 well-equipped men in the Washington area that was called the Army of the Potomac.

In October, however, McClellan's training program was disrupted—temporarily, at least—when word was received that Confederate forces under General Joseph E. Johnston had moved north into Leesburg, Virginia, dangerously close to Washington. McClellan ordered General Charles P. Stone's division, which included the Massachusetts 15th, 19th, and 20th Regiments, to make a "slight demonstration." Stone and his troops marched up the Maryland side of the Potomac, and on the night of October 20, one company of the 15th Regiment crossed over to the Virginia side and came upon a strategic bluff more than a hundred feet high. By noon the next day, the entire regiment had made the crossing, and commanded by Colonel Edward D. Baker, senator from Oregon and close friend of Lincoln, the Union troops began climbing from the beaches toward the top of the bluff. It was a poorly organized assault, and the Confederates on the summit opened up with deadly fire that drove the unprotected Federals down the bluff and into the waters below. When relief units finally arrived, they had little to do except carry off the wounded and bury the dead, including Colonel Baker.[78] There, at Ball's Bluff, was established the smallest National Cemetery in the Civil War, where twenty-seven men from Massachusetts regiments were buried. But these figures do not tell the whole story: in the 15th Regiment, 227 men were listed as missing, along with 135 men of the 20th. Many of these 362 men were wounded and most had been taken prisoner by the Confederates. In the 20th Regiment, almost two-thirds of the men who were captured were also casualties, and most remained in prison several months before they were exchanged.[79] Their heavy losses caused both the 15th and the 20th to undergo extensive reorganization. Among those who had been captured were the colonel of the 20th, William R. Lee, Major Paul Revere, Assistant Surgeon Edward Revere, and Adjutant Charles L. Peirson, who later wrote a vivid account of the action. Among those severely wounded in the engagement was twenty-year-old Captain Oliver Wendell Holmes, Jr., future Justice of the U.S. Supreme Court, who confounded the physicians by recovering from two chest wounds, only to be wounded again a year later in the Battle of Antietam. Most of the men in the 15th Regiment came from Worcester County, and the 20th Regiment had officers and enlisted men from towns and cities as far apart as Lowell and Nantucket and Pittsfield.[80] As a result, news about the casualties at Ball's Bluff brought sadness to

families all over the state, and resulted in a call for a congressional investigation.[81]

Looking for some way to offset the defeat at Ball's Bluff, military leaders
decided to follow up the earlier Union successes at the Hatteras Inlets by sending a force to Ship Island on the Mississippi River, where sat a small fort the
Confederates had abandoned in September 1861. Late in that year, troops
from Massachusetts were transported to the island, where they were put
ashore on December 3. They established "Fort Massachusetts" and were garrisoned there until spring 1862, when they embarked for the expedition against
New Orleans and the Mississippi ascent.

It was clear that the federal government was beginning to turn to the Bay
State for leadership in naval affairs. During the Civil War the Commonwealth
supplied more men for the Union navy than any other state but New York. By
the end of 1864, Massachusetts had received draft credit for 26,198 men in
the navy, although some were reenlistments. The Massachusetts Adjutant General's office indicates that Massachusetts supplied 19,983 sailors and marines
and that 1,757 of 7,500 volunteer naval officers came from Massachusetts.
These were about one-fifth of the naval personnel, and slightly fewer than one-
fourth of the volunteer officers. New Bedford alone sent to the navy more than
1,300 men from a population of 22,300.[82]

Several outstanding naval officers came from Massachusetts. Captain Gustavus Vasa Fox, a native of Saugus, and a Regular Navy officer, had been in
charge of the naval units that attempted to relieve Fort Sumter in April 1861.
Shortly afterward, Secretary of the Navy Gideon Welles named Fox as his assistant, and in that capacity he served with distinction throughout the war. An
excellent planner and a good judge of his officers' abilities, Fox is given much
credit for planning the successful Mississippi expedition.[83] Charles Henry
Davis, also a Massachusetts native, served as fleet captain in the expedition
against Hatteras Inlet and Port Royal in November 1861. In February 1862,
he commanded a gunboat flotilla in the Upper Mississippi above Fort Pillow,
and in June 1862 his fleet won the battle at Memphis, Tennessee. Occupying
Memphis was both a strategic and an economic success, for within a few
weeks thousands of bales of precious cotton were on their way north to manufacturers eager for these raw materials. Davis, by that time a rear admiral,
spent the last two years of the war as Chief of the Bureau of Navigation.[84]
Another naval leader, Captain John A. Winslow, later a rear admiral, was also
a Massachusetts native. He captained the *Kearsarge,* which finally destroyed
the *Alabama,* one of the most notorious Confederate privateers that had been
wreaking havoc upon Union shipping.[85]

In other naval activities, Massachusetts men had also made their presence felt. In March 1862, the country was electrified by the news that the *Virginia,* an iron-plated Confederate vessel, had attacked Union ships blockading Hampton Roads. Two Union wooden ships, the *Congress* and the *Cumberland,* were destroyed by the *Virginia* on March 8, 1862, and many Bay Staters were lost. Lieutenant George W. Morris captained the *Cumberland,* a sloop with twenty-four guns, and Lieutenant (later Admiral) Thomas A. Selfridge, Jr., served as executive officer aboard the same vessel.[86] Both men, as well as many in the crew, were from Boston. On the following day, March 9, the *Virginia* returned to destroy other blockading vessels, but the new Union ironclad, the *Monitor,* which had been launched only a month before, now engaged the Confederate craft in a fierce gun battle. Although the two warships exchanged shots for more than four hours, neither could claim victory, for neither received much damage. Once again men from Massachusetts served on the *Monitor;* the gunner was Lieutenant Samuel Dana Greene of Rhode Island and Massachusetts, who had a brilliant naval career following this historic battle. The North continued to build "monitors," as the new ships were named, and enabled the North to offset the immediate danger from Southern ironclads and thus maintain naval supremacy in the coastal waters.[87]

Closer to home, the people of Massachusetts did not neglect their naval security. The Charlestown Navy Yard was busy throughout the war, enlisting sailors (7,658 during the war's first year); training naval personnel; constructing, repairing, and maintaining war vessels; and manufacturing rope and other naval stores. Governor Andrew had strengthened the forts in Boston Harbor at the beginning of the war, but other forts also needed attention. Reports that Confederate privateers were seen cruising in Long Island Sound and in Buzzards Bay early in 1861 stimulated plans for attending to coastal defenses in the New Bedford area. At Clark's Point, a sand battery was constructed and three twenty-four-pound guns were mounted. At Fort Phoenix in Fairhaven and at Fort Taber at Clarke's Point (now Fort Rodman), companies of home and coast guards and an artillery company were organized to man the guns, patrol the coast, and garrison the forts. Not until spring 1862, however, when the *Merrimac* appeared to threaten the entire Atlantic coast, did the state legislature take action. Although the Navy Department had informed Governor Andrew that it wanted all naval vessels reserved for the nation's use, it did advise the state to erect some kind of physical obstructions in the harbors to keep out any enemy vessels. Much to Governor Andrew's annoyance, almost another year passed before funds were finally appropriated for coastal defenses. Earthworks were constructed at Provincetown and Plymouth on the South Shore, and at Newburyport, Gloucester, and Salem on the North Shore.[88]

Despite a Union blockade that officially extended from Virginia to Texas,

Confederate cruisers managed to elude the federal warships, put to sea, and engage in privateering. Southern ships attacked Northern vessels and inflicted great damage, usually confiscating cargo, removing crew members, and then setting the vessel afire. Ship owners from Boston, Salem, Gloucester, and New Bedford who were engaged in West Indian, Caribbean, and South American trade suffered heavy losses throughout the war. In whaling the losses were especially great. When the Civil War broke out, whaling vessels from Nantucket, New Bedford, and Salem were scattered all over the globe, and they were especially vulnerable to random attacks. Of the fourteen whalers destroyed by the Confederate raider the *Alabama,* eight were from New Bedford. In the Pacific, the *Shenandoah* destroyed many whalers, and continued to inflict damage several months after the war ended.[89] All in all, twenty-eight whaling vessels from New Bedford were destroyed, and barrels of sperm oil valued at $500,000 were taken or destroyed by the enemy. Destruction of Bay State ships clearly contributed to the New England whaling industry's decline, and also diminished Massachusetts as a leader in commerce and trade. "Every great war has brought an upheaval in Massachusetts commerce, some for the better," concludes Samuel Eliot Morison, "but the Civil War conspicuously for the worse."[90]

The U.S. Navy was aware that Confederate ships were slipping out of such Atlantic ports as Charleston and Savannah, then sailing down to Bermuda and the Bahamas to pick up cargoes of arms and supplies. In summer 1861, the navy decided to sink a flotilla of forty-five old wooden ships, loaded with heavy stones, at the mouths of enemy harbors. With this objective in mind, the navy sent agents to New England ports—New London, Mystic, Sag Harbor, Nantucket, New Bedford—to negotiate for old ships at a cost of somewhere between $3,000 and $5,500 each. Because some 7,500 tons of stone were also needed, the government contracted with a New Bedford merchant to furnish it at fifty cents a ton. Many farmers in the nearby towns and villages dismantled their old stone walls in their eagerness to cash in on this profitable opportunity. Very soon, the ships were ready and loaded, with two-inch holes along their waterlines plugged with bolts until the time came to remove them and sink the ships.[91]

The so-called Stone Fleet left New Bedford late in November and early in December 1861. On December 20, sixteen of the vessels were moved into Charleston Harbor, the plugs were removed, and the ships were sunk. Shortly after, fourteen more vessels were towed to the entrance of Maffitt's Channel, about six miles east of Fort Sumter, and sent to the bottom.[92] Although British and French newspapers attacked the Stone Fleet as a barbarous action, a matter of vengeance rather than an act of war, the expedition turned out to be a fiasco. The old ships' wooden hulls were quickly broken up by tides and currents, and the heavy stones embedded themselves deeply in the sand. Except for making the blockade runners resort to slightly more devious routes, the Great Stone Fleet failed to accomplish its purpose.[93]

In the meantime, as the Bay State played its part in the war at sea, Governor Andrew got involved in an interstate problem with Governor Thomas A. Hicks of Maryland. Following the Baltimore riot the previous April, Governor Hicks was more favorably disposed toward President Lincoln, kept the state legislature from voting for secession, and helped keep Maryland in the Union. In the November elections, a pro-Union legislature was chosen, and Hicks summoned the body into session at once to vote in favor of the war. The chairman of the Committee on Militia was then instructed to confer with the Massachusetts governor about "the condition of the widows and orphans, or any dependents on those patriots who were so brutally murdered in the riot of the 19th of April," because the Maryland legislature was "anxious to wipe out the foul blot of the Baltimore riot."

Governor Andrew promised to study the matter, stating in his letter: "The past cannot be forgotten; but it can be, and will be, forgiven, and, in the good province of God, I believe that the day is not distant when the blood that was shed at Baltimore by those martyrs to a cause as holy as any for which sword was ever drawn, shall be known to have cemented, in an eternal union of sympathy, affection, and nationality, the sister states of Maryland and Massachusetts." Following Andrew's subsequent report, the Maryland legislature voted $7,000 for the families of the men killed or wounded in the riot, and Andrew arranged to distribute the money. The full correspondence between the governors, and between Andrew and the legislature, was published in Baltimore and in Boston, winning for both Hicks and Andrew much favorable publicity.[94]

Although relations between Governor Andrew and Governor Hicks came to an amicable resolution, an unsavory dispute between Andrew and General Butler ended much less satisfactorily. Long before the war, Benjamin Franklin Butler thrived on controversy. As a successful lawyer in Lowell and Boston he had became known as a champion of the underdog, upsetting influential mill owners by trying to reduce working hours for immigrant workers. In the state legislature he led the minority faction, ferociously attacking his opponents' personal and public lives. In 1860 he was a delegate to the Democratic National Convention, voted to nominate Jefferson Davis, and later supported the candidacy of John C. Breckinridge. And in fall 1860, he had the temerity to run against John Andrew in the state's gubernatorial election on the Southern Democratic ticket.[95]

Just after the war began, having transformed himself into an outspoken defender of the Union, Butler used his influence with Senator Henry Wilson to obtain an appointment from the governor to command the Massachusetts

John Albion Andrew was a graduate of Bowdoin College and a successful lawyer before entering politics and achieving leadership in the Massachusetts Republican party. A strong opponent of slavery, Andrew was elected governor of Massachusetts in 1860, dispatched Massachusetts regiments to Washington, D.C., and mobilized the resources of the Bay State in support of the Union cause. President Lincoln always regarded Governor Andrew as his most constant and loyal supporter. (The Bostonian Society)

Brigade. Soon after Butler went south with the troops, Governor Andrew regretted his decision—and he would continue to regret it throughout the war. At Annapolis, when Butler heard rumors about a possible slave revolt, he offered troops to Governor Hicks to help suppress the insurrection. Governor Andrew, a zealous abolitionist, was visibly upset when he heard this news, and engaged in heated correspondence with Butler that was subsequently released to the newspapers.[96] Andrew was further infuriated when he learned that Butler had not freed slaves who had fled to safety in Fortress Monroe. Instead, he had classified them as "contraband of war," which he announced he would willingly return to any loyal Southerner.[97]

Late in summer 1861, the War Department authorized Brigadier General Thomas W. Sherman to raise an army for a special expedition to the Carolina coast. Governor Andrew agreed to supply Massachusetts troops for Sherman's regiment. A short time later, General Butler received authorization from Secretary of War Cameron to raise six regiments in New England for an attack on the Gulf Coast.[98] When Governor Andrew learned of Butler's recruiting activities, he announced that his first commitment was to General Sherman. Until the regiments designated for Sherman were filled, said Andrew, he would allow no new regiments to be formed without his permission. Andrew offered Butler command of the 26th Regiment, which was then being organized by Colonel Edward F. Jones of Pepperell, who had previously commanded the 6th Regiment. Although Butler gladly accepted command of the 26th, he indicated that he not only intended to raise two new regiments of his own, but expected to select the officers for these units himself. This being a violation of established procedure, Andrew protested vehemently against Butler's attempt to use federal influence to usurp the state governor's prerogatives.[99]

Despite Andrew's strong objections, Butler went to Washington and obtained a new general order creating a separate Military Department of New England that would be under his command. He then raised two regiments, the 30th, the "Eastern Bay State Regiment," and the 31st, the "Western Bay State Regiment." He also enlisted an artillery company and three cavalry companies. He himself named the officers for all these units.[100] The 26th, in the meantime, had left Massachusetts together with the 9th Connecticut Regiment, to head for Ship Island and the beginning Gulf Campaign. In January, the 30th and 31st Regiments, along with the artillery and cavalry units, left the state—but the officers in all these units were still without commissions issued by Governor Andrew, who continued to protest against Butler's outrageous actions. He sternly warned that any soldiers recruited by Butler were not eligible for state aid, and he carried his protests directly to Washington.[101] Finally, in January 1862, with Butler refusing to budge, the War Department decided to abolish the newly created Department of New England and formally agreed that the governor of the Commonwealth should issue commissions for the officers in Butler's units. Andrew, however, obviously still stewing over the affront to his authority, refused to commission many of the high-ranking officers Butler had named, and forced the general to find other places for them on his staff. Although the governor had won the argument, the four-month public correspondence between the two men gave people on the home front an unfortunate example of petulance and pride at a time when families, confronting lost sons and wartime suffering, expected much more.[102]

Just before Thanksgiving, Boston came alive with excitement over the news that the Fort Warren prison in Boston Harbor held two important political prisoners—Confederate agents who had been on their way to Europe.[103] In October 1861, the Confederate government, still hoping for recognition abroad, decided to send James Murray Mason of Virginia to London, and John Slidell of Louisiana to Paris, to work toward that end. The envoys traveled to Havana, Cuba, where early in November they took passage on a British naval packet, the *Trent*. One day out of Havana, the U.S. warship *San Jacinto* stopped the *Trent*, and U.S. Navy Captain Charles Wilkes removed Mason and Slidell and carried them to Boston Harbor on November 24, 1861, where they were confined in Fort Warren. The two Confederate agents were quartered in the front room of Quarters Number Seven, with arrangements for their two male secretaries in an adjoining room.[104] Although Wilkes's action was probably a breach of international law, most Americans cared little about diplomatic niceties in wartime. Starved for a military victory of any kind, the public hailed Wilkes as a national hero.[105] Newspapers praised him, at banquets in many northern cities prominent dignitaries paid homage to the popular captain, and the U.S. Congress passed resolutions in his honor. On the other side of the Atlantic, however, the British public was outraged at the flagrant insult to their national honor. War talk filled the air; 10,000 British troops were dispatched to Canada; and the Secretary of State for Foreign Affairs, Lord John Russell, drew up a strongly worded note demanding return of the Confederate agents and a formal apology from the U.S. government. President Lincoln confronted a delicate problem: if he did *not* apologize for Wilkes's action, he faced possible war with Great Britain; if he *did* apologize to the British, he risked angering the Northern public, to whom Wilkes was a national hero.[106]

A Boston man handled most of the complicated negotiations between the American State Department and the British War Office over "the *Trent* affair." Charles Francis Adams, grandson of one president and son of another, was born in Boston in 1807, graduated from Harvard College in 1825, briefly practiced law, but spent most of his early career in politics. As a Whig legislator he served three years in the Massachusetts house and two more in the state senate before his antislavery views persuaded the Free-Soil party to offer him its vice-presidential nomination. After moving to the Republican party, in 1858 Adams was elected to the U.S. Congress, where his calm demeanor and moderate views made him something of a question mark among his more explosive Radical colleagues. Indeed, in the exploratory attempts to find common ground with the Southern secessionists during the troubled winter of 1860–1861, Adams's conciliatory attitude and his apparent willingness to consider alternative proposals produced a nasty personal split with Senator Charles Sumner and caused many other Radicals to accuse him of selling out the Republican platform.[107] President-elect Abraham Lincoln's first Cabinet choice was his Chicago rival, William S. Seward of New York, as Secretary of State, a choice with which he may not have been truly comfortable but one that immediately strengthened his Cabinet's appeal. Seward, in turn, had hoped that Lincoln would also give Charles Francis Adams a position in the new Cabinet; but when that did not happen he strongly recommended the fifty-four-year-old Bostonian for the post of ambassador to Great Britain. Adams was a lifelong friend and a tireless political worker who had supported Seward in many of his endeavors and who had stumped the Northwest with him during the 1860 campaign.[108]

In many ways, Adams was a natural for the post in London, both for his highly regarded academic and professional background and for his unique family traditions. His grandfather John Adams had been prominent in the American delegation that worked out the final Treaty of Paris that successfully concluded the American Revolution and recognized the former thirteen colonies as the independent United States of America. His father, John Quincy Adams, had been on the American team sent to the Belgian town of Ghent in 1814 to negotiate with the British to end the War of 1812, and later served nearly eight years as Secretary of State in the Monroe administration, where he formulated the principles that became the Monroe Doctrine, placing him among the highest-ranked secretaries of state in American history.[109] A widely read, broadly traveled, and politically experienced politician-statesman, Charles Francis Adams brought an impressive heritage to a difficult task: reconciling American pride with British determination. Mainly because of his patient and skillful handling of the *Trent* affair, British-government leaders were finally persuaded not to take drastic action. His prolonged diplomatic negotiations gave the U.S. government time enough to work out a diplomatic solution to the complex problem. Lincoln finally apologized that Captain Wilkes had not followed the proper procedure (he should have brought the vessel itself in to port for adjudication); the prisoners were released; and Secretary of State Seward complimented Great Britain for having at last acknowledged the principle for which the War of 1812 had been fought—freedom of the seas. Although the British government was never quite certain whether it had received an apology or another insult, it chose to regard the unfortunate incident as closed rather than risk conflict with the United States.[110] The immediate crisis had passed and tempers had been allowed to cool down, it was true, but trouble between the United States and Great Britain was by no means over, and Charles Francis Adams would have many more incidents that would call upon his considerable diplomatic abilities.

Late in 1861, the cold weather was closing in and the Union armies were preparing to go into winter quarters—usually an encampment where a military unit would rest from its exertions during the year, and prepare for the customary spring offensive. Civil War soldiers, writing later, invariably recalled that this first winter was the best they would have until the war was over. The 2nd Massachusetts Regiment was encamped at Seneca Creek, near Dainestown, Maryland, late in October 1861. They lived in Silbey tents, large unheated canvas houses that held about sixteen men. The sickness rate, especially measles and typhoid fever, was high in this swampy area. Finally, on December 4, the regiment was transferred to a site near Frederick, Maryland, where it remained until February 28, 1862. Here the men cleared the underbrush and surplus trees, leveled some of the land, and turned the woods into a "delightful grove, where the sun shone all day, to the great improvement of health." The 2nd went into winter quarters "by degrees." First, they lived in their tents and slept on straw on the bare ground. Then boards for tent floors were delivered. Later the wooden sides of the hut were constructed about three feet high, and the tents were pitched on this foundation. Stoves were installed in the middle of the tent, and the smoke rose through a makeshift chimney. They had comforts from home—gifts of food, clothing, pincushions, pillow covers, needle cases, and all kinds of religious tracts. Two thousand pairs of gloves, sent by Mrs. Harrison Gray Otis and her women volunteers, were received gratefully, although some of the socks made by the young female students at a Cambridge private school were, according to the colonel, "like the world when it was without form and void." Most regiments celebrated the holidays with makeshift camp feasts, during which the men produced plays and sang songs. Many regiments in the camps celebrated Thanksgiving with special foods and supplies sent from home for the occasion.[111]

Although during the 1860s Christmas was not usually an important holiday in Massachusetts, many soldiers now living with German and Irish soldiers, who celebrated the day with feasting and exchange of gifts, caught the Christmas spirit and entered enthusiastically into the celebration. But these periods of pleasurable recreation were few in the soldier's daily life in wartime. "There was not much time for play, or idleness, or dissatisfaction," wrote the regiment's historian. "These men were well-fed, thanks to the Ladies' Association at home; were well-sheltered; were nursed when sick; were well drilled and disciplined; were, in short, well cared for when they obeyed, and well punished when they erred; and so the machine, well regulated, moved under an intelligent will." Other Massachusetts regiments followed similar patterns, depending on their place of encampment. The 7th Massachusetts Regiment, recruited primarily in Taunton, had been stationed at Camp Brightwood in Washington, D.C., at the intersection of Seventh and Fourteenth streets, about five miles from the city's center. The unit was visited by so many dignitaries and subjected to so many reviews and inspections, according to the regimental historian, that its principal military work was "guard mounting and dress parade." When the fall came, each company in the 7th Regiment detailed men to go into the nearby woods to fell trees, trim them, and cart them to the camp. Then at Brightwood, other details built log cabins to shelter the regiment for the winter. Fortunately for the woodchoppers and the amateur carpenters, most of the lumber was cottonwood, which is easily cut and split. Each barracks building was about 25 feet long and 10 feet wide. On the end wall and at each side of the building were three tiers of bunks. A heavy pot stove stood in the middle of the floor to warm the barracks and provide heat for drying socks, shoes, and other clothing. Troops on garrison duty in permanent army forts probably had the best-constructed quarters, but complaints were few about life in the barracks and about food during that first winter. Little did these men know that this first winter would probably be their only "comfortable" one in the entire war.[112]

As 1861 drew to a close, Governor Andrew must have looked back upon his first administration with satisfaction. By the end of the year, thanks greatly to his personal leadership, Massachusetts had been able to send out twenty-two regiments for three years of service, with another regiment ready to leave early in January 1862. A cavalry regiment and two sharpshooter companies had been organized and four Massachusetts companies had garrisoned Fort Warren. When we add the six companies of Massachusetts men in the New York state regiment, the 300 who enlisted in the Union Coast Guard at Fortress Monroe, and the 7,658 sailors who had enlisted at the Charlestown Navy Yard, in only nine months Massachusetts had furnished more than 41,000 volunteers for the nation's defense. Despite his recent unhappy experience with General Butler, Governor Andrew could take great pride in the Bay State's contribution to the national security, and could derive additional satisfaction from his successful dealings with Maryland and its governor.[113]

Charles Sumner graduated from the Harvard Law School, but left the study of law for the more exciting arena of political action. Sumner went to the U.S. Senate in December 1851, and became such a vigorous opponent of slavery that he was severely beaten in 1856 after a speech against the Kansas-Nebraska Act. During the Civil War, Sumner was the leader of the Radical Republicans who pressed for the Emancipation Proclamation, the Thirteenth Amendment, and postwar measures intended to bring about racial equality. (The Bostonian Society)

4 ~~~~~~ The Dark Clouds Gather

It was a year of promise and disappointment.

Even before the winter of 1861–1862 ended, Massachusetts troops had once again gone into action. General Butler's successful amphibious operation in the previous fall at Fort Hatteras, together with Flag Officer Dupont's successful expedition against Port Royal, convinced the War Department that it was time to exploit these victories. In February 1862, a combined force under Rhode Island's General Ambrose Burnside was dispatched to attack Confederate fortifications on Roanoke Island, North Carolina. Five Massachusetts infantry regiments took part in the fighting and in subsequent offensive actions against the enemy at Newbern and Washington, North Carolina. Throughout the campaign, Bay State regiments were prominent and suffered about half the force's casualties—127 killed and 500 wounded. Despite these losses, Burnside's success in seizing Roanoke Island and Newbern made the Union blockade much more effective. Of the chief ports on the South Carolina coast, only Wilmington, North Carolina, and Charleston, South Carolina, remained in Confederate hands.

By the time spring arrived, according to William Schouler, adjutant general of the Commonwealth, Massachusetts military units were spread all the way "from the valley of the Shenandoah" to "the lowlands of Louisiana."[1] Thirteen infantry regiments, three light-artillery batteries, and two sharpshooter companies were part of the Army of the Potomac; three regiments were stationed with the Army of Virginia in the upper Potomac; six regiments were attached to General Burnside's army in North Carolina; three infantry regiments, three cavalry companies, and two light-artillery companies were assigned to the Department of the Gulf. One infantry regiment and one cavalry regiment were stationed in South Carolina; other artillery units were defending Washington, D.C., and on garrison duty at nearby Fortress Monroe. In the first six months of the year, 4,587 additional men were recruited in Massachusetts for the army and sent to the front. All this arming was accomplished before July 1862, when President Lincoln issued his newest proclamation, calling upon the country to provide 300,000 additional men to serve for three years, or the duration of the war. On March 13, 1862, a delegation from Massachusetts, led by Representative Charles R. Train and including Nathaniel Hawthorne, the well-known author, called upon President Lincoln and presented to him an "elegant" buggy whip made by a Bay State manufacturing plant. Lincoln expressed his thanks, admired the gift, and added: "It displays a perfection of workmanship which I really wish I had time to acknowledge in more fitting words, and I might then follow your idea that it is suggestive, for it is evidently expected that a good deal of whipping is to be done." But then he added in a more conversational tone: "As we meet here socially, let us not think only of whipping rebels, or of those who seem to think only of whipping Negroes, but of those pleasant days which it is to be hoped are in store for us, when, seated behind a good pair of horses, we can crack our whips and drive through a peaceful, happy, and prosperous land."[2]

But peaceful, happy days were a long way off as President Lincoln turned to the distasteful task of persuading General George B. McClellan to take the offensive. During fall 1861, when the weather was most suitable for marching and fighting, McClellan had continued his elaborate training programs and had undertaken no major offensive operations. Now that early spring was under way, Little Mac showed no inclination to bring the Army of the Potomac into battle. Pointing to recent successes in the West, where General Ulysses S. Grant had captured Forts Henry and Donelson in February, and had then defeated Confederate forces in the battle of Shiloh two months later, critics increased their complaints about General McClellan's "masterful inactivity."[3] Early in 1862, President Lincoln tried to set Washington's Birthday, February 22, as the date for a general forward movement by Union troops in Virginia, but McClellan still refused to march on Richmond. Finally, however, he agreed to take the offensive, using a roundabout water route that would land his troops on the Confederate capital's eastern flank, on the peninsula between the York and the James rivers. In a well-executed maneuver, McClellan transported about 112,000 men to the peninsula early in April, but instead of driving immediately on the Richmond defenses' eastern flank, he settled in for an elaborate, month-long siege of a Confederate fortress at Yorktown, employing almost 10,000 soldiers from Massachusetts. When the Confederates finally abandoned the fort on May 5, McClellan was ready to move ahead with his advance, confident that the Confederate capital's fall was a foregone conclusion.[4]

While McClellan was getting ready for the final drive against Richmond, activities were taking place elsewhere. Throughout the winter of 1861–1862, General Benjamin F. Butler's Massachusetts troops had remained encamped at Ship Island, about ten miles from the Mississippi River.[5] Here, Butler and his men waited to start a land-sea expedition that would strike against Confederate fortifications along the lower Mississippi. Commanded by the crusty sixty-year-old Admiral Farragut, a Southerner who had refused to abandon the Union, and who was ably seconded by Commander David Porter, a naval fleet moved into the Gulf and headed for the great river mouth. Running his Union frigates past the shore batteries of Forts Jackson and St. Philip at night on April 23, 1862, Farragut's heavy guns destroyed the outer defenses and forced the evacuation of New Orleans. General Butler and his men, mostly from New England, were left behind as an occupation force while Farragut and the fleet continued to sail northward.[6]

As a career politician now serving as a civil administrator, Butler demonstrated remarkable competence in improving living conditions in New Orleans. He suppressed lawlessness, constructed drainage systems, reduced the incidence of deadly yellow fever epidemics, and promoted commercial activity. For all his efforts, however, the Yankee general got little support and even less praise from Crescent City residents, who resented his heavy-handed version of martial law, and who accused him of lining his pockets by speculating in southern cotton.[7]

Among other things, the occupation of New Orleans pointed up the complications in obtaining cotton supplies from the Confederacy. Despite constant military demands to end all trade with the enemy, President Lincoln was pressured by northern textile interests to procure enough cotton to fulfill government orders and contracts.[8] The Boston Board of Trade had already begun negotiating with the Quartermaster General about contracts for army uniforms, and in October 1862 a Boston business delegation came down to Washington en masse to urge speedy occupation of Texas so that New England mills could "obtain a supply of cotton."[9] Although he acknowledged that hard-line field commanders like Grant and Sherman would be "disturbed," Lincoln ordered his chief of staff, General Henry Halleck, to see that "all possible facilities are afforded for getting out cotton. It is deemed important to get as much as we can into market."[10]

From his vantage point in New Orleans, General Butler showed himself more than eager to cooperate with the government's policy. It was impossible, he stated, to overrate the importance of supplying cotton to northern manufacturers, "to say nothing of the effect on European powers." "I have endeavored in every possible way to open trade in cotton through the rebel lines," he added, stressing his assumption that this move was "consonant with the wish of the Government." Butler, one of the largest stockholders in Lowell's Middlesex

Mills, went on to promise "safe conduct, open markets and prompt shipment" for all southern cotton. Moreover, he boasted, he would see that each planter got his money—even if he were "Slidell himself!"[11] Thus a fabulous trade began, made easier because by 1862 and 1863 many Confederates were willing to sell their cotton to the first buyers. Desperate for cash, planters sold off their surplus cotton to European buyers and even to those whom Confederate newspapers were denouncing as "enemies and traitors" from the North. Late in 1862 it was reported that Judah P. Benjamin, Secretary of State for the Confederacy, had authorized the private sale of cotton to Yankees. Secretary of War Randolph not only permitted Mobile citizens to trade with Butler, but expressed to Jefferson Davis his opinion that trading with enemy ports was forbidden only to citizens—not to the government. Complaining that this was "the first really dark period of our struggle for independence," John B. Jones, clerk for the Confederate War Department in Richmond, condemned this news as nothing less than "treasonable traffic" with the enemy.[12] Before long, Union sailors were also actively and ingeniously involved in the New Orleans cotton traffic. The tars used their own money to buy up as much cotton as they could (and even used converted navy equipment to gin and bale it themselves), and they then borrowed incoming army mules to haul away their lucrative bundles, stamped "C.S.A." on one end and "U.S.N." on the other. Disgruntled army personnel insisted that these initials stood for "Cotton Stealing Association—United States Navy."[13]

The exercise of military power by Yankee officers, combined with unscrupulous speculation by profiteers, produced a wave of bitter animosity among the native New Orleans residents. Hot-tempered men publicly defied Union authority, and haughty women openly gestured insults against federal troops. Young Henry Warren Howe told his relatives back home about sitting on the sidewalk with buddies watching people pass by and admiring the "colored folk" dressed so finely, with their "high colored turbans," when an "aristocratic" white lady took pains to walk by the soldiers several times, flaunting a "secesh flag" wound around her waist. "She said she would tear the United States flag before our eyes, if she only could get one," the Yankee soldier wrote.[14] General Butler finally decided that the time had come for decisive action. He publicly hanged a man named Mumford who had hauled down the Union flag from the customs house, and he issued his famous "Woman Order," declaring that any female who displayed any form of "insult" or "contempt" toward any of his men would be charged with being "a woman of the town plying her avocation."[15] Southern chivalry was shocked to its core at this flagrant insult to Southern womanhood, a price of $10,000 was placed on "Beast Butler's" head, and European nations condemned the Union general's uncivilized "barbarity" in waging war on innocent women. Although Butler resolved his immediate problem, he had committed a scandalous blunder whose lasting propaganda effects would be difficult, perhaps impossible, for Union authorities to counteract all through the war.[16] Indeed, the pressure on President Lincoln became so great that in December 1862 he had to remove the general whom critics unkindly called the "American Cyclops" (Butler had a cast in one eye) from the one job he was probably capable of doing well, and sent the politician-general back to military operations in the field, where he was inclined to do very badly. Perhaps to suppress any feelings of satisfaction among local residents over Butler's transfer, Lincoln replaced him with another Yankee—this time Nathaniel P. Banks, former governor of Massachusetts and now a major-general of volunteers. Young Henry Howe and his fellow soldiers were quite surprised at this change in command and the swiftness with which it was accomplished. "I tell you what," he wrote back to his relatives in Boston, "there are many blue faces round here. No one knows why this thing has been done." [17] For the moment, however, Butler was greeted as a hero throughout the North, for the Union victory at New Orleans had at least given the people in Massachusetts something to cheer about.

On July 4, 1862, Massachusetts celebrated Independence Day enthusiastically because it seemed an appropriate moment to reaffirm the people's patriotic spirit. Independence Day itself was beautiful, cool, and sunny. Families flocked to the cities and towns all over the Commonwealth to take part in patriotic festivities. Boston was decorated with flags and bunting. Slogan-emblazoned banners hung from public buildings and private homes: "Union—Constitution—Law" and "Obey the Laws—Support the Constitution of the United States" were popular themes. On Boston Common, a Liberty Pole attracted much attention. During the American Revolution the Pole had been famous as a rallying point and now, eighty-five years later, it served the same function. All kinds of patriotic programs and exercises took place. Ranks of soldiers and cadet militia companies from the city schools marched through the streets accompanied by bands. At the Academy of Music, speakers reminded citizens of their duty and recalled proud episodes in the nation's past, and several hundred schoolchildren sang a special ode called "Old Glory." In the evening, at a grand Faneuil Hall dinner, Boston mayor Joseph M. Wightman sounded a most appropriate theme: "Let Massachusetts sons be animated with the spirit . . . that whatever the cost, this rebellion shall be crushed." But the day had gaiety as well as military symbolism. Young and old could enjoy all sorts of entertainment, such as a sailing regatta on the Charles River, a display of magic tricks at Tremont Temple, a special balloon ascension from Boston Common, and a band concert in the evening.[18]

The war was never far from the people's minds, however, and the occasion's temporary merriment was subdued by ominous reports about events taking place hundreds of miles to the south. The public's exaggerated confidence, so evident in the war's early months when most people were predicting "peace in ninety days," had quickly disappeared and grimness had settled over the home front. The people of Massachusetts were now anxious and troubled as they followed the uncertainties in the fighting. Spring 1862 had opened with the expectation that under George B. McClellan's command, federal armies would sweep easily on to Richmond. But June brought utter disillusionment. Because of his prolonged Yorktown siege, McClellan had lost the initial advantage gained by speed and surprise. The month-long delay allowed Confederate General Joseph E. Johnston to concentrate his main forces in Richmond and prepare for all-out defense of the capital. At the same time, he sent Stonewall Jackson northward into the Shenandoah Valley to create such a frightening diversion that Lincoln would not dare send reinforcements to McClellan. The Southerners were ready and waiting for McClellan to make his move.[19]

With his base at White House Landing and his army straddling the Chickahominy River, McClellan moved forward to within five miles of Richmond. Despite a surprise Confederate assault on May 31, the Federals drove the Rebels back into the city's defenses. With General Joseph E. Johnston severely wounded and Confederate forces badly mauled, it looked as though Richmond would certainly fall. But a period of heavy rains and impassable roads persuaded General McClellan to halt his march and wait for the terrible weather to clear. "I only wait for the river to fall," he wrote confidently on June 2, "to cross with the rest of the force and make a general attack."[20] Meanwhile, the task of defending Richmond had fallen to General Robert E. Lee. He recalled Stonewall Jackson from the valley, sent J. E. B. Stuart on a remarkable sweep around McClellan's army, and then combined with Jackson in a surprise assault against McClellan's force. From June 25 to July 1, Lee launched attacks that drove the federal troops away from Richmond and back toward the coast.[21] McClellan took up strong defensive positions at Malvern Hill, however, and when Lee ordered a frontal assault, it was torn to pieces by massed Union artillery.[22] At Malvern Hill Colonel Thomas Cass, commander of Boston's Irish Regiment, the 9th, was badly wounded. Carried to the rear for first-aid treatment, then taken home to Boston, Cass died of his wounds on July 12, 1862.[23] Command of the 9th Regiment passed to Lieutenant Colonel Patrick R. Guiney, a native of Tipperary, Ireland, a successful lawyer in Boston before enlisting as a private in April 1861. Guiney rallied his men and fought bravely under the green banner until the Confederates had finally withdrawn from the field.[24] Next day, McClellan brought his forces back to Harrison's Landing, while Lee pulled his exhausted Army of Northern Virginia back to Richmond for a much-needed rest. For the time being, at least, Richmond remained in Confederate hands. Although even by the first week in July the home front did not know just how profound the military disaster was—1,734 Union soldiers killed, 8,062 wounded, 6,053 missing—enough dismal news had filtered through to alert the public that more bad news was coming.[25] The terse military communiqués and the preliminary reports coming in from the front caused perceptive newspaper readers to realize that something had gone badly wrong.[26]

In Washington, D.C., the Lincoln administration recognized that recent heavy losses made a further buildup of the nation's military strength necessary. The president issued a call for 300,000 men to sign up with the army for three years; within a month he made another request for 300,000 men to serve for nine months. At the same time, without fanfare, Secretary of State William Seward toured major cities, and on July 2 arrived in Boston, met with Governor Andrew, and informed him that the first quota for Massachusetts was fixed at 15,000 men; the second quota at 19,000. The Bay State responded immediately, and on August 5 Amos A. Lawrence, the wealthy industrialist, assured President Lincoln by telegram that Massachusetts welcomed the opportunity to support the Union. At about the same time, Charles Eliot Norton, Harvard art professor and keen observer of society, wrote to the famed English novelist Elizabeth Gaskell, commenting on the latest response: "The spirit, the patience, and the good sense of our people are worthy of the highest admiration. I wish you could see and feel, as we do, this truly magnificant display of national character."[27]

Raising more troops was an idea universally applauded, but the manner in which they were to be raised often aroused controversy. Government officials in Washington were already suggesting a draft, but Governor Andrew and other state leaders rejected the idea, insisting that Massachusetts men would willingly enlist. Moreover, the governor felt that conscription was not in keeping with the spirit of the Constitution, and he made his views known to the president. Instead, the Commonwealth organized an extensive grass-roots enlistment campaign to demonstrate that the volunteer spirit was still alive. On July 14, Mayor Wightman presided at a special Faneuil Hall war meeting that Edward Everett stirringly addressed, ending with the cry: "Let the response go forth from Faneuil Hall, trumpet-tongued, the Army of the Potomac shall be reinforced!" The plea had been made; the offensive for manpower had been launched. Edward Everett took up the cause with a crusader's zeal and spoke at meeting after meeting in the next six weeks. During the same period most cities and towns in the Commonwealth held recruitment rallies similar to that in the state capital.

A special pattern was followed in recruiting: first an event was organized in the town's main square, including band music and patriotic speeches, followed by a phalanx of people contacting prospective enlistees. Every Boston

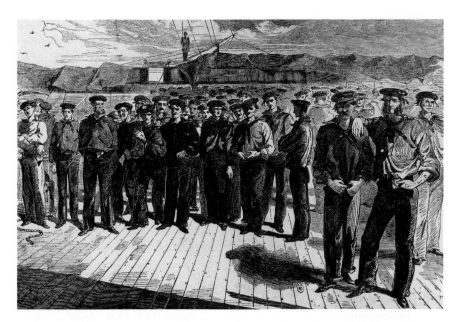

A scene showing the crew of the U.S. sloop Colorado, *sailing out of Boston in June 1861. As a seaport town, Boston was always conscious of its vulnerability to naval attack by such daring Confederate raiders as the* Alabama *and the* Shenandoah. *Governor Andrew strengthened the coastal defenses of the various forts in Boston Harbor, and also constructed additional fortifications in other cities along the Massachusetts coast. (Courtesy of the Boston Public Library, Print Department)*

ward sponsored war meetings, pitching enlistment tents in busy thoroughfares. The drive's climax came during the last week in August. Shops closed every afternoon at 2:00, church bells pealed, and everyone turned to the task of enlistment. On several occasions, patriot fever ran a bit too high—mobs of men threw bricks at windows and hooted at shopkeepers who were tardy in suspending their operations. On August 27, parades, a music program, and a giant evening rally aroused the population. Next evening, General John C. Frémont, the popular if not very successful general who had been Republican nominee for president in 1856, spoke to a surging crowd at Tremont Temple. Emotion gripped the audience, the air crackled with excitement, and listeners threw their hats into the air and shouted joyously for everyone and everything the famed "Pathfinder" mentioned.[28] The earnest endeavors achieved more than just noise and excitement: they got the desired result. Within three months of the president's call, Massachusetts had filled its quota, and 4,000 men stepped into the depleted regiments. Altogether, Massachusetts had contributed 79,000 men to the country's service from the war's start to the end of 1862.

With such extensive recruiting, the tramp of marching men was an omni-present sound in the Commonwealth. The 18th, 33rd, 35th, 44th, and 45th Massachusetts Regiments left for the South. Camp Meigs in Readville re-sounded with the officers' sharp commands, civilians' sad farewells, and the hum of excited soldiers' voices. The men who enlisted came from many back-grounds. Some came from Harvard, Tufts, and Amherst classrooms. The Har-vard class of 1862 had ninety-seven students, of whom thirty-eight enlisted; and of the ninety-two class of 1863 members, thirty-eight joined the colors as well. Most of the recruits, however, had worked on farms, in factories, or in shops. Patriotism touched rich and poor, educated and uneducated, newly im-migrated and established old families. In Lowell, Edward Abbott, a son of prominent Yankee forebears, graduated from Harvard College in 1860 and practiced law. When the war came, he joined the army and at age twenty-two rose to major. In summer 1862, he and seven of his men were killed at Cedar Mountain. The young Thomas Clafley also lived in Lowell, but grew up in a "paddy camp" in a district called "The Acre," where Irish immigrants lived a good distance from the planned Yankee mill village.[29] A young Irish immi-grant, he had only a grammar school education before going to work in a local shop. Devoted to his new country, he left his wife and family and enlisted as a private in the 20th Regiment. At Antietam, he was promoted to lieutenant for gallantry in the field; a few months later at Fredericksburg, after he was again cited for bravery and raised to brevet captain, his life ended.[30] And so it went in town after town throughout Massachusetts. Men of all backgrounds joined in the common cause. Most expected they would be called upon to serve only a few months; many remained forever united in death as Union army heroes.

While Massachusetts continued to enlist men, Lincoln weighed a new mil-itary offensive after McClellan's failure in the Peninsula campaign. Clearly dis-satisfied with McClellan's performance, the president decided to try a new commander. To relieve pressure on McClellan's 85,000-man army, still en-camped at Harrison's Landing, Lincoln consolidated Union detachments in the Shenandoah Valley (about 45,000 men), called it the Army of Virginia, and placed it under General John Pope. Early in August, he ordered McClellan to move northward and link up at Fredericksburg with Pope, who was marching south. The plan was to place a massive Union army of 130,000 men about forty-five miles north of the Confederate capital, midway between Washington and Richmond.[31]

Refusing to allow these two Union armies to join forces, General Rob-ert E. Lee drove northward with his main force against Pope before the slow-moving McClellan could arrive with the Army of the Potomac. With great speed, Lee sent Jackson sweeping around Pope's right flank and soon after sent Longstreet on another sweep following Jackson's route. Union forces struck out blindly at the fast-moving Confederates, but they could not figure out Lee's confusing tactics. Fighting for their lives in the unbearable early August heat, troops from the Bay State gave a good account of themselves in an action that was fast becoming a losing cause. On August 2, General Nathaniel Banks of Massachusetts, with 8,000 men, launched an assault against Jackson at Cedar Mountain, a blow that nearly disrupted the Confederate movement. Banks had attacked without sufficient reserves, however, and when the Confederates counterattacked, the Union forces were forced to retreat. The 2nd Massachusetts Regiment suffered particularly heavy losses in this engagement: 35 percent of the unit's complement were killed or wounded. Later in that month the brigade, led by seventy-five-year-old Edwin Vose Sumner, and consisting of the 1st, 11th, and 16th Massachusetts Regiments along with units from New Hampshire and Pennsylvania, made a gallant charge against the center of Jackson's lines but once again failed to stop the Confederate advance.[32] At a promontory called Bald Hill, Colonel Fletcher Webster, at the head of his 12th Massachusetts Regiment, fell mortally wounded. With Confederate forces attacking from all sides, General Pope ordered an immediate retreat to Washington, and by September 3 the Union troops reached the capital after suffering nearly 15,000 casualties. A summer of expectations had withered; federal troops were now completely demoralized.[33]

Following his victory in the Second Battle of Bull Run, General Lee decided it was time to carry the war directly into enemy territory. On September 4, 1862, the Army of Northern Virginia crossed the Potomac River and encamped near Frederick, Maryland. Moving north with his main force toward Hagerstown, he sent Jackson and Longstreet back across the Potomac to guard against a flank attack by federal troops at Harpers Ferry. With Washington in a panic over Lee's drive into the North, President Lincoln put General George McClellan once again in overall command of the Union forces and ordered him to intercept Lee at all costs. To cut off Lee's northern advance, McClellan stepped up his pace and pushed his men through the ripe Maryland wheatfields, following the enemy's progress. Realizing that McClellan might move behind him and catch his troops stretched out on a line of march where they were most vulnerable, on September 15 Lee pulled his forces back to Sharpsburg on Antietam Creek for a strong defensive stand while he waited to be reinforced by Jackson and Longstreet. Fortunately for the Rebels, McClellan delayed his offensive until September 17, before launching powerful but uncoordinated assaults against the Confederate line, using only five of his six army corps.[34]

Bay State units participating in the Battle of Antietam suffered heavy casualties, especially the 15th, 19th, and 20th Regiments, which were in the Second Division under that *vieux beau sabreur* (as one historian labeled him), General

Edwin Vose Sumner. The men of the 2nd Massachusetts Regiment were also at Antietam, and on a damp, misty September morning were preparing breakfast in a nearby cornfield when suddenly Confederate troops came roaring in on their flank. Soldiers from Indiana and Wisconsin, standing alongside the Bay State troops, were raked by deadly enemy fire. Colonel Andrews of Massachusetts shifted his own troops to assist the 3rd Wisconsin Regiment, which was at the center of the attack, and turned back the Confederate charge. The aroused Massachusetts men moved forward through the cornfield pursuing the retreating enemy, and let out a cheer as one of their sergeants seized the standard of the 11th Mississippi Regiment and waved it aloft—the traditional prize of war. A small part of the battle had ended, but similar clashes were taking place all over the sprawling battlefield. It was the bloodiest day of fighting in American military history. During that day, more than 23,000 Americans fell, and almost 12,000 of them died, either immediately or later from their wounds.[35] By nightfall, after twelve hours of fighting, Lee was hanging on the ropes after suffering well over 12,000 casualties, but he still held his ground and was preparing to repulse more Union attacks on the following day. McClellan, however, decided that he had accomplished his assignment in stopping Lee and saving the North. He refused to resume the attack, and allowed Lee to take his badly shattered army back across the Potomac to comparative safety in northern Virginia.[36]

It took a little longer than usual for accurate reports about the terrible losses at Antietam to reach the Northern public. Because General McClellan had ordered all newspaper reporters excluded from the front lines, rumors and news leaks were generally suspect. Then, too, military record keeping was neither rapid nor efficient: no official account of casualties was kept, no proper hospital lists, no methodical burial records or graves registration. Parents waited in vain for news of their sons; wives wept in anguish to hear from their husbands. Only when trains and boats began bringing home from the battlefield the dead and wounded, and when local newspapers began printing names of those killed, wounded, or missing in page-long columns, was the North fully aware of the battle's enormity and the huge Union losses. "Several of our best officers were killed; many were wounded," wrote the governor's adjutant, William Schouler; "and the fatality which attended the rank and file was terrible."[37] Not until September 22, five days after the battle, did the *Boston Traveller* start describing the gruesome details—"the dead and dying lying thick and in rows where they had fallen on the enemy's centre." Groups of surgeons, followed by women in ambulances, were heading toward the battlefield, said the paper, to tend the wounded soldiers who had been collected in churches and other public buildings.[38] Being a weekly newspaper, *The Boston Pilot* did not come out with a full story about the fighting at Antietam until

September 27, when it proclaimed the battle "The Most Stupendous Struggle of Modern Times." In its October 4 issue, it elaborated further upon the extraordinary number of casualties—"the dead strewn so thickly that as you ride over the field you cannot guide your horse's steps too carefully"—reporting that the 13th Massachusetts Regiment had lost nine of their seventeen officers, and including on its front page a long list of Bay State men killed, wounded, or missing.[39]

Every battle is horrible both for those who have participated in it and those who have witnessed its gruesome aftermath. During the night after Antietam, fifty-six-year-old Dr. Oliver Wendell Holmes, distinguished professor of anatomy at the Harvard Medical School and well-known author of *The Autocrat of the Breakfast Table,* received an anonymous telegram informing him that during the battle his son, Captain Holmes, had been wounded in the neck. At once the doctor set off southward, and after two days reached the Sharpsburg area, where he wandered across the plain of desolation searching for his missing son, who had volunteered for the 20th Massachusetts Regiment in April 1861, just before his graduation from Harvard.[40] Stepping over the dead bodies that still littered the ground, Holmes groped in the darkness for some sign of his son, making his way across a battleground covered with fragments of clothing, haversacks, canteens, caps, and scattered personal equipment and scraps of food. "It was like the table of some hideous orgy left uncleaned," wrote the distraught father, "and one turned away disgusted from its broken fragments and muddy heeltops." Further reports about young Captain Holmes's whereabouts took his father to Harrisburg and then to Philadelphia until, by accident, he came upon his wounded son in a railroad car. "In the first car, on the fourth seat to the right, I saw my Captain," Holmes later recalled. Suppressing the father's natural urge to rush and embrace his lost son with a great cry of joy after such a long and painful search, the doctor drew himself up, walked quietly forward, tapped the young man on the shoulder, and asked simply: "How are you, Boy?" The young captain looked back over his shoulder, smiled, and replied: "How are you, Dad?" "Such are the proprieties of life," explained the Autocrat of the Breakfast Table, "as they are observed among us Anglo-Saxons of the nineteenth century."[41]

President Lincoln, knowing that McClellan had the advantage in his bigger army and superior offensive position, was bitterly disappointed that McClellan had permitted Lee to escape with his army intact. At the same time, however, Antietam did give Lincoln the opportunity to take a step he had been contemplating for some time—emancipating the slaves. The decision was a long time in coming, and Bay State leaders had been agitating for it since the war began.

Throughout his public career and into his presidency, Lincoln had declared

Oliver Wendell Holmes, Jr., son of the famous author and medical authority, volunteered for the infantry in April 1861, in July was commissioned a second lieutenant with the 20th Massachusetts Regiment, and later rose to the rank of captain. Wounded three times in battle, Holmes returned to civilian life and graduated from Harvard Law School. After serving as Chief Justice of Massachusetts, in 1902 he was appointed by President Theodore Roosevelt to the United States Supreme Court. (Courtesy of the Boston Public Library, Print Department)

that, although he was personally opposed to slavery and its expansion into the territories, he would not touch slavery in the states. When war broke out in 1861, Lincoln again stated that he was fighting the war to restore the Union—not to free the slaves. Most Bay State Republicans, however, demanded immediate emancipation almost as soon as the war started. The so-called Radical faction, especially, saw the war as an unparalleled opportunity to abolish the nation's greatest evil. And a proclamation of emancipation, they argued, would also severely damage the Southern war effort. Not only would it encourage slaves to escape, and thereby disrupt the plantation system, but it would force the Confederacy to assign troops to retrieve runaway slaves, draining the military forces of valuable resources. Senator Charles Sumner, speaking before Massachusetts Republicans in Boston, called for the administration to end slavery. "It is often said that War will make an end to slavery," he said. "This is probable. But it is surer still that the overthrow of slavery will make an end of the war." [42] Reflecting this point of view, Charles Francis Adams expressed frustration with administration policy, remarking: "We cannot afford to go over this ground again." "The slave question," he insisted, "must be settled this time once and for all." [43]

Always the consummate politician, however, Lincoln was convinced that the Northern population's attitude was not yet sufficiently antislavery to support emancipation. For the president to move out too far ahead of public opinion on the slavery question, he felt, might well cost him support from conservative Republicans (and there were many) as well as War Democrats, whose votes he needed to create a united front against the Southern rebellion. Then, too, any drastic steps in favor of freeing the slaves would most certainly drive the slaveholding border states out of the Union and into the Confederacy's waiting arms. During 1861 and into 1862, therefore, Lincoln made it quite clear that emancipation was not one of his priorities. Massachusetts Republicans reacted bitterly to Lincoln's apparent indifference toward emancipation, and were further dismayed by his failure to respond to announcements by such Democratic military leaders as General McClellan and General Robert Patterson that they would refuse to confiscate Southern "property" (including slaves) captured by their troops. A colleague of Governor John Andrew observed that the Massachusetts governor, usually one of Lincoln's staunchest supporters, was "greatly discouraged, disturbed, and even disgusted by the delays at Washington, and the obstructions thrown in the way by those in authority." [44]

Some semblance of optimism among the Radical Republicans returned during summer 1861, however, in response to actions taken by General John C. Frémont, now commander of Union forces in the Western Department. Unable to achieve significant gains in that region, and in an effort, perhaps, to create disorder among the Rebel military forces, Frémont issued an order declaring free all slaves within his military jurisdiction. Massachusetts Republicans enthusiastically applauded Frémont's announcement. Here was a man, they cried, willing "to strike a real blow at the hated institution" of slavery.[45] "This step of General Frémont," Gerrit Smith, a leading Bay State Radical, told an acquaintance, "is the first unqualified and purely right one . . . which has taken place during the war."[46] Radical newspapers such as the *Springfield Republican* and the *Worcester Spy* echoed this approval of Frémont's decree.[47] President Lincoln, however, did not share the Radicals' enthusiasm for Frémont's proclamation for at least two reasons: First, if he allowed Frémont's order to stand, it might establish a dangerous precedent and encourage other commanders to exercise similar powers without first clearing their actions with the White House.[48] Second, Lincoln feared that officially endorsing Frémont's slavery decree would alienate Northern conservatives and provoke the border states into joining the Confederacy. Accordingly, early in September 1861, Lincoln rescinded Frémont's declaration.

Massachusetts Radicals, along with Radical Republicans everywhere, were deeply disappointed with Lincoln's repudiation of Frémont, but refused to abandon their objective of securing abolition. They decided to join their Radical counterparts in the other Northern states to turn the Lincoln administration around in favor of emancipation. In this undertaking the Radicals were perhaps surprised to find themselves supported by many leaders in Boston's business community who had earlier tried to work out a compromise with the South but who were now calling for all-out prosecution of the war. The city's Board of Trade proclaimed that all Northerners were obligated to support the country's cause, and in September 1861 the local business community sponsored a mammoth rally at Faneuil Hall to show their solidarity on behalf of the war effort. Amos A. Lawrence served as the meeting's vice-president, along with such other businessmen as George Luther Stearns, Edward Atkinson, Edward S. Tobey, and James M. Beebe. Supporting the war itself, several businessmen also conceded that the slave would probably have to be freed to preserve the Union.[49] Many of them worried, however, that a movement favoring emancipation could become disruptive if it developed too early, and especially before public opinion was ready to accept such a radical move. The nation's people "had no conception of the evils of slavery," complained John Murray Forbes, who also feared that if slaves became encouraged by the prospect of freedom they might organize an insurrection of their own. Until emancipation was clearly seen as a military necessity, said Forbes, he hoped that "abolitionists, radicals, and disorganizers" would hold their tongues.[50]

Meanwhile, however, several businessmen showed willingness to use their talents to build up public sentiment favoring emancipation. In September 1861 two friends who had worked with Amos A. Lawrence in the old Kansas crusade, Dr. Samuel Gridley Howe and George Luther Stearns, met with several leading abolitionists in Howe's Boston office. They decided to organize the Boston Emancipation League as a vehicle for preparing the public mind to accept emancipation as inevitable. The League planned to sponsor lectures, put on discussions, circulate pamphlets, and supply Northern newspapers with articles and editorials advocating emancipation and criticizing the Lincoln administration's lack of response on the slavery issue.[51] Following their probusiness philosophy, however, the League promoted abolition not on sentimental or humanitarian grounds, but "as a measure of justice, and as a military necessity." Practically, emancipation promised to be "the shortest, cheapest, and least bloody path to permanent peace," they insisted, as well as "the only method of maintaining the integrity of the Union."[52] The League also established a newspaper, *The Commonwealth,* edited by Frank Sanborn and Moncure D. Conway, with a clear and stated purpose: to create popular opinion favorable toward emancipation.[53] Wendell Phillips, long an abolitionist spokesman, participated actively in the emancipation cause, delivering rousing speeches exhorting the public to support a policy of freeing the slaves and denouncing Lincoln's caution in dealing with the slavery issue.[54] Beyond these local public relations efforts, in Washington Senator Charles Sumner vehemently criticized the president's refusal to take steps toward emancipation and urged him to reverse his policy.[55] Sumner's antislavery colleague Senator Henry Wilson also expressed his dissatisfaction with the administration's policy on slavery, and in a speech on the Senate floor raised the thorny question of constitutional authority: "The President cannot lay down and fix the principles upon which a war shall be conducted," he argued. "It is for Congress to lay down the rules and regulations by which the Executive shall be governed in conducting a war."[56]

The steady pressure that the Massachusetts Radical Republicans and their colleagues exerted throughout the North, together with signs of antislavery sentiment that he perceived to be growing among the Northern population, caused President Lincoln to begin moving toward emancipation. Such a shift first suggested itself early in April 1862, when the president pledged his support for an international treaty that called for more effectively suppressing the international slave trade. Still more encouraging to the Bay State Radicals was an order Lincoln issued on April 13, refusing to return runaway slaves who had safely crossed Union army lines. But the first really significant victory for the Radicals came on April 16, 1862, when President Lincoln signed a law abolishing slavery in the District of Columbia. Hailing this action as "one of the greatest victories of the war," the Massachusetts Radicals exuberantly applauded Lincoln's decision, which they regarded as historic, and Charles Sumner enthusiastically referred to the new law as "the first installment of that great debt which we all owe to an enslaved race." [57]

Though they applauded these initial efforts, the Massachusetts Radicals were more determined than ever that Lincoln should move even faster toward complete emancipation. They were more than a little discouraged by the General David Hunter controversy. In May 1862 Hunter, commander of Union forces in the Department of the South, declared free all slaves within his jurisdiction. President Lincoln, for many of the same reasons that had led him to overturn General Frémont's similar order the previous summer, compelled General Hunter to rescind his decree. Predictably, Bay State Radicals voiced their displeasure with Lincoln's decision, and one local Republican observed caustically to a colleague: "It is strange when a rattlesnake is attacking us that we should be so delicate about the stick we hit him with.[58] Although clearly frustrated with Lincoln's lack of decision on slavery, Governor John Andrew held his tongue and refused to criticize the president in public. "Let none of us who remain at home presume to direct the pilot, or to seize the helm," he wrote, firmly believing that human slavery would inevitably be rendered extinct.[59] But the Hunter episode seemed to shake his confidence, and in a speech in Boston he sadly stated his belief that from the day the government "turned its back" on General Hunter, the "blessing of God has been withdrawn from our arms." [60] Still another prominent Massachusetts Radical, Matthew Warrington, acknowledging that Lincoln was personally against slavery, voiced his disappointment with the president's latest action. "So thought Frémont; so thinks Hunter; and so I really believe thinks Lincoln," speculated Warrington. "Only his terrible habit of procrastination may put at naught his wisdom and foresight.[61] Businessman John Murray Forbes had just returned from visiting his son, an officer in the 1st Massachusetts Cavalry, stationed at Beaufort, South Carolina. He also reacted bitterly to the president's decision to revoke Hunter's order, having already expressed hope that Lincoln would not make "another Frémont blunder." "Perhaps after we have expended a few thousand more lives and millions of dollars," Forbes wrote to the general, "the people will agree to use slaves against the rebellion." [62]

In spite of the Hunter episode, however, most Boston Radicals believed that the unfortunate incident was merely a temporary setback for their cause. Along with Lincoln's recent policy freeing slaves in the nation's capital, they were encouraged by the increasing antislavery sentiment throughout the North. Augustus Holmes graphically stated in a letter to his fellow Radical Charles Sumner that the Emancipation League and other Radical groups in the Bay State had already begun to get positive results, although the outcome might not yet be apparent. "There is a defense of blubber about the arctic creature through which the harpoon must be driven before the vital parts are touched," he wrote, using a seafaring analogy that a New Englander might quickly appreciate. With Lincoln's first steps, he suggested, the "harpoon is, I think, at last through the blubber." [63]

The Democratic party in Massachusetts was only too well aware that the harpoon was beginning to penetrate the blubber, and feared that President Lincoln would finally yield to the abolitionists' pressure and free the slaves. Over and over, Democratic spokesmen reiterated their position that the war should be fought solely to return the rebellious states to the Union, and not to free the slaves. The Boston Irish, especially, reacted bitterly to Lincoln's April decree that abolished slavery in the District of Columbia and also forbade returning runaway slaves who crossed Union lines. "The North is becoming black with refugee Negroes," complained *The Pilot*'s publisher, Patrick Donahoe, obviously disgusted. Conjuring up awful visions of runaway slaves taking essential jobs away from poor immigrant workers, he declared: "These wretches crowd our cities and by overstocking the market of labor do incalculable injury to white hands." [64] Irish leaders tried to persuade the state legislature to pass laws preventing fugitive slaves from coming to the Commonwealth of Massachusetts, but they were unsuccessful. *The Pilot* angrily questioned how long soldiers could support the Union cause if they saw that the war was going to be fought to free the slaves. "The soldiers are not in the march of abolition," insisted the paper. "They did not enlist for anything save the vindication of the Union." [65] For the blacks themselves, insisted *The Pilot*, nineteen of twenty would not accept emancipation because "they love their masters as dogs do," and because plantation life was the life "nature intended for them." The only hope for the country's salvation, Donahoe concluded, lay in the Democratic party. "Give it power, and everything will soon be reversed." [66]

Those who opposed emancipation protested in vain, however, for reports coming out of Washington made it clear that Lincoln was moving closer to the fateful decision. For one thing, Lincoln recognized the growing sentiment against slavery among the Northern states' population. One evidence of this shift was that Northern business interests, once decidedly opposed to emancipation, were now agitating for programs that would transform the outmoded and unproductive slave-labor system into a modern and disciplined free-labor system. In supporting emancipation, the businessmen continued to emphasize the practical benefits that freedom would bring to black people and to white people as well. With free labor at work, the increased cotton production and the flourishing output of agricultural products would add immeasurably to the national income and make it possible to reduce taxes. In this way, Edward Atkinson assured his colleagues, just by destroying slavery, "this war can be made to pay." [67]

But by midyear, even some of the local businessmen had begun to reflect the idealism usually associated with the abolitionists. Amos A. Lawrence professed to see the Almighty's workings in the growing momentum for emancipation. "If God ever indicated His will in advance, He seems to have done so in this war," said the cotton tycoon. "And God means to give freedom to the slaves." This from a former Cotton Whig who, in 1851, insisted that the abolitionists would have to be "knocked in the head" to return fugitive slaves to the South.[68] George Luther Stearns agreed with his colleague that slavery contravened "the eternal laws of God," and Edward Atkinson declared that hardly a man in Boston would not thank God if he heard that the slaves had risen up in a "successful insurrection."[69] Calling upon their experiences in the mid-1850s with the Emigrant Aid Companies, several Boston businessmen went further and proposed daring ventures that would send Free-Soilers into Confederate territory to promote the Union cause and procure much-needed cotton supplies for the war effort. John Murray Forbes proposed a scheme to transport "a respectable class of people" into Missouri; Eli Thayer was pushing plans to send a military expedition to Florida, where he would establish a free-labor colony; Edward Atkinson was going to great lengths to persuade the administration to support his plans for a full-fledged military expedition into Texas that would strike a strategic blow at the enemy coast and also make it possible to colonize Texas with Union soldiers, who would grow cotton efficiently and productively.[70] The Lincoln administration paid lip service to most of these schemes, going as far as to authorize former Massachusetts Governor Nathaniel Banks to head an expedition to the Texas Gulf Coast, but no decisions were reached at this time. The military situation during late summer and early fall 1862 was obviously much too precarious to undertake any new and highly speculative ventures. With General Burnside making plans to take Richmond, with General Grant and the Army of the West moving south against Vicksburg, with Admiral Farragut and the fleet cruising up the Mississippi, diverting precious manpower from these important missions would be much too dangerous.

Boston businessmen did, in one place, have a fairly free hand to experiment with their ideas on free slaves and free enterprise. After Union forces had taken over Port Royal and the Sea Islands along the South Carolina coast, the white population, famed for producing long-staple Sea Island cotton, fled to the mainland, leaving behind 10,000 slaves. The Boston people saw in this prime location their chance to create a working model showing what the South could look like after the war had abolished slavery. The government was primarily interested in the islands as a valuable source of cotton to meet its war needs, but Edward L. Pierce, a Boston lawyer and close friend of Senator Charles Sumner, cared much more about the opportunity to help the abandoned black people become educated, industrious, and self-supporting citizens. Turning to his friends and colleagues in Boston for help, Pierce got his first response from Rev. Jacob Manning, assistant pastor of Boston's Old South Meeting House. Early in February 1862, Manning met with seventeen parishioners, adopted a constitution, and organized the Boston Education Commission. Following Pierce's intentions, the commissioners announced that they intended to seek "the industrial, social, intellectual, moral, and religious elevation" of the African Americans on the Sea Islands, who were then being released from bondage.[71] Many men who had previously served together in the Emigrant Aid Company during the 1850s now had leading parts in the Education Commission. William Endicott, Jr., was named treasurer; Edward Atkinson served as secretary; John Murray Forbes, Samuel Cabot, Jr., George Higginson, and Patrick Tracy Jackson, Jr., were active members. The eminent Edward Everett Hale was a vice-president, and Governor John Andrew agreed to serve as the first president. Amos A. Lawrence, a contributor, said he hoped "the experiment will now be tried of abolishing slavery as a military necessity."[72] Combining the Protestant work ethic with that distinctive Boston commitment to education's infinite powers, the members announced that they intended to instruct the freed people in "the rudiments of letters and science," and also in such virtues as temperance, self-respect, industry, promptness, and good order. Collaborating with the American Missionary Association in New York, the Education Commission prepared to send missionaries to teach the newly freed people "civilization and Christianity" as well as "order, industry, economy, and self-reliance." On March 3, 1862, fifty-three young men and women—thirty-five of them from Boston, many with degrees from prominent New England schools—left Boston and New York for South Carolina. Edward Pierce was there to "distribute" the newcomers among the Sea Island plantations, and John Murray Forbes went along to observe at first hand how the experiment was progressing. Supporters back in Boston and New York sent private donations to assist the missionary effort; the federal government provided public funds for purchasing supplies and equipment and to defray travel expenses.[73]

Even as the conservative business community was demanding a stronger emancipation policy, the Lincoln administration was becoming acutely aware that the Radical element in the Republican party was growing in both size and influence. Lincoln realized that he would need support from these abolitionist members of his party to win approval for his war measures in Congress, and eventually for reelection in 1864. In Boston, unsettling signs appeared that abolitionist sentiment was wearing dangerously thin and threatening to break entirely if the president did not come out with an emancipation proclamation of some kind. Wendell Phillips, who had been moving further from the administration all summer, on August 1, in a speech at the South Shore town of

Abington, Massachusetts, angrily dismissed Lincoln as "a first-rate *second-rate* man*," and savagely attacked the administration as having neither "vigor" nor "purpose." It simply "drifts with events," he said contemptuously.[74] Adding to rising discontent over his failure to confront slavery's immorality, it was apparent that Lincoln was being influenced by Radical arguments that freeing the slaves would disrupt the Confederate war effort and would also be a stimulant to offset a string of military defeats. The delicate international situation in 1862 also contributed to Lincoln's decision to free the slaves. From the day hostilities began, Great Britain had been noticeably sympathetic to the Confederate cause, especially because southern cotton was essential to England's textile industry. As long as the North was fighting solely to preserve the Union and not to free the slaves, the British government saw no reason why England should not maintain a mutually satisfying relationship with the Confederacy. By summer 1862, Lincoln saw emancipation as a means for changing the war's objective and thereby at least neutralizing this sympathetic support for the South. As early as July 13, 1862, Lincoln confided to his Secretary of State, William Seward, and his Secretary of the Navy, Gideon Welles, that he had finally come to see that freedom for the slaves was "absolutely essential" to preserve the Union, and on July 22 he informed his Cabinet that he planned to issue an emancipation proclamation.[75] Before making such an announcement, however, he wanted a suitable military victory so that his action would not appear to be a desperate act of reprisal before imminent defeat. As he followed McClellan's movements early in September, the president clearly expected a major Union victory. "I will wait only on the military situation," he told his Postmaster General, Montgomery Blair. "If God gives us a victory in the next battle, I will consider it an indication of the Divine will that it is my duty to move forward in the cause of emancipation."[76]

Although Antietam was certainly not the grand victory he had hoped for, the defeat of Robert E. Lee did give Lincoln the most appropriate opportunity to issue his decree. On September 22, 1862, acting as commander-in-chief of the armed forces, he adopted "a fit and necessary war measure for suppressing . . . rebellion." Lincoln issued a preliminary announcement declaring that if the seceded states had not returned to the Union by January 1, 1863, all slaves in rebellious states would be "then, thenceforward, and forever free." He also announced that freed slaves, "of suitable condition," would be used in the armed forces, and he pledged that the government of the United States, both civil and military, would recognize and maintain the freedom of all former slaves.[77]

Admittedly, the Emancipation Proclamation had no immediate or practical effects on African Americans themselves, for it did not apply to the border states that had not seceded, and was not put into effect in the seceded states.

Still, the document's long-range significance is beyond doubt. With the Emancipation Proclamation, a milestone had been passed in the nation's history. The document helped establish a significant truth, both at home and throughout Europe, that the Civil War was no longer merely a political struggle to defeat a rebellious faction; it was now a holy crusade to abolish the scourge of slavery and set all people free. The Radicals of Massachusetts were somewhat disappointed with the proclamation's limited scope, and a little uncertain about whether it would be implemented on January 1, 1963. Lincoln, after all, was known for his political astuteness, and Bay State Radicals had come to suspect the president's ability to say one thing while planning another. Indeed, as late as August 14, 1862, even after he had informed his Cabinet members that he was planning to issue a proclamation, newspapers reported that he was considering the possibility of a government-financed colonization project in Central America. Meeting in the White House with a group of African-American leaders from the District of Columbia, Lincoln told his guests that although he regarded slavery as "the greatest wrong inflicted on any people," he feared that considering current racial attitudes, black people had little chance of achieving equality in the United States. He asked them to consider recruiting volunteers who would emigrate to somewhere in Central America, where they would have more freedom and better opportunities. Most African Americans ridiculed Lincoln's proposals, and Frederick Douglass accused the president of "contempt for the Negroes." "This is our country as much as it is yours," retorted one angry Philadelphian, "and we will not leave it." White Radical Republicans opposed colonization as racist and inhumane and saw the shocking proposal as simply one more reason for watching Lincoln carefully to make sure he put his proclamation into effect on January 1.[78]

Despite their suspicions, the Radicals enthusiastically received the news about Lincoln's decision as the final step toward complete emancipation. "It is a poor *document* but a mighty *act;* slow, somewhat halting, wrong in its delay till January," wrote Governor John Andrew to a fellow Northern Radical, "but grand and sublime after all. 'Prophets and Kings' have waited for this day," he wrote with obviously deep emotion, "but died without the sight."[79] Although William Lloyd Garrison at first expressed disappointment at the document's incompleteness, he nevertheless rejoiced in the Proclamation as "an important step in the right direction, and an act of immense historic consequence."[80] In a similar tone, Senator Charles Sumner delivered an oration in the U.S. Senate heartily praising Lincoln's long-awaited decree;[81] and in Boston's Music Hall, Wendell Phillips declared that the time had finally arrived when he could rejoice under the Stars and Stripes.[82] And in a burst of intellectual largesse, Ralph Waldo Emerson, hitherto cool toward Lincoln, was prepared to let bygones be bygones. He announced he was now willing to forget "all that we thought shortcomings, every mistake, every delay," because he could see the president had been permitted "to do more for America than any other American man."[83] Thus, late in 1862, the Massachusetts Radicals could take pleasure in achieving two great victories. First, they felt they had succeeded in pressuring President Lincoln to remove from his command in the Army of the Potomac General George B. McClellan, a Democrat they accused of being both an incompetent military leader and a Southern sympathizer. More important, however, President Lincoln's historic proclamation of September 22, 1862, made the Bay State Radicals feel they had succeeded in transforming the war's basic objective from merely restoring the Union to establishing freedom for all Americans.

All this, of course, was political fodder during the 1862 elections, in which Governor John Andrew stood for reelection as the Republican candidate. Publicly, he had announced his unqualified support for the national administration during the late summer months; in fact, however, he let it be known that he considered that the president had been too cautious in his attitude toward slavery and too slow in deciding upon emancipation. In speech after speech, Andrew had pleaded that the administration issue an edict freeing the slaves, and predicted that the president would do so at any moment. Even as he spoke, however, it was clear that Andrew, one of the president's most loyal supporters, was losing confidence, and was no longer sure that Lincoln was equal to the task. He was convinced that Lincoln needed his friends' help in reorganizing his administration, getting rid of the Democratic generals, and developing a more positive agenda on the slavery question. Andrew felt the time had come for him to begin trying "if possible, to save the Prest. from the infamy of ruining his country," and toward this end he set in motion plans for convening a conference of his fellow governors at Altoona, Pennsylvania, late in September.[84]

Andrew's political opponents took completely different positions. When the war broke out, those who were called War Democrats had rallied behind the president and supported the war.[85] A larger group of Democrats reluctantly accepted the war, it is true, but only as long as it was being fought to preserve the Union the way it was before the war began. As Lincoln used greater and more extensive war powers, those who now called themselves Peace Democrats worried that a prolonged conflict would turn out to be"the Trojan horse of tyranny."[86] Some in the Democratic party continued to oppose emancipation and increasingly criticized the wartime restrictions President Lincoln had imposed on civil liberties. So far, however, they had failed to articulate a coherent agenda. A compromise group came up with a political program somewhat similar to that being put forward by the forty-two-year-old former Ohio congressman Clement L. Vallandigham—a "prince of dissidents," as the historian

Fletcher Pratt labeled him.[87] A strict-construction Jeffersonian with decided sympathies for the Southern way of life, Vallandigham blamed the war entirely on the Republican abolitionists' fanaticism, and denounced the Lincoln administration as a despotism that had suspended constitutional law and violated civil rights. Setting himself up as leader of the Peace Democrats, he pandered to other critics with such simplistic mottoes as "stop the fighting," "make an armistice," "withdraw your army from the seceded States," and "the Union will re-establish itself."[88] Opponents of the administration formed a Massachusetts chapter of the People's party and chose Brigadier General Charles Devens as their gubernatorial candidate.[89] Devens was a hero in McClellan's recent Peninsula campaign, but was better known to local antislavery people as the U.S. marshal who in 1851 had sent the black fugitive Thomas Sims back to slavery. Lacking a suitable candidate of their own, the state Democratic party agreed to support Devens, the People's party candidate, thereby forming a temporary political alliance with some of the most extreme and outspoken anti-Lincoln forces. Most voters, however, were never quite sure what the new antiadministration alliance stood for, or what its position was on the war effort, with its nebulous party platform calling for "The Constitution as it is and the Union as it was."[90]

When President Lincoln finally came out with his Emancipation Proclamation late in September, shortly before the elections, General Devens and his followers suddenly found their position weakened and Governor Andrew appeared to be a remarkable prophet because he had foretold the president's decision. Massachusetts expressed its desires clearly, overwhelmingly reelecting Andrew, who received 79,835 votes to his opponent's 52,587.[91] Senator Charles Sumner was also a candidate for reelection in 1862. Aggressively championing the slave's cause and often calling with abrasive rhetoric for emancipation, he had aroused anger among his party's more moderate members. Nevertheless, he easily won the Republican endorsement. The abolitionist spokesmen Wendell Phillips and John Greenleaf Whittier actively campaigned for Sumner, and Horace Greeley, editor of the *New York Tribune,* among the country's most influential newspapers, claimed that Sumner's return to the Senate was of inestimable value to all American citizens. At a time when U.S. senators were not elected by popular vote, the Massachusetts Great and General Court (the state legislature) chose Sumner by the one-sided vote of 227 to 47.[92]

Despite welcome reports about individual successes in states like Massachusetts, however, the election returns from other parts of the country gave Lincoln and the Republicans very little to cheer about. The off-year elections in 1862 had cut deeply into Republican power throughout the North, reflecting both general disgust with the Army of the Potomac's failure to crush

the Rebel forces, as well as many a bitter response to Lincoln's recent Emancipation Proclamation. That "ill-timed proclamation," protested Senator John
Sherman, "contributed to the general result," and Horace Greeley complained
that the president's announcement had taken him too far ahead of the people.
Reviewing the disturbing Republican political reverses, the conservative editors at the *Boston Daily Advertiser* put it down as repudiating the course pursued by the party's "radical managers," and an expression of "distrust of their
policy and guidance." [93] Though many disconsolate Republicans stayed home
and sat on their hands, Democrats flocked to the polls, shouting that the Republicans had "gone too far!" Democrats picked up thirty-five congressional
seats previously held by Republicans, took the statewide elections in Illinois,
Indiana, and Pennsylvania, and captured the governor's chairs in New York
and New Jersey. Even though vastly outnumbered in New England, Democrats
still got almost 45 percent of the vote in all the state races, and walked away
with nearly 50 percent of the vote in the congressional contests. [94] All things
considered, therefore, the Republicans' victory in Massachusetts was especially gratifying to President Lincoln in a month that saw his party go down
to defeat in so many other states. New England may have wavered a little in
supporting the national administration, but it finally remained solidly in the
Republican column, thereby becoming instrumental in providing the Republican party the votes it needed to control Congress. [95]

Political successes, control of Congress, emancipation of slaves, inspirational words and speeches—all would mean very little unless President Lincoln
could come up with a general who could achieve victory on the battlefield.
After removing McClellan from command early in November—greatly surprising and bewildering the Army of the Potomac troops, who idolized Little
Mac—Lincoln replaced him with General Ambrose Everett Burnside, an
impressive-looking officer with resplendent side-whiskers. [96] Setting out to take
Richmond by marching south, Burnside took his army to the Rappahannock
River at Fredericksburg. There he found Robert E. Lee and his Army of Northern Virginia entrenched in heavily fortified positions along heights overlooking
the river. Burnside decided that his most effective strategy would be to use his
superior numbers to smash his way straight through the Rebel positions. He
sent General William Franklin with the I and VI Corps to bridge the left flank,
and General Edwin Sumner with the II and IX Corps to bridge the stream and
occupy the right flank, hoping that from their flanking positions these troops
could provide covering fire for their comrades, who would be launching assaults directly across the river. Under Sumner's command, the 19th and 20th
Massachusetts Regiments fought their way into Fredericksburg on the right
wing and drove the Confederate defenders out of the town. "I cannot presume
to express all that is due to the officers and men of the regiment for the un-

flinching bravery and splendid discipline shown in the execution of the order," wrote Captain Macy in his official report. "Platoon after platoon was swept away, but the head of the column did not falter. Ninety-seven officers and men were killed or wounded in the space of fifty yards." It was an almost impossible assignment, but the men from Massachusetts had taken the town. Further Union attempts on both flanks to overrun enemy positions met with tragic results, however, as deadly fire from Rebel guns opened great gaps in the advancing columns and every Union regiment left rows of dead federal soldiers.[97]

And then followed a day of utter disaster. On December 13, General Burnside ordered General Winfield Hancock to send the main body of Union infantry across the Rappahannock in suicidal assaults against Lee's massed guns atop Marye's Heights. At Fredericksburg, Meagher's Irish Brigade gained national admiration for their great courage and incredible losses. Fearing that the Irish regiments would be the next ones forced to make this suicidal assault, one soldier consulted Rev. William Corby, chaplain of the 88th New York Regiment. Father Corby tried to calm the young man's fears: "Your generals," he told the lad, "know better than that."[98] But they did not. At 2:00 P.M., the Irish Brigade received the order to cross the open plain and attack the Confederate positions on the heights. From three sides, enemy batteries poured relentless fire upon the advancing columns, with devastating effect. The storm of shot and shell was "terrible," Peter Welsh of the 28th Massachusetts Regiment wrote to his wife back in Boston afterward, "mowing whole gaps out of our ranks, and we having to march over their dead and wounded bodies."[99] Confederate General James Longstreet called the Irish soldiers' gallant assault against Lee's entrenched positions "the handsomest thing in the whole war," and General George Pickett later told his wife how he watched "those sons of Erin . . . rush to their deaths." "We forgot they were fighting us," he wrote, "and cheer after cheer at their fearlessness went up all along our lines."[100] But it was to no avail. All day long the blue lines struggled across the open waters, crawled up the exposed shores, and then crumpled like cut wheat before the withering fire from Confederate cannon and muskets. And all the while, the men of the 20th Massachusetts Regiment stood firm on the flank, fired their weapons, and gave the attackers as much covering fire as possible. By 4:00 in the afternoon, it was all over. More than 12,000 Union solders lay dead or wounded in the ice-choked waters or on the bloody beaches below the heights, where Lee's forces remained securely in position. The Battle of Fredericksburg was one of the worst defeats in the U.S. Army's history, and when his generals made it clear that they would not again order their men into battle, a furious General Burnside had no alternative but to call his Army of the Potomac back to Washington. Despite his attempts to blame others for his appalling lack of military competence, Burnside was removed from command and President Lincoln was forced to renew his search for a general.[101]

Boston citizens could hardly believe that another disaster could follow so quickly upon the terrible losses at Antietam only three months earlier, especially because most Boston newspapers followed General Burnside's advance very closely and gave readers optimistic promises—a great victory for the Union side.[102] On Monday morning, December 15, two days after the battle, the *Boston Post* told its readers that the news from Fredericksburg was "not as encouraging as we hoped for" from the latest reports about Union assaults against Confederate fortifications. "It is appalling to think of our noble soldiers marching up to the rebel batteries in solid columns to be cut down, like grass before the scythe, by shell, cannon, and rifle." And yet the paper held out hope that the sacrifices might yet produce a victory.[103] A day later, the *Boston Daily Advertiser* was still printing encouraging reports about Burnside's movements against Lee and his defenders.[104] Complaining that reports coming out of Washington about the battle were "meagre, confused, and unsatisfactory," the *Post* began to express "great anxiety" and the "deepest concern" at the possibility of disaster, and the *Advertiser* came out with "startling intelligence" about Burnside's evacuation from Fredericksburg.[105] By this time the news was out about Burnside's defeat and the enormous casualties that accompanied it. Describing the "awful events" that were now becoming apparent from subsequent news reports, the Democratic *Post* took the opportunity to strike out at the Republican administration. Burnside probably did his best, said the paper, but what could he do if he was carrying out orders from Washington? If President Lincoln continues to direct military strategy in the field "from his chair in Washington"; if the Secretary of War refuses to supply his generals with the necessary materials; if General Halleck is motivated more by jealously than by patriotism, said the paper, then disaster will follow disaster until "wiser and more patriotic men" govern the country. The *Post* editors also implied that "we told you so" because Lincoln had appointed Burnside to command the Army of the Potomac after he had dismissed their own favorite Democratic general—George B. McClellan.[106]

Perhaps because it was a weekly that came out on Saturday mornings and worked from earlier reports, *The Boston Pilot* took a long time to come to grips with the military defeat at Fredericksburg. Not until after Christmas, in its December 27 issue, did *The Pilot* finally alert its Irish-Catholic readers to the "Great Disaster" that had befallen the Army of the Potomac, with the "Terrible Slaughter of the Best Blood of the Country." In a front-page story that ran parallel with a special feature on "The Nativity of Christ on Christmas Day," the newspaper gave all the ugly details about the Union defeat. And on the next page, in a special-feature column titled "Records of Irish-American Patriotism," the editor praised the gallantry of General Meagher and his Irish Brigade, who were in the hottest part of the "slaughter-pen." *The Pilot* then joined the other Boston Democrats in blaming the "deplorable events" at Fredericksburg on the "bureaucratic officiousness" of an inefficient Secretary of War and his general-in-chief, and in ultimately holding President Lincoln himself legally responsible for his immediate subordinates' blundering.[107] It was painfully clear to the people in Boston that one more opportunity to defeat General Lee, capture Richmond, and crush the rebellion had gone by the board.

Hard on the heels of the defeat at Fredericksburg, the year drew to a close with the nation in a somber mood. President Lincoln, in deepest dejection, observed: "If there is a man out of perdition that suffers more than I do, I pity him." Voices of discontent were loud and forceful in Washington as in the state capitals. Newspapers reminded their readers about the seemingly endless reverses suffered by federal military forces, and citizens called to mind their loved ones who had been killed or wounded. Lincoln told a friend at the year's close: "I must save this government if possible. What I cannot do, of course, I will not do; but it may be as well understood, once for all, that I shall not surrender this game leaving any available card unplayed." Although the cards must now have seemed stacked against him, Lincoln would not throw down his hand. He was in this game for keeps.

Despite their shocked reactions to the unexpected Fredericksburg disaster, Bostonians too quickly regained their composure and resumed their normal preparations for the Christmas holiday season. The continuing war news from the front filled local newspapers, along with advertisements for Christmas gifts—photograph albums, writing cases, backgammon boards, dominoes, pens and pencils, pocket knives, wallets, books for young and old, chinaware, silverware, and magnificent new sewing machines for the home.[108] The social scene also took on a more routine atmosphere, especially with the news that the renowned Shakespearean actor Edwin Booth was making special appearances in Boston. On Wednesday afternoon, December 16, he was scheduled to appear at the Boston Music Hall in *Much Ado about Nothing,* a day later he would perform in *Richard II,* and on December 18 he would give a farewell performance in *Hamlet.* A "spectacular" drama, *Magnolia: The Planter's Daughter,* was playing at the Boston Museum, and playgoers could attend an evening performance of *Faint Heart Never Won Fair Lady* at P. T. Barnum's Museum. During the day, visitors to Barnum's were treated to a display of a live, "mammoth" hippopotamus and a "great living roaring" black sea lion—events certainly calculated to obscure the more depressing details in the war news.[109]

Amid the holiday celebrations and anticipation of the year's end, the papers put aside their party disputes and political rivalries long enough to focus on their common desire to defeat the Confederacy and restore the Union. The *Boston Post* decried the local prejudice against the Democratic party and called upon patriotic men of all parties to move away from their "ultra" members and work with the armies to put down the rebellion. When patriots "sink the prejudices of party and rise to a platform of action," said the *Post,* they will the sooner "do their duty to their country." [110] *The Boston Pilot* also called for a renewed sense of unity among its readers on the eve of a new year. The editor expressed regret that Northerners had been at war with "brethren of the same blood and race," but had done so to "hand down to our children the heritage entrusted to us by the fathers of the Republic." The Irish race had always fought "gloriously" for the Stars and Stripes, emphasized the paper, and would continue to do so until the Union and the Constitution were restored to "the proud position it had before the breaking out of the rebellion." [112]

And on Christmas day, the *Boston Daily Advertiser* urged its readers to recapture the "bright vision of the brilliant future which awaits this country" after the rebellion has been suppressed and the Union's power restored. "We must work patiently until the glorious end arrives," said the paper, "not discouraged by disappointments, not querulous about leaders, not obstinate about opinions—giving to the government, each man in his sphere, his most earnest and energetic support." [113]

If President Lincoln, despite the setbacks in December, was still determined to stay in the game and play for keeps, the evidence was sufficient to indicate that his supporters in Boston were also determined to see the game through to the finish.

NOW IN CAMP AT READVILLE!

54th REGIMENT!

MASS. VOLUNTEERS, composed of men of

AFRICAN DESCENT

Col. ROBERT G. SHAW.

 Colored Men, Rally 'Round the Flag of Freedom!

BOUNTY $100!

AT THE EXPIRATION OF THE TERM OF SERVICE.

Pay, $13 a Month!
Good Food & Clothing!
State Aid to Families!

RECRUITING OFFICE,

COR. CAMBRIDGE & NORTH RUSSELL STS.,

BOSTON.

Lieut. J. W. M. APPLETON, Recruiting Officer.

RWELL & CO., Steam Job Printers, No. 37 Congress Street, Boston.

After the adoption of the Emancipation Proclamation, Massachusetts Governor John Andrew obtained authorization to organize the first regular army regiments of African-American troops, which he expected would "elevate or depress the estimation in which the character of the Colored American will be held throughout the world." Black volunteers were recruited throughout the Northern states and taken to Camp Meigs in Readville, where they formed the 54th Regiment and later the 55th Regiment. (Massachusetts Historical Society)

5 The Tide Turns ~~~~~~

It was the year of Jubilee.

As colder weather closed in during late fall in 1862, Bay State troops were getting ready to spend a second season in winter quarters—only this year even farther from home. The winter months provided an opportunity for the men to recuperate from the rigors endured in the previous campaigns, to snatch any rest and recreation they could during the holiday season, and to prepare for the inevitable spring offensive. For now, the men carried out their routine duties, sweeping barracks, cleaning tents, and tending to their gear.

When Massachusetts soldiers first went into service in 1861 they were dressed in all sorts of attire. By late 1862, however, a regulation uniform was in common usage. A soldier was usually dressed in an overcoat and cape of light blue, sometimes black; a dress coat or tunic of dark blue, single-breasted, with a narrow stand-up collar; and an army blouse of the same color for fatigue duty. Both items of clothing were trimmed with brass buttons. Included were light blue trousers, much-criticized brogan shoes, and a dark blue cap with patent-leather visor and strap. The regulation hat was black felt with the crown dented from front to back; often one side of the brim was caught up with a metallic figure indicating the company and regiment. Around the crown was a three-colored silk-and-wool cord and silk tassels that gave the headgear a jaunty air. The soldier's arms and equipment varied, but usually included a musket, or more often a rifle of the Springfield type or the heavier English-made Enfield, a bayonet, leather belt, leather scabbard and cap box for percussion caps, and over the right shoulder was a strap to which was attached a cartridge box. The enlistee was also given a haversack of waterproof material, a knapsack of black enameled cloth, a tin dipper, tin plates, knife, fork, and spoons, two woolen blankets and one of rubber. There was much grumbling among the soldiers about too much shoddy equipment being provided by contractors.[1]

As the holiday season approached, the men eagerly awaited packages from home. The most prized items were foodstuffs such as chocolates, canned sardines, and cookies, which relieved their monotonous, unappetizing army diet. Men in camp made every effort to celebrate the holidays properly. The 45th Massachusetts Regiment, stationed at New Bern, North Carolina, determined to have a real New England Thanksgiving dinner, and prepared for the feast by foraging in the countryside and buying up whatever produce was available. After prevailing upon some of the local women to cook the choice parts of the dinner, the men sat down to a rather sumptuous meal. Much to be commended was the good judgment and lack of bitterness in the toast one man offered: "The states of Massachusetts and North Carolina, may the day soon come when both shall unite in one glad thanksgiving for a people united and peace restored, and when our sister Southern states shall respond with a hearty Amen."[2]

The soldiers showed much imagination as they came up with all sorts of improvisations. The 45th Regiment staged two lively events for their recreation. A masked ball, with tickets at ten cents per person, was heavily attended. Although most of the men wore their dress uniforms to the event, a few of the more imaginative members created bizarre costumes. One private put together a uniform entirely of newspapers and came as "the press"; another man turned his sash into a turban and made a grand entrance as a Turkish pasha. A band played for the assemblage, and a glee club performed musical numbers. To the offhand observer the scene in the barracks-turned-ballroom may have seemed a little ridiculous, but to the participants the gala event gave a necessary boost to sagging spirits. The regiment also produced an original operetta entitled *The Recruit*, which the men enthusiastically flocked to see in a hall fitted with footlights and a curtain borrowed from a local theater. Evening band concerts were held fairly often and were a pleasant respite from the duties of the day.[3] Irish soldiers from the 28th Massachusetts Regiment even enjoyed a St. Patrick's Day celebration on March 17, 1863, along with other members of the Irish Brigade. Attended by General Joseph Hooker and other dignitaries, the festivities included horse races and other competitions, followed by theatrical productions, recitations, songs, and toasts that lasted well into the night, according to Peter Welsh from Charlestown.[4]

These were occasions when soldiers far from home got a chance to lose some of their provincial attitudes as they talked with fellow servicemen from other parts of their own country, as well as from Ireland and Europe, and saw strange scenery and different customs. Most of them looked upon their military careers as defined by disturbance, boredom, inconvenience, and even suffering and tragedy; at the same time, however, they were years of excitement and high adventure which would never be repeated and which they would remember for the rest of their lives.

~ ~ ~

ON NEW YEAR'S DAY, 1863, the Emancipation Proclamation went into effect. Back in Boston, bells rang out during the day from churches throughout the city; in the evening, there was a huge gala at the Boston Music Hall. People arrived early as black Americans and white Americans joined to ring in the year they believed to be a new era in the social history of America. Major figures among the city's literati were present—Ralph Waldo Emerson, Henry Wadsworth Longfellow, John Greenleaf Whittier, Edward Everett Hale, Charles Eliot Norton, Harriet Beecher Stowe—but everyone was still nervous about whether President Lincoln would keep his promise. Restlessness pervaded the hall as the guests waited for the official news about the proclamation to come over the telegraph wires from Washington. Suddenly a messenger burst through the doors shouting, "It is coming! It is on the wires." "A thrill shot through the crowd," recalled one eyewitness; "the enthusiasm was intense." The transmission completed, a young abolitionist read the Emancipation Proclamation aloud to the crowd.[5] He had hardly finished when the auditorium vibrated with cheers and applause for Abraham Lincoln and William Lloyd Garrison. When Ralph Waldo Emerson ascended the rostrum, the excited mass fell silent. Lean, patrician, and clear-voiced, the literary philosopher epitomized the highest type of citizen. With feeling and dignity, he read "The Boston Hymn." By word and by work, he said, Boston had earned the right to be associated with the slave's redemption. It was a song of liberty and justice, wild and strong:

> Today unbind the captive,
> So only are ye unbound;
> Lift up a people from the dust,
> Trump of their rescue, sound!
>
> Up! and the dusky race
> That sat in the darkness long,—
> By swift their feet as antelopes
> And as behemoth strong.[6]

The rich musical program that followed was almost anticlimactic; it included Beethoven's majestic Fifth Symphony and the glorious "Hallelujah Chorus" from Handel's *Messiah*. When the emotional evening ended, the celebrants felt that they had called upon Boston's finest human resources to welcome their African-American brothers and sisters out of bondage.

When the historic document had been officially promulgated, Governor

John Andrew traveled to Washington and somehow got written permission from Secretary of War Stanton to raise additional bodies of volunteers that "may include persons of African descent, organized into special corps." With the order in hand, Andrew hurried back to Boston and set in motion the steps necessary to organize as soon as possible an African-American infantry regiment before Stanton changed his mind.[7]

In September 1861, Secretary of the Navy Gideon Welles had authorized enlistment of blacks in the navy, but the color line was clearly fixed by low pay and menial jobs in which blacks served mainly as firemen, coal heavers, cooks, and stewards.[8] The War Department, on the other hand, consistently refused to accept Northern blacks as soldiers, even when black regiments had been organized in Kansas by James Land, in occupied areas of southern Louisiana by Ben Butler, and from among freedmen in the South Carolina Sea Islands by General Rufus Saxon. Abolitionists and Radical Republicans had pushed steadily for enlisting black soldiers as one more way to defeat the Confederacy, and black leaders emphasized that military service would demonstrate African Americans' bravery and help them earn the right to full citizenship. During summer 1862, Robert Morris, the well-known attorney, had gone to the State House with a delegation of influential black Bostonians, offering to raise a regiment of black volunteers led by black officers.[9] Governor John Andrew refused the offer, saying the state constitution specified that only white men could command a regiment. Morris retorted angrily that if that was so, then perhaps blacks should not enlist at all if the opportunity should ever arise.[10]

To help him recruit enough volunteers for his all-black regiment, Governor Andrew persuaded his friend George Luther Stearns to head a committee to superintend recruiting of black troops and raise any funds necessary for travel and publicity.[11] With backing from public-spirited citizens of both races, Stearns's committee quickly collected $5,000, which was used to publish announcements in newspapers throughout the North calling for enlistments in the new 54th Regiment. To speed the work, Stearns employed recruitment agents, relying heavily upon such African-American leaders as Frederick Douglass and Highland Garnet of New York, Martin Delany of Pittsburgh, and William Wells Brown and Charles Lenox Remond of Boston. Because Governor Andrew's recruiting committee was composed of private citizens, no one could legally complain that Massachusetts was sending agents into other states to lure their men away.[12] "The delicacy of the situation, as well as its absurdity," observed the contemporary historian Luis Emilio, "lay in the fact that these other governors, though themselves refusing to enlist the negro, still claimed him, as soon as he manifested his intention to enlist elsewhere, as potentially part of their quota." Technically speaking, Andrew sent no Massachusetts recruiting officers outside the state; practically, Stearns's agents went everywhere through the Middle States and even penetrated beyond the Mississippi.[13]

Realizing that the 54th Regiment would be the first of its kind to be established in the North, Andrew was well aware that its success or failure would go far "to elevate or depress the estimation in which the character of the Colored American will be held throughout the world."[14] He was particularly eager to have young officers who would be "gentlemen of the highest tone and honor," and indicated that he would look for such men "in those circles of educated antislavery society which, next to the colored race itself, have the greatest interest in this experiment." Having established for himself this idealistic model, Andrew wrote to Francis G. Shaw of New York, a committed abolitionist and descendant of one of Boston's most prosperous families, proposing that his son, Robert Gould Shaw, then serving as a captain with the 2nd Massachusetts Infantry, be named colonel of the new 54th Regiment.[15] Andrew felt that the twenty-five-year-old Shaw had the proper qualifications to lead the unit he hoped would be "a model for all future colored regiments." Young Shaw accepted the commission, and on February 15, 1863, arrived in Boston to prepare to assume his duties.[16]

Next day, February 16, Shaw met with Governor John Andrew and rode in the governor's carriage through the frosty Boston streets while they talked about efforts to recruit enough volunteers to meet the regiment's quota, a thousand men. On that same night, Shaw's second in command, Lieutenant-Colonel Norwood Hallowell, son of a wealthy Philadelphia Quaker, together with several leading abolitionists including Frederick Douglass and Wendell Phillips, held a rally at the Joy Street Church in Boston's black neighborhood to energize the community to support the war and to promote recruiting for the black regiment.[17] The response among local African Americans, however, was not as enthusiastic as the recruiters had hoped. That black troops had formerly been rejected was humiliating, and many blacks were bitterly determined to stay out of the war entirely. Then too, many in the black audience were clearly disappointed to learn that the new regiment would have white officers. Several black Bostonians in attendance that night expressed their frustration that black men would not be allowed to elect their own officers of their own color. Robert Morris, the black lawyer, repeatedly objected to the word "white" in the laws. When one of the white abolitionists sought to placate "Brother Morris" by assuring him that black soldiers would be treated respectfully by white officers, Morris snapped back: "Don't you call me "brother" until you have taken the word "white" out of the Constitution!"[18] The reaction against white officers was reinforced by anxiety over possible bloody retaliation by Confederates. Any black men enlisting in the Union army, wearing a blue uniform, and carrying a loaded firearm, knew full well that he faced deadly reprisal. In December 1862, Jefferson Davis had declared that all Negro slaves, "if captured in arms," would be handed over to state authorities and dealt with "according to the laws of said States." And on May 1, 1863, the Confederate Congress resolved that any white officers commanding Negro troops would be "deemed as inciting servile insurrection" and if captured could be sentenced to death. Although these resolutions were not put into effect as final policy, numerous instances were recorded of captured black prisoners of war being wantonly murdered by their Confederate captors.[19]

Despite these obstacles, however, recruiting continued slowly but steadily. Broadsides appeared, appealing to men "of African descent" to join the 54th Regiment by going to the recruiting office at the corner of Cambridge and North Russell Streets in Boston; in return, each man would receive a $100 bounty.[20] Although at first many Boston blacks had responded somewhat negatively, by spring 1863 the black community was fully behind the 54th Regiment. At least 137 young black men, about 40 percent of military-age black males in Boston, enlisted in the black regiment.[21] Just after he arrived in Boston, Colonel Shaw decided it was time for him to supervise the training at Camp Meigs, at Readville, a town a few miles south of the city, on the Boston and Providence Railroad line. The camp was laid out on a broad plain, well suited for drilling large bodies of men, and wooden barracks were lined up against the pine-covered slopes of Milton's Blue Hills. During spring and summer, the drill field had a pleasant, rustic appearance; during the winter, however, the camp was a bleak stretch of flat ground that heavy rains and melting snows quickly turned into a sea of mud. By the time Colonel Shaw arrived, the men—now consisting of four companies—had been issued their uniforms, and they presented a "soldierly appearance." The camp itself was still "topsy turvy," with the barracks cleaned but unheated, and with very little food for meals.[22] Gradually ironing out the problems, Shaw put his men through rigorous basic training and instructed them in the rudiments of soldiering. When winter snowstorms and icy winds swept across the open fields, the drilling continued inside the wooden barracks. By early May, the parade grounds had finally hardened, and columns of blue-coated black soldiers drilled with crisp precision. Recruiting still went on, men still arrived at Camp Meigs, and the regiment was filling out.[23]

By May 14, the 54th Regiment finally was fully staffed. Indeed, so many African Americans were now continuing to pour in to the Commonwealth that it was decided to organize a second black regiment, the 55th. Success for Governor Andrew's project was particularly gratifying because, though general recruitment was declining, the 54th and the 55th had full ranks even without bounties for inducement. Meanwhile, the men of the 54th, 1,000 strong, had been equipped with Enfield rifles, the noncommissioned officers were fur-

The valor of the 54th Regiment on the battlefield, especially in the assault at Fort Wagner, proved conclusively that black soldiers could fight courageously and well. Despite unequal pay and various forms of discrimination, the 54th Regiment successfully paved the way for the enlistment of some 178,000 black troops who wore the Union blue and helped win the Civil War. (Massachusetts Historical Society)

nished with swords, and May 18 was set for the formal presentation of the colors. Among the invited guests were William Lloyd Garrison, Wendell Phillips, and Frederick Douglass, whose two sons were members of the regiment. At 11:00 A.M., Colonel Shaw called his regiment to order, four flags were made ready for presentation, and after a brief opening prayer Governor Andrew stepped forward to address the new regiment. "I stand or fall as a man and a magistrate," said the governor, "with the rise and the fall in history of the Fifty-Fourth Massachusetts Regiment." This was an opportunity, he asserted as he presented Colonel Shaw with the colors, "for a whole race of men."[24] In a brief response, Shaw thanked Andrew for the flags and expressed his hope for an opportunity to show the governor that he had not made a mistake in "intrusting the honor of the State to a colored regiment—the first State that has ever sent one to the war." A national flag was then presented by the young black women of Boston; another flag showing the state colors was presented as a gift from the Colored Ladies' Relief Society; a third flag, donated by "a large and patriotic committee," was made of white silk with the figure of the Goddess of Liberty and the inscription "Liberty, Loyalty, and Unity."[25] After reviewing the troops, the governor handed Shaw a telegram from the Secretary of War ordering the 54th Regiment to report to General David Hunter, who was at Hilton Head, commanding the Department of the South.

Four days later, at 9:00 A.M. on May 18, the 54th arrived in Boston by train at the Providence Depot, in what is now Park Square. Taking his place at the head of his regiment, preceded by Patrick Gilmore's marching band, Colonel Robert Gould Shaw led his regiment up Boylston Street, around Boston Common, and then onto Tremont Street, cheered by thousands of spectators. Turning left onto Somerset Street, the regiment looped around Pemberton Square and then down to Beacon Street, where it paused before the State House to greet Governor Andrew and his staff.[26] As the black regiment moved down Beacon Hill toward Charles Street, Shaw's relatives, gathered in the family home at 44 Beacon Street, watched proudly from behind the windows of the second-floor balcony as the young colonel rode by. At the bottom of the hill the regiment turned left on Charles Street and marched through the gate onto the Boston Common parade ground, where the troops passed in review before Governor Andrew and his officials. At noon, the regiment marched across the Common to the West Street gate, and made its way proudly down the length of State Street to Battery Wharf, where the men boarded the transport *De Molay*, which would take them to their destiny in South Carolina.

Not content with having formed his all-black regiment, Governor Andrew continued to demonstrate deep interest in the African-American soldiers' welfare. In spite of objections by some officers, he persuaded Secretary of War Stanton to grant a commission to the 54th's black chaplain. He also secured assurances that the men in these regiments would receive the same pay as all other soldiers, and equal treatment.[27] This pledge, however, was sadly neglected in subsequent months. White privates were paid $13 a month and provided a clothing allowance of $3.50. Black privates, on the other hand, were paid only $10 a month, and had $3 deducted in advance for their clothing, leading Governor Andrew on one occasion to explode in anger while writing to Senator Charles Sumner: "For God's sake, how long is the injustice of the Government to be continued toward these men?"[28] Despite bitter opposition by blacks and abolitionists, and near mutiny in the 54th Regiment, the inequality persisted more than a year, until June 1864, when Congress retroactively equalized military salaries.[29] Lincoln explained to Frederick Douglass in summer 1863 that lower pay for blacks was a "necessary concession" he had to make to popular prejudice until whites could be shown evidence that blacks were effective combat soldiers.[30] Black troops also experienced discriminatory treatment in performing their military duties. They were assigned excessive fatigue details, used for the most menial tasks, and invariably stationed where white soldiers had already been decimated by such diseases as typhus, typhoid fever, yellow fever, and malaria. This unhealthy garrison duty, combined with grossly inadequate medical care, contributed greatly to the black mortality rate, which was 40 percent higher than that of white soldiers in the Union army.[31]

On July 18, 1863, the 54th Massachusetts Regiment took part in the assault on Charleston, South Carolina, a city guarded by heavily fortified islands. The Massachusetts regiment's specific objective was to capture Fort Wagner on Morris Island. After an exhausting march of several hours, the regiment reached the point of attack. In the gathering dusk, with Colonel Shaw at the front of his men, they charged toward the fortifications, across 600 yards of open sand, facing heavy, concentrated fire from the Confederate batteries. Shaw reached the parapet, but fell into the fort mortally wounded. After two hours of fruitless attack, with a third of the officers and almost half the enlisted men killed or wounded, the federal troops retired. The soldiers of the 54th Regiment, by their blood and valor, had become heroes. Massachusetts mourned its loss. Robert Gould Shaw was regarded as the ideal patriot, whose devotion and unselfish sacrifice gave needed life to sagging spirits in New England.[32] Ralph Waldo Emerson expressed sincere condolences to Shaw's family, and commemorated the fallen soldiers in his poem "Voluntaries." Of the poem's 121 lines, these seemed most touching and appropriate as a final eulogy for young Shaw:

> So nigh is grandeur to our dust,
> So near is God to man,
> When Duty whispers low, *Thou must*,
> The youth replies, *I can*.[33]

At Honey Hill, near Charleston, in summer 1864, the other Massachusetts African-American regiment, the 55th, gave the country another display of high bravery and dedication. Massachusetts men were associated with several African-American units. General Butler in 1862 drew black soldiers into his command, and Thomas Wentworth Higginson raised the first unit of former slaves, which became known as the First South Carolina Regiment. A Harvard graduate (1841), an advocate of woman suffrage, and an abolitionist supporter of John Brown, Higginson was serving as captain in a Massachusetts regiment when General Rufus Saxton offered him command of the First South Carolina Volunteers, a regiment composed entirely of black troops. After taking part of his regiment on a raid along a South Carolina river in January 1863, Higginson reported to the War Department his conviction that successful prosecution of the war lay in "the unlimited employment of black troops." The *New York Tribune* agreed with Higginson's assessment and commented that similar reports about black soldiers' successes in the field were sure "to shake our inveterate Saxon prejudice against the capacity and courage of negro troops." [34]

Encouraged by the success of the 54th and 55th regiments, and urged on by several of his Brahmin friends, in September 1863 Governor John Andrew proposed to Secretary of War Stanton that he be authorized to recruit "a Massachusetts cavalry regiment of colored men." He insisted that the African-American members of this new elite unit be designated as state volunteers, not classified as "U.S. Colored," and that its officers be drawn exclusively from Massachusetts.[35] He further insisted that he be allowed to appoint the white officers himself, drawing them from Massachusetts regiments already in the field, so that this new cavalry unit would have "brave, devoted and noble fellows, like those who were selected for the 54th and 55th (infantry) volunteers." [36] To serve as colonel of the new regiment, Andrew called upon Henry Sturgis Russell, a Harvard graduate, close friend of Robert Gould Shaw, and son-in-law of John Murray Forbes. Harry Russell had already seen active fighting with the 2nd Massachusetts Cavalry, and Andrew considered him an experienced cavalry officer and a gentleman "of the highest tone and honor." [37] Stanton replied that he was "entirely in favor of the measure," and by December 1863 the governor began recruiting men for the 5th Massachusetts Cavalry Volunteers, the only African-American cavalry regiment ever raised in Massachusetts. Andrew set up a special recruitment committee with such prominent

Robert Gould Shaw was selected by Governor Andrew to be the leader of Massachusetts' all-black 54th Regiment. On July 18, 1863, Colonel Shaw was killed leading his men in a gallant assault against Fort Wagner, South Carolina. Shaw was buried on the battlefield with his men, but on May 31, 1897, their courage was commemorated on Boston Common with a bronze memorial by the famous sculptor Augustus Saint-Gaudens. (Courtesy of the Boston Public Library, Print Department)

black leaders as Martin R. Delany, John Mercer Langston, Henry Highland Garnet, William Wells Brown, and Frederick Douglass, whose son Charles eventually served in the 5th Cavalry. The recruiters accomplished most of their work during winter 1863–1864, so that by spring 1864 the 5th Cavalry was sent to the front, where they performed a great deal of fatigue duty at Point Lookout, Maryland, and guarded Confederate prisoners of war, who did not take kindly to being ordered about by black soldiers.[38]

The Emancipation announcement was exciting, and the spectacle of black troops in blue uniforms was breathtaking, but President Lincoln was aware that everything was futile unless he destroyed the power of the Confederate armies. "Defeat and failure in the field," he stated somberly, "make everything seem wrong." [39] On January 25, 1863, therefore, Lincoln replaced the ineffective General Burnside with General Joseph Hooker, a Hadley, Massachusetts, native who had won a good reputation as a division and corps commander. Through training and discipline, Hooker helped restore morale in the Army of the Potomac, which had been so badly shattered in the Battle of Fredericksburg a month earlier. With more than 150,000 men, by early spring he was making plans to envelop Lee and his army in a gigantic pincer movement that would send General John Sedgwick and 40,000 men swinging east toward Fredericksburg while he took the rest of the army in a westward arc around Lee's left flank.

Refusing to be caught in the trap, Lee sent a small force to hold off Sedgwick while he used his main force to strike at Hooker's army at Chancellorsville on May 1, 1863. Sending Jackson and Longstreet around Hooker's right flank, Lee smashed through the enemy lines and inflicted a devastating defeat upon the Union army. As in so many other engagements, regiments from Massachusetts had a significant part in the fighting, and were among the 16,000 federal troops killed and wounded. Once again the long lists of casualties in the local newspapers and the many unsettling rumors arriving from the battlefield added to the reaction that William Schouler recalled as "the general feeling of disappointment and sorrow which pervaded loyal hearts." [40] Directly following the military disaster at Fredericksburg in December 1863, the bloody Chancellorsville defeat seemed to support administration critics' complaints that Lincoln could not direct the war efficiently, that Union generals were uniformly incompetent, that General Robert E. Lee was invincible, and that the North would never be able to defeat the South in battle. Civilian morale was at an all-time low as the lengthening casualty lists reflected the Union forces' incredible suffering. Telling his wife afterward how the 28th Massachusetts Regiment, as part of the Irish Brigade, had fought to rescue the 5th Maine battery on May 3, Peter Welsh could not conceal the terrible losses. "Our brigade brought in a battery by hand off the field," he wrote. "The horses were all killed, and what men belong to it that were not killed or wounded run and left it." [41] "The Irish spirit for the war is dead! Absolutely dead!" cried *The Boston Pilot* upon learning about Irish casualties at Chancellorsville. "There are a great many Irish yet. But our fighters are dead," it moaned. "Their desperate valor led them, not to victory, but extinction. . . . How bitter to Ireland has been this rebellion!" [42]

With all the setbacks on the battlefield, however, during the disheartening winter and spring of 1863, Bay Staters who still supported the Lincoln administration displayed a good deal of stamina and resilience. Edward Everett, always a shrewd observer of what was going on, reported: "The most extra-ordinary feature of the times is the immobility of the public mind under the most serious reverses. Hooker's disappointing failure and retreat, beyond a lit-tle fluttering on the Stock Exchange at New York," he wrote, "produced not the slightest apparent effect upon the community." For those who did not sup-port the administration, however, the Chancellorsville disaster was only one more example of the inability of Lincoln and his officials to save the Union. Although back in January many people in the North had greeted with great rejoicing the Emancipation Proclamation and the subsequent recruitment of black soldiers, many others denounced these actions as further examples of the ineptitude and irresponsibility of the Lincoln administration. Boston Dem-ocrats formally protested against the Emancipation Proclamation because of its "unconstitutionality" as well as its "inexpediency," and denounced Lin-coln's unjustified and unauthorized expansion of the purpose of the war.[43] For-mer Democratic statesman Caleb Cushing used the *Boston Post* to publish a statement by an unidentified Union army officer, who predicted that if this turned out to be a war for the "emancipation, education, and improvement of the slaves," then the Union army would break up in twenty-four hours.[44] Bay State Democrats also opposed the Emancipation Proclamation because it amounted to confiscating private property without due process of law, thus constituting a clear violation of the Fifth Amendment. Reflecting prevailing Democratic opinion, the *Post* declared: "The President has no authority to free the slaves en masse, either by Constitutional law or by the war power."[45] And finally, many Democrats expressed the belief that emancipation would only prolong the conflict between North and South and strengthen Confederate determination to resist to the bitter end.[46] *The Boston Pilot,* representing Irish-Catholic opinion, echoed the Democratic sentiment and denounced the Eman-cipation Proclamation as "violently opposed to the Constitution."[47] Instead of realizing that the "infallible" means for ending the war was to "withdraw its causes," the paper blamed the Lincoln administration for having "deliberately increased it."

The decision to recruit African Americans into the Union army further antagonized Irish Americans. "I see by late papers that the governer of Massa-chusets has been autheured to raise nigar regiments," wrote Peter Welsh of the 28th Regiment to his wife back in Boston. "I hope he may succed, but I doubt it very much," he continued. "The feeling against nigars is intensely strong in this army, as is plainly to be seen wherever and whenever they meet them. They are looked upon as the principal cause of this war, and this feeling is especially strong in the Irish regiments."[48] And at times racial feelings went beyond words and broke out in violence. One day, Charles R. Douglass, son of the well-known African-American spokesman Frederick Douglass, was waiting at the railroad station for the train to take him back to his cavalry unit at Camp Meigs. An Irish soldier standing nearby overheard him praising General Meade and assumed he was criticizing General McClellan, always a popular figure among the Irish regiments. The Irishman stepped up in front of Douglass, brandished his fist in his face, and asked angrily: "Ain't McClellan a good General . . . you black nigger! I don't care if you have got the uniform on!" Douglass exploded in rage, ripped off his jacket, and "went at" the man. He was not afraid, he later told his father, because he had his pistol with him "and it was well loaded." Young Charles had already made up his mind to "shoot the first Irishman that strikes me—they may talk, but keep their paws to themselves." Fortunately for all, a policeman came up, pulled the two men apart, and asked what the trouble was. When Douglass explained what started the fight, the policeman marched the other soldier away. "That made all the other Irish mad," Douglass wrote, "and I felt better." [49]

On the home front, *The Boston Pilot* continued to denounce the president's plans to recruit African Americans for the Union army as "a lasting disgrace to the nation," scoffing at the very idea of blacks as soldiers.[50] Nature intended the African American to be the white man's slave and nothing else, insisted the newspaper, and for this reason the Negro race was much happier "in slavery than in freedom."[51] The Catholic weekly deplored most bitterly efforts by those it labeled "negrophilists" and "nigger-worshippers" to convince black people that they were the equals of white people, and supported the growing opposition to Lincoln. "Call them Copperheads—or any other ungentlemanly term you like," it said; they are the only "true representatives of Republican freedom today in this country."[52] The paper now called upon its readers to withdraw completely any support they had given to the Lincoln administration. "At one time we did support Lincoln; but then he had the full promise of Constitutionalism about him," declared *The Pilot,* "but he changed, and so have we. It is now every man's duty to disagree with him."[53]

Disenchantment with the Lincoln administration grew even faster when the federal government passed a conscription law in March 1863. During June and July, in accordance with the new law, all men twenty to forty-five years of age were enrolled for the draft. The total in Massachusetts came to 164,178. Of this number, the names of 32,079 men were drawn, of whom 22,343 obtained exemptions and 3,046 failed to report. Of the number drafted, 6,690 were obligated to serve. Of these, 743 offered to serve personally; 2,325 procured substitutes; and 3,623 paid the government $1,085,800 to avoid military service altogether. Most who were drafted, as well as those who were substitutes, were assigned to Massachusetts regiments in the field to replace those who had been lost in battle or whose enlistments had expired. Governor Andrew had opposed the idea of a draft, considering it ill-advised. Not only did

he feel it antagonized many people needlessly, but he also doubted its effectiveness in raising troops. He preferred the more positive approach: increasing
inducements to enlist, especially with the bounty system. On July 18, Andrew
requested permission from the Secretary of War to allow him to enlist as
volunteers Massachusetts men who had been drafted, and to provide them
with a state bounty. His request, however, was not granted. Another thing that
bothered Governor Andrew was that Massachusetts was not receiving credit
for all the servicemen who came from that state. Except for New York, Massachusetts provided more sailors for the U.S. Navy than any other state, nearly
one-fifth of the complement. But the Commonwealth received no credit for
this official manpower contribution to the war effort. At the end of 1863,
more than 17,000 Massachusetts men were in the navy, but not until July 4,
1864, was Andrew able to prevail upon the federal government to acknowledge that naval volunteers from the Bay State (by now 22,360) were in fact
part of Massachusetts men under arms. In counting quotas that the government assessed from the states, getting credit for naval enlistments was most
important.[54]

Against Governor Andrew's wishes, however, the new conscription law
went into effect. It was restricted to able-bodied men aged twenty to forty-five,
and was supposed to apply only in districts that had not fulfilled their assigned
troop quotas. No man was placed in the federal service until selected by the
draft, but even then a wealthy young man could either hire a substitute to go
in his place or purchase outright exemption for $300. Because the conscription
law was vague and considered particularly unfair to the poor, opposition was
widespread and sometimes violent. In many parts of the country, but especially
in East Coast states like New Jersey, New York, and Massachusetts where Irish
immigrants protested against the draft's inequities, many "insurrections" arose
against enforcement of the law. But New York City had the most frightening
outbreak of violence after a fight in the draft office exploded into a vicious
attack on the city's black population. For three days, July 13 to 15, 1863,
bloody rioting swept the city—telegraph lines were cut, buildings destroyed,
property looted, and innocent African Americans brutally murdered. Order
was not restored until U.S. Army troops were brought up from Gettysburg to
put down the rioting.[55]

Throughout Massachusetts, but above all in Boston, with its large Irish
population, officials worried that the same factors producing riots in New
York City—anger with the Emancipation Proclamation and reaction against
the unfair conscription law—would also produce disorders.[56] John Fitzpatrick, the Catholic bishop, had left the city for a visit to Belgium, but he
assigned his chancellor, Fr. James Healy, to administer the diocese in his absence. As soon as he heard the first reports of the rioting in New York, Fr.

Healy became apprehensive about the possibility of trouble.[57] After learning that several local priests had been speaking out in their churches against the draft law and using language "calculated to inflame the minds of their hearers," the young administrator concluded that it would be "strange to me if we escape some such trouble."[58] Healy's fears were soon realized. In the afternoon of July 14, only one day after the New York riots broke out, irate women set upon two provost marshals who had called at a home on Prince Street in the city's North End. When men came home from work in the nearby gas works and beat up several local policemen, the mêlée quickly expanded into a wholesale riot. By late afternoon, the crowd had swelled so that the police were forced to retreat to their station house, in which they were barricaded by the screaming mob. Mayor Frederic W. Lincoln used the police telegraph to assemble the three militia companies in the nearby Cooper Street Armory.

Governor John Andrew was taking part in the Harvard commencement exercises in Cambridge when he heard about the riot and immediately returned to Boston. Sizing up the situation, he used his authority as governor to call in regular U.S. Army troops from the harbor forts and local camps. Although the 55th Regiment was the only regiment at Camp Meigs then at full strength, Andrew decided that the black regiment could not be "safely employed" to put down a riot of "free white American citizens."[59] Three companies of troops from Fort Warren, under Major Stephen Cabot, came ashore a little after 6:00 in the evening and reported to Governor Andrew, who directed them to Mayor Lincoln. One company was sent to protect an armory on Marshall Street; the other two marched down North Margin Street, moved into the Cooper Street Armory, and set up two six-pound cannon facing the doors. When the rioters tried to break into the building, Major Cabot ordered his men to fire a single blast through the closed door, killing several in the mob, and putting the rest of the attackers to flight.[60] Still determined on further mischief, however, the rioters headed for Dock Square and several gun shops. Fortunately for the safety of the city, an advance guard of policemen arrived first and held back the mob until additional regular troops could be brought over from Fort Independence to clear the area, set up field pieces at several strategic locations, and station armed guards along the streets.[61] Meanwhile, the Harvard classes of 1852 and 1857 were holding a reunion at the Parker House hotel. Hearing all the excitement, in a spontaneous burst of patriotism they marched in a body up School Street to the State House to be mustered in for emergency all-night duty. Thus ended the Boston riot for the night.[62] "As we go to press, the military are at their posts and all is quiet," reported the *Advertiser*. "Little knots of people, however, still linger about Cooper and the adjacent streets but threaten nothing serious."[63] No one knew for certain whether trouble would break out again next day.

"Great apprehension" remained throughout the city in the two or three days following the brief Boston rioting. Rumors that the Irish were planning new disturbances brought offers from nativist vigilante groups in neighboring communities to come in to help city authorities put down any new outbreaks of violence.[64] Fortunately, however, no further trouble arose. Public figures made eloquent appeals to citizens to remain calm; Catholic priests patrolled the immigrant neighborhoods and dispersed potential troublemakers; newspapers such as the *Advertiser* called upon "all honorable and good men" to support the authorities and stamp out this "frantic movement" that threatened to replace law with anarchy.[65] Slowly the tensions began to ease, and the city gradually returned to normal. Mayor Lincoln made it a point to express thanks for the "good influences" exerted by the Catholic chancellor, Fr. Healy, and by Fr. Brady in the North End, as well as by other clergymen, who "laboured to preserve quiet among their congregations."[66] Clearly, however, the violence in America's cities dramatically showed the growing dissatisfaction in many quarters with the Lincoln administration's way of managing the war, the decision to use black troops in the Union army, and the continuing military losses during winter and spring 1862–1863.

This undercurrent of opposition, even in a city as traditionally loyal as Boston, made some prominent citizens feel that the time had come to counteract these negative sentiments and rebuild public opinion to favor the president and the war. Early in 1863, Unionists heard unsettling talk among Bay State Democrats about the possibility of a negotiated peace, and observed the warm welcome they gave to General George B. McClellan when he visited the city early in February. Obviously, local Democrats tried to arouse support for McClellan, who they hoped would oppose Lincoln for the presidency in 1864. They sponsored several public receptions for the Democratic general, and some leading merchants and bankers closed their businesses in his honor. After eight days of "triumphant visiting," McClellan was presented a dress sword by George Lunt, Democratic editor of the *Boston Courier*. The political purpose behind McClellan's Boston visit was not lost on Bay State Republicans. "Evidently a President is wanted," observed the *Springfield Republican* sourly, and the *Worcester Spy*, another Republican newspaper, came down hard on the Democratic party for its "admiration" for General McClellan. They liked him not because of any "distinguished merit," said the paper, but simply because the Democrats hated the Lincoln administration so much that they would use McClellan as a "convenient instrument" if he served their purposes.[67]

No apparent counterargument was heard against all this antiadministration talk and pro-McClellan activity at places such as the Somerset Club, the Friday Club, and other locations where conservative residents regularly gathered. As a result, such prominent Bostonians as John Murray Forbes, Charles

Eliot Norton, and Oliver Wendell Holmes felt it was time for gentlemen in the city who believed in supporting Lincoln and prosecuting the war to form their own patriotic association.[68] Boston was notoriously a "club city," where "gentlemen of property and standing" met to enjoy pleasant surroundings, a good dinner, an excellent brandy, a fine cigar, and an evening of stimulating conversation. Forbes complained that Boston social clubs were uncompromisingly conservative, led by men "who think themselves aristocratic and gentlemanlike" and who therefore still identified with the Southern slaveholders.[69] Late in January, therefore, an invitation went out calling a meeting to organize a "Union" club, the letter being signed by Forbes; Charles Eliot Norton, editor of the *North American Review;* Samuel G. Ward, Boston agent for Baring Brothers; Jonathan I. Bowditch, a partner with Edward Austin in a firm engaged in the China trade; and Martin Brimmer, a Boston philanthropist. On February 4, 1863, those who signed the invitation met with several other businessmen at Samuel Ward's home, where they agreed to organize a Union Club in Boston and to limit membership to those who held "unqualified loyalty to the Constitution" and who were ready to pledge "unwavering support of the federal government in suppressing the rebellion." By the time the details had been worked out, the list of subscribers included Amos A. Lawrence, Henry Lee, J. Wiley Edmands, and Alphaeus Hardy, along with a hundred other Boston business and professional men. To further enhance the new group's prestige, they agreed to purchase the Park Street residence of the late Abbott Lawrence for $55,000, and then named the old Whig conservative Edward Everett as the Union Club's president. In his opening address, Everett had an appropriately militant message: "The cause in which we are engaged is the cause of the Constitution and the Law, of civilization and freedom, of man and God."[70]

The Union Club's charter, though, forbade direct involvement in political action, and so Forbes believed the club's "strongest members" should form another association for that purpose. On March 10, 1863, a number of prominent Boston businessmen, all staunch Republicans and Union Club members, met at Martin Brimmer's house at 48 Beacon Street to organize the New England Loyal Publication Society. Charles Eliot Norton was selected as editor of the enterprise, which twice a week published and distributed information about events of the day, excerpted from various newspaper articles and editorials, to inform public opinion. Before long, however, Norton was publishing his own broadsides (sheets of paper printed on one side and folded), and within a year had sent out as many as 159 of them to newspapers all over the North. Although initial circulation ran to only 1,000 to 2,000, the materials were reprinted in weeklies all over the country, and Norton believed they eventually reached as many as a million people.[71]

With a similar aim, in spring 1863 Boston women, led by Elizabeth Cady Stanton and Susan B. Anthony, prominent feminist leaders who had also been active in the abolitionist movement, organized the Women's Loyal National League to promote loyalty and to propagandize for emancipation. With local abolitionists calling for Congress to pass an emancipation act to reinforce the president's recent Emancipation Proclamation, the women decided that their League's main objective would be to circulate petitions urging that such an act be passed. Encouraged by the mounting enthusiasm for their cause, the women boldly predicted they would get at least one million signatures on their petition by the time the 1863–1864 congressional session came to a close. Considering that nowhere near so many signatures had ever been amassed for a petition, the goal was unattainable, but Stanton and Anthony forged ahead with great determination. Women abolitionists all over the North rallied to the League's cause, and Senator Charles Sumner permitted the women to send out blank petitions under his senatorial franking privilege.[72] To further expand its publication efforts, the League employed lecturing agents who would travel through key areas in the North, give speeches, organize meetings, circulate petitions, and establish auxiliary societies. By fall 1863 the League's petition campaign was in full swing, slowed only by a shortage of funds. Susan B. Anthony succeeded in persuading the American Anti-Slavery Society's executive committee to use some its own resources during the winter of 1863–1864 to fund an expanded corps of lecturers to further the work of the Women's Loyal National League.[73]

Fearing that once the war was over the Emancipation Proclamation would become invalid, abolitionists decided, starting in December 1863, to press for a constitutional amendment to abolish slavery forever in the United States. From then on, antislavery organizations included the demand for a constitutional amendment in all petitions. In February 1864, after Stanton and Anthony had sent the first installment of petitions bearing 100,000 signatures to Senator Sumner, the Women's Loyal National League included in all its petitions a request for a constitutional amendment. When Congress adjourned in June 1864, the League had sent in petitions bearing as many as 400,000 signatures—far short of the million signatures promised, but a truly impressive accomplishment for that period. Both Senator Charles Sumner and Senator Henry Wilson later assured the women in the League that their petition campaign had greatly assisted the struggle to secure congressional passage of the Thirteenth Amendment.[74]

But the Women's League was influential not just for the changes it accomplished, but also for demonstrating American women's rapidly changing role during the war years. From the time the fighting began, women had immediately and enthusiastically rallied to the Union cause and begun doing all those traditional things women did, and were expected to do, in time of war. In the quiet of their homes, or in large groups in schoolrooms or church parlors to form what became known as sewing circles, women constantly turned out needed articles such as bandages and quilts, along with such knitted goods as socks, mittens, scarves, and caps. In the small town of Lexington, for example, fifty to a hundred women met every week and by war's end had sent more than 40,000 articles, including 20,000 rolls of bandages, to the battlefront. And the *Springfield Republican* reported that the Franklin County soldiers' aid society had forwarded "two valuable boxes of hospital supplies for the sick and wounded soldiers" and that the "ladies of Erving" had held a levee at which they raised $50 for the soldiers' benefit.[75] Very often the women would attach a personal note or an encouraging message to the materials they made: "This blanket was carried by Molly Aldrich, who is 93 years old, downhill and up-hill, one and a half miles to be given to some soldier." In a box of bandages was this message: "Made in a sick room where the sunlight has not entered for nine years, and where two sons have bade their mother goodbye as they went to war."[76] In Boston, too, women were busily engaged in supporting the war effort. The *Boston Traveller* published a front-page announcement calling upon the "Ladies of Boston" to hurry to the Tremont Temple with their "needles and thread" so as to "prepare comforts for wounded soldiers."[77] Mrs. Harrison Gray Otis, wife of the city's most distinguished political figure and perhaps the most prominent woman in Boston in her own right, organized a committee to accept donations of money and articles to be used for the soldiers' comfort and convenience.[78]

As the tempo of the fighting increased and casualties began to rise beyond all expectations, it was clear that women would be needed in many other roles—especially to provide nursing and hospital care for soldiers at the front and in Washington area hospitals. Prior to the Civil War, no procedures had been established to supply organized care for wounded soldiers. The army sometimes resorted to slightly wounded soldiers, or those unfit for active duty, to care for their wounded comrades. Except for the nursing care provided in a few urban hospitals by the Catholic order of the Sisters of Mercy, anything like professional nursing care was totally inadequate.[79] In one of those strange historical coincidences, the bloody passage through Baltimore by the 6th Massachusetts regiment on April 19, 1861, brought two Bay State women to the national scene to begin adventures that would significantly affect women's history in the United States.

One of these women was sixty-year-old Dorothea Dix, who was born in Hampden, Maine, but who lived most of her life in Massachusetts. Because her parents' rigid discipline left little room for affection, at age thirteen Dorothea moved to Boston, where she lived with a grandmother and found comfort in the Unitarian faith. She involved herself in service activities, visiting the East Cambridge jail and the Boston Female Asylum and discovering the terrible conditions in which the mentally ill were forced to live. After a trip to England in 1836, she returned to Boston and began two decades of traveling, investigating, and reporting on the conditions afflicting insane men, women, and children in Massachusetts.[80]

Visiting New Jersey in April 1861, Dix heard about the attack on the Massachusetts troops. In three hours she was on a train to Washington, and when she arrived she headed for the White House. There, she "reported herself" for duty to the surgeon-general, along with some nurses, ready for free service "wherever we may be needed." Seeing the need for trained nurses, she spoke directly to President Lincoln and Secretary of War Cameron about her program for a professional nursing corps. On April 23, 1861, Cameron appointed the Bay State woman Superintendent of Women Nurses for the Union army, and authorized her to organize Union military hospitals to care for wounded soldiers, supply nurses, receive supplies, and draw from Army stores.[81] Dix immediately threw herself into the new assignment with the same singleness of purpose as in her previous work for the mentally ill. She made a point of accepting as nurses only women "who are sober, earnest, self-sacrificing, and self-sustained; who can bear the presence of suffering and exercise entire self-control, of speech and manner; who can be calm, gentle, quiet, active, and steadfast in duty." When some of the women volunteers turned out to be unmarried, young, and attractive, Dix made qualifications even clearer. "No woman under thirty need apply to serve in government hospitals. All nurses are required to be plain looking women. Their dresses must be brown or black, with no bows, no curls, no jewelry, and no hoops."[82]

Despite her personal devotion to the task and her intense sensitivity to the pain and suffering she saw in the army hospitals, Dorothea Dix encountered opposition from physicians, nurses, and the military. On the one hand, Dix was a female dealing with two entrenched bastions of authority—the military and the medical—which could not accept the idea of any female exercising independent action or authoritative decision making. In her customary singleminded and self-assured manner, Dorothea Dix was trying to do both. She ran into a wall of resistance composed of army officers who saw no role at all for females in the military service, and medical surgeons who considered women meddlers and threats. According to Mary Rice Livermore, a Boston woman working for the U.S. Sanitary Commission, the surgeons in the hospitals did not work "harmoniously" with Miss Dix. The doctors, wrote Livermore, were "jealous of her power, impatient of her authority, condemned her nurses, and accused her of being arbitrary, opinionated, severe, and capricious."[83] Many older nurses, too, resented this outsider, who had no training as a nurse, coming into the hospitals and setting up her own peculiar qualifications for nursing.[84]

But Dorothea Dix herself had shortcomings that provided a convenient reason for some of the resentment and criticism. She appeared to have little administrative talent and did not delegate effectively; she was overly scrupulous and continually at loggerheads with medical officers. Her constant preoccupation with details and the unswerving determination that had worked so well in reforming hospitals and asylums proved counterproductive when she confronted the military and medical bureaucracies. Washington officials considered her a "muddled executive," a "mother hen"—a meddlesome old biddy.[85] Even George Templeton Strong of the Sanitary Commission became annoyed by Dix's complaining whenever "we do not leave everything else and rush off the instant she tells us of something that needs attention." [86] Concluding that her own "pathetic sympathy with suffering" was out of place in a war that was ever more bureaucratic, Dix decided that this was not the work "I would have my life judged by." [87] Although her power in Washington circles gradually eroded, she remained in government service until the end of the war, when she returned almost immediately to helping the mentally ill.[88]

The other Massachusetts woman who had been galvanized into action by the April 19 attack on the Bay State troops in Baltimore was forty-year-old Clara Barton. Born in North Oxford, Massachusetts, Clara was the youngest of five children in a well-educated family. Her father, Captain Stephen Barton, was a war hero and a successful mill owner from whom Clara acquired admiration for military heroism; her mother, Sarah, was a disturbed woman whose eccentricities often led to outbursts of violent rage.[89] Clara spent several years teaching in a New Jersey public school, but in 1854 she took a job in Washington, D.C., as a copy clerk in the U.S. Patent Office—one of four women working in the only federal agency that would employ women at that time. Although she received pay equal to that of the male employees, she complained in her diary about the men who made it a practice to line up in the halls and who "stared, blew smoke in the women's faces, spat tobacco juice, and gave cat-calls, or made obnoxious remarks." [90] Despite such annoying episodes of sexual harassment, Barton enjoyed her work and excelled at it.

In 1861, three days after the Baltimore attack, Clara Barton walked over from the Patent Office to the Senate building, where the Bay State troops were quartered, and discovered that some of the young men came from her hometown in Worcester County. Sitting in the vice-president's chair, Clara read to the troops the account of the bloody Baltimore encounter as it appeared in the *Worcester Daily Spy*. Stimulated by this experience in working firsthand with the troops, Barton advertised in the *Spy* for women at home to send her money and supplies to help the men. The response was overwhelming—Barton had to rent a warehouse in Washington to store the goods. She then became a one-woman relief agency, cooking food, buying stores out of her own salary, and distributing supplies to soldiers at hospitals and nearby military encampments.[91] In July, after the Union defeat at Bull Run, Barton went immediately to the Washington hospitals to care for the wounded soldiers. She was mostly satisfied that the men who made it as far as the hospitals were well taken care of by the women nurses there. She was appalled, however, to hear how terribly the soldiers suffered while waiting to be transported from the battlefields to the hospitals.

Determined to get relief to the men on the battlefield as rapidly as possible, Barton finally talked the Quartermaster General into giving her permission to travel behind the Union lines. Taking most of the summer to build up her supplies of food and provisions, Barton arrived at the front lines early in September, while the second Battle of Bull Run was still raging. "The men were brought down from the field and lain on the ground beside the train, and so back up the hill till they covered acres," she wrote. By midnight, Barton recalled 3,000 helpless men lying in the open on crude hay mattresses. Barton and her helpers worked through the next day giving water, coffee, crackers, bread, and sandwiches to the wounded troops, and bandaging their wounds while ambulances took them to the trains that would transport them to hospitals. After Second Bull Run, Barton went on to nurse the sick and tend the wounded at Harpers Ferry and then Antietam, becoming famous as the "Angel of the Battlefield"—the woman who would "follow the cannons" and treat the wounded soldier on the battlefield.[92] When the war was over, Clara Barton took to the lecture circuit and was in great demand as a speaker at lyceums, literary societies, and veterans' organizations affiliated with the Grand Army of the Republic. Few people seemed upset that Miss Barton was speaking before large, "mixed" audiences—for a sizable fee, at that—which would have been impossible for a woman to do in the decades before the Civil War.

Other prominent Bay State women engaged in hospital work, and much literature attests to their humanitarian accomplishments.[93] Louisa May Alcott, who would become famous after the war writing such sentimental works of fiction as *Little Women* and *Little Men*, went to Washington late in 1862 to work in the hospital that was overflowing with wounded men from the recent Fredericksburg disaster. Although she became ill and was forced to leave after a month, she left a vivid recollection of pain and suffering in her *Hospital Sketches*. Overwhelmed by the anonymity and the randomness she saw in wartime deaths, she decided to focus on the details of pain and suffering so that the soldiers would not go down in history as nameless or faceless numbers.[94] Mary Ashton Rice Livermore was another Boston native who made a substantial contribution to the Union war effort. An early feminist and temperance advocate, she married Daniel Livermore, a Universalist minister, moved to Chicago during the 1850s, and continued her activities in numerous charitable programs. When the war began, Mary Livermore helped establish the Chicago chapter of the U.S. Sanitary Commission, and after the war worked steadily for woman suffrage.[95] Mrs. Stephen Boyd, wife of the chaplain with the 14th Massachusetts Regiment, worked from 1862 to 1864 at Fort Albany, part of Washington's defenses, where she nursed wounded soldiers. In 1864 Boyd took charge of a system of hospital visitors, a corps of women volunteers who traveled to every hospital, observed sanitary conditions, and recorded the patients' complaints. Helen Louise Gilson went to the battle sites with her uncle, Frank Fay, mayor of Chelsea, who cared deeply about immediately supplying medical attention to the soldiers who fell in the front lines. Although his niece was too young to enter Dorothea Dix's nursing corps, she carried on her work under her uncle's guidance. She accompanied the Army of the Potomac, served on hospital ships, nursed wounded soldiers at Gettysburg, and later served in Virginia at City Point hospital, where she established a kitchen for 900 African-American troops.[96]

Despite dedicated contributions by these and other women volunteers, however, it soon became clear that more efficient, centralized, and much more professional humanitarian assistance was necessary. One major support group grew out of a Young Men's Christian Association meeting in New York, which organized the Christian Commission as an agency to coordinate the wartime efforts volunteered by hundreds of local church groups. Seeking to help as much with spiritual solace as physical recovery, commission members visited the sick, comforted the wounded, wrote letters home, delivered family gifts, read the Bible, conducted prayer meetings, and held Sunday services. Strongly supported by church groups, business leaders, and government officials, and relying greatly on dedicated work by Northern women, the Christian Commission accomplished remarkable feats of organized charity throughout the war.[97]

The second major organization committed to coordinated medical relief work was the U.S. Sanitary Commission, an association created by prominent New York citizens to promptly and efficiently distribute clothing, food, and medicine to the Union army. Frederick Law Olmsted, a landscape architect and former correspondent for *The New York Times* who would later design Boston's extensive park system, became the commission's chief executive, and soon called on his Boston businessman friend John Murray Forbes for advice and assistance. Forbes was impressed by the commission's rational and businesslike approach, and devoted much time to raising funds for its expansion. He put together his own committee of twenty local businessmen, lawyers, ministers, and physicians to form a local branch of the Sanitary Commission. The Boston unit was chaired by J. Huntington Wolcott, a wealthy partner in Amos

A. Lawrence's cotton business, and included such well-known figures as Edward Everett Hale, Dr. Samuel Gridley Howe, Francis Jackson, Jr., Martin Brimmer, George Higginson, John Lowell, and Edward Atkinson, many of them former members of the Emigrant Aid Company. Like typical businessmen, the commission leaders played down "the vague sentiment of philanthropy" of the work in which they were engaged and emphasized their operation's practical, no-nonsense, dollars-and-cents objectives.[98] Though the Sanitary Commission commended volunteer efforts by well-meaning amateurs such as Dorothea Dix and Clara Barton, they felt that individual volunteers' lack of coordination and training did more harm than good. Emphasizing efficiency and bureaucracy, the Sanitary Commission used paid agents to carry out the organization's functions, employed professional canvassers as fundraisers, and employed paid professionals as staff. Saving fighting men's lives by the most organized and economical techniques possible, they argued, would reduce the war's overall costs and allow the soldiers to engage in productive labor as healthy and able-bodied workers once the war was over.[99]

The most active commission members, by this time, were women, who sought to provide for men wounded on the battlefield essential medical and hospital services not furnished by either the War Department or the Army Medical Corps. They worked to get adequate supplies of medical equipment and bandages to the battlefields in time to save lives; they undertook to remove wounded soldiers from the battlefields to military aid stations by wagon trains or hospital steamers; and they engineered transportation for disabled troops to permanent hospitals or to convalescent stations. During 1862, commission transports took tens of thousands of sick and wounded soldiers from the Virginia battlefields in much cleaner and more comfortable surroundings than they would otherwise have had.[100] And while they were carrying out their own functions, commission members also inspected sanitary conditions in army camps and government hospitals, reported on physicians' and nurses' efficiency, and worked to reduce scurvy, typhoid, and other diseases in poorly maintained hospitals. With its work being done overwhelmingly by women, the Sanitary Commission proved to be enormously successful, gained extensive public support, and almost matched the $6 million in receipts reported by the Christian Commission.[101]

Certainly the Lincoln administration needed all the help it could get, from men or women, from volunteers or professionals, during the spring of 1863 as the Confederates brought war's horrors closer to the North. Following his victory over General Hooker's forces at Chancellorsville in May, General Robert E. Lee again decided to carry the war into the heart of Union territory. Early in June, Lee funneled his Army of Northern Virginia northward through the Shenandoah and Cumberland valleys, crossed through Maryland into

Pennsylvania, and headed toward Harrisburg. When Hooker proved incapable of dealing with the new Confederate threat, Lincoln turned to General George Gordon Meade, an experienced commander, to take over the Army of the Potomac and to stop Lee at all costs. Moving with speed and determination, Meade marched his forces from Fredericksburg northeast toward Harrisburg, and on July 1, 1863, made initial contact with the Confederates just outside the little town of Gettysburg, Pennsylvania.

On the second day, July 2, while Confederate forces attempted to overrun Union positions at the line's northern end, the 28th Massachusetts Regiment engaged in heavy fighting at the southern end of the line to secure the strategic heights at Little Round Top. "We lost heavily; the killed, wounded, and missing of our little regiment is over a hundred," the Irishman Peter Welsh told his wife back in Boston. "Out of five regiments that form this Brigade," he said, "there is but men enough here present to make three full companys." [102] Next day, July 3, the Confederates directed their assault at the center of the Union line. After a thunderous cannonade that for an hour and a half shook the earth, 15,000 men, veterans of the Army of Northern Virginia, moved out of the woods and, commanded by General George Pickett, began a steady march toward the Northern lines. When they came within range, however, federal artillery and rifle fire tore great holes in the Confederate lines. In spite of heavy losses, the Confederate attack broke through the Union defense's center and overran a battery of cannon. But the ragged gap was quickly plugged as Union reinforcements, including the 19th and 20th Massachusetts regiments, came charging into the breach, shouting "Fredericksburg!" "Fredericksburg!" Colonel James Clay Rice, a Yale graduate who had distinguished himself a day earlier by helping to secure Little Round Top, saw the underbrush filled with dead Confederate soldiers. Soldiers in gray and blue uniforms clashed in hand-to-hand combat until the Confederate lines finally broke, and the men retreated across the bloody valley. [103] The Union forces had held the line; the threat of invasion was over. Robert E. Lee led the remnants of his shattered army back to safety in northern Virginia.

The great Gettysburg victory on July 3, 1863, gave the annual Fourth-of-July celebrations in Boston next day an especially festive air. For several days the local newspapers had been filled with accounts of the Union and Confederate troop movements, and the general population was awaiting news of the outcome with great anticipation. The official dispatch from General Meade, finally confirming that the Union forces had won a great and decisive military victory, sparked wild rejoicing throughout the city, as did the congratulatory address from President Lincoln that followed. "At every street corner," reported the *Boston Traveller*, "knots of people gathered to peruse or listen to the latest accounts of victory." [104] In nearby Framingham, an abolitionist gathering cheered long into the night to celebrate the defeat inflicted on General Lee and his Confederate forces. On July 4, the holiday festivities in Boston started with the customary ringing of bells for half an hour at sunrise, at noon, and at sunset. Salutes from artillery batteries went off as scheduled. A concert with mostly national anthems went on at the Academy of Music, Faneuil Hall had dancing, and five "magic shows" were conducted by Professor Harrington in Tremont Temple. The military parades were even more colorful and exciting than a year earlier, and 108 Tremont Zouaves marched behind a new "elegant regimental flag" pieced together, so the report read, by "Their Lady Friends." Professor Oliver Wendell Holmes spoke long and eloquently to a large crowd in the afternoon. The annual racing regatta on the Charles River attracted the usual interest, and the perennial balloon ascension was more impressive than ever, with two balloons sailing off into the heavens between 5:00 and 6:00 P.M. Evening celebrations featured a fireworks display with a Crimson Meteor Rocket and a Grand National Tableau outlining an equestrian statue of George Washington. Perhaps the most exciting event was the illumination, from the State House cupola, of a new powerful "electric light"—a dazzling display equal to 25,000 candlepower, "reflectors included." Despite warnings by the newspapers that the police would "prevent the unauthorized discharging of firearms, squibs, and crackers as well as mock parades and the blaring of horns," a goodly number of boys managed to get into trouble. Some burned themselves with gunpowder, and one or two suffered fatal injuries before the day was over. Fifty little children became lost in the crowds and had to be escorted to the police station to await their anxious parents. Several citizens had their pockets picked while walking across Boston Common, just to round out a typical day in the city.[105] And if the Gettysburg news was not enough to lift the Northerners' spirits, the next day brought the welcome news that General Ulysses S. Grant had succeeded in taking the Confederate fortress in Vicksburg, Mississippi, opening up the great waterway to Union shipping all the way to the Gulf of Mexico.

Unfortunately, news about the inevitable heavy casualties that came after the great Union victories did much to temper enthusiasm and dampen happy celebrations. Newspaper accounts were sketchy and inaccurate at first, yet everyone knew that many soldiers must have given their lives and that countless Massachusetts boys lay severely wounded on the battlefields at Gettysburg. On July 5, E. S. Tobey of the Boston Stock Exchange succeeded in raising $1,000 for immediate aid, by way of the Adams Express Company, as a means of sending the wounded first-aid supplies. On July 7, the U.S. Christian Commission reported to Mr. Tobey that although 140 representatives had already distributed 300 boxes of supplies to the wounded at Gettysburg, they would have to count on the Boston area alone to supply $10,000 for promptly relieving the suffering. Tobey had anticipated this need, however, and by that very evening $8,900 had been subscribed. The following days, weeks, and even months were to see numerous contributions from Massachusetts applied to the vast cleanup at Gettysburg, including support for the projected National Cemetery. Although many bodies of Massachusetts boys killed on the field were returned to the Bay State for interment in family plots, by November 1863, at the time of the formal dedication services, 158 Massachusetts soldiers were honorably buried on the slopes of Cemetery Hill.

Summer 1863 brought the important Union victories at Gettysburg and Vicksburg, and also news that the British government had decided to give no further aid to the Confederacy. From the very beginning of hostilities, fear that Great Britain would recognize the Confederate States of America had greatly worried Charles Francis Adams of Massachusetts, U.S. ambassador to Great Britain. For two years he had been negotiating almost constantly with British authorities, trying in vain to persuade them *not* to sell war materials to the South, *not* to break the Northern blockade of Southern ports, *not* to advance loans or credit to the Confederacy. Adams could see, however, that intervention was possible as long as the British thought the Confederacy had a good chance of gaining its independence. Too many people in England, as Adams saw it, considered the war a purely political struggle and sympathized with the South's ambitions for national independence. Then too, many English capitalists saw wonderful opportunities for commercial profit if the South should become a separate and independent nation.[106]

At any rate, the British continued to sell goods to the Confederacy, sometimes shipping cargoes to the Bahamas, where Southern blockade runners could pick them up, and sometimes selling products to freebooters who would run the blockade. Even as late as summer 1863, hardly a week passed without Boston newspapers reporting at least one auction of British goods seized from a captured blockade runner. The British government had even gone so far as to permit companies to build and outfit armed frigates for the Confederacy, the most famous of which were the *Alabama* and the *Florida*. The South was also negotiating to purchase vessels of an even more frightening type—the so-called Laird rams. This ironclad steamer, with a powerful pointed ram at its prow, would make a devastating blockade runner and might also be used to plough into the wooden-hulled Union naval vessels guarding Northern ports.[107]

How to prevent the Confederates from obtaining the warships being constructed for them in English shipyards was a question that puzzled the Lincoln administration. If Union vessels interfered with British shipping—especially with the *Trent* affair still a very touchy issue—war with Great Britain was a distinct possibility. As one idea for avoiding use of naval power, the administration seized upon a suggestion by John Murray Forbes of Boston that the administration let him go to England, pretending that he was making purchases for Siam or China, though he would actually be buying up war vessels "under construction for the rebels." Traveling as a private merchant, "untrammelled by naval contractors and such nuisances," Forbes argued that he could get away with such a subterfuge.[108] The administration was intrigued by the idea, but could see difficulties in the scheme. Which vessels, for example, were the most dangerous? How many would be purchased? Would they include the Laird rams? Who would make the final decision? Then, too, they asked what would happen if the British discovered that Forbes was not a private buyer, but was an undercover agent for the Union government?

Despite the scheme's complexities, the administration decided to go ahead with the plan. On Saturday morning, March 14, 1863, Forbes received a telegram from Secretary of the Treasury Salmon P. Chase asking him to come that evening to the Fifth Avenue Hotel in New York City: "I desire to confer with you on important business immediately. Answer." Forbes replied with a simple "Yes," and that night met with Chase, Secretary of the Navy Gideon Welles, and W. H. Aspinwall, the New York businessman he had met two years earlier during the Washington Peace Convention who would accompany Forbes on his trip to England.[109] To supply credence to the men's cover as independent businessmen, Secretary Chase agreed to have them traveling to England to raise a £1-million loan from the Baring Brothers banking house, putting up $10 million in U.S.-government bonds as security. Forbes and Aspinwall were instructed to contact Freeman H. Morse, American consul in London, and Thomas H. Dudley, American consul in Liverpool, the two men most actively involved in supplying the administration with information about Confederate activities in England. The Americans would, of course, call upon Ambassador Charles Francis Adams and pay their formal respects, but they were instructed not to tell him the real reason for their visit to Great Britain so that Adams's legal negotiations with British authorities would not be compromised. Adams was to be told that Forbes and Aspinwall had come to Europe to raise troops for the Union army.[110]

Taking the first Cunard steamer out of Boston after the New York meeting, Forbes arrived in England by the end of March, and after a quick survey of Anglo-American relations came up with four major conclusions: (1) letters of marque (authorizing private citizens to capture merchant ships of another nation) would only cause further trouble with England, and therefore should not be issued; (2) Admiral Charles Wilkes, the American naval officer involved in the *Trent* affair and now commanding the U.S. West India Squadron, was an obstacle to good relations and should be removed from command ("Everything he does," wrote Forbes, "hits twice as hard in irritating John Bull as the same thing done by anybody else"); (3) even though all the mercantile and upper classes are "entirely against the North," the emancipation movement in the United States "is coming to our rescue"; (4) the Union should emphasize emancipation, strike hard at the Confederates, and "set our teeth" to avoid giving the British ruling classes any pretext for picking a quarrel with the North.[111] A week later, on April 4, 1863, Aspinwall arrived in England with the bonds to join Forbes. Even within that short time, however, the situation had become more difficult. A $15-million loan (secured by cotton futures) had just been granted to the South, relieving the Confederate government, at least temporarily, of its most acute financial difficulties and lessening the possibility that the Rebels would allow the British to sell off any of their vessels.[112]

Even more damaging, perhaps, was publication by the *London Times* of rumors that the two Americans were actually in the country to buy up "the gunboats now building in England for the rebels."[113] Now that their cover had been blown, Forbes and Aspinwall decided not to get involved with the warships. Instead, they made a great pretence of concentrating on their financial mission, eventually negotiating a £600,000 loan.[114] The two men meanwhile devised alternative strategies for preventing British ships from going to the Confederates. Forbes provided additional funds for the two American consuls, Morse and Dudley, to set up a network of "confidential agents" to observe operations at English shipyards. Forbes also wrote to Secretary of State William Seward, suggesting that reprints of Northern newspaper editorials be sent to him so that he could supply them to editors at the two liberal papers in England, the *Star* and the *Daily News*.[115] Forbes and Aspinwall continued to work on influencing British public opinion, writing constantly to prominent figures in the business, literary, and especially government worlds, hoping that Lincoln's new emancipation policy would help turn the tide to favor the Union.[116]

As long as Union forces showed themselves incapable of defeating the Confederate armies, however, English critics continued to insist that the Southerners were bound to win their independence. Hooker's terrible defeat at Chancellorsville in May 1863 struck a particularly heavy blow at Forbes's efforts to convince the British about Northern superiority. Shortly after news about the Union defeat reached Europe, Forbes was attending a dinner party during which he struggled to hold his temper while the Englishmen around the table made "many chilly remarks" about how futile it was for the North to continue its struggle to save the Union. His host asked Forbes for more information about the battle of Chancellorsville—especially the "heart-rending rumor" that Stonewall Jackson had been accidentally killed by his own soldiers. Forbes could no longer contain his temper: "I don't know or care a brass farthing whether Jackson was killed by his own men or ours," he exploded, "so long as he was thoroughly killed, and stands no longer in the way of that success upon which the fate of everybody and everything I care for depends!" The Englishmen were stunned at this unexpected outburst and sat at their places without saying a word. "Had a naked Indian, in war-paint with tomahawk and scalping-knife, appeared at the dinner-table," wrote Forbes afterward, "the expression of horror and dismay at my barbarous utterances could hardly have been greater." [117]

Despite these anxieties, however, the English climate of opinion was gradually changing. The Emancipation Proclamation had unquestionably altered the war, transforming a conflict of political oppression into a crusade for human rights—a cause that was popular with the English masses. On June 30, 1863, a Parliamentary resolution to give official recognition to the Confederacy failed to pass, and when the news of Gettysburg and Vicksburg reached the British Isles, faith in the cause of Southern independence faded rapidly. The prolonged meetings between Charles Francis Adams and English representatives, protesting the sale of the Laird rams to the Confederacy, finally produced results. On September 5, 1863, the British government seized the controversial vessels. The cause for which the Boston statesman had worked so long had finally been won. [118]

News about the Union victories at Gettysburg and Vicksburg, coupled with reports that Great Britain was no longer a danger to the Union blockade, convinced many in the North that the tide of battle had finally turned. Even though for well over a year people in the North had experienced defeats, reverses, and great suffering, through it all they had maintained their confidence. Although no one could doubt that still more battles would be fought and victories won, a general feeling prevailed that the worst of the crisis had passed and ultimate victory was in sight. In the West, the Stars and Stripes floated over the entire length of the Mississippi River; Union armies were now poised for a thrust into the South's heartland. Of utmost importance was Ulysses S. Grant's rise as an outstanding strategist and perhaps, finally, the Union general who could match Robert E. Lee's genius. The Confederacy, forced back into a purely defensive position, faced hunger, privation, and isolation. The Union, with seasoned troops and unlimited resources, for the first time in many months realized that victory was attainable.

It was certainly not the end. No Bostonian who had witnessed the fierce determination of Southern resistance and the high caliber of Confederate leadership over these two years could possibly think that the terrible war would be over quickly or painlessly. But indications were clear that it might well be the *beginning* of the end—and that was something devoutly to be wished.

A contemporary engraving from Harper's Weekly *showing Boston women filling cartridge shells on an assembly line at the Watertown Arsenal. The extraordinary requirements of the Civil War in terms of industrial production and an expanded work force provided unusual opportunities to Northern women for a greater range of jobs, experience, and income. (Courtesy of the Boston Public Library, Print Department)*

6   So Near, So Far
~~~~~~~

*O*ne more push might topple it.

     After the welcome news about the Union victories at Gettysburg and Vicksburg in July 1863, followed by the gratifying reports that Great Britain would no longer provide aid to the South, President Lincoln had every right to expect that the Confederacy might succumb to one final blow. After Lee's defeat at Gettysburg, the president assumed that the Army of the Potomac was in excellent position to deliver that last mighty blow.

     Once again, however, Lincoln was bitterly disappointed. He was furious when he learned that General Meade had allowed Lee to slip safely away into Virginia. "Our army held the war in the hollow of their hand," he fumed in utter frustration, "and they would not close it." [1] When he finally became reconciled to the prospect that the war would continue indefinitely, he found he could take some comfort in reports that Union General William S. Rosecrans had brought his troops south from Murfreesboro, Tennessee, to occupy the strategic railroad junction at Chattanooga, which the Rebels had abandoned. But even after this good news, he was doomed to further disappointment. Confederate General Braxton Bragg, responding to Rosecrans's move, had taken up strong defensive positions south of the city, anchoring his left flank at Lookout Mountain and settling his right flank along Missionary Ridge. From these commanding heights, Bragg was fully prepared to starve into submission the Union garrison in Chattanooga.

     While military progress ground to a halt along all fronts, Boston and other Northern cities had to continue the dull routine of continuing to fight a war that seemed both endless and pointless. Around New England, marauding Rebel privateers were still seen as a potential threat, and the relatively weak Bay State coastline occupied local residents' attention. [2] On March 30, 1863, the General Court had appropriated $1 million for coastal defense, and the

U.S. Congress had raised additional funds for the same purpose. Around Boston, local fortifications were strengthened; in Newburyport, Gloucester, Salem, Marblehead, and Plymouth, earthworks were overhauled; in Provincetown plans called for constructing a masonry fort.[3] A vital element in defending Atlantic ports was getting authorization for the Boston businessman John Murray Forbes to travel to England to purchase heavy coastal defense guns. Previously, Captain Henry A. Wise of the Bureau of Ordnance in Washington had contacted Forbes about purchasing antiquated eleven-inch guns the government had captured from the Confederacy. Forbes was far from impressed when he saw this outmoded armament, however. "They are the 6 cheapest guns in the world," he snorted. "They seem to have been appraised on the same principles as you would appraise an elephant, very cheap to anyone who wants them!"[4] Forbes turned down the offer, and set off across the Atlantic to see if he could do better. Once he had reached England, Forbes was impressed by some brand-new Blakely rifled cannons. He made preliminary arrangements to purchase twenty of the big guns, nine and eleven inches in caliber, to be delivered by September 15, but the contract was never completed.[5] First, Blakely had never made such big guns before, and the problems in large-scale production were much greater than anyone had expected. Then too, transporting the heavy weapons by rail to the coast and then loading them aboard an oceangoing vessel meant delays and increased cost. But the biggest problem was secrecy. For Great Britain to sell heavy coastal guns to the U.S. government would violate neutrality as much as selling armed frigates such as the *Alabama* to the Confederacy. Forbes made arrangements, therefore, to have the guns secretly commissioned as though they were being sent to Russia and, as an extra precaution, they were to be unfinished. The plan was to have them completed by the Putnam Machine Shop in Fitchburg, Massachusetts, when they arrived in the United States. The difficulties in acquiring the guns grew, however, and Confederate sea power weakened, so that by 1863 the entire project was abandoned.[6]

Despite reassurances that the Confederates were losing ground, Bostonians were still worried about inadequate defenses for the Northern harbors. Ignoring earlier promises, Washington had taken few concrete steps to remedy the situation. Boston residents complained that they were needlessly exposed to easy attack by Confederate ironclads, and insisted that forts along the coast be armed and garrisoned. They also demanded ironclad warships of their own so that they could defend their harbor and protect their ships in Massachusetts waters. In September Governor Andrew petitioned the federal government to establish an official coastal defense for Boston. Washington accordingly sent General Joseph G. Totten, a seventy-five-year-old veteran of the War of 1812 and now chief of the U.S. Bureau of Engineers, to devise an appropriate defense plan and make recommendations for Boston's security. He did consult with state and local authorities on details in his assignment, but they failed to arrive at any definite conclusions.[7]

While these discussions on defense measures were in progress, two incidents caused excitement throughout the Bay State and further increased demands for better coastal protection. Two fires broke out in Boston, one in East Boston, destroying the Atlantic Works, the other in South Boston, leveling the Globe Machine Works—both of which had been constructing monitors for the government. Boston residents feared that these disasters were acts of sabotage, and demanded a full-scale investigation. Some reassurance came in October when the good news arrived that the federal government was ready to begin work on the city's harbor defenses. To head up the project, Governor Andrew assigned Colonel William Raymond Lee, a graduate of West Point and considered one of the best engineers in the Commonwealth, as chief with the rank of brigadier general.[8] As things eventually worked out, the Bay State was never obliged to protect itself against a Confederate naval attack, but such a raid was always a threatening possibility.

Another irritant for Bay State citizens was the growing casualty lists in their daily newspapers. The bloody battles at Chancellorsville in May and Gettysburg in July had claimed the lives of a great many Massachusetts soldiers. Although local casualties fortunately had decreased during the autumn months while Lee and Meade were entrenched along the Rapidan, newspapers continued to publish lengthy obituaries of Massachusetts men killed in the previous engagements. Local residents still followed the newspaper reports anxiously as they read about activities of the 2nd and 33rd Regiments of Massachusetts Volunteers, which were serving with General Hooker at Chattanooga. Hardly a family now did not have a brother, father, son, husband, sweetheart, or someone in the service. And more soldiers died of disease and infected wounds than suffered death on the battlefield, creating constant uneasiness for the loved ones' safety. Fear of receiving an official black-bordered envelope was something families lived with every day. As mothers and daughters spent time making clothes and bandages for needy soldiers, their patriotic activities commanded public attention and praise. In the *Boston Advertiser* was a typical notice about practical results from their good work:

The Boston Agent for the Massachusetts Soldiers Relief Association acknowledges to have received from the West Amesbury Ladies Union Sewing Circle the following contributions—39 shirts, 9 pairs drawers, 4 sheets, 2 pillow cases, 3 dressing gowns, 34 handkerchiefs, 12 towels, 9 bandages, 5 pairs slippers.[9]

On occasion, an individual would make a specific contribution to the war effort that received special attention. Miss Philena M. Upton of Leicester sent Governor Andrew a handsome scrapbook she had made for hospitalized soldiers—for which the governor thanked the lady profusely and publicly. Another way of indicating patriotic support for the war effort was for men who could not serve in the army to pay the government $125 for a "representative recruit." Seventy-year-old Edward Everett was one among hundreds of loyal Massachusetts citizens who tried to do his bit by contributing a "representative recruit" for the cause.

With so many men in the service—83,932 by the end of December 1863, and 17,304 serving in the navy—the Bay State economy was undergoing substantial changes. The textile industry, the mainstay of the New England economy, was hit hard by the war's sudden outbreak and the Confederate states' virtual embargo on cotton, which paralyzed northern trade and disrupted New England textile operations. Fortunately, as with Great Britain, many mills had stocked up on the 1860 bumper crop and had enough raw material on hand to stay in operation for a time; thus, manufacturing circles felt deep apprehension but no real panic.[10] Most people also clung to the general belief in a short war—"peace in ninety days"—typifying most Northerners' early confidence. Although the defeat at Bull Run sent cloth sales to unprecedented lows as 1861 ended, the news about Grant's capture of Forts Henry and Donelson, the *Monitor's* victory over the *Merrimac,* and then the occupation of New Orleans in spring 1862 restored much confidence. New England relaxed again and waited for news of the Confederate surrender. Oliver Wendell Holmes confided to his friend John Motley: "The almost universal feeling is that the rebellion is knocked on the head." Amos A. Lawrence promised his sister that the Stars and Stripes would wave over the entire Atlantic seaboard before New Year's day. Newspaper readers were assured that the "rebellion is crumbling" and that the "backbone of the rebellion is broken."[11] The fighting might continue a *little* longer, of course, but the enemy's final "subjugation," the *Springfield Republican* announced confidently, would be "comparatively easy."[12]

Such idyllic dreams came to a sudden end when summer 1862 brought news about awful Union military reverses, clearly demonstrating that this was not to be a short war. Wall Street reacted in alarm; textile sales dropped 75 percent in one month; mill owners suddenly found themselves, as Amos A. Lawrence put it, "looking forward into empty space."[13] For the first time, the New England textile men were deeply worried. Mill workers were leaving rapidly, either going off to war or taking higher-paying jobs in defense industries. Even worse, however, was the prospect that they would not be able to get any more cotton. The Union blockade would undoubtedly cut off all exports from the South, and England could obviously outbid New England for any cotton that managed to get through the blockade. Contrary to expectations, the occupation New Orleans had so far failed to produce anything like the massive supplies of cotton anticipated by northern mills. With inventories on hand quickly slipping away, the cotton shortage became acute. By June 1862, more than 3 million of the 4.5 million cotton spindles in the Northeast had ceased to operate. By August, the *Providence Journal* reported that cotton production was not even one-quarter that of normal times, and every week "it is growing smaller. Mills are stopping in every direction." [14] Looking forward to 1863, it was clear that the entire cotton industry was in profound trouble.

The woolen industry, by contrast, proved to be one of the largest and most profitable branches of manufacturing to develop during the war, by substituting wool for cotton textiles in army uniforms, overcoats, underwear, blankets, and other military necessities. The number of woolen factories grew enormously in New England during the war, some of them new structures, others converted from former cotton mills. At the war's height, annual military consumption of wool reached 75 million pounds, and 138 million pounds were used for domestic purposes. The wartime total consumption was more than 200 million pounds, against 85 million pounds in peacetime. [15] Manufacturing woolen products, however, was not without its problems. Many soldiers complained of being issued poor uniforms that had been made not of wool at all, but of something called "shoddy," a material made up from rags and sweepings of all colors and descriptions, chopped up into pulp and pressed together to form a cloth material. Such cloth had no resistance at all, and quickly disintegrated on the soldiers' backs as they marched through bright sunshine or heavy rain. The word "shoddy" quickly became a common label for wartime fraud and corruption and was applied to all government contractors who made huge profits at government expense by turning out cheap and imperfect materials. [16] The wool business profited by easily available raw materials and innumerable factories, but also by the rapid, new technology of "ready-made" clothing that was now applied in manufacturing uniforms. Much of this success was built by the new sewing machine, invented by Elias Howe of Spencer, Massachusetts, and put on the market in 1849. This machine greatly stimulated clothing manufacture by shortening the time in which an item could be produced, increasing the number of items that could be turned out, and making it easy for unskilled workers to learn the new technology. [17]

The shoe industry likewise benefited by applying the sewing machine, whose mechanical operations were adapted to sewing leather by Gordon McKay, a native of Pittsfield, Massachusetts. With this new machinery, shoe production, which had been a small-shop enterprise, quickly became a large manufacturing industry. Now one operator with a sewing machine could sew several hundred pairs of shoes a day—a hundred times faster than had for-

merly been possible. Indeed, when steam power was applied, many new machines could be hooked up and set in operation at one point, accelerating
production even more. In Lynn, Haverhill, Danvers, and other north shore
Massachusetts towns, as well as in localities south of Boston such as Wey-
mouth, Rockland, Whitman, Brockton, and Bridgewater, new shoe factories
greatly expanded production throughout the war years.[18]

The need for military equipment also stimulated industrial production in
many parts of the Bay State. As the war began, almost a third of the muskets,
carbines, pistols, and swords used by the Union army had been purchased in
foreign countries, much to the disgust of local protectionists, who objected to
domestic industries' loss of income.[19] By the war's second year, however, the
foreign contracts had pretty much dried up, although consignments of war
goods for which contracts had already been made continued to arrive for many
months. In the government armory in Springfield, Massachusetts, where 3,000
workers were employed, 350,000 rifles were turned out annually—more than
1,000 per day—and twice as many were manufactured under government contract in private factories.[20]

In many parts of New England, new factories appeared and began turning
out all sorts of products, including heavy machinery, steel ships, armaments,
weapons, shoes, and other much-needed wartime equipment. Across the channel, at the lower end of the South Boston peninsula where many immigrant
Irish laborers lived, foundries, factories, and machine shops responded to the
demand for manufactured products. The South Boston Iron Works, started in
1809 by Cyrus Alger, was extremely active turning out rifles, cannon, and
spherical shells with time fuses. With the outbreak of the war the Alger plant
had doubled its capacity and, according to one source, was kept operating day
and night. Increasing its production of guns, cannon, ammunition, and other
forms of ordnance, the plant also produced an experimental missile, the
"schenkle projectile." Alger's plant cast 272 Rodman cannon, including 100
large 15-inch models, which were particularly useful as coastal-defense guns.
Once cast or forged, these cannon were loaded onto barges or sloops and
taken across the harbor to Castle Island. Here they were test-fired—probably
at first by technicians from the foundries, for the first army artillery unit did
not arrive at Fort Independence until late in April 1863.[21] Guns that came
from this Boston plant "sank the *Merrimac* and the *Alabama*," one historian
wrote, "and played a conspicuous part all along the coast from Norfolk to
New Orleans." So great was the wartime demand that in 1863, young Francis
Alger built a new factory, enlarged the machine shop, and added three new
45-ton air furnaces to take care of war orders.[22]

The City Point Works, a plant originally founded in 1847 by Harrison
Loring to manufacture marine engines, boilers, and paper-mill equipment, was

another South Boston plant that was kept busy filling war orders as Loring expanded his operations to construct iron ships. After the battle between the *Monitor* and the *Merrimac,* the federal government urged Loring to build as many ironclad monitors as he could as soon as possible. He immediately began work on the *Nahant,* the first monitor built in New England, after which he turned out an improved model, the *Canonicus.*

Still another South Boston firm that contributed to the Union war effort was the Globe Works Company, incorporated in 1845 by John Souther as a plant for manufacturing railroad engines, but which in 1860 he converted to manufacture steam excavators used in constructing railroad lines. During the Civil War, pressed into wartime service, the Globe Works constructed the U.S.S. *Housatonic,* provided the hull and machinery for one of Loring's iron monitors, and furnished the machinery for a sloop of war and two sidewheel steamers. Not all Bostonians were enthusiastic about applying new technologies to oceangoing vessels, however. The *Boston Post* vehemently denounced the trend toward the newfangled ironclads, and called for a return to the old-time sailing vessels. "It is humiliating to us as a nation that the average speed of our naval vessels seems to be decreasing," complained the paper. "The best ships are the older vessels and the private steamers and merchant men." Ironically, this myopic pride in America's aesthetically beautiful, sleek wooden sailing vessels delayed the country's eventual conversion to steam and to more modern steel vessels. For the time being, however, the heavy equipment produced in this small but vital South Boston manufacturing center contributed substantially to the Union war effort, and also caused the small peninsula's population to rise from about 22,000 in 1860 to more than 30,000 in 1865, and provided that district's predominantly Irish Catholic population with a welcome source of income and a start for family savings.[23]

The remarkable expansion in iron foundries, steel works, shipyards, and other forms of heavy industry across the way in South Boston contrasted sharply with the economic picture in Boston's downtown area. Unlike manufacturing centers such as Lowell, Lawrence, and Fall River, Boston had few large factories, massed plants, or huge industrial concentrations. The city's economic base still consisted of individual shops and small manufacturing plants that employed thousands of craftsmen, mechanics, and laborers. With an estimated 40,000 workers in the city in 1850, the working class constituted most of Boston's population, and by the end of the Civil War, 45,000 workers were recorded in manufacturing pursuits alone, along with more than 11,000 domestics, 9,000 day laborers, and 7,900 clerks. As it expanded traditional industries and occupations, the Civil War also spawned a remarkable number of new enterprises. The photography business, for example, became prominent in daily life. The war, separating young men from their loved ones, created a huge market for small photographs, called *cartes de visite,* mounted on a piece of cardboard measuring 2½ by 4 inches. These items were cheaply produced and sometimes sold for as little as $1.50 a dozen.[24] Photographers themselves began to advertise extensively, and every military man, whatever his rank or branch of service, was encouraged to have his likeness preserved for posterity. Officers in full-dress uniforms complete with shining swords would pose for full-length or three-quarter-length photographs, and enlisted men would have their pictures taken for their parents and arrange to have tintypes converted into brooches for the girls they left behind.[25] Ira S. Pettit, a young farmer from upstate New York who had enlisted in the 11th Regiment of Infantry a week after his twenty-first birthday, was sent to Boston in July 1862, and was stationed at Fort Independence. After receiving his first uniform and a "new Springfield rifled musket," Ira wanted his photograph taken. He had to wait until he got an overnight pass just before Christmas to go to Boston and have his picture taken (without his weapon) for $3. After sending the photographs home as a belated Christmas present, he stayed overnight in the big city with supper, lodging, and breakfast the next morning for 62 cents.[26] For the benefit of those who had a little more money, one of the few artists left in town would paint miniature portraits. Michael H. Leary, a twenty-two-year-old Boston resident who had joined the 9th Massachusetts Regiment and had gone off to Virginia, was promoted to sergeant in April 1862. Back in Boston, obviously proud of her dashing young soldier, Nellie Desmond wrote to Michael and asked him to be sure to have a "miniature taken" at the earliest opportunity.[27] Printing and processing so many photographs during this period produced a new industry and gave more women than ever the opportunity to take jobs as clerks in photographic studios and learn about printing's intricacies.

Women who worked as milliners did a thriving business during the war; the new ready-made clothing and shoe stores found a responsive market among the city's growing working-class population; jewelers served customers who had money to spend on luxury items; tobacconists offered products that were always in demand either on the home front or among the troops on the battlefield. And in every daily newspaper, auctioneers and real-estate agents advertised the latest bargains in well-built homes. Other occupations also flourished during the war. Copies of important political speeches of the day were for sale in pamphlet form. Religious tracts and low-cost Bibles for the serviceman—with duly documented evidence on how a Bible in a uniform pocket had stopped a bullet and saved a soldier's life—were for sale in most bookshops or directly from the publisher—at a discount, of course. Spiritualists and mediums, taking advantage of wartime emotions, offered to help families get in contact with soldiers who had died; fortune-tellers promised to ensure the loved one's safety on the battlefield—for a nominal fee, of course.[28]

Newspapers were filled with advertisements by pseudophysicians and fast-talking quacks who promised miraculous cures for various ills and maladies, and offered for sale medicines compounded under "secret" conditions that would provide the most amazing panaceas ever known to man. One *Boston Traveller* issue carried an advertisement calling upon "Wives, Mothers, and Sisters" to tuck a few boxes of *Holloway's Pills and Ointment* into the knapsack for their husbands, sons, and brothers serving in the army—at only 25 cents a box.[29] For those who made profits in wartime enterprises, Boston banks and investment houses encouraged further investment in trust funds, the new steel industry, coalfields, railroads, and any one of the new petroleum companies that had been organized in Boston and other major cities throughout the Commonwealth to exploit the oilfields in Pennsylvania. For the more conservative investor, stockbrokers offered U.S. Gold Bonds, and U.S. Five Per Cent Notes at market prices.[30]

As the Commonwealth became recognized as one of the Union's major industrial centers, its population grew rapidly. In the decade prior to the Civil War the number of inhabitants had increased 23 percent, and several towns—Somerville, Brookline, Marlboro, Melrose, Lawrence, and Natick—doubled. The American Civil War was unusual in that the North had few painful shortages of food, clothing, or even luxury goods. Indeed, even at the height of the war, the North was actually shipping surplus grain to Europe. For most of the city's middle and upper class, life went on pretty much as before, with few adjustments or dislocations caused by the war. Those who had no direct relationship with the fighting continued to live ordinary lives, went to work each day, met people, fell in love, married, raised families, attended church, went to school, and took part in local politics.

For the less well-to-do, and for those in the working class, however, day-to-day life in wartime had many more anxieties. Workers in all sections of the Bay State, including all ethnic groups, flocked to the army to join in opposing the attack on the nation. In proportion to the North's population, according to modern authorities, more industrial workers served in the Union army than any other group except for professionals. Because so many workers enlisted, labor unions were weakened, many burgeoning industrial conflicts were pushed into the background, and management had greater opportunities to hire nonunion workers at lower wages. Enlistments by factory workers also opened up jobs for unskilled and unemployed workers, many of whom were willing to work for reduced wages.[31] In addition to the workforce changes brought about by vacancies and replacements, technology definitely influenced industrial employment. Judging by the increase in patents issued at the height of the Civil War (more than 5,000 in 1864, compared with 4,778 in 1860), the national conflict greatly accelerated inventive designs and mechanical inno-

vations. The new technology provided the army and navy with advanced weap-
onry that transformed the conflict into the first "modern" war, and also
furnished more efficient laborsaving devices that replaced workers who had
left their industrial jobs to serve in the armed forces.[32] Gradual changes in the
workforce, combined with rapidly rising costs for food and essential consumer
goods, led to a decided decline in the average worker's standard of living.
Skilled mechanics, who had made about $1.50 a day before the war and gener-
ated an annual income of about $450, increased their daily wage to $2.25 a
day and earned more than $600 a year. Unskilled workers, however, still made
anywhere from 60 cents to $1 a day and earned much less than $400 a year,
and day laborers brought in much less than $200 a year. The wage rates were
so unsatisfactory for skilled and unskilled workers alike because wartime consumer prices went up far more rapidly than any of their wages.[33] Turkey was
17 cents a pound; roast beef could be had for 22 cents a pound. Eggs rose
from 15 cents a dozen in 1861 to 28 cents late in 1863; butter went up to 30
cents a pound; potatoes rose from $1.50 a bushel to $2.25 a bushel during the
same period; bread prices almost doubled. Rent was about $75 a year; clothing
for the family amounted to $60; two and a half tons of coal and a supply of
wood cost $25.[34]

Although wartime economic conditions were difficult for male blue-collar
workers, for females in the labor market conditions were much worse. Wom-
en's wages, much lower to begin with, increased by less than half as much as
those for men. In some businesses, in fact, their pay actively declined as wartime costs skyrocketed. Women in New York City who worked as seamstresses
saw their wages go down from 17.5 cents a shirt in 1861 to a mere 8 cents a
shirt in 1864. Then they were receiving an average of $1.54 a week for working
a 14-hour day. "To a surprising degree," the economic historian Emerson D.
Fite observed in 1910, "women were already the rivals of men in the industrial
world when the war started," pointing out that the 1860 census reported that
of the 1.1 million persons employed in manufacturing pursuits, some 285,000
were women.[35] For well over thirty years, women's labor had been essential to
cotton, woolen, and paper mills, shoe and rubber manufacturing, and productivity in other manufacturing enterprises. Perhaps because such women as the
well-known Lowell "Mill Girls," who worked the spindles at the textile factories, had become so intimately associated with industrial production, a male-
dominated society was able to accept women's employment in mills as "wom-
en's work"—a natural part of the modern work ethic. Outside these major
industrial establishments, however, women had been employed mainly in manufacturing jewelry, gold pens, watches, ready-made clothing, matches, per-
fumes, fireworks, hats, bonnets, and similar small-scale enterprises in which

Because of the shortage of civilian manpower during the Civil War, Northern women took over many occupations usually performed by men—as can be seen in this scene of women serving as post office workers at a fair in aid of the Sanitary Commission. Women also received a wide range of administrative and managerial experience in numerous regional and national organizations that carried over to the postwar era. (Courtesy of the Boston Public Library, Print Department)

light work and delicate craftsmanship were considered appropriate for women.[36]

During the war, however, vacancies, enlistments, and casualties associated with the conflict made it possible for women to begin taking over men's jobs in types of work that had not usually been associated with females. Single women, widows, women whose husbands were away at the front, and immigrant women took work on local farms and filled positions in the country schoolhouses. They also appeared as printers on newspapers and magazines, secretaries in government offices, bookkeepers in commercial firms, clerks in dry-goods stores, shoe shops, and commercial houses in which it had been more customary to see men behind the counter.[37] It was clear that most men did not approve of "the petticoats" moving into trades and occupations they traditionally considered the male worker's exclusive domain. In many respects, of course, this attitude reflected the traditional gender orientation in a period that praised the "cult of domesticity," with such ideals as the secluded and genteel wife whose responsibilities were the home and the children, and argued forcefully against paying any woman for employment outside the home.[38] But a practical aspect too appeared in the hostility men displayed against women workers—the fear that female competition would force down wage rates and inevitably push male workers out of the market. Whether they were being honest or simply disingenuous, local journeymen declared they had no objection to women being employed in shops as long as they received the prevailing wage rather than a reduced wage that would, in turn, depress rates for men workers.[39]

Despite pressures of war and the changing economy, Boston itself was experiencing major structural and topographic changes. After recovering from the disruptive effects of the War for Independence, Boston had spent the first half of the nineteenth century reviving its commercial economy, investing in the new textile industry, expanding its banking enterprises, experimenting with railroads, and transforming itself from a small colonial seaport town into a substantial urban metropolis. Increased prosperity stimulated rapid growth in population, which rose steadily from 61,392 in 1830, to 93,383 in 1840, to 136,881 in 1850, and to 177,840 in 1860. This growth generated a remarkable boom in building and construction that sustained itself through the mid-1800s with few interruptions. The new Charles Bulfinch State House, constructed in 1798, stimulated development of a fashionable residential district around Beacon Hill that was further expanded when the other hills were reduced to provide residences for wealthy businessmen and retired sea captains. During the mid-1820s, Mayor Josiah Quincy undertook extensive renovation of Boston's old waterfront and provided the city with an impressive new market district adjacent Faneuil Hall. To provide even more room for the city's ever-increasing population, and especially for its wealthy businessmen (Forbes and Greene estimated that in 1851 Boston already had forty-one men who were worth half a million to three million dollars each), developers dumped tons of gravel into the muddy waters along the south side of the thin strip of land (the "Neck") that connected the old Shawmut Peninsula to the Roxbury mainland. As early as the 1830s, this district, called the South End, began to take shape as an attractive and well-designed community to which wealthy Boston families could move when room ran out on Beacon Hill and in the other old sections in the city. When Bulfinch's popular Tontine Crescent and the accommodations at Franklin Place were demolished during 1857 and 1858 to make way for blocks of stores and warehouses, and as the days of Colonnade Row as a pleasant residential area along Tremont Street were definitely numbered, well-to-do patrons sought out suitable townhouses in the new South End's shady parks and green squares. This move was facilitated because late in 1856 the Metropolitan Railroad's horsecar lines had begun to operate from downtown Scollay Square to Roxbury, thereby bringing the South End into convenient contact with the city's center.

Surprisingly, despite Bostonians' intense and consuming absorption with innumerable details of the horrendous Civil War, the city's building boom continued unabated. Indeed, the wartime structures' increasingly grandiose style and elaborateness seemed to characterize an almost frenzied desire among city leaders to demonstrate that Boston had finally grown enough that it could be truly considered a world-class city, on a par with any other major cities. Paris, particularly, became the standard by which Bostonians now began to measure their city's status in the modern world. "Very slowly in the 1850s and then with a rush after 1860," writes the modern architectural historian Douglass Shand-Tucci, "Boston suddenly surrendered to a passion for things French."[40] Letters and memoirs from many traveling Bostonians during these years testify that Napoleon III's brilliant court had come to exercise international influence. Having vaulted to power in a national plebiscite that hailed him as Emperor of the French, Napoleon III skillfully disguised the dictatorial methods applied by his police-state regime by sponsoring remarkable public works late in the 1850s that stimulated industry, provided jobs for workers, and impressed foreign visitors. On the city of Paris, especially, he lavished vast sums that allowed his town planner, Baron Haussmann, to construct expansive boulevards and magnificent public buildings that quickly made it the most beautiful city in the world—a mecca for tourists and pleasure seekers. The new Louvre, housing the nation's magnificent art collection, became a universal architectural icon for fine-arts lovers throughout the world, and the imposing new opera house, with its ornate decorations and brilliant gaslights, was a glowing symbol of the Second Empire.

This view shows the South End's Blackstone Square, with the spire of the Shawmut Avenue Universalist Church in the background. One of the most elaborately designed areas of the South End, this was one of a series of attractive squares that featured elegant parks and central fountains in hopes of attracting wealthy patrons to what was originally expected to be Boston's most fashionable residential area before the Back Bay was filled in. (The Bostonian Society)

Boston's newest planners set out to emulate this glorious City of Lights, and architectural projects during the wartime years clearly incorporated the Parisian styles, as American architects began finishing their education at the Ecole des Beaux Arts in Paris. The Boston architect Gridley J. Fox Bryant, whose father had designed the Granite Railway in nearby Quincy a generation earlier, was certainly influenced by what was going on in France when he provided Boston with a new City Hall on School Street in 1862. The Democratic mayor, Joseph M. Wightman, threw his support behind the idea of a monumental city hall that would be worthy of the name American Athens, and after his defeat in December 1862 his successor, Frederic W. Lincoln, Jr., added his own encouragement to the project.[41] Inspired by the Tuileries and the Louvre, Bryant and his associate, Arthur Gilman, created for the city a stately building in Concord granite, very much in the Second French Empire style, with coupled columns and pilasters on the facade and topped with a signature mansard roof of wood covered with copper. A new Post Office building on Milk Street, also constructed by Bryant and Gilman around 1862, displayed columned pavilions of superimposed orders similar to those of the public buildings in Paris. A short time later, their Boston Equitable Building on Milk Street displayed strong Parisian influences, as did Bryant's design for the city's first Horticultural Hall, completed in 1865 on Tremont Street just across from the Old Granary Burying Ground. In 1864, the architect William G. Preston conveyed definite European influences in the Renaissance style he used in constructing the handsome Museum of Natural History on Berkeley Street.[42]

Still perceived as the area into which the future population would naturally gravitate now that little room remained for wealthy people in the older parts of the city, the South End experienced a brief but exciting period of construction during the war years. Gridley Bryant chose "the modern style of Renaissance architecture" when he designed the new City Hospital on the South End's Harrison Avenue in 1861. Constructed in the French style, the main administration building in the center, with its impressive dome and portico, was flanked by mansard-roofed pavilions and created a dramatic focal point for what the historian Walter Muir Whitehill later called "the handsomest development" in the South End.[43] When the city's rapidly growing Roman Catholic population made it impossible for the small downtown church on Franklin Street to accommodate so many parishioners, Bishop John Fitzpatrick decided to build a new and much larger Gothic cathedral on Washington Street in the South End, to be designed by the well-known church architect Patrick C. Keeley of New York. Keeley also designed for the city's Jesuits the imposing granite Church of the Immaculate Conception on Harrison Avenue, which was completed in 1861 and which, Douglass Shand-Tucci writes, was a splendid example of how "the best mid-century American architects translated the Classical tradition into the idiom of their own time."[44] And two years later, in 1863, the South End was also the site for the first building that housed Boston College, operated by the Jesuits and designed for sons of Irish immigrants. The Jesuits believed that the South End, with its "better class of houses," would be a promising part of the city for such an institution, and, because of the horsecar railroad, it would be easily accessible to students "from all parts of the city and vicinity."[45] A number of new Protestant churches also appeared in the South End during the Civil War period, heralding its role as the neighborhood of the future. A new Unitarian church was built on West Newton Street; the South Congregational Church constructed a new building on Union Park Street in 1862; building for a Methodist church was completed in 1862 on Tremont Street; the first Presbyterian Church went up on Columbus Avenue; and a new structure for the Evangelical Lutheran Zion Church was at the corner of Shawmut Avenue and Waltham Street.[46]

But the South End's rise as the most promising and lucrative real estate development for Boston's foreseeable future was suddenly and unexpectedly eclipsed by spectacular development in the Back Bay district. That development was motivated by the private impulse for immense real estate profits and also by the public desire to clear up a bad health problem caused by the Charles River dams along the north side of Boston Neck, just below Beacon Hill. For years, ebb and flow on the tidal flats left the sewage dumped into the basin exposed to the sun and open air, producing, a city health report said, "nothing less than a great cesspool" that acted as a giant receptacle for "all the filth of a large and constantly increasing population."[47] To alleviate this disgusting health hazard, and to provide new space close to the city's center for residences and "dwelling houses," in 1857 a special state commission recommended the "Filling up and sale of [Back Bay] lands." The landfilling began in 1858, when earth from the Needham sandhills and gravel pits, nine miles to the west, was moved to Boston in railroad cars to begin creating 580 acres of brand-new land (the project was eventually completed about thirty years later).[48] The commissioners developed the new part of the city in accordance with an impressive design, usually credited to the architect Arthur Gilman, envisioning long vistas, residences in the Second-Empire style, and a broad central boulevard reminiscent of the Champs Elysées. The main thoroughfare, Commonwealth Avenue, was 200 feet wide and ran west from Arlington Street at the foot of the Public Garden. Beacon Street and Boylston Street extended westward on either side of the boulevard, and two new streets given the old colonial names Marlborough and Newbury also ran parallel to Commonwealth Avenue.[49] From the very beginning, the Back Bay was clearly to be the most fashionable and luxurious residential section in the expanding city, and the extensive French influence further reflected the Parisian elegance that wealthy Bostonians were convinced would make their city, a modern analyst says, "the cultural center of the United States, and one of the greatest cities in the world."[50]

The Civil War years also saw in the formative Back Bay an interesting local counterpart to the more famous wartime Morill Land Grant Act of 1862, which was intended to advance the cause of higher education by providing to the states federal land grants for colleges. The Commonwealth of Massachusetts deposited money received from selling new Back Bay lands into the Bay Lands Fund. Half the money was used to maintain the newly created state property; the other half was parceled out to academic institutions. Fifty percent of that was put into the Massachusetts School Fund; 20 percent was given to Harvard's Museum of Comparative Zoology; 12 percent was donated to Tufts College; the remaining 18 percent was divided equally among Williams College, Amherst College, and Wesleyan Academy in Wilbraham. As a prerequisite for receiving this financial aid, most of these schools had to provide scholarships for students. In 1861 the state also granted an entire block of land on Berkeley Street to the Boston Society of Natural History, which soon constructed a three-story museum on the site; and to the recently incorporated Massachusetts Institute of Technology, which also erected a building to house its scientific facilities. Following the state's lead, several private institutions invested in culturally developing the Back Bay area, including the Boston Water-Power Company, which was granted a plot on the corner of Dartmouth Street and St. James Avenue for constructing a rather bizarre Victorian-Gothic structure that served for a time as the city's Museum of Fine Arts.[51] Even amid the greatest and most devastating war the nation had ever known, Boston's face and personality were undergoing substantial changes. For good or for bad, a new cosmopolitanism was about to descend upon one of the oldest cities in North America.

Along with these topographic and architectural innovations, the Civil War years coincided with one of the most exciting and original periods in New England's literary history. The "Flowering of New England" during the 1840s and 1850s had inspired Massachusetts poets, essayists, novelists, philosophers, historians, clergymen, and established literati generally to create a brilliant period in American letters and scholarship. Boston had truly become the Athens of America, and was proud of the high esteem in which its literary figures were held by the rest of the nation and most European intellectual circles. In almost every way the leading Massachusetts writers and thinkers were proudly nationalistic in their literature, and almost totally consumed by the effect the war was having on American life and society. "The war . . . has assumed such huge proportions that it threatens to engulf us," wrote Ralph Waldo Emerson, pointing out that from now on neither the scholar nor the hermit would be exempt from "the public duty." And about the war itself, Emerson had no doubt or hesitation: "It is not a revolution," he wrote, "but a Catalinian conspiracy."[52]

The Massachusetts intelligentsia supported the Union mostly for the same reasons as most of their fellow citizens, but their intense intellectual interests further heightened their devotion to the country. They considered the United States neither an artificial creation nor a mere confederation; they saw the nation as a distinctive organism with a highly advanced and distinctive culture of its own. Emerson's famous Phi Beta Kappa lecture, *The American Scholar,* written a generation before the war, had been a plea for a uniquely American cultural community that would be free of all dependence on the Old World's

outworn teachings and obsolete practices. Clearly, Emerson continued to believe in the distinctive and creative American genius. The absorbing interest in
the expanding frontier and the vast reaches of the Far West displayed by his
literary friend Henry David Thoreau, and by the historian Francis Parkman,
who had himself journeyed over the Oregon Trail in 1846, also showed how
conscious these writers were of America's uniqueness and its manifest destiny.
Even intellectuals who were students of European history and literature—
scholars such as William Hickling Prescott, his fellow historian John Lothrop
Motley, and the celebrated linguist George Ticknor—in no way rejected
America. On the contrary, they had a true cosmopolitan spirit and recognized
that the accumulated wisdom of the ages benefited the United States in shaping
its own cultural patterns. Even the self-sufficiency and self-absorption that
some Massachusetts intellectuals displayed, so tinged with local pride, was in
actuality a facet of nationalism. They believed that the Bay State had a unique
task to perform: to harmonize and advance the nation and to invigorate the
citizenry's moral fiber.

Contemporary events caused some of the literati to become even more
intensely active. The slavery issue, especially, had touched most of them very
deeply during the antebellum years, and now the real possibility of emancipation at some time in the very near future stimulated them to even greater
creative efforts. In the war's opening months, they implored the Lincoln administration to put an end to slavery, and when they did not feel their requests
were being heeded they put pressure on political leaders in Congress. Furthermore, they used their literary talents to educate the general American public
to their point of view. In January 1862, at the Smithsonian Institution in Washington, Ralph Waldo Emerson took the occasion to make a fiery address on
slavery, which was reported in full in the newspapers and was read by the
Lincoln administration.[53] In the same uncompromising spirit, Emerson wrote
in his private journal: "Better that the war and defeats continue until we come
to that amputation [the end of slavery]." In his poem "To John C. Frémont,"
John Greenleaf Whittier bestowed a public benediction upon the man who
took it upon himself in August 1861 to free slaves under his command. Although Frémont's actions were overruled by his superiors, Whittier clearly considered the general a courageous man in the vanguard of righteousness:

> Thy error Frémont! simply was to act
> A brave man's part without the statesman's tact.[54]

Whittier's works were published in the *Atlantic Monthly* and the *New York
Independent,* and of course were reprinted by newspapers in all parts of the
country. Without doubt one of the sharpest attacks on the institution of slavery
was this Whittier poem:

We wait beneath the furnace-blast
The pangs of transformation.
Not painlessly doth God recast
And mould anew the nation
    Hot burns the fire
    Where wrongs expire.
    Nor spare the hand
    That from the land
    Uproots the ancient evil.[55]

These verses were read to President Lincoln, and he was greatly impressed by their powerful imagery. The poem was set to the music of the well-known old hymn "Ein feste Burg ist unser Gott," ["A Mighty Fortress Is Our God"] and quickly became a favorite vocal selection in family circles throughout the North. The sheer quantity of material he produced may make John Greenleaf Whittier the Civil War's poet laureate.[56]

To writers in Massachusetts, the Civil War was unquestionably a contest between good and evil. They assured the nation's people over and over that their course of action was morally right and that Almighty God was on the side of those who served His cause. In such a spirit, Oliver Wendell Holmes cried:

Whose God will ye serve, O ye rulers of men?
Will ye build you new shrines in the slave breeder's den?
Or bow with the children of light as they call
On the Judge of the Earth and the Father of All.[57]

And in his work "To Canaan," Holmes compared the Union soldiers—perhaps with his own gallant son in mind—to those Old Testament warriors who had pledged their lives to God:

Where are you going young soldiers
With banner, gun, and sword?
We're marching to Canaan
To battle for the Lord.[58]

The shattering defeats and personal tragedies that the Union troops suffered early in the conflict evoked poignant emotion throughout the literary world. Henry Wadsworth Longfellow reflected his sadness in his journal: "I thought in the night of the pale upturned faces of young men on the battlefield and the agonies of the wounded; and my wretchedness was very great." In a similarly dejected mood he wrote, in "Killed at the Ford":

He is dead! the beautiful youth
The heart of honor, the tongue of truth

> He, the life and light of us all,
> Whose voice was blithe as a bugle-call
> Whom all eyes followed with one consent.[59]

James Russell Lowell reacted to friends' and relatives' death and maiming on the battlefield with both loud lamentation and quiet grief, but he was sustained by the belief that their willing sacrifice indicated the vitality in American society:

> Dear Land! whom triflers now make bold to scorn
> Thee! from whose forehead Earth awaits her morn,
>   How nobler shall the sun
> Flame in the sky, how braver breathe thy air
> That thou bred'st children who for thee could'st dare
>   And die as thine have done.[60]

In days of disaster, literary men appealed to the public to stand firm and continue the struggle for total victory. After the U.S.S. *Cumberland* was sunk by the *Merrimac,* Longfellow commended the dead heroes who had gone down with the doomed vessel, but also called upon the living to go forward:

> Ho! brave hearts that went down in the seas!
>   Ye are at peace in the troubled stream
> Ho! brave land! with hearts like these,
>   Thy flag, that is rent in twain
>   Shall be one again
>   And without a seam.[61]

But a Boston woman, Julia Ward Howe, found perhaps the most powerful way to express wartime idealism with her stirring "Battle Hymn of the Republic." Wife of Dr. Samuel Gridley Howe, reformer, humanitarian, and early supporter of John Brown, Julia Ward Howe visited an army camp near Washington, D.C., late in November 1861 and undoubtedly heard familiar strains from a well-known song, started by the Boston Tigers at Fort Warren at the war's beginning and now being used as a popular marching song because of its sprightly cadence and its catchy tune. "John Brown's Body" could be heard in varied renditions, from a pious camp-meeting hymn to a rollicking and often ribald drinking song. Mrs. Stowe woke up in the middle of the night, determined to set down new words to the old song. "The Battle Hymn of the Republic" was published in the *Atlantic Monthly,* and right from its opening line declaring that "Mine Eyes have seen the Coming of the Glory of the Lord," it became the war's anthem. By viewing the tragic conflict as a fulfillment of God's destiny for mankind, her inspirational vision captured the most sublime ideals that the Civil War was all about. Julia Ward Howe continued to produce patriotic verse so as to raise the nation's morale, and in the *Atlantic Monthly* appeared her tribute "The Flag":

> There's a flag hangs over my threshold
>   whose folds are more dear to me
> Than the blood that thrills in my bosom
>   its earnest of liberty
> And dear are the stars it harbors
>   in its sunny field of blue
> As hope of a further heaven that lights
>   our dim lives through.[62]

James Russell Lowell's literary career during the war typified those of a good many among the best writers of the day, in that he could respond energetically to a specific theme and yet had difficulty in sustained writing. Lowell had not written poetry since the Mexican War, but in 1862 he had a message for the nation. Once again he resorted to his trademark Down-East Yankee dialect as a vehicle for his homely advice, and in a new series of *Biglow Papers* he urged his countrymen to renounce slavery forever, rebuked Great Britain for its hostility toward the Union, and demanded more idealism and less sham in American political life. By summer 1862, however, after successive, discouraging Union defeats, he admitted he had exhausted his thoughts on the war and could write no more: "Better no crop than small potatoes." When urged to turn out more poetry, he replied disconsolately: "Give me a victory and I will give you a poem, but I am now clear down in the bottom of the well, where I see no Truth too near to make verses of."[63] By the end of 1863, however, he had been refreshed by the Union victories at Gettysburg and Vicksburg, and in "The Latest Views of Mr. Biglow," he exulted in Lincoln's decision to issue the Emancipation Proclamation, although he still regretted the lack of that final, climactic victory that would bring the war to an end, and missed the one bold military leader who would make that victory possible.[64] Like the men on the battlefield, Lowell and the other Bay State writers became discouraged and depressed; yet the dejection was temporary, and their patriotic spirit always responded to the nation's emotional needs.

The men who shaped the New England mind believed that ultimate good would finally come out of the fratricidal war, and that it would take form as a more democratic and dynamic American society. Emerson observed that it was the unfortunate lot of some great nations to undergo trials and tribulations at times, but concluded that even something as terrible as a civil war could bring forth fundamental issues that must be resolved. Harvard professor Charles Eliot Norton expressed the belief that the American people were abidingly faithful to justice and freedom. Total dedication to high moral principles was not possible at all times in a nation's history, he conceded, but he felt it was essential that a people respond gallantly when the occasion demanded it. Fortunately, in Norton's opinion, the American people had met the challenge and had risen to the call.[65] Oliver Wendell Holmes was sure that the war had added something entirely new to the American scene: it had bound the entire population in a brotherhood that had not been possible previously. Thanks to such modern technological improvements as the railroad, the telegraph, and the daily newspaper, he observed, the North's entire population was now totally and ideologically committed to the nation and was acutely conscious of the issues involved in the war. New England poets had surely become the nation's conscience, and yet they did not reach their full measure of talent in either war poetry or prose. They were at their best in observing human society's peaceful drama in its day-to-day operations, and in reflecting upon nature and the human relationship to that phenomenon. John Greenleaf Whittier's "The Battle Autumn of 1862" presented the desire by the writers of the day to return to the habitat and subjects so familiar to them:

> Ah! eyes may well be full of tears
>   And hearts with hate are hot;
> But even-paced come round the years,
>   And Nature changes not.
>
> She meets with smiles our bitter grief,
>   With songs our groans of pain;
> She mocks with tint of flowers and leaf
>   The war-field's crimson stain.
>
> Still in the cannon's pause, we hear
>   Her sweet thanksgiving-psalm;
> Too near to God for doubt or fear
>   She shares the eternal calm.[66]

Despite discouraging news reports of military reverses and depressing literary accounts of battlefield casualties, Boston residents tried to retain some lightheartedness and levity—as if to remind themselves that this is what people usually do in ordinary times. Despite a good deal of pain and suffering, society danced and frolicked; parties were as gay and lavish as ever. Obviously disapproving, Ralph Waldo Emerson commented in his journal: "With the South, the war is primary; with the North, it is secondary; secondary of course to their trade, then also to their pleasure. The theaters and concerts are filled as usual." Perhaps the very intensity with which they sought pleasure revealed, in fact, a desire to escape from the present's grim realities and recapture for a moment the tranquil past's carefree hours. Soldiers home from the front in their dress uniforms attended gala affairs where they would have an opportunity to recount their daring exploits and charm their eager listeners, especially the young women. War always has a real fascination for those who have not observed firsthand its stark and frightful force. Cambridge divided its attention between Camp Cameron, where regiment after regiment gathered, and Harvard College, which continued its age-old academic routine despite steady attrition from students going into the army. The young undergraduates listened to lectures, studied their lessons, sang such favorite songs as "Litoria," and played pranks upon one another. During one militia training session, students rolled cannonballs along the floor between the mattresses of sleeping comrades. The old habits and practices perhaps blended a little incongruously with the hectic pace produced by the war.[67]

The romance, excitement, and poignancy of war was also reflected in the poetry and music of the day. Broadsides with poems on war and sentimental items were offered for a few cents. One enterprising printer had prepared a single-leaf printing of Lovelace's "To Lucasta, Going to the Wars" for the man in the service to send to his beloved explaining his enlistment. In this printing, the lines: "I could not love thee, Dear, so much / Loved I not honor more" were printed in capital letters, so that the full effect would not be lost. Truly, the Civil War, in many ways the most horrible war ever known, was the last war in which such sentimentality—evident in the day's songs and music— abounded. Almost any event called for a song, and Oliver Ditson and Company of Boston published many of them. At the corner of Washington and School streets, in the old gambrel-roofed building later famed as the Old Corner Book Store, the Oliver Ditson Company had since 1835 been part of Boston's musical history.[68] Most of the songs they produced were sad and sentimental, referring to impending death, to a soldier's love for his mother, his wife, or his fiancée. Some dealt with nostalgia for the simple things the soldier felt in the camp or in the field. Most songs were melancholy and cheerless, and moved even the strongest men to tears. Indeed, a hundred years later they still carry a sadness almost unknown in more recent wartime music. Without competition from such forms of mass communication as radio, recordings, or television, the sheet music for Civil War songs sold in phenomenal numbers. The moving words that Julia Ward Howe wrote for "The Battle Hymn of the Republic" transformed a rollicking marching tune into one of the war's most inspirational songs, and assured this Boston woman of a permanent place in American history. Another Massachusetts native, George F. Root, owed almost all his fame as a composer to his Civil War music, although he continued to write hundreds of songs after the war. All knew by heart the words to all these songs and they sang at home, at church socials, at gatherings of soldiers on furlough or on leave. The troops sang them in the camps, in the tents, and on the march. The war made American music, and particularly American songs, truly popular. Not until the phonograph and the other media of mass communication came along would any one factor be so influential in spreading American music.[69]

Boston's theater and the concert stage, too, continued to present diverse offerings during the war years. Many enjoyed the light and frothy variety stage with such attractions as an Irish song-and-dance team, a group performing the Highland Fling, and a trapeze act featuring a boy's breathtaking gyrations. Dr. Colton, a comedian, administered laughing gas to twelve men and women, who proceeded to jump, sing, and cavort all over the stage, delighting the spectators. Commodore Nutt, 29 inches tall, weighing 24½ pounds, and claiming to be the smallest man in the world, arrived in Boston with much publicity and was drawn through the streets in a tiny carriage hitched to ponies. An Italian opera company came to town and appropriately launched the glittering fall season, featuring Carlotta Patti, sister of the more famous diva Adelina Patti. A few months later, an American opera group advertised another series of productions with Clara Kellogg, the brilliant and popular American singer, as its star. In dramatic presentations, Boston audiences wept when they viewed the melodrama titled *The Octoroon,* a timely play presented by Mrs. Barrows's Stage Company, in which such emotionally charged events as slave auctions and lynchings were prominent. Many of these same audiences greeted with sincere affection Edwin Booth, probably the best-known American actor, who had just recently concluded a triumphant tour of English theaters. During a three-week engagement he put before the cheering citizenry a dazzling array of plays, concentrating upon Shakespeare's tragedies *Hamlet, Romeo and Juliet,* and *Othello,* but also appearing in such romantic productions as *Richelieu* and *Don Cesar de Bergón.* And another member of the famous Booth family made a premier appearance in Boston in May 1862, starring in Shakespeare's *Richard III.* A local reviewer called his performance uneven—brilliant in some spots, but fuzzy in others—but Boston theatergoers nonetheless were pleased with the play and every evening packed the Boston Museum to see the young actor perform.[70] Fate was indeed strange; Boston thundered its applause for John Wilkes Booth!

ALTHOUGH THE civilian population might have felt a little more confident about the war's outcome after the summer 1863 military victories, the missing follow-up successes caused a gradual but perceptible erosion in political support for the Lincoln administration. The administration's decision to emancipate the slaves, followed by the draft, produced outbursts of protest and violence in many parts of the country, and threatened Lincoln's fragile grasp on the North's political leadership. As early as January 1863, the *Boston Courier* reported that things looked gloomy for the Lincoln administration and the Republican party, and it expressed indignation at alarming reports on "the peace schemes of the Northern traitors and submissionists."[71] With military progress stalled, and Union forces unable to come up with the knockout punch that would bring the war to a close, the Lincoln administration was pummeled by friend and foe alike. Democrats, on the one hand, continued to blast the Emancipation Proclamation as an unconstitutional act by a dictatorial president that changed the war's progress and made reasonable negotiations with the Southern states impossible. Radical Republicans and committed abolitionists, on the other hand, vigorously objected to the Proclamation's incompleteness and cast doubt on Lincoln's sincerity in working for freedom and equality for all. Amid persistent talk about peace overtures to the Confederacy, many Republicans feared that the price for peace at this time would be compromise on slavery. "God save us from any such calamity!" exclaimed Senator Charles Sumner.[72]

And Republicans had good reason to worry about emancipation's future, because the succession of Union defeats, from Fredericksburg in December 1862 to Chancellorsville in May 1863, reinvigorated Democratic opposition in many parts of the country. Indeed, in Ohio, Clement Vallandigham, the outspoken leader of the Copperhead movement, had been nominated for governor.[73] The coming 1863 elections were crucial for Lincoln and his party. At stake were important local offices in many parts of the North and especially governorships in such states as Maine, Massachusetts, Pennsylvania, Ohio, Wisconsin, Minnesota, Kentucky, Iowa, and Lincoln's own home state, Illinois. If the strong Democratic showing in the 1862 fall elections should be repeated in 1863, the chances that the Republicans could win the next presidential election would be in danger. And if that happened, said one White House supporter, "Mr. Lincoln will not wind up the war [and] a new feeling and spirit will inspire the South."[74] Clearly capitalizing on the North's war-weariness, Peace Democrats stepped up their preparations for the local 1863 elections, but really focused on issues for the 1864 presidential campaign.[75] The Democrats' long-range strategy was apparent as early as February 1863, when they wined and dined General George B. McClellan. Although Democrats insisted that the general's visit to Boston was not at all a "public affair," no Republican doubted that McClellan was being groomed for a run at the presidency in the following year. That "charmed circle," observed the *Worcester Spy*, referring to Boston's old conservative Whigs, "whose sun rises in Chelsea and sets in Back Bay," had set out to find a candidate with enough popular appeal to defeat Abraham Lincoln.[76] And the *Springfield Republican* agreed: "Evidently a president is wanted," it remarked caustically.[77]

Republicans took seriously the signs of increasing strength among the Democrats and the declining enthusiasm among their own members. Considering the administration's big political losses in the previous year, the party simply could not afford to let its public support slip lower. The newly formed Union Club was one refreshing response by the city's loyal businessmen to help restore confidence in the Lincoln administration. The Loyal Publication Society also helped by counteracting the disturbing talk about a negotiated settlement that followed Hooker's awful defeat at Chancellorsville early in May. In the broadsides he sent out during this period, Charles Eliot Norton argued that this "peace-at-any-price" approach was not only a practical impossibility, but would encourage the Confederacy and prolong the war. This idea of "any peace," he argued, would be nothing less than a confession of national defeat. "We have nothing to ask," he declared flatly; "the rebels nothing to give but submission."[78]

Fortunately for the Lincoln administration, July brought the exhilarating news of military victory—first at Gettysburg and then at Vicksburg. These two welcome successes did much to restore Republican confidence and dampen any prospects the Democrats had for gains in the 1863 elections. But Bay State Democratic leaders forged ahead anyway, clearly intent on using their convention as an opportunity to organize their forces and hone their arguments for 1864. At their convention in Worcester early in September, the Democrats stated that it was "the duty of every citizen to sustain the National Government"; but it then went on to define the Union as composed of "independent sovereign states." Their party's paramount object, they maintained, was to "restore the Union as it was, and to maintain and abide by the Federal Constitution." Although they claimed to oppose "all secession," at the same time they said they were equally opposed to the national government's interfering in the several states' local and domestic affairs. Taking a strong states'-rights position, they announced themselves opposed to the federal government's assuming "any implied power" to use the Civil War to free the slaves, to subjugate the South, or to extend martial law into states that were not in rebellion.[79]

Anticipating a constitutional issue that would become a sticking point in future debates over Reconstruction, the Democrats rejected the Republican idea that any state would be declared out of the Union just because its citizens had engaged in rebellion. "Whenever any state shall lay down its arms and submit to the laws and the constituted authorities," they declared, "the people thereof [shall] be entitled to return and enjoy all the rights and privileges given by the laws and Constitution to the citizens of the several States." If a sovereign state that had withdrawn from the Union should decide to return to it, said Dr. George B. Loring of Salem expansively, "then the doors shall be thrown open and she shall be welcomed back once more."[80] Declaring that the November elections would be a contest between "Conservatives and Radicals," between "the friends of the Constitution on the one hand, and the Administration and their sympathizers on the other," they nominated Henry Paine, a former Whig, as their candidate for governor. Without admitting that recent military successes had greatly reduced Democratic chances in 1863, Judge Josiah Abbott emphasized the 1863 gathering as the first important step in a movement that would unite the forces of those opposed to "the unconstitutional acts of the party in power" and provide the basis "a year hence" in sweeping that party "into oblivion." Summing up the results of the Democratic gathering's results, the *Boston Post* headline announced to its readers: "The Government sustained, but the administration censured." [81]

Two weeks later, Worcester was also the site of the Republican state convention. Great enthusiasm reigned as party regulars sought to continue their policies for finally bringing the "irrepressible conflict" to a victorious conclusion. Confident of their local officials' reelection, their optimism was further heightened by news that the Republican party had won a resounding victory in Maine. "The Maine election may be regarded as conclusive evidence that Copperheadism has no chance in a loyal state," asserted the *Boston Transcript*. "The Democratic party will have to place itself squarely upon a war platform before it can command the support of the patriotic masses." Determined to head off, once and for all, any further talk about negotiating with the enemy, the Republicans pledged "unwavering and unconditional support" for the national government. Henceforth, they announced, they would treat as enemies those who suggested making peace with the Rebels on any terms other than total submission to national authority and suppression of their "pretended Confederacy." Expounding on the contest "between slavery and liberty," the delegates endorsed the Emancipation Proclamation as an appropriate instrument of military necessity, and also as a guarantee to the world at large that the American contest was for civilization and Christianity.[82] In their official platform, the Republicans suppressed any suggestion that a compromise might save slavery, or that the Emancipation Proclamation might not survive the end of the war. They assured their party that neither individual rights nor personal freedom would ever be destroyed. With an air of optimistic excitement, the Republicans renominated John Albion Andrew by acclamation as their candidate for governor.[83]

Throughout October, the two parties fought it out furiously, attacking each other's candidates and denouncing each other's platform. From the White House, Lincoln watched all the races closely, monitoring firsthand reports that came in from Republican workers in the field.[84] In Kentucky, General Burnside aided the candidacy of Governor Thomas Bramletter, an acceptable Union Democrat, by proclaiming martial law and throwing Democrats into prison.

In Pennsylvania, government clerks were released from work and Union soldiers were furloughed to return Governor Andrew Curtin to office. In Ohio, clerks and soldiers were also made available so that they could vote for Republican John Brough, to whose candidacy Salmon P. Chase, Lincoln's Secretary of the Treasury, devoted a great deal of time and effort. And in his own home state, Illinois, Lincoln studied details about the political struggle with great anxiety. Unable to leave Washington to take the stump in person, the president wrote a carefully scripted public letter defending his policies, calling for unconditional support for the Union, and defending his Emancipation Proclamation as a perfectly constitutional measure.[85] Despite the gravity of the issues, both parties expressed annoyance and frustration at the general public's disappointing lack of interest in the campaign. By the time the November elections came around, however, the Republicans were in a much stronger position than they had been at their September convention. To relieve the frustrating stalemate at Chattanooga, President Lincoln had named General Ulysses S. Grant supreme commander of all Union armies in the West, replaced the ineffective Rosecrans with General George H. Thomas, and ordered reinforcements into Tennessee. Contrary to most pessimistic expectations, Grant reached Chattanooga on October 23, opened up a new supply route from the north, which the troops called the "cracker line," and then moved against Braxton Bragg's mountain positions south of the city. On November 24, Union forces under General Hooker drove the Confederates from Lookout Mountain; next day, General Thomas's men stormed the trenches at the base of Missionary Ridge, and then charged uphill under heavy fire to drive the Rebels from the heights. With Confederate forces now in full retreat, Union troops took control of Chattanooga and consolidated their hold through most of Tennessee.

For the Lincoln administration, news about Grant's rescue operations could not have come at a better time. Inspired by the unexpected display of raw military power in the West, the Republicans carried their banners into the polling booths and took the day. From Maine, Governor Israel Washburn announced proudly that the outcome in his state demonstrated "the square and unqualified support" for the Lincoln administration. Iowa reported that the Republicans in that state had "swept the state overwhelmingly"; loyal Pennsylvania voters had put Governor Curtin back into office. From Ohio, Secretary of the Treasury Salmon P. Chase took great delight in telegraphing President Lincoln the gratifying news that Vallandigham's defeat was "complete, beyond all hopes." When the final returns were reported in Massachusetts, Republican governor John Andrew had won an overwhelming victory—70,000 votes to 29,000—and had even carried Boston, with its bloc of Irish-Democratic voters, by an unprecedented margin of 2,411 votes. Frederic W. Lincoln, the proadministration candidate, was easily reelected to another term as mayor of the city, defeating his rival, Thomas Rich, by 6,206 votes to 2,142.[86] Local Democrats sourly acknowledged defeat, grumbling that the Bay State was too thoroughly "joined to her idols" to be subject to "conversion" as yet. We must wait, they sighed philosophically, for events to bring about a "complete revolution in her political position." From Vienna came a letter from the noted Massachusetts historian John Lothrop Motley, saying that he considered the elections of 1863 "of more consequence than the battles. . . . However the tides of battle may ebb and flow . . . the progress of the war is steadily in our direction." Motley felt that slavery was bound to be "wasted away," and with it would go all threats to the Union. "As to Massachusetts," he told his mother, "I should as soon have thought of the sun's forgetting to rise as to her joining the pro-slavery Copperheads."[87]

In mid-October, though the election campaign was on, the Lincoln administration felt obliged to call for an additional 300,000 volunteer troops for a three-year tour of duty. This time the Massachusetts quota was set at 15,126 men. Governor Andrew realized more than ever that if he was not allowed to raise the state bounty, enlistments would surely falter. Except for the men drafted as replacements, no organized Massachusetts regiments had been sent to the front since late spring—the only exception being the 55th Regiment, the black volunteer unit that had grown from oversubscription to Colonel Shaw's 54th Regiment. This was a poor showing indeed, but symptomatic of the general war-weariness that had crept into almost every aspect of Northern life during fall 1863. Only 6,353 volunteers enlisted and mustered between January 1 and October 17, 1863, including the black regiments, according to the governor's report to the General Court on January 8, 1864. Where would 15,000 more men come from? Andrew decided to call a special session of the legislature, which convened on November 11, 1863. By this time, Congress had raised the U.S. bounty to $402 for those who had already served not less than nine months, and to $302 for new recruits. The Massachusetts legislature now offered an additional $325 for new recruits, as well as for any veteran who might reenlist for three years or for the duration of the war. An enlistee might take only a $50 bounty, and also receive $20 a month from the state for the time he served. Penalties were assessed against any Massachusetts man enlisting in a unit sponsored by another state. Massachusetts itself, however, continued to welcome enlistees from other states.[88]

Governor Andrew's foresight in increasing the bounties ordered for volunteers seems to have been borne out by a steady increase in enlistments. On February 1, and again on March 14, 1864, President Lincoln called for 200,000 more men. The Massachusetts quota for both calls was set at 22,000 men. The Bay State responded very promptly. The 4th and 5th cavalry regiments were organized and sent to the front, as well as the 11th, 14th, and 16th light-artillery battalions. The 5th, 6th, 8th, and 42nd Regiments were also sent off, the new 60th Regiment was enlisted, and nine infantry companies were raised for 100 days' duty on Massachusetts coastal defenses. Besides recruiting new volunteers, the War Department had sent directives to all states requesting them to encourage reenlistment by veteran soldiers. Beyond the increased bounties being offered by the individual states and the federal government, men who reenlisted were made eligible for a thirty-day furlough. Approximately 6,200 veterans from Massachusetts took advantage of this opportunity to continue their military service.

Several unsavory developments, however, came out of this increase in bounties for new enlistments. First, the number of bounty-jumpers increased greatly—men would enlist, receive their bounties, and then skip town to try the same scheme in another state. Stiff penalties, of course, were levied on such offenders. Many of the men were also officially classified as deserters, and some regimental records show a number of deserters out of proportion to enlistments.[89] But perhaps the greatest evil was a private enlistment company, with headquarters in Boston, set up to bring in immigrants from Europe to serve in the Union army. This enterprise originated in fall 1863, when John Murray Forbes talked with some of his business associates about encouraging foreign immigration to Massachusetts as a way of building up the state's manpower quota. Early in January 1864, a group of businessmen formed a committee for that purpose, like that of the old Emigrant Aid Society, with E. S. Tobey serving as chairman and Edward Atkinson as secretary. The plan was to get employers to pay them to obtain skilled workers from Europe, who would be attracted by advertisements promising them homesteads, high wages, or generous bounties if they enlisted in the army. This "emigration" scheme quickly fizzled out, however; employers were reluctant to contribute funds, and the general public turned a cold shoulder to the idea.[90]

Several entrepreneurs, however, were attracted by the speculative possibilities in Forbes's plan, and they organized their own private company. They hoped to use the large state- and local-government bounties to attract "voluntary emigrants" from the Continent. The company made contacts with European immigrants and paid for their transportation to America in return for their signing an agreement to serve in a Massachusetts regiment. After paying for the emigrants' passage, the Boston company would then extract a percentage from the bounty as profit. Governor Andrew was greatly disturbed when he learned that greedy opportunists, "encouraged to the speculation by the large bounties," had brought over more than 200 "voluntary immigrants" from Prussia and Switzerland, and then, only a few months later, brought in three shiploads of men from Germany—nearly 1,000 men—"with hardly a word of English among them." This importing of "shiploads of foreign mercenaries," said the governor angrily, caused strong reaction against the Bay State in other parts of the country, and showed Massachusetts "in its ugliest light." [91] Misunderstanding was rife about individual arrangements, and the whole affair became scandalous.[92] Some of the foreign emigrants later claimed that Massachusetts agents had either forced them into service against their will, or deceived them with false promises and misrepresentations. The governments in the German states involved complained, as did such American cabinet officials as Secretary of War Edwin Stanton and Secretary of State William Seward, who protested against the unwarranted interference in their areas of authority. The colonels in the regiments to which these men were assigned were equally unhappy. Most of the new European recruits could not speak English or understand orders, and many were massacred in the Wilderness campaign only a few months later.[93]

Machinations by greedy individuals profiteering from immigrants' desperation, corruption among unscrupulous manufacturers turning out shoddy goods, and reports of shrewd speculators overcharging the government outrageously for everything from spoiled food to broken-down horses, only increased disenchantment among the general public grown weary with a war in which everyone seemed out to feather his own nest. Was it worth making sacrifices any more? Was any end to the conflict foreseeable, or would it go on forever? Was it fair for some men to go out and put their lives on the line while others stayed home and made big profits? Did the Civil War have any real meaning, or was everyone now just going through the motions?

According to Abraham Lincoln's recent biographer, the historian David Donald, the president himself was acutely aware of this general disillusion and disenchantment, and spent much time after the battles at Gettysburg and Vicksburg thinking about the need for him, as president, to come out with some kind of "broad statement" on the larger significance of the war—some inspirational theme to explain why the struggle was worth fighting and dying for.[94] Others, too, were obviously aware of the pessimistic national mood, for late in September, Boston businessman John Murray Forbes wrote to the president, suggesting that he should seize "an early opportunity" to address "the public mind of the North" as well as "such part of the South as you can reach," on the basic issue of the war. This was not just a contest of "the North against the South," Forbes insisted, but a struggle by "the People against the Aristocrats."[95]

President Lincoln clearly shared Forbes's convictions, and decided that the formal dedication of a national cemetery in Gettysburg, Pennsylvania, scheduled for November 19, 1863, would serve quite well as an appropriate occasion for such a statement. The main speaker was Edward Everett of Massachusetts, considered one of the country's most elegant and polished speakers. President Lincoln was also invited to make a "few appropriate re-marks" during the services, but whether the president would come was uncer-tain, for he had made almost no official visits outside Washington since the war began. Lincoln, however, decided to accept the invitation so that he could speak about the war's larger meaning at the place where so many young Ameri-can dead were being interred. "Short, short, short," Lincoln said about the remarks he would make at the Union Cemetery dedication ceremonies, un-doubtedly appreciating that his part in the proceedings was intended to be minor. But he was determined to say something memorable.[96] With nearly 15,000 people in attendance, the dignitaries took their places on the platform and the solemn event went off as planned. After an opening prayer, followed by a funeral dirge, Edward Everett gave his formal oration, which took nearly two hours to deliver. After another dirge, Lincoln stepped forward, opened with the words "Fourscore and seven years ago. . . ," and delivered the piece that John Hay called his "half dozen words of consecration" to an enthusiastic audience, who interrupted the president's brief remarks with applause at least four times, according to a reporter from the *Boston Advertiser*. Although Lin-coln did not feel that his remarks had been as effective as he wished ("it went sour," he later remarked), others recognized that they had heard a masterpiece of eloquent prose. Edward Everett certainly saw the power in Lincoln's words, and in a note next day told the president that he would have been pleased indeed if he had come as close to the central idea of the day in two hours as Lincoln had in two minutes.

As the ceremonies at the Gettysburg cemetery came to a close, and military operations ground to a halt in the wintry snows, it was time for the president's annual message to Congress, scheduled for December 8, 1863. According to David Donald, the main body of the message itself was fairly routine, con-sisting of pasted-together reports from his department heads and lacking his usual "literary elegance." Only in the final portion, addressing the future of the Southern states, did one hear Lincoln's "distinctive voice."[97] The president offered full pardon, with restoration of all rights and property (except slaves) to all Rebels, excepting high-ranking Confederate officials, who would take an oath of future loyalty to the Constitution and pledge to obey congressional acts and presidential proclamations relating to slavery. He further promised to extend recognition to a Southern state when it reestablished a government loyal to the Union that was supported by as few as one-tenth of its 1860 voters who would take the oath of allegiance.[98]

This proclamation proved to be an interesting and controversial topic of discussion for Bay State residents during the holiday period. The *Boston Jour-nal* reported "great anxiety" in Boston streets among people who wanted a copy of the president's message, especially when they learned that it dealt with amnesty. The *Journal*'s counting rooms were crowded with Bostonians who seemed as impatient to get the latest edition of the newspaper as they usually were to get the latest returns after a hotly contested election. Opinion in Massachusetts differed widely over Lincoln's proposed amnesty plan. Most Republicans, on the one hand, appeared to think the program a sensible and moderate way of approaching a difficult problem. Most Democrats, on the other hand, denounced the plan as nothing more than an insidious plot to "enslave the whole people by crushing out the very vital principle of Republican institutions." They apparently felt that the one-tenth plan would transfer state governments in the South into the hands of a small coterie of Republican sympathizers who did not reflect the people's will. "Does there live one so absurd an idiot," asked the *Boston Courier,* "as to believe the South can be so reclaimed to the Union?"[99]

The Christmas period in 1863, therefore, was a time of mixed emotions. It was difficult for most people to be "merry" as long as the war continued, and as long as the question of the Union was still unresolved. But the news from the front was gradually improving, the Confederacy seemed to be living on borrowed time now, and President Lincoln was already formulating plans for postwar reconstruction—obviously envisioning an imminent end to the fighting. For the first time since the days of Fort Sumter, the people of Massachusetts began to feel that they might look forward to a Christmas in the near future when all Americans would celebrate this traditional holiday in the spirit of peace and happiness that it had before 1861.

The Union Club on Park Street, across from the Boston Common and only a short distance from the Massachusetts State House, became a center of Union sentiment in the city. Founded by prominent Bostonians such as John Murray Forbes, Charles Eliot Norton, and Oliver Wendell Holmes, the Union Club provided a private place where businessmen and financiers could meet and plan programs to support President Lincoln, the Republican party, and the war effort. (Courtesy of the Boston Public Library, Print Department)

7 Changing Patterns
~ ~ ~ ~ ~ ~ ~

*N*ow *was the time to finish it.*

The year 1864 began auspiciously. Many people sensed the confidence and buoyancy that only the smell of victory can bring. "Never since I have been in public life," Senator Charles Sumner wrote to the future British prime minister William E. Gladstone on January 1, 1864, "has there been so little excitement in Congress. The way seems, at least, open. Nobody doubts the result. The assurance of the future gives calmness." James Russell Lowell, in the January issue of the *North American Review,* agreed that by now the war's progress had outstripped all expectations, and that "the country is unanimously resolved that the war shall be prosecuted, at whatever the cost." [1]

Despite this air of assurance, however, the military campaigns, at least in the eastern theater of operations, had bogged down. New military leadership was a crying need. On February 29, Congress revived the lieutenant-general grade, and authorized the president to appoint to the post whomever he might choose. Most observers expected that the new man would be General Ulysses S. Grant. Lincoln eagerly concurred with public sentiment, and promptly appointed Grant general-in-chief of all the Union armies. [2]

Not until March 8, however, did Lincoln first meet Grant in person, at an evening White House reception. In the large gathering was Theodore Lyman of Boston, son of a former city mayor, recent Harvard graduate, and member of General Meade's staff. The forty-two-year-old Grant, he observed, was "rather under middle height, of a spare strong build; light brown hair; and short, light-brown beard." The new general's eyes, he noticed, were a "clear blue; forehead high; nose aquiline; jaw squarely set, but not sensual." [3] And then there was Lincoln himself, eight inches taller than the general, but even homelier in appearance, eagerly searching the new lieutenant-general's face for signs of the determination required to lead Northern armies to victory. The

White House reception became a wild affair once Grant's presence was known. People shouted and crushed about him; ladies' dresses were mussed; the furniture was disarranged. Next day the formal ceremonies took place, and then Grant went to work in his deliberate, matter-of-fact way. "He's the quietest little fellow you ever saw," Lincoln confided to a friend shortly after their first meeting. "The only evidence you have that he's in any place is that he makes things git! Wherever he is, things move!"[4] Having little firsthand knowledge about the new military commander, people in Boston, like people all through the North, were apprehensive about this new appointment. "What has happened?" asked the *Boston Transcript.* "How will he work out?"

Although some of Grant's friends advised him to remain in the West, Lincoln had indicated that he wanted his new general to stay nearby, and so Grant set up his headquarters with the Army of the Potomac. General George Meade still retained command of that army, but by attaching himself to the unit Grant automatically became the ranking general in charge.[5] While new efforts were being made to revitalize the armed forces' fighting spirit, a presidential election year was already under way. As the year 1864 opened, it seemed that Abraham Lincoln would have little difficulty commanding his party's support for a second term. Indeed, if the presidential election took place next week, said *Harper's Weekly* in a January issue, "Mr. Lincoln would undoubtedly be returned by a greater majority than a President since Washington." James Russell Lowell, a prominent leader of the nation's literary circles, published an article in the *North American Review* entitled "The President's Policy," in which he compared Lincoln with King Henry IV, hailed him as an outstanding statesman, and predicted that Lincoln would have nothing to fear in the November elections.[6] And in Boston the people seemed to reflect these warm sentiments. Bostonians had firm trust in Lincoln and believed that if he remained at the Ship of State's helm the Union would be preserved, the city would remain prosperous, and its young men would return home victorious. Boston Mayor Frederic W. Lincoln, in his inaugural speech on January 4, 1864, proclaimed: "In common with the rest of the Union, we share the evils that affect the nation, but at the same time, we have much reason for congratulation upon the general prosperity of the particular community in which we live." Governor John Andrew reiterated this optimistic theme in his own inaugural address four days later, when he stated that 1864 was a year "which opens full of hope . . . succeeding one . . . of unexampled moral and military progress."[7]

The optimistic hopes for the president's political future quickly dimmed, however, as military successes failed to fulfill the enthusiastic promises. Despite the welcome victories at Gettysburg and Vicksburg in the previous summer, and the successes in Tennessee early in the fall, Union armies had not been able to capitalize upon the Confederate defeats. Republican party leaders were openly criticizing the manner in which President Lincoln was directing the war, and concluded that he was no longer capable of delivering the final blows that would bring the Confederacy to its knees. They publicly blamed him for appointing ineffective Democratic generals such as George B. McClellan, who had let Lee escape after the battle of Antietam, and George G. Meade, who had committed the same error after Gettysburg, and who even now was sitting in Washington when he should be "on the road" toward Richmond.[8] By spring, Lincoln himself had deep doubts about his ability to secure his own party's nomination at their convention in June, much less to win the national election in November. He had found his political status weakened after he issued his proclamation of amnesty in December, making known his conciliatory terms about letting the Southern states back into the Union after the war. Radical Republicans were furious at Lincoln's "soft" amnesty proposal, and responded in July with the Wade-Davis Bill, which declared that the seceded states were "out" of the Union and could not be restored until Congress made the appropriate determination.[9] When Lincoln deliberately pocket vetoed the Radicals' bill on July 4, many observers felt it was tantamount to a declaration of war between the president and his party's Radical wing. From that moment on, Radical leaders were determined to replace Lincoln with some other political figure who would carry out the party leaders' wishes.[10] Some thought that Secretary of the Treasury Salmon P. Chase, whom Horace Greeley regarded as a stronger and bolder candidate, was much more committed to emancipation and racial equality. Other Republicans supported the mercurial Massachusetts figure Benjamin F. Butler; still others favored General John C. Frémont, the disgruntled soldier-adventurer, who attracted much support from antislavery groups.

Unfortunately for Lincoln, announcing at the end of the year his postwar reconstruction policy provoked a grave split among moderate and radical Republicans, and also among Boston's vocal abolitionist groups. Ever since the Emancipation Proclamation was announced, Wendell Phillips had grown impatient with what he regarded as Lincoln's half-hearted approach to emancipation and his total failure to grasp the war's revolutionary implications as a way of promoting full equality for African Americans. Phillips's friend William Lloyd Garrison had also criticized many presidential policies, but he was generally inclined to withhold public disapproval of Lincoln's antislavery sentiments in the belief that much had already been accomplished and that further advances were bound to come under the president's slow but steady prodding.[11] The apparent leniency in the president's December amnesty proclamation, however, was the final straw in convincing Phillips that Lincoln was not really sincere in his racial attitudes and that he might well go back on his emancipation policies once the war was over. Convinced it was time that Lincoln be removed and replaced by someone much more committed to full racial equality, Phillips broke with Garrison and took the lead in organizing an outspoken anti-Lincoln faction among his fellow abolitionists.[12]

As early as January 1864, the split between Phillips and his anti-Lincoln supporters and Garrison and his pro-Lincoln backers flared into the open at the Massachusetts Anti-Slavery Society's annual meeting. Phillips offered a resolution charging that the Lincoln administration was ready to sacrifice "the interest and honor of the North" to secure a "sham peace," and was prepared to abandon the freed slaves in the South and leave them "under the control of the late slave holders." President Lincoln, claimed Phillips, had "no desire, no purpose, no thought" about lifting the freed slave to any higher social or political status than that of a mere laborer "superintended by others." This was not, he concluded, the man to undertake the difficult task of reconstruction. Garrison did his best to soften the harsh wording in Phillips's resolution, but when the final vote was taken the Massachusetts Anti-Slavery Society adopted Phillips's original resolution, putting themselves on record as opposing Abraham Lincoln's renomination by the Republican party.[13] Following their resolution, many Radical abolitionists came out for Salmon P. Chase. They announced that they were dissatisfied with Lincoln's inefficient handling of the war, opposed to his lenient approach to reconstruction, and resentful of the influence he allowed men such as William H. Seward and Montgomery Blair to have upon White House policy. Chase, they agreed, would offer a tougher approach both to finalizing the war and to orchestrating a tougher reconstruction policy.[14]

For all their elaborate planning, however, the more extreme members of the Republican party were frustrated in their plans to derail the Lincoln bandwagon. The railsplitter from Illinois was still much too popular with the general public to be outvoted, and he was much too astute a politician to be maneuvered out of the picture. To forestall possible candidacy by the Bay State's Ben Butler, but at the same time to capture any votes this canny lawyer-politician-general might deliver, Lincoln appeared to toy with asking Butler to run as his vice-presidential candidate. In February, Lincoln had a long talk with Butler's chief of staff, General J. Wilson Shaffer, during which he put down in writing his conviction that he had confidence in Butler's ability and in his "fidelity to the country and to me." In March, Lincoln sent a delegation, headed by Simon Cameron, to Fortress Monroe to ask Butler if he would consent to becoming Lincoln's running mate in the fall elections. Butler replied that he would not. The Bay State lawyer was too shrewd a politician himself not to see what Lincoln had in mind. If he accepted second place on the ticket, Lincoln's renomination would be secure; without Butler, Lincoln's place on the ticket was in doubt. And at this time some Republican leaders were trying to persuade Butler himself to run for the main office. A Butler "boom" could well be under way, and Butler was certainly not the man to stop it. Tell Mr. Lincoln, he told Cameron, that "while I appreciate with the fullest sensibilities his act of friendship" . . . I must decline." He suggested "laughingly" that Cameron might inform Lincoln that the only condition under which he would accept the vice-presidency would be if the president would die "within three months after his inauguration."[15] Butler, of course, was to live to regret his decision. Only two months later, during the campaign for Richmond, his shortcomings as a soldier would become painfully apparent once again, leaving his military fortunes as low as his political future.

Having skillfully dispensed with one Republican alternative, Lincoln moved deftly against his other potential rival—Salmon P. Chase. A New Hampshire native and a Dartmouth College graduate, Chase had moved west to Ohio, entered politics, and in 1849 was elected by the Free-Soilers to the U.S. Senate. In 1855 the new Republican party leaders chose him as their candidate for governor of Ohio, and in 1860 he was again returned to the U.S. Senate.[16] An ambitious and able man, Chase became Lincoln's Secretary of the Treasury, and obviously had his eye on the presidency. For three years he used the Treasury Department to build a well-financed and carefully organized political machine for his nomination in 1864, an ambition that certainly was fueled by reports of growing Republican dissatisfaction with Lincoln. In December 1863, a Chase committee was quietly established in Washington, and by February 1864 the organizers considered the political climate supportive enough to come out publicly. Announcing that the "one-term principle" should prevail in Lincoln's case, they insisted that Chase was now the candidate to lead the nation into the victorious years of reconstruction.[17] Before long, however, the Chase insurgency found itself under deadly attack from all quarters. Lincoln had not neglected to establish his own patronage and power bases in Washington, and now gave the word for other Cabinet officials to open up on Chase. Postmaster-General Montgomery Blair used his own patronage sources with great effect in supporting the president; his brother Frank Blair delivered a blistering speech on the House floor charging the Treasury Department with implication in corrupt practices related to cotton-trading permits. At the same time, intensely loyal proadministration groups back in Ohio lashed out at Chase for not supporting Lincoln and for undermining the Republican party's unity at a time of great peril.[18] Overwhelmed by the attacks' intensity and fearful for his political future, on March 5 Chase withdrew his name from consideration for the presidency and humbly offered to resign his position in the Cabinet.[19] By this time most Republicans had given up looking for an alternative nominee and were climbing aboard the Lincoln bandwagon.

In Boston, the conservative Republican *Boston Transcript* complained that "the loyal people of Massachusetts regret to see plotting and scheming in various high quarters in regard to the next President." "As far as we are advised," wrote the editors, "few prominent Massachusetts men figure in the contentions between rival Presidential aspirants." Republicans in Boston generally disapproved of the way in which their party was being weakened by a "contemptible struggle," and the *Transcript* hailed Salmon P. Chase's withdrawal from the race as a "noble move" that would ensure party unity.[20]

Some Radicals still felt that if the Lincoln bandwagon could not be stopped it might be derailed. They pinned their hopes on General John C. Frémont, who was still smarting from Lincoln's humiliating reversal of his slavery edict back in 1861 and was disgruntled that the president had failed to assign him to an important military command.[21] In August 1862, Frémont had come to Boston to speak to a huge crowd in the Boston Music Hall, where he was flanked on the platform by several abolitionist leaders who already saw this antislavery military figure as a possible presidential candidate in 1864. Indeed, in 1863 Frémont purchased a summer home in Nahant, Massachusetts, where many prominent Bostonians owned property and spent their summers. Throughout the year, he consulted frequently with Bay State abolitionist leaders. He became especially friendly with Wendell Phillips, who revitalized his antislavery views and encouraged his presidential ambitions.[22] On March 4, 1864, a Frémont Club was formally organized in Boston, where resolutions were passed denouncing Lincoln's reconstruction plans and calling for equality of all men before the law.

Other abolitionists, however, refused to follow Phillips into the Frémont camp and continued loyal to the president. William Lloyd Garrison, in particular, continued to publicly support Lincoln, fearful that an open split in the abolitionist ranks at this critical time would drive a wedge into the Republican party and encourage Rebels and Copperheads everywhere. In the March 18 issue of his *Liberator*, Garrison repeated his warnings about the dire effects divisions and factions could have in the Republican party. Although Abraham Lincoln was not always "perfect," he conceded, nevertheless there was "much to rejoice over and to be thankful for." He pleaded with his fellow abolitionists to overlook the president's shortcomings and recognize what he had already accomplished. A thousand "incidental errors and blunders are easily borne with," he wrote, "on the part of him who, at one blow, severed the chains of three millions three hundred thousand slaves."[23] But Phillips and his radical followers would have none of it, and at the American Anti-Slavery Society's annual meeting in New York City early in May the members adopted another sharply worded resolution offered by Phillips, affirming that abolitionists could see "no evidence" that the Lincoln administration intended to put the

Wendell Phillips, son of Boston's first mayor and a graduate of Harvard College, became a strong supporter of William Lloyd Garrison and an eloquent speaker for the abolitionist cause. After the announcement of the Emancipation Proclamation, Phillips broke with Garrison and became increasingly critical of President Lincoln for not moving more quickly to outlaw slavery altogether. (The Bostonian Society)

freedom of the African American on such a basis "as will secure it against every peril." For Phillips, reelecting Lincoln in 1864 would produce "the end of the Union in my day or its reconstruction on terms worse than Disunion."[24] When Frémont was able to get enough eastern abolitionists and western German-Americans to organize a third party, some local abolitionists went off to Cleveland at the end of May to attend a political convention of the "Radical Democratic Party." After an impassioned letter from Wendell Phillips was read to some four hundred cheering delegates, they nominated General Frémont as their presidential candidate.[25]

William Lloyd Garrison, in the meantime, attended the Republican convention at Baltimore in June 1864, at which Abraham Lincoln was almost unanimously renominated. The Boston abolitionist came away satisfied that the Lincoln administration was on the right path when the convention adopted a resolution pledging that the Republican party would guarantee to extinguish slavery in the United States by a constitutional amendment. Looking forward to the Confederacy's imminent defeat and the restoration of the Union, Republican party leaders worked to reestablish their party nationally. To get around the "Republican" label, which by this time was synonymous with "Northern," they adopted the name National Union party. To draw votes from the border states, and to demonstrate their party's national character, Republicans selected Andrew Johnson, the loyalist senator from Tennessee, now a War Democrat, as their vice-presidential candidate.[26] Some consolation for Radical Republicans who still had reservations about campaigning for Lincoln came late in August when, at their Chicago convention, the Democrats nominated General George B. McClellan, and then adopted a "peace platform" written by the Copperhead (Peace Democrat) leader, Clement L. Vallandigham. The extreme Radicals may not have been enthusiastic about a second term for Lincoln, but this McClellan-Vallandigham combination was enough to make them abandon their reservations and go for the incumbent.[27]

The Democrats, in the meantime, enthusiastically supported their candidate, General McClellan, and their newspapers hammered away at President Lincoln's inefficiency. Boston newspapers were generally much less vehement in their attacks upon Lincoln himself than Democratic presses in other northern cities. The man from Illinois was no longer lampooned as the "coarse, vulgar joker," "gorilla," "buffoon," or "third-rate lawyer who once split rails and now splits the Union"; he was, rather, characterized as a well-meaning but misled misfit who was running the government ineptly and inefficiently. "The fault," remarked the *Boston Post* accusingly, "has been in the directing power at Washington." *The Boston Pilot,* on the other hand, blamed the administration for burdensome debts, heavy taxes, depreciated currency, division in the parties, and a "despotism that over-rides personal rights." One charge that the

Boston Democrats kept repeating was that Lincoln had gone back on his original promises. He had abandoned his moderate approach to the war; he had
given up on his opposition to emancipation; he had turned away from the idea
of restoring the Union to the "status quo ante bellum." He had, in short, sold
out entirely to the extremist Radicals and the fanatical abolitionists in his
party.[28]

The Democrats' strategy was, they hoped, to drive so divisive a wedge
between the Republican president and the Republican party leaders that the
Democrats would win by default. They saw that by encouraging a major power
struggle among the Republican factions who were supporting such rival candidates as Lincoln, Chase, Butler, and Frémont, they might be able to create a
fatal weakness that would end Radical control of the government. Then moderate and conciliatory Democrats could take up the responsibilities of government, reconcile conflicting political factions, preserve constitutional freedom,
and prevent the social revolution they feared would result from four more
years of Radical rule. The Democratic *Boston Post,* reporting on George B.
McClellan as the party's nominee, commented that local reaction greeted the
news "with an enthusiasm we have never before seen surpassed." "The sun
went down," it continued, "on as satisfied a people as often dwells in any
city."[29]

Lincoln may have succeeded in getting his party's nomination in June, but
his reelection in November was becoming extremely problematic because of
successive Union military defeats. During spring 1864, Boston, like most other
northern cities, watched with great hope as Ulysses S. Grant, the new general
from the West, prepared to launch a powerful offensive against the Confederate forces. One Union army was to march through the Shenandoah Valley,
destroying its fruitful resources and diverting Confederate forces from the
Richmond area. A second army under General William T. Sherman was to
proceed southwest from Chattanooga in a drive through Georgia that would
destroy Atlanta and slice the eastern half of the Confederacy in two. "For the
first time in the war we had a commander-in-chief," wrote William Schouler,
the Bay State's adjutant general. "The war of the Union was no longer to be
fought by twenty different commanders, each acting upon his own responsibility, and without concert of action," he noted approvingly.[30] General Grant himself chose to accompany General Meade and the Army of the Potomac in a
direct march against Robert E. Lee and the Confederate capital, Richmond.[31]

Early in May 1863, both Grant and Sherman launched their spring offen-
sives designed to crush the Confederate armies. Boston newspapers showed
little interest in Sherman, but kept a close watch on Grant as he crossed the
Rapidan River in a move against General Lee's right flank. Lee, however, struck
out hard against the Union forces as they stumbled through dense thickets

known as The Wilderness. For two days the two armies fought a furious battle in the dark gloom of the tangled undergrowth as hundreds of small brushfires flamed and smoldered about them.

Reporting that the "pending contest in Virginia absorbs general thought for the moment," newspapers told how the people in Boston waited eagerly for news about a great Union victory as early communiqués suggested "exciting" and "gratifying" successes for the Northern forces. Shortly, however, Boston learned that Grant had not been able to turn Lee's flank, and that the Army of the Potomac had "received a very heavy blow from Lee's army." The city settled back to watch the new commander's progress with a bit more anxiety and doubt.[32]

Seeing that he could not break through the Wilderness barrier, Grant moved his army farther around Lee's right flank, toward the village of Spotsylvania Courthouse. But Lee quickly shifted his own army to meet Grant's latest maneuver. Once again Bostonians followed reports about the Union offensive with hopeful enthusiasm, expecting to hear at any moment that Grant had defeated Lee and had captured Richmond. At the Merchants' Exchange a "clothesline telegraph" was rigged up to keep Boston businessmen in constant touch with the latest military developments. For five days, from May 8 to May 12, Grant's men hammered away at the stubborn Confederate defenses, only to be repelled by Lee's veterans, who shifted expertly to meet each new assault. After five fruitless days of battle, Grant once again shifted his army southward. The anticipated victory had not developed, and it was obvious that Boston's citizens were beginning to lose their confidence in General Grant.[33]

Lee skillfully countered Grant's latest movements, and maneuvered the Confederate force inside the Richmond fortifications, its right flank along the Chickahominy River, its center drawn up at Cold Harbor. On June 3, Grant ordered a frontal assault against the Confederate center at Cold Harbor, only to have massed Rebel artillery shatter the Union charge with incredible losses—nearly 7,000 casualties in an hour.[34] Now many Northerners openly criticized Grant's leadership. He had failed to defeat Lee; he had failed to take Richmond; and, worse yet, he had already recorded nearly 60,000 casualties since he first crossed the Rapidan. Although such Republican newspapers in Boston as the *Journal* tried to bolster public confidence in Grant, the Democratic *Post* sneered at the "constant sickening flow of partisan delusion as to successes, in order to create capital for the party in power."[35] President Lincoln realized, however, that although Grant's losses were admittedly high, he was also inflicting heavy casualties on Lee's army—casualties that the Confederacy could never hope to replace. Grant had been relentless in reducing the enemy's size and in forcing Lee and his army back into the Richmond defenses. Lincoln therefore paid little attention to the public clamor for Grant's dismissal, and refused to remove from command the man he had chosen to win the war.

In mid-June, Grant suddenly shifted his forces across the James River and sent them driving for Petersburg, the strategic railroad center some twenty miles south of Richmond. This unexpected maneuver caught Lee by surprise, and news of the Union offensive caused Northerners to hope for the final victory that would bring the tiresome war to an end. But poor planning and bungled orders by Union commanders gave the Confederate defenders time to hold the enemy off while Lee maneuvered the Army of Northern Virginia to defend this important city. Petersburg withstood four days of battering, cost Grant 8,000 more men, and forced both sides to dig in for a nine-month siege—the longest in the entire war. "It is evident that the people regard the check at Petersburg as a serious blow to the campaign," grumbled one Boston newspaper, complaining about the inaccurate reporting that raised false hopes and painted inaccurate pictures of the military situation.[36] It was obvious that having had their hopes and expectations raised to great heights on several occasions, only to have them dashed to the ground, Boston residents had now lapsed into general melancholy. Grant could do no better than any of the other generals against Robert E. Lee. This war could drag on forever. One minute the Johnny Rebs appeared to be defeated; the next minute they popped up again.

As if to lend truth to their suspicions about the enemy's ability to spring to life again, in the first week of July Bostonians were shocked by the news that Confederate general Jubal Early was racing northward through the Shenandoah Valley toward Washington, D.C.[37] As the *Boston Advertiser* issued a call for an additional 5,000 Bay State volunteers to perform garrison duty in the forts around the nation's capital, Early and his troops boldly clattered to within ten miles of Washington. "The country is ashamed," wrote the *Advertiser,* "that at this stage of the war we should have a rebel force beating back a Union general on this side of the Potomac."[38] The Democratic *Boston Post* was especially critical of the Lincoln administration for allowing this "Rebel invasion" to frighten Washington and disrupt the whole state of Maryland's business and commerce. This was one more proof of the current administration's incompetence, said the paper, which called upon President Lincoln to dismiss immediately every member of his Cabinet.[39] Although Grant eventually sent two divisions from Petersburg to drive Early back into Virginia and placed General Philip Sheridan in command of the Army of the Shenandoah, these changes did little to lift the pall of gloom that had settled over most of the North. Indeed, the dark clouds grew still blacker when the end of the month brought even more tragic news from the Petersburg area.

In a desperate attempt to break through the stubborn Confederate lines, on June 25 Union forces dug a 500-foot-long tunnel under the Rebel fortifications and packed it with 8,000 pounds of gunpowder. At 4:45 on the morning of July 30, 1864, the earth shook with a tremendous roar. Huge masses of dirt, boulders, timber, and human bodies were hurled into the air, creating a crater 60 feet wide, 170 feet long, and 30 feet deep. As the Union troops charged forward, however, they had to clamber down one side of the deep crater and then claw their way up the other side while the Confederates stood along the rim and poured deadly musket and cannon fire down upon them. It was like shooting fish in a barrel.[40] The Union forces suffered 3,798 casualties at the Battle of the Crater—of whom 504 were killed, 1,881 wounded, and 1,413 captured or missing. The disaster was especially shocking to Massachusetts readers because of reports that black troops had suffered some of the heaviest losses.[41] Specially trained members of a black division had originally been scheduled to lead the assault, and were eager "to show the white troops what the colored division could do." At the last minute, however, General Meade decided to send the white troops in first, so that when the black troops followed after the explosion, they caught the full blast of the fierce Confederate counterattack and were slaughtered by the enraged Rebel soldiers.[42]

From start to finish the plan was a fiasco, one more inglorious setback that caused people in the North to become even more disheartened. "It begins to look to many folks in the North," said *The Boston Pilot*, "that the Confederacy perhaps can never really be beaten, that the attempts to win might after all be too heavy a load to carry, and that perhaps it is time to agree to a peace without victory." [43] "Neither Richmond, Charleston, Mobile, nor Atlanta have been captured," mourned the *Boston Post*, which reported "evident disappointment" and "deep dissatisfaction" among the general public at the way in which the war was going.[44] This sense of public discouragement was further evident in that interest in the war itself seemed to be waning fast. Although the newspapers had now shifted focus from the Eastern front to Sherman's and Sheridan's activities in the West, and cannon salutes were fired on Boston Common at any report of Union successes, it was difficult to rekindle the old spirit and enthusiasm. Recruitment had slowed and showed no signs of picking up. In fact, the number of men signing up as volunteers for the army had fallen off so much that by fall the numerous recruiting offices throughout the city had to be closed for lack of business; only one central office in Haymarket Square remained open.

Another reason for the growing disillusion that had set in during late summer and fall of 1864 was that the war's dreadful sacrifices were being felt in every city and town throughout the state. The Massachusetts contribution to the war effort had been overwhelming from the very start. Bay Staters had been the first organized units to answer President Lincoln's initial call to arms in April 1861. Four regiments had marched off proudly to relieve the nation's capital, followed shortly by a fifth regiment, a light battery, and a battalion of rifles. Over the next three years Massachusetts, discounting all short-term enlistments, had contributed twenty-five infantry regiments, four of heavy artillery, five of cavalry, and fifteen light-artillery batteries. Altogether, more than 87,362 men had signed up for three-year enlistments. Many of the three-year enlistments were now up, and as veteran regiments came home to be demobilized their slender ranks gave tragic testimony to their gallantry and devotion and brought home to the public, starkly and dramatically, freedom's heavy price. Many infantry units had already lost more than 20 percent of their men in individual engagements; one regiment, the 15th, had lost 40 percent of its complement at Antietam. As returning Bay State regiments marched through Boston's streets during fall 1864, the crowds of people waiting cheerfully and expectantly to celebrate their young heroes' return suddenly gasped in heartbreak at the sight of the pitiful handful of veterans, all that was left of regiments once swelled by the city's eager young men. When the "Fighting Nineteenth" arrived back in Boston, the newspapers observed that only 75 veterans were left of a regiment that had marched out of the city back in June 1861 with 1,915 men. Indeed, the 19th had to be consolidated with the shattered remnants of the 15th and the 20th to bring its numbers up to slightly more than 100 men. And in December, the 28th Regiment of Massachusetts returned to Boston to be mustered out. Of the original 1,000 Irish men who had left three years earlier, only 119 had made the long journey home.

News releases only added to the prevailing spirit of gloom and depression. The *Journal* reported that 220 men of the 39th Regiment, captured on the Weldon Railroad in August, had been transported to the notorious Libby Prison, where they were said to be living under "deplorable conditions."[45] Another item related the sad news that of the 71 members of the Massachusetts 2nd Cavalry who had been captured by guerrillas in Virginia and sent to the prison at Andersonville, Georgia, all but two had died. Bostonians shook their heads in sad discouragement when they read the news that in one week in September, 783 coffins had been issued at Newbern, North Carolina, for soldiers who had died of yellow fever. And perhaps some of the more perceptive caught the brief but significant business item reporting that the American Artificial Limb Company in Boston had declared a semiannual dividend of 5 percent—an increase over the previous year. Indeed, almost every day the *Boston Post* carried advertisements for artificial arms and legs being manufactured by companies with the unsettling announcement that they were operating "under the patronage of the U.S. Government."[46] After the great victories in 1863, the year 1864 had started out on a high note with bright hope and great expectations. By late spring and early summer, however, it was evident that the absence of Union victories, the growing casualty lists, and the new high command's failure to bring the war to a swift and glorious conclusion had produced decided pessimism and dissatisfaction. No one could find a clear indication that the terrible conflict would not drag on interminably.

Amid military failure and political uncertainty, one of the few bright spots was the general prosperity the war had brought to the New England economy. The port of Boston had become a forest of masts. Goods and produce of all kinds arrived every day from all parts of the world, and the city's newspapers devoted much of their space to the latest shipping news, and also voiced their complaints about the Union navy's failure to capture such Confederate privateers as the *Alabama,* the *Georgia,* and the *Tallahassee,* which constantly preyed upon Northern vessels. The demand for goods to outfit the gigantic army that the Civil War had created had greatly accelerated the incipient industrial revolution that had already taken hold in New England a quarter of a century earlier. Northern industry's expansion as a result of the exigencies of the first modern war in world history was almost explosive in force. New machinery was invented to equip new factories; the interchangeable-parts principle made the Springfield rifle supreme; now that the Sault Sainte Marie canal was open, the Pittsburgh foundries had an unlimited supply of inexpensive iron with which the foundries in South Boston could turn out cannon, anchor chain, railroad rails, and iron plating for monitors. The northern textile mills turned to woolen production now that cotton was generally unavailable. New plows, mowers, reapers, and steam-driven threshing machines enabled the farmer to meet domestic wartime needs and to provide valuable overseas exports to Great Britain and France. Advertisements in the *Post* and the *Journal* indicate that Boston was still in great demand as a leather and textile center. The McCormick reaper received its share of attention as did the Howe sewing machine, which was improving so rapidly that new models were appearing every year.

Further evidence of Boston's wartime prosperity could be seen in the city's numerous charitable endeavors. A Sailor's Fair opened on November 10, and in only a few days raised $157,000 toward its projected goal of $200,000 for a Sailor's Home. On November 17 the *Boston Post* reported that more than $3,000 had been raised to provide Thanksgiving dinners for soldiers and sailors.[47] On that same date, the Boston Provident Association made a public appeal for the poor—ironically, because the general economy was doing so well. It reported having only $4,000 in its treasury, an unusually small amount for that season: "The number of poor this winter is likely to be larger than ever on account of want or unemployment and the price of the necessities of life." The U.S. Christian Commission of the Young Men's Christian Association had spent more than $6,000 a day during the previous month ministering to soldiers; and on November 19 the *Post* announced that the commission had set for itself a goal of $1 million to meet expenses for the winter's work.[48] By December 1, $105,782 of this amount had already been raised in a Thanksgiving Day collection. Even the Catholic-sponsored House of the Angel Guardian had raised $15,000 over expenses from its less substantial supporters.

Another sign of local prosperity was the appearance of new financial institutions in the city at the war's peak. On December 17 a Boston newspaper observed that three new banks, the North National, the Shawmut National, and the Broadway National, had been chartered. The word "National" in these new banks' names was significant, for during 1863 Secretary of the Treasury Salmon P. Chase (always a "sound" money man) had finally persuaded Congress to pass a national banking act. When the Republicans first came to power in 1860, only local banks, chartered by the states, had been in operation; and they had in circulation 7,000 varieties of paper notes. By the wartime act of 1863, local banking associations were authorized to be formed under federal authority, empowered to issue notes on the basis of U.S. bonds up to 90 percent of par value. The local banks could buy federal securities, receive interest from the government on their holdings, and then, on the strength of these securities, issue paper bills. This wedge into the traditional local-currency system did much to secure a fairly stable national currency system—a vital necessity for the business expansion that the war had stimulated throughout the North. One local illustration of the way in which wartime enterprises were stimulating new areas of economic development could be seen in the nearby South Boston peninsula, where employment opportunities brought about by the war had produced higher prosperity. Several prominent citizens petitioned the state legislature for a charter to establish a local savings bank. Once Governor Andrew approved the legislation, the South Boston Savings Bank opened its doors for business on September 1, 1863, with the president of the bank and several other members of the corporation demonstrating their faith in the new enterprise by depositing a combined total of $550. The next name in the ledger was that of a twelve-year-old boy, Frank D. Morse; his name was followed by other depositors whose occupations were listed as Broker, Dep. Sheriff, Brewer, Merchant, Physician, Grocer, Lumber Dealer, and just plain Gentleman.[49] The great age of industrial capitalism was just around the corner, and signs of that expansionist period were already beginning to bubble up from the great national conflict.

The *Boston Post* columns very clearly depicted "business as usual" in Boston commercial centers, spending little time on the horrors of war. Government contracts were steadily helping many war fortunes to accumulate from profits derived from wooden and metal limbs for survivors mutilated in bloody battles, and from uniforms made from shoddy. Fraudulent contractors who

John Murray Forbes started his financial career as a successful China merchant before going into the construction of railroads. Forbes was one of the first Massachusetts Whigs to become a member of the Republican party, and during the Civil War he helped organize black regiments, formed the Union Club, and organized the Loyal Publication Society. Forbes helped President Lincoln and the Union military war effort by purchasing ships and weapons abroad. (The Bostonian Society)

flaunted their ill-gotten gains were derided and scorned by the general public. On November 8, the *Boston Post,* in a reprint from the New York *Sunday Times,* moralized:

> Shoddy appears in its glory at Central Park. Its "fire new" liveries, its glossy studs, flashy carriages, ornamented with fancy coats of arms made to order . . . its elaborately bedecked ladies of tone are to be seen there every sunshiny afternoon in full flare. How many soldiers must have been badly equipped, how many spavined horses palmed off on Uncle Sam, and what lots of plundering done to pay for the gaudy show.[50]

The "Shoddies" might well be scorned, but as yet the nation had not clearly defined legitimate profit—especially in a national crisis. Already the nation's natural resources were being regarded as obviously belonging to the clever and the quick. The September 2 *Journal* devoted a column and a half to the Northern Pacific Railroad Company's organizational meeting, which had been called to order by Willard Sears. A prominent and respected Bostonian, Mr. Sears explained that the project would take at least seven years and would call for an initial outlay of $120 million. It would be a sound investment, he assured his listeners. The proceeds from the land alone, after reimbursing all the original outlay, was calculated to yield a profit of 40 percent a year.[51] Congress, in its eagerness to settle the West, had granted the company 49,360,000 acres of land—20 square miles for each mile of road through Wisconsin and Minnesota; 40 square miles through the newly created Dakota, Montana, and Idaho territories, as well as through Washington Territory. At a nominal fee, $10 an acre, the land alone was expected to bring in $439,360,000 in profit. Despite wartime pressures and demands, the western territories were being settled with amazing speed. Some men were going west to avoid the draft; others were bounty jumpers who had acquired a stake and were getting away before the law caught up with them. Many, however, were genuinely looking for a chance to better themselves and find more land and greater opportunities for their families in the great expanse of the American West.

Not everyone shared in the wartime prosperity, however; nor was everyone able to handling newly acquired fortunes carefully. The September 1 *Journal* commented that a Mr. David Niles had lost $10,000 from his coat pocket; and the same paper elsewhere reported that a trunk with $40,000 had been stolen from a messenger for The Bank of Mutual Redemption. The man had carelessly left the trunk on the counter while transacting business at the Shoe and Leather Dealers Bank.[52] Such news items, reporting incredible sums lost from coat pockets, were surprisingly frequent. Even by today's standards, such sums seem large, but consider their magnitude in 1864: state aid voted for the wife and dependents of any volunteer in the national service was set at "one dollar per week for each dependent . . . not to exceed twelve dollars per month on account of any single volunteer." The base pay for an enlisted private in the U.S. Army was only $13 a month. In striking contrast with the frequent and careless loss of large sums of money were newspaper reports such as one in the October 25 *Boston Post:* "Ellen Perry was sentenced to one month in the House of Correction for stealing three pounds of corned beef." [53]

For many poor and working-class Bostonians, times were hard, for costs of living escalated as never before as a result of wartime scarcities. On December 13, the Board of Aldermen announced new rates for taxis: "For one or more adult passengers within the City Proper or from one place to another within the limits of South Boston or East Boston, fifty cents each. Between the hours of 11 P.M. and 7 A.M. the fare for one adult passenger shall be one dollar." Later in that month, the Metropolitan Horse Railroad, which traveled the route to and from Roxbury, upped its fare to six cents "due to the high cost of the care of horses and the heavy tax laid by the Government on car passengers." A notice on December 30 stated that gasoline was scheduled for an increase in price; and a day later the city truckmen announced that they were raising their rates by 2.5 percent. [54] The high price of potatoes became a "matter of general complaint" during the Thanksgiving period, especially because they were found to be selling for as much as 89 cents to $1 a bushel in Boston, but in towns less than 100 miles away they could be had in any quantity from 30 cents to 50 cents a bushel. The September 1 *Journal* reported that "butter had declined 5 cents per pound at St. Albans, Vermont." If people would only be "sparing" in its use, suggested the paper, "speculators, now strong for a rise, will be glad to sell at reasonable prices." [55]

The rising cost of coal was always a problem for any New England city, but with winter closing in, the newspapers called special attention to coal, which in Boston was then selling for as much as $16 a ton. Several citizens took it upon themselves to investigate, and the September 19 *Journal* reported on the inspection tour these Bostonians had made to the Pennsylvania coal regions. The coal miners, they reported, were charging $2 a ton to get the coal out and into the cars. The company paid 25 cents a ton to the owners. Lehigh coal, when placed in the cars, cost $2.25 a ton. By the time the coal had reached Mauch Chunk, Pennsylvania, eight miles away (and downhill all the way, the *Journal* added), the price had gone up to $8.50 a ton—showing that it was not the miners but the transportation company directors who were causing the high prices. "The cure for this evil is an opposition Railroad in the area," the Bostonians advised. [56] The September 11 *Journal* reported that a meeting would be held to take measures for procuring coal at less than the prevailing rates. "If anything can be done to supply coal to the poor and middling classes at less than $16 a ton it deserves encouragement." The group formed a cooperative association that finally succeeded in reducing the price to $13.50 a ton.[57] By September 24 another group, the Labor Reform Association, announced that it would sell coal to members for $13.50 a ton. Nonmembers would be charged (in addition to the $13.50) one cent on each dollar's worth of coal purchased.

Everyone had a different explanation for the high cost of living. Merchants blamed "the market"; others gave more cynical reasons. On September 23, the *Post* charged that the Lincoln administration had deliberately withheld from the press decisive military news until Wall Street speculators had been given "full opportunity to feather their nests."[58] Undoubtedly this charge was based upon the fluctuating price of gold, which usually followed the ups and downs in the nation's military fortunes. The price of gold reached an all-time high of $250 an ounce during the gloomy August days when the war's outcome was in grave doubt; but when Atlanta fell early in September, the price began to decline, and by September 25 it was down to $187 an ounce. Reporting this rapid drop, the *Journal* took occasion to reveal to the public that merchants had been holding back on their goods until the price of gold decreased, and asked if these same merchants would now lower their prices, too. "Why is this?" asked the writer indignantly. "If gold must be the standard for them, and they must adjust their prices by it, surely goods and provisions ought to be cheaper now than they were a week ago."[59] The *Boston Post*, however, had a different solution to the problem of high prices, blaming them not on inflated currency or business speculation, but on high taxes. In a November 4 article it detailed eight distinct taxes placed upon the raw materials that went into manufacturing one pair of patent-leather pumps—exclusive of the stamp tax on all sums of more than $20, or the taxes on checking accounts.[60] The Democratically controlled newspaper warned its readers that a 5 percent income tax was scheduled to be imposed by the Republicans if they won the 1864 elections.

As if reflecting the dissatisfaction and unrest that prevailed in late summer and early fall 1864, when news from the battlefronts was still far from encouraging, Boston was caught up in sporadic racial and labor difficulties. Although much of the Boston community had rejoiced when the Emancipation Proclamation was formally implemented as 1863 began, little serious effort had been undertaken in the city to broaden racial equality. The typical Bostonian's impression of the African American still rested on the misleading stereotypes in popular and well-attended minstrel shows and in the numerous "darky" jokes regularly passed along by the humor columnists in most newspapers. Open trouble brewed between black residents and Irish immigrants, and newspapers reported frequent clashes between these groups on the waterfront. Until now, the Irish had been on the lowest rungs of the local economic ladder, and they handled most of the heavy and menial work, for which they were grossly underpaid. With the slaves freed, and with more blacks moving north, many immigrants feared that their hard-won jobs were in immediate danger from former slaves who would accept even lower wages and longer hours.

Friction between Irish Americans and African Americans, however, was only one small part of labor unrest within the city, perhaps because the proportion of African Americans in Boston was so much smaller than in other comparable-sized northern cities. Perhaps, too, the frequency was lower because Governor Andrew and state-government officers had so actively supported emancipation and worked for equality in the black regiments. The growing number of women in the city's labor force, on the other hand, did help change attitudes and elevate tensions. The armed services had absorbed much of Boston's traditional male labor force, leaving most of the replacement workers to face antiquated working conditions and low wages—especially amid rapidly rising prices. For the first time, women began to enter the industrial workforce in significant numbers, further changing the city's laboring classes and introducing gender into a predominantly male bastion. Many young people, too, were forced to assume family responsibilities during the war years by taking any jobs they could get, the results of which we can gather from a report in the *Boston Journal* observing that "of the first class of one of the Grammar Schools in East Boston but one boy has returned to school since the summer vacation." [61]

Slowly the city noticed signs of real economic turmoil and social unrest, especially among dissatisfied female workers. "The police were called to No. 49 Court Street, Saturday," reported one newspaper, "to remind about forty shop girls who were endeavoring to induce other girls not to do work at a given rate, that such conduct was hardly the thing and that they had better desist, which the dears did." [62] Late in November, however, further evidence of labor unrest appeared when the city's newspapers faced trouble of their own, initiated by the Boston Printer's Union. The papers defiantly stated that "The proprietors of the several establishments, though at some inconvenience, propose to issue their papers without the assistance of those who have seen fit to assume this belligerent attitude." The newspapers proceeded to hire new typesetters, and then announced that "a large number of the best workmen, who were dragged into the movement against their better judgment, have resumed work, satisfied that their true friends are their employers." The newspaper strike was short-lived, and the editors reported that it had been "a most disastrous fiasco." [63]

This new weapon for labor discontent—the strike—caused obvious alarm and anxiety in local business circles. The *Journal* expressed pleasure in announcing powerful opposition to a strike then in progress in the Pittsburgh coal mines. "The advance demanded [by the miners] would be ruinous to the business interests of the city, unwarranted by circumstances, oppressive to the poor," stated the paper. The date was September 1, before an investigation revealed that the high price of coal was due to transportation costs, not miners' wages or owners' profits. In New York City, the dry-goods clerks demanded a 50 percent increase in their pay. In Chicago, striking printers working for the *Chicago Times* had been summarily discharged by the proprietors, who put forty young women in their places. Faced with a similar confrontation on November 30, the *Boston Post* publicly announced that it would not "surrender" control of its business operations to an association that would try to "coerce us into compliance with whatever terms it may please to dictate." On the contrary, the owners assured their readers they were resolved to "exercise some power in the direction of the labor in our office," and were determined to be a party in deciding "the conditions upon which it shall be formed." [64] On December 1, the *Post* reported that it intended to organize its own office in such a manner that "every man in it will enjoy the right of disposing his skill and labor as he pleases and to his own best advantage." It forthwith advertised for new printers who "need not hesitate to apply under apprehension from members of the Union, as we have taken ample measures to see that all connected with our office are protected in enjoyment of their rights of labor." [65]

It was obvious that a restless but as yet unfocused labor movement had begun to take shape in the city. In four brief years, given impetus by the war, the new industrial age was already taking shape. Great quantities of capital had piled up; a national currency had been created; an ample supply of labor had been imported. New factories had been organized with new forms of mass production; new approaches had been taken to labor relations; new techniques had been applied to industrial management. And a new industrial morality had appeared. That morality condoned wide-scale corruption, felt no shame when selling shoddy to the army, accepted as normal both a 40 percent annual profit on an investment and the Ellen Perrys who were reduced to stealing food in order to eat. In 1850 most of the people still were the self-sufficient farmers in whom Jefferson had placed his trust. As the Civil War ended, however, this "backbone of the nation" was no longer in the majority. Increasingly, as he mortgaged his farm to pay for new machinery and purchase more mechanical equipment, the yeoman farmer ceased to be self-sufficient. A new class had come into being with industrialization: the laborer dependent upon his wages.

The swift and momentous transition from an agricultural to an industrial economy, "the breath of a new and roaring age intricate with man's new found devices," had already begun to uproot the established way of life in America. By 1864, the pattern had been set. Abraham Lincoln's reelection in the coming

November elections was essential to the Republican party's continuing in power for another four years, but it was also crucial to keep the nation's economic revolution going. If the Democrats won, the pattern would probably be slowed; it might well be reversed. The Democrats, after all, had traditionally blocked the protective tariff, opposed free homesteads, denounced a national banking system, and fought federal aid to internal improvements. But if Lincoln remained in office, the Republican party would be almost certain to continue these programs and policies, which had already stimulated the changing patterns in American economic life.

The fast-approaching presidential elections, however, took place against a frustrating military situation that did little to help President Lincoln's chances for a second term. Despite initial assurances of great success, General Ulysses S. Grant had failed to deliver on his promises. The Union armies were still bogged down at Petersburg, the Federals had failed to clear the Shenandoah, and General Sherman was making only slow progress on his march eastward from Chattanooga. Confederate General Joseph E. Johnston had forced the huge Union army to advance across Georgia at a snail's pace so that by the end of June it had not even reached Atlanta. By summer's end in 1864, therefore, the Lincoln administration was coming under increasing attack for having selected Grant as the Union commander and for failing to prosecute the war effectively. Many Radical Republicans felt that this was final evidence that Lincoln was unable to act as the forceful leader of their party, and began renewing their earlier efforts to come up with another candidate with more color and appeal. Even such a loyal supporter as Governor John Andrew was getting nervous about persistent rumors that Lincoln might knuckle under to some local Hunker Republicans who favored a negotiated settlement that would allow the South to keep slavery. The Massachusetts governor felt constrained to join with some so-called War Republicans in talking about ways to persuade Lincoln to step aside in favor of a more aggressive candidate who would have a better chance of winning in November.[66]

The Democrats also used the discouraging news from the front as a basis for attacking the inefficient war effort, the enormity of the casualty lists, and Lincoln's ineptitude as commander in chief. The *Post* reported that Northerners displayed "evident disappointment" that "neither Richmond, Charleston, Mobile, or Atlanta had been captured" by Union forces, and placed heavy responsibility for this failure upon Lincoln himself. The Richmond campaign, the *Post* said, had "certainly been dictated by President Lincoln," who was responsible for its failure because "General Grant had been ordered to proceed to Richmond in a way not possible for him to go."[67] The Democrats' inference was very clear: Lincoln's bungling interference, which earlier had deprived

General George B. McClellan of victory in his Peninsula campaign, was now interfering with General Grant's operations.

As the summer drew to a close and election day grew nearer, the Democrats stepped up their barrage against the Republican president. They called him the "perpetuator of iniquitous acts"; they accused him of attacks against state sovereignty; they charged him with outrages against personal liberties because of "arbitrary arrests" and with violating freedom of the press. The *Post* charged that the Lincoln administration had secretly adopted a policy of withholding the truth about military reverses and issuing false reports to the nation's press to keep itself in power. "The Administration is bent on a perpetuation of its power," claimed the Democrats, "and a Secretary of War has deliberately imposed upon the community relations not true; hence it has been almost impossible to get at the truth as to the military situation through official telegrams." The time had come, said the *Post,* to "turn out Lincoln" and replace him with a man "of dignity and singleness of devotion to the country." This would be the most "glorious achievement" that could happen "on this planet."[68] *The Boston Pilot* echoed the growing resentment among its working-class readers who protested the way in which rising wartime prices were driving down their wages and their incomes. Under the "iron heel of despotism," the country's poor people were becoming poorer, and the rich were becoming richer. "Lincoln's administration is a failure," announced the paper. "Two-thirds of the American public have allowed one-third to rule them."[69] Throughout Boston, tensions continued to mount, and numerous rallies and political gatherings ended in bloody fistfights and wholesale riots. Although Boston Democrats were distinctly a minority, they appeared to have made up for their inferiority in numbers by extremely vocal and active campaigning for General George B. McClellan. McClellan Clubs sprang up all through the city; "ratification meetings" were frequently reported; and parades or flag-raisings were almost daily occurrences.

Although Bay State Republican leaders seemed confident of an easy victory for Abraham Lincoln, the grass-roots voters of Boston took their campaigning seriously. Rock-throwing was a favorite pastime among rival political groups, and arrests for "rowdyism" and disturbing the peace were an accepted part of most political gatherings. A typical incident occurred at the height of the campaign early in October as a McClellan "caravan" left Marblehead by train en route to Lynn. The Democratic newspaper, the *Boston Post,* reported that the train was "stoned" as it left the Marblehead station; and after the group had arrived in Lynn "all terms of insult to be found in the blackguard's vocabulary were applied to the Democrats in the procession, followed by stones and other dangerous missiles cast at the men . . . seriously injuring citi-

zens and destroying the emblem they wore. These offenses were not perpetrated by a few individuals," emphasized the paper, "but by hundreds,
countenanced by many more in their company." The *Post* demanded an immediate apology from the responsible parties, and insisted that the Republican
party itself should take the blame.[70] Although other accounts of the incident
reported only that "a rock" had been thrown through the train door in Marblehead, a severe disturbance had taken place that night in Lynn, and had not
been an isolated instance of violence during the local campaign. A great deal
of "loose hilarity about the streets" was reported as the people of Boston
waited to hear results from elections in other states in mid-October. As a precaution, on the eve of the November elections, the Board of Aldermen confirmed the nomination of fifty-eight special police officers "in order to fully
insure the preservation of the public peace."[71]

Fortunately for President Lincoln, by early fall the military news took a
decided turn for the better, and the general public began to see the long-range
effects the relentless Union offensive was having upon the hard-pressed Confederate defenders. General Philip Sheridan, the fiery cavalry commander, defeated Jubal Early at Winchester and Fisher's Hill in September, and then
overwhelmed the Confederates at Cedar Creek in the next month.[72] To prevent
the Rebels from using the fertile valley to conduct their destructive raids into
the North while living off the land, Sheridan put the torch to the valley and
reduced the fertile lands to blackened rubble. "Here I am in the 'Valley of
the Shenandoah,'" wrote young Lieutenant Henry Warren Howe of the 30th
Massachusetts Regiment to his grandfather back in Boston. Now a hardened
veteran of three and a half years' service that had taken him from the Louisiana
bayous to the western Virginia hills, where he had recently taken part in battles
at Winchester, Fisher's Hill, and Cedar Creek, Lieutenant Howe found land
that had once been "a beautiful country, teeming with fields of grain and all
other productions necessary for the support of man and beast" now all "laid
waste from the effects of a devastating war."[73]

While readers in the North were buzzing over these dramatic victories,
news came in from General Sherman and his Army of the West, which, up to
now, had been frustrated by Confederate "Joe" Johnston's delaying tactics. In
mid-July, however, President Jefferson Davis, impatient with Johnston's failure
to halt Sherman's march, turned command of the Confederate forces over to
the more aggressive General John B. Hood. Although the new Confederate
commander staggered Sherman with a series of assaults, the Union commander counterattacked and eventually drove the Confederates down into
Alabama. With Atlanta undefended, the Union troops moved into the city un-
opposed, and on September 2, 1864, Sherman sent President Lincoln a laconic
telegram: "Atlanta is ours and fairly won."[74]

With Sherman's capture of Atlanta, with Phil Sheridan clearing the Shenandoah, and with Grant throttling the Richmond defenders at Petersburg, the months of political gloom gradually lifted.[75] "How absolutely this success was to turn the scale in Lincoln's favor," wrote Governor John Andrew later, "one could, at the moment, only guess." Andrew was, in fact, so elated by the encouraging news from the front that a little later he organized a "war meeting" at Faneuil Hall to celebrate Sherman's capture of Atlanta, along with Admiral Farragut's victory at Mobile Bay. "The response was all that could be desired," he recalled. "The hall was packed" as Republicans turned out in great numbers to display their support for reelecting Lincoln. John Murray Forbes was there, along with such party stalwarts as Samuel Ward, Martin Brimmer, Edward Tobey, John Lowell, Jonathan Bowditch, and Patrick T. Jackson. But there too were previously uncommitted businessmen who were now clearly leaning to favor the incumbent. Gardner Brewer, a wealthy wholesaler; Daniel Denny, a successful dry-goods merchant; Henry P. Kidder, of Kidder, Peabody and Company; and a shipowner named William F. Weld added to the growing demand for returning Lincoln to the White House.[76] Facing such overwhelming support, the usually taciturn Governor Andrew was seized by "the cannon fever," his biographer writes, and spoke both eloquently and passionately for supporting all the Republican candidates as a way to bring the war to a victorious conclusion.[77]

By the time the November elections rolled around, Lincoln seemed sure to sweep to victory easily. McClellan made a strong showing in Northern cities with German-American and Irish-American voters, who helped give him an impressive 45 percent of the popular vote. But the Republicans were able to roll up a substantial vote of their own that drew heavily upon the "voters of New England descent" in many parts of the country, as well as enthusiastic support from young soldiers.[78] From the earliest returns, according to historian David Donald, it was clear that the Republicans had won a "huge victory." On November 8, 1864, Lincoln won reelection by carrying every Union state except Delaware, New Jersey, and Kentucky—running up 212 electoral votes to McClellan's meager 21.[79] Governor John Andrew could not contain his excitement over the happy outcome: "We have knocked down and stamped out the last Copperhead ghost in Massachusetts," he exclaimed in a telegram to Frank Howe, undoubtedly further satisfied that he himself had swamped his Democratic opponent by a similar margin.[80] Republican newspapers throughout the Bay State also crowed with delight. The "little 'un" (McClellan) had been "disposed of," they chortled, and were delighted that President Lincoln's reelection had "finally squelched out the Democratic pary." They expressed the hope that all those who had voted for Lincoln and the Union party would now cease waging their "factious opposition" to the war and unite with the

Republicans in a patriotic effort to restore the Union and put a final end to slavery. On Thursday morning, November 10, the Democratic *Boston Post* published a brief statement acknowledging that the "great battle" had been fought, and that the victory had been won by "our opponents." "We submit, not with an ill grace," wrote the editor, "to what must be considered the voice of the people." Beyond that, the paper carried no editorials or political news of any kind on its front page, which was covered with advertisements.[81] The antiadministration *Boston Pilot* also appeared to accept the outcome with good grace, and suggested that now it was time for its readers to "settle down to the ordinary pursuits of life." In a rather conciliatory gesture, considering its earlier opposition to Lincoln on such questions as the draft, emancipation, and employment of black troops, the Catholic weekly called upon its people to give the administration all the support it needed for the next four years in its efforts for "the integrity of the constitution, the preservation of the Union, and the restoration of peace in the land."[82]

With the elections over, Lincoln safely reelected, and the military picture brightening, Massachusetts residents began to relax and enjoy the holiday festivities with more enthusiasm than they had during the war's darker days. Although fall 1864 had boasted an extraordinary Indian summer (the temperature on November 30 had risen to 67°F), December brought extremely cold weather and several severe snowstorms. The horse trolleys were forced to discontinue operations for days because of so much packed snow on the streets, but despite the inconvenience the people greeted the Christmas season in a carefree mood. "Sleighing appears to be fully appreciated, for the broad streets are thronged with gay riders and runners." All was bright, cheerful, and happy—as Christmas should be. Shopping was brisk; streets and shops were "crowded," "thronged" masses of people jammed the markets bent chiefly on procuring a fat goose for Christmas dinner. "We have never seen richer displays of goods suitable for Christmas or New Year's gifts than can now be found in our city's stores," boasted a local newspaper. "A person can get anything he wants." Prices were reported to be "moderate—the times considered," and booksellers agreed that this holiday season had been their best. The day after Christmas was a Monday, and all the banks, courts, schools, and most of the stores were closed as people enjoyed an extra day of leisure. By this time the temperature had dropped to a tingling −15°F. Looking ahead to the new year, most Bostonians relaxed, confident that the war was nearing its end, the men would all be back home again, and the Union would soon be restored to normal. Certainly no one could possibly have predicted the tragic events that lay ahead.

On December 22, 1865, a public ceremony, "The Return of the Colors," was held in Boston. The regimental flags of every Massachusetts regiment were carried to the State House. As each formation came to a halt before the capitol, a color-bearer marched up the steps and presented the flags to Governor Andrew. The banners were then taken into the State House, where they were draped around the pillars of Doric Hall. (Hall of Flags, State House, Boston)

8　The Final Trumpet
~ ~ ~ ~ ~ ~ ~

It was all over now.

On January 2, 1865, Boston began its official new year by inaugurating Mayor Frederic W. Lincoln, Jr., who devoted part of his address to the city's outstanding role in the Civil War. He praised its soldiers for their loyalty and courage, its merchants and manufacturers for expanding their material resources to aid the war effort, and its civilian population for the numerous relief societies they had put into operation over the past three years.[1]

On the same day, the Emancipation Proclamation's second anniversary was celebrated with a military parade and a dinner. Afterward a meeting in Tremont Temple featured the abolitionist Senator Henry Wilson as the main speaker. This celebration seems to have been almost entirely organized by the city's African-American population, although many white people also attended. Anticipating that its long-cherished dream was about to be realized, on January 27 the Massachusetts Anti-Slavery Society held its thirty-second annual meeting at the Melodeon, a Washington Street theater, with Edmund Quincy presiding. Wendell Phillips praised the members for what they had already accomplished, but reminded them that much remained to be done. The meeting also accepted the resolution William Lloyd Garrison offered: when a constitutional amendment abolishing slavery was actually passed, the membership should "terminate the existence of the society."[2]

Emancipation advocates had additional reason to rejoice when, on Wednesday, February 1, the news arrived that Congress had adopted the Thirteenth Amendment, officially abolishing the institution of slavery in the United States.[3] Ratified by three-fourths of the states, this amendment would become part of the U.S. Constitution in December 1865, thus carrying out the guarantees the Radical Republicans had given to Garrison and other abolitionists at the national convention. When word was received that President Lincoln had added his signature to the amendment, signs of jubilation appeared throughout Boston. Upon orders from Governor Andrew, a one-hundred-gun salute was fired on Boston Common on February 2, churchbells rang, chimes pealed, and the national colors were displayed on public and private buildings.[4] Two days later, a Grand Jubilee Meeting at the Music Hall celebrated passage of the amendment, with speeches by William Lloyd Garrison and Benjamin F. Butler. In a typical display of party rivalry, the Republican newspapers hailed the amendment as a "triumph of reason and justice," while the Democratic papers questioned its legality and prophesied that this measure, along with all those enacted by Congress during the rebellion, would be "null and void" when the rebel states were back in the Union.[5]

Soon after the festivities died down, Bay Staters' attention was drawn to the military front when newspapers carried the startling news that General Benjamin F. Butler, former Democratic congressman from Lowell, Union occupation commander in New Orleans, and more recently a potential rival for the presidency, had been removed from his command by President Lincoln's order after failing to take Fort Fisher. That fort was the principal sea defense for Wilmington, North Carolina, and a port from which blockade runners frequently operated. Late in December, a combined land and sea force converged on the fort. The fleet was commanded by Admiral David Porter, the army by General Butler. After an intensive naval bombardment on December 24, Admiral Porter decided that the fort was sufficiently crippled to permit a landing assault. Butler claimed, however, that the defenses were still too strong to allow an assault, and withdrew his forces without attempting to secure a beachhead. The naval command was furious, blamed Butler for the entire expedition's failure, and demanded his removal. On January 8, 1865, General Edward O. C. Ord succeeded General Butler in command of the Army of the James. Interestingly, perhaps because he had deserted his original party and turned Republican, local Democratic newspapers criticized Butler as a "political general" and held him personally responsible for the fiasco at Fort Fisher. Republican papers, on the other hand, treated "Ben" more kindly, reminding their readers that he had already rendered valuable service to the Union cause.[6] By mid-month, however, the controversy had subsided when Union forces, after a massive assault, finally captured Fort Fisher. The Boston Post expressed the opinion that this capture demonstrated the military genius of Grant and Sherman and removed any lingering fears that Great Britain or France might intervene in the American conflict.[7]

Early in 1865 the Republican press gave special attention to reports of atrocities and cruelties inflicted on northern soldiers at the Confederate prison at Andersonville, Georgia. This was a subject that touched northern readers deeply and personally, and led to fierce denunciations of such "outrageous and disgraceful" actions and to demands that those responsible for such cruelties against "our soldiers" must be severely punished. Clara Barton was approached by a former Andersonville prisoner, Dorence Atwater, who had been assigned by Confederate prison officials to record the names of Union soldiers who had died. Fearing that his death records would be lost or misplaced once the war was over, Atwater made a copy of his own, hoping to notify relatives of the more than 12,000 men who had been interred at Andersonville. Knowing Barton's reputation as an advocate for the troops, Atwater asked for her assistance. The Massachusetts woman responded enthusiastically and during July and August 1865, Barton, Atwater, and a detachment of laborers and soldiers traveled to Andersonville cemetery and proceeded to identify and mark the graves of the Union dead. Thanks to their efforts, only 460 graves had to be marked "unknown U.S. soldier." [8]

Boston newspapers such as the *Boston Courier* took a rather cautionary approach to stories coming out of the South, and warned their readers that many reports of "atrocities" had been greatly exaggerated. If Northern troops had occasionally been subjected to "barbarities," said the paper, such practices were neither uniform not systematic. More positive assistance to those in dire need, said the editors of both the *Courier* and the *Boston Journal*, might be achieved by sending supplies of clothing, food, cooking utensils, sewing materials, and other basic necessities to the starving colored population in Washington, D.C., as well as to black people throughout the South. Calls for charitable assistance became more frequent as the Union armies won more victories and as additional Confederate territory passed under Federal control. Most prominent among these were the appeals made during January to aid the inhabitants of Savannah, Georgia, which by that time was occupied by General Sherman's Union troops. The Boston newspapers depicted Savannah's civilian population as destitute, starving, and homeless, and expressed the hope that the Boston community would respond to these appeals with charity and zeal. A public meeting for this purpose was held at Faneuil Hall on January 9, with the renowned orator Edward Everett asking the people of Boston to respond promptly to Savannah's appeal.[9] As a result of this meeting, $21,307 was raised in three days, and packages of food, clothing, and other supplies were sent to the people of Savannah.

At least this one incident seemed to indicate to the people in the North that the war was in its final stages. With Confederate armies being steadily driven back on all fronts, and the civilian population in major Southern cities reduced almost to starvation, final surrender obviously could not be far off. This anticipation of victory was further stimulated early in the year by persistent rumors that Francis P. Blair, Sr., an adviser to President Lincoln and a close friend of Jefferson Davis and his family, had made several trips to Richmond, apparently acting as an unofficial go-between for the warring governments. These rumors took on greater meaning when, on January 12, Blair held a personal interview with the Confederate president in Richmond, but hopes dimmed when it was learned that Davis had refused to negotiate without promise of independence.

Expectations for an end to the fighting were soon aroused again when, on February 3, President Lincoln and Secretary of State Seward met with Vice-President Alexander Stephens and two other Confederate peace commissioners at Hampton Roads. Once again, however, discussions broke down when the Confederates insisted upon Southern independence and Lincoln would consider nothing less than restoring the Union. Republican newspapers in Boston generally praised Lincoln's conduct, questioned Jefferson Davis's motives (the *Boston Transcript* suggested he was desperately stalling for time), and considered the conference a further indication of weakening Confederate morale. Democrats, on the other hand, accused Lincoln of being completely unreasonable in his demands upon the South. Furthermore, they claimed to see the meeting as a distinct tactical advantage for the Confederacy: by meeting with Rebel leaders at all, the Union representatives had unwittingly given formal recognition to the Confederacy as a belligerent.[10] Whichever side they took, however, Bostonians seemed agreed that the struggle's outcome would not be determined by meetings, negotiations, or conferences—but by sword and battle. With this thought in mind, Bay State citizens once again turned to the generals and the battlefields.

By this time, Sherman's massive sweep through the heart of the Confederacy had captured the full attention of the Northern press. Bostonians watched excitedly as Sherman's forces cut through South Carolina and moved closer to Charleston, the port city. "He has a keen eye and most expressive face, and no nonsense about him," wrote a correspondent for the *Boston Daily Advertiser* after interviewing Sherman at Savannah. "He deals with those villainous rebels in the right vein, and takes down their hightone most effectively."[11] By February 20, Columbia, the capital, had fallen into Union hands, and once that happened, Charleston could no longer be defended. With Sherman's army coming up fast, General J. W. Hardee, commanding the Confederate forces in South Carolina and Georgia, ordered Charleston evacuated and its resources destroyed. Buildings, warehouses, and cotton storage sheds were torched; torpedo boats and blockade runners were scuttled or burned. Meanwhile, after first taking possession of Fort Sumter and other harbor defenses, the advancing Union forces received the city's surrender, promising that Union troops would render every possible assistance in "extinguishing the flames." Into the stricken city, with smoke and flames still rising from the skeletal ruins of blackened buildings, marched the Union soldiers, with the 21st U.S. Colored Troops in the lead, followed by a detachment of two companies from the 54th Massachusetts Regiment. After distinguishing themselves at Battery Wagner, where they had led the gallant charge, the African-American unit from Boston had taken an active part in the fighting around Charleston. Along with many former South Carolina slaves who now composed the 3rd and 4th South Carolina Regiments, the Bostonians were among the first Federal troops to enter the city where the war had begun.[12] Confident and disciplined, the Union troops marched into the fallen city in close-order formation and then, in a business-like manner, stacked their weapons and set about manning the pumps, putting out the fires, and saving whatever property could be rescued. The sight of so many African-American troops so prominent in the clean-up deeply impressed Charles Coffin, a reporter for the *Boston Journal.* "On this ever memorable day," he wrote with obvious emotion, "they made manifest to the world their superiority in honor and humility." Here were former slaves, now in uniform, he observed, "with the old flag above them, keeping step to freedom's drum beat, up the grass-grown streets, past the slave shambles." Then, laying aside their rifles, they worked the fire-engines, and "in the spirit of the Redeemer of men, saving that which was lost."[13]

Three days later, troops from the 55th Massachusetts Regiment, the second black unit recruited by Governor Andrew, entered Charleston, singing "John Brown's Body" as they marched to their assigned barracks, with Lieutenant George Thompson Garrison, son of the famed Boston abolitionist, commanding one of the companies. Seeing so many additional African Americans in blue uniforms caused even further rejoicing among the city's black population as they showered the troops with prayers and blessings and occasionally rushed into the columns to embrace them and kiss their hands. On March 3, two weeks after the initial occupation, Charleston's African-American women held a formal ceremony in which they presented to the black regiments three flags. With the Stars and Stripes flying in the breeze, the Union troops were drawn up in parade formation on the bright green grass before the South Carolina military academy, The Citadel. The immense irony in the situation was not lost upon the Boston abolitionist Wendell Phillips, who was beside himself with joy. "Can you conceive a bitterer drop that God's chemistry could mix for a son of the Palmetto State," he asked, "than that a Massachusetts flag and a colored regiment should take possession of Charleston?"[14]

Back in Boston, readers had kept up with the daily reports on Sherman's relentless advance. Then, on February 21, the headlines carried the news that Charleston had been taken. In one of the war's most frenzied outbursts of joy, Bostonians used Washington's Birthday to touch off a jubilant celebration over Charleston's fall. The Stars and Stripes crackled in the crisp air from public buildings, private residences, churches, stores, and hotels throughout the city.

One-hundred-gun salutes sounded from Boston Common and Dorchester Heights. Three companies of the Boston Light Infantry (the Tigers) started out from their Pine Street armory, marched along Washington, Franklin, Devonshire, Milk, India, and State streets, and then back to their quarters in the South End. Throughout the city, as well as in Roxbury, Cambridge, and Charlestown, followed steady rounds of commemorations, concerts, demonstrations, exercises, and dinners. Most shops and small businesses were closed down for the day, but the city happened to be having its annual "Trade Sale of Dry Goods." The major department stores were open, and Washington Street was thronged with people either celebrating the rebellion's imminent collapse or shopping to their heart's content—or both.[15]

General Sherman was universally hailed as a "genius" and a "military master," and the *Boston Journal* announced him to be without parallel in this or any other modern war, a warrior who was accomplishing his task "gloriously and promptly."[16] The atmosphere of the moment was heady with excitement, for people could not believe their good fortune at the "glorious" news reports that kept piling up. "Victory follows victory so swiftly," wrote the *Boston Daily Advertiser* editor, "that the glory and importance of one is not fairly appreciated before the public mind is diverted from it by the news of a fresh triumph."[17]

Only ten days later, even as the optimistic spirit still prevailed, President Abraham Lincoln prepared to embark upon his second term of office. Like the people, Lincoln could see that the end of the war was close at hand, and in his second inaugural address he revealed his own ideals and attitudes about the defeated South and also tried to shape the American people's minds and feelings. With words and phrases that continue to rank with the greatest written prose, Lincoln patiently endeavored to explain how two sides, diametrically opposed in their beliefs and values, could have clung so steadfastly to their convictions and called upon Almighty God to witness the righteousness of their cause. But God, said Lincoln, had His own purposes, and His own way of rendering justice—and this terrible conflict would not end for either side until "every drop of blood drawn with the lash would be paid by another drawn with the sword." Viewing the war, therefore, as a just and provident punishment by Almighty God for the evils both North and South had perpetrated in the past, Lincoln saw that war's end as an opportunity for both sections, purged and cleansed by an awful fire, to finally reunite—"with malice toward none; with charity for all."[18]

Except for some complaints by Democrats that Lincoln had not been specific enough in stating the future terms of "forgiveness," most Boston newspapers greeted Lincoln's second inaugural address with respect and attention, praising it for brevity and for invoking Divine Providence. Inauguration Day saw festivities continue in the city. Most businesses closed early, services were held in the churches, and a salute was fired on Boston Common. In the evening, the places of amusement were well attended, and in some parts of the city the public was treated to displays of fireworks and rockets. The only thing that marred an otherwise festive occasion were reports that Andrew Johnson of Tennessee, the new vice-president, had been intoxicated at the inauguration ceremonies. Reaction to this shocking behavior ranged from expressions of "mortification" to outright demands for his impeachment. A. G. Browne, Jr., personal secretary to Governor Andrew, made it a point to write to the governor from Washington to halt the growing apprehension that the vice-president was a "drunkard." Johnson, explained Browne, was the tragic victim of an unfortunate accident, which occurred when the vice-president had taken a little liquor that disastrously affected a system badly weakened by a six-month bout with typhoid fever.[19]

With the Inauguration Day events over, the people were once again free to turn back to military events and to speculate upon their significance. Speculation, in fact, was about all Northern readers had to rely on, for almost no information was known about Sherman and his army after they had advanced beyond Charleston. People thus had a little more time to observe developments in northern Virginia, where Grant was maintaining his relentless siege around the Petersburg defenses. By now, a definite feeling was in the air that victory was close and that all that was needed was one battle to end it all. "A hopeful spirit pervades the entire community," observed *The Boston Pilot.* "There is great reason to believe that the end of our great struggle is near at hand." [20] And they had good reason for this hopeful spirit. With Grant encamped to the east, and Sherman coming up from the south, General Robert E. Lee saw that he must either escape the closing pincers—or perish. On March 25 he attacked Fort Stedman at the eastern end of the Union lines, but was driven back toward Richmond.[21] A week later he struck at Grant's left flank near Five Forks, but again the Army of Northern Virginia was beaten back into its defenses. It was clear that the Confederate defenders could no longer hold out against the growing power wielded by Grant and his forces.[22]

On Sunday, April 2, Jefferson Davis was attending services at St. Paul's Church when he was handed a telegram from General Robert E. Lee, informing him that the Army of Northern Virginia was being withdrawn from its defensive positions at Petersburg. The meaning of the message was quite clear: because Richmond could no longer be defended, and Lee and his army were moving westward, hoping to make a defensive stand elsewhere, the city would have to be evacuated and the officers of the Confederacy forced to flee the capital. By afternoon, news of the evacuation had spread throughout the city, and with members of the government already on their way out of town, other residents were streaming toward the railroad station, taking any money, property, and other valuables they could carry. By nightfall the city was in flames, the fires touched off by order of Confederate General Richard S. Ewell and gleefully spread by hoodlums.

At daybreak on April 3, about an hour after the last contingent of Rebel soldiers had made their way through the smoke and burned the Fourteenth Street bridge behind them, Union troops came marching into the burning city, tramping along Main Street with flags flying and drums beating. At the head of the column came the 5th Massachusetts Cavalry, the elite black cavalry regiment formed by Governor John Andrew, and now commanded by Colonel Charles Francis Adams, Jr., grandson of President John Quincy Adams.[23] Flanked by two white regiments, the 5th was soon followed by companies from the 29th Connecticut Colored Volunteers and the 9th U.S. Colored Troops. The black residents of Richmond were overcome with joy. To see men of color marching along in formation, their heads high, with rifles over their shoulders, was one thing. But to see mounted black cavalry troopers, waving their flashing sabres aloft, was almost too much to grasp. The black residents' cheers were deafening, and white citizens were, wrote Confederate War Clerk John B. Jones, an inveterate diarist, "annoyed that the city should be held mostly by Negro troops."[24] Besides hauling down the Confederate flag from the state capitol and running up the Stars and Stripes, however, the Union troops had little time or inclination to lord it over their beaten foes. Stacking their rifles and laying aside their gear, they began working the fire pumps, formed bucket brigades, poured water on the flames, pulled down some structures, blew up others—all trying to get the flames under control. At the same time they monitored crosswalks, arrested looters, protected private property, policed the streets, and restored law and order to the city.[25] The *Boston Daily Advertiser* took obvious pleasure in describing for its readers the actions of "drunken Rebel soldiers" who vandalized their own city, and reporting the "utmost cordiality of feeling" between the residents and the soldiers. The local citizens, said the newspaper, apparently are "delighted with the boys in blue."[26] Allowing for some parochial exaggeration, even a member of one of the city's most prominent families had to concede that the Yankee troops' conduct was exceptional: "The military was for the most part courteous," she wrote, "and the people gladly cooperated . . . to restore order."[27]

More than any other Union victory so far, news that the Confederate capital had fallen sent Boston into wild rejoicing. "Never before," said the *Boston Journal*, "have we known the bare announcement of a great event to prove so satisfactory as the capture of Richmond." State Street and the Merchants' Exchange were thronged with excited people, recalled William Schouler, and bulletin boards outside the newspaper offices proclaimed: "Richmond Occupied by the Union forces." After some of the initial excitement had died down, a meeting was organized in the Merchants' Exchange and the Reverend Mr. Hepworth was called upon to offer a prayer. The people silently bowed their heads and listened to "the outpourings of gratitude and thanksgiving" for such a welcome victory. Then everyone joined in an emotional rendition of "America."[28] Outside the building were "demonstrations of delight." Flags were thrown up all over the city, and at noon Gilmore's Band was stationed in front of the Exchange building and played popular airs while an immense crowd swayed to and fro in time to the music "like the waters of the ocean," cheering and hugging each other with uncontrolled joy. Shortly after 1:00, all the bells in the city were rung and then, by Governor Andrew's order, a one-hundred-gun salute was fired on Boston Common. State Street and Washington Street were filled with people who embraced each other happily and discussed the latest news with breathless excitement. Throughout the city, newspaper offices, hotels, bars, and all public places were filled to overflowing with people who laughed and chattered noisily. Gilmore's Band marched to various places throughout the city to perform in honor of the occasion; at night, illuminations and fireworks lit up the sky, and even the police officials cooperated in the general spirit of goodwill and festivity by not exacting the usual fines from celebrants who became too intoxicated.[29] *The Boston Pilot* also joined in the celebrations, hailing the fall of Richmond and also pointing out to its readers that Sherman's army was still "steadily and sturdily" forcing its way northward. "Its strong Irish-American 'contingent,'" said the paper proudly, "participates in all its battles, triumphs, and honors."[30]

And the celebrations were by no means confined to the city. In Roxbury, the State Guards marched through the streets all evening, accompanied by large groups of residents, and in Elliott Square, houses were all illuminated and the people treated to a grand display of fireworks. At 9:00, a one-hundred-gun salute was fired, after which the churchbells in the town were rung from 9:00 until 10:00 P.M. In Charlestown, too, the news was heralded by ringing churchbells and flag displays everywhere. At noon, 4,000 workmen at the Charlestown Navy Yard had assembled in front of the commandant's residence and listened to the admiral make a patriotic speech. When it was over, the workmen applauded, gave three rousing cheers for General Grant and the "Potomac Army," and then fired off a salute from the Navy Yard guns. In the evening illuminations and fireworks followed. And over in Cambridge, evening meetings were held to cheer the wonderful victory and praise the Union troops. The mayor announced that the city's bells would be rung, and called upon residents to illuminate their houses and publicly display the red, white, and blue, and the Walcott Guards marched through the streets, cheering for the Union and for General Grant.[31]

One noticeable feature in the Boston celebrations was that General Grant was beginning to receive some of the praise that had been withheld from him, as papers commended him for his sound judgment, his effectiveness, and his execution of military maneuvers. Already people were discussing postwar reconstruction policies upon which the South would be permitted to return to the Union. But these considerations were quickly thrust into the background when the news came that on April 9, with his army whittled down to 30,000 men, his supplies nearly exhausted, and encircled by combined Union forces, General Robert E. Lee had bowed to the inevitable and surrendered to General Grant at Appomattox Courthouse. For all practical purposes the war was over.

On April 10, the *Boston Daily Advertiser* proclaimed PEACE! in bold capital headlines on the front page of its morning edition. Under a line engraving of an American Eagle was the announcement that GENERAL LEE AND HIS WHOLE ARMY had surrendered.[32] "The joyful news of the surrender of General Lee and the entire army under his command has thrown Boston and the whole country into a state of enthusiastic excitement and rejoicing," agreed the *Boston Journal*.[33] That it was raining in Boston did not dampen the city's enthusiasm. Flags appeared everywhere, people fired guns in public, stores were decorated, schools, banks, and public offices were closed. Impromptu celebrations were held at Franklin Street, at Winthrop Square, and at Union Park, with impassioned speeches and patriotic band music. And at night the city was once again treated to illuminations and fireworks. "Everybody was allowed to get drunk," complained Fr. James Healy, the Catholic chancellor of the diocese. "Liquor dealers dispensed their fluids gratis, and the Judges dismissed the arrests without trial."[34] "Our usually staid citizens let themselves loose yesterday upon learning that Lee and his army had surrendered to General Grant, and that the war was virtually ended," reported the *Boston Daily Advertiser*. "It was one of the greatest days Boston ever saw, and was like a dozen 'Fourths of July' concentrated into one day."[35] Boston newspapers regarded this victory as a promise of coming peace, and hailed the honorable arrangements worked out between General Grant and General Lee as one of the noblest spectacles in the war. "It was arranged with the delicacy and generosity which became honorable opponents who respected each other." The *Boston Post* editors even went so far as to suggest that for his military successes during the past two years, Ulysses S. Grant merited the title of "the second George Washington."

With the war perceptibly at an end, discussion over reconstruction plans now grew more heated, and Lincoln himself added to the growing controversy. To the crowd of jubilant people who came to "serenade" him in Washington on Tuesday night after he had returned from conversing with General Grant at City Point, Virginia, the president spoke thoughtfully, soberly. He did not revel in the military victory just achieved; instead, he dwelt upon the complex problems to be solved in the coming months. Urgently he pleaded that the nation get at the business of restoring the Union as quickly and as painlessly as possible, and not become embroiled in pointless arguments about such legal technicalities as whether the Southern states had been "in" or "out" of the Union. "Finding themselves at home," he said, obviously trying to break the semantic logjam, "it would be utterly immaterial whether they had ever been abroad."

The Boston press mirrored the divided sentiments on how to treat defeated Confederates and the future of the seceded states. Bay State Republicans who were loyal to the administration agreed that it was their duty to stand by the president and support his amnesty program "no matter whether we think it ill-advised or not." [36] Radical Republicans such as Charles Sumner and abolitionist spokesmen such as Wendell Phillips, however, opposed the president's ideas on amnesty and reconstruction because they failed to guarantee African Americans future civil and political rights, and also because they failed to agree that the seceded states were out of the Union. The rebel was a U.S. citizen, insisted the *Springfield Republican,* and could be forgiven and restored "if he repents," but would be excluded from all citizenship rights "if he continues obdurate." [37] And all the while, Boston Democrats loudly complained that Lincoln's approach would destroy the very "germ" of American liberty. Because the Union was composed of independent sovereign states, it argued, it was impossible to "thrust any state out of the Union" because some of its citizens had resorted to rebellion.[38]

With war's horror now behind him, and the obviously controversial reconstruction problems lying before him, a desperately fatigued Lincoln agreed to a momentary respite from the cares of office and accompanied his wife to Ford's Theater to enjoy the relaxing witticisms in *Our American Cousin.* As the president leaned back in the comfortable rocking chair to enjoy the amusing comedy, a silent figure stepped into the box, raised his arm in a quick, sure movement, and sent a bullet crashing into the nodding, unprotected head of Abraham Lincoln.

On Saturday morning, April 15, Amos A. Lawrence was just sitting down to breakfast at his home in Brookline when the maid burst into the dining room with the terrible news that the president had been assassinated. Even as she stood there wringing her hands in consternation, the Brookline bell began to toll, and soon the mournful peal sounded through every city and town in the Commonwealth. ASSASSINATION OF PRESIDENT LINCOLN!! was the *Boston Daily Advertiser*'s headline announcing the news to Boston residents and reporting that official Washington was "Mad with Excitement." [39] All citizens, regardless of their attitudes toward Abraham Lincoln or his official policies, were stunned and aghast at this appalling event that had come, one newspaper phrased it, "like a thunderbolt from a clear sky." The faces of men and women that, only the day before, had been radiant with joy over the war's end, were now bathed in tears and twisted in anguish. "As one passes along the street," observed the *Boston Journal*, "strong men are met with their eyes dimmed with tears." People were packed in crowded masses on the sidewalks, in the newspaper offices, and in the reading rooms, shaking their heads in disbelief and desperately hoping that perhaps, at the last moment, they might hear that the reports were wrong and that Lincoln still lived.[40]

But no, the flurry of incoming news only confirmed the awful fact: President Abraham Lincoln was dead. Flags that yesterday had fluttered over the joyous city celebrating victory now drooped at half mast while bells tolled out their mournful dirge. "It is indeed a sad day in Boston," said the *Boston Journal*. The only sounds that could be heard were muffled groans of "horrible!" "awful!" "cruel!"—with an occasional oath that the Rebels would pay dearly for this terrible deed. One of the many ironies in that tragic time was that on the very Saturday on which Boston heard the news about the president's assassination, the actor Edwin Booth, brother of the assassin, John Wilkes Booth, was to have opened in *Hamlet* at the Boston Theater. The stricken tragedian canceled the engagement because his brother had committed the heinous crime, and also in homage to a "justly honored and patriotic ruler who has fallen in an hour of national joy."[41]

The next day, April 16, was Easter Sunday. Even as the martyred president's corpse lay in the northwest wing of the White House, dressed in the plain black clothes he had worn at his recent inauguration, Boston churches were more crowded than they had ever been. After services, the streets were thronged with people who moved along slowly, silently, and without expression, like shadow figures in a strange dream, awakening only to look up anxiously from time to time to inquire whether more news had come, any new developments. As if in response, the *Boston Daily Advertiser* printed a special Sunday edition, reporting the latest news coming in from Washington about the conspiracy that had murdered President Lincoln and seriously wounded Secretary of State William Seward.[42]

On Wednesday, April 19, Abraham Lincoln's funeral took place in the nation's capital. Ironically, this was the very day that, only a week earlier, Governor Andrew had urged President Lincoln to proclaim as a day of national thanksgiving for the capture of Richmond. He had suggested April 19 because it was the anniversary of the Battle of Lexington as well as the day the 6th Massachusetts Regiment fought its way across Baltimore to come to Washington's defense. Now, on April 19, the Massachusetts governor attended the funeral ceremonies for the president in the East Room of the White House.[43]

And then, in a great and solemn pageant, the beloved president's remains were removed from the White House and taken to the Capitol as throngs of people looked on in silent sadness and wept openly.

Back in Boston, the day was clear and sunny; everything in the city was closed down on the day of the funeral in solemn tribute to the occasion; every house displayed some public symbol of mourning. Horsecars were withdrawn from service for the day, and operation of the cars on the steam railroad was suspended between 12:00 and 2:00 P.M. Churches everywhere held special noontime services, which were attended by overflow throngs who, rich and poor alike, were dressed in black as they filed into the churches, somber and silent. At 2:00 the bells in the city tolled, and then minute guns fired their farewell salutes. Later in the afternoon, several thousand residents held an impromptu ceremony on Boston Common in one final effort to express their grief for their fallen leader.[44]

Slowly, ever so slowly, as the shock began to wear off, Bostonians awakened from stark tragedy's numbness and looked around them at what was going on. Andrew Johnson of Tennessee had been promptly sworn in to office at 10:00 in the morning on April 15 (less than three hours after Lincoln had been pronounced dead) by Chief Justice Salmon P. Chase. Although some Bostonians had reservations about Johnson's abilities, his southern birth, and his uncouth personal characteristics, most expressed confidence in his ability to lead the nation in the days ahead. These feelings were bolstered almost immediately by the new president's first public announcement, promising dire punishment for those responsible for the assassination, and calling for forceful measures against the Confederacy's leaders. These pronouncements did much to help the populace in the North pull itself together and throw its support behind President Johnson. "The Army is very much excited at all the news of the assassination of our President," young Nathan Appleton wrote to his mother, "but our first feelings over, we feel we must arrange things as best we can. Truly we Americans are a mighty people."

For most Bostonians, the last sounds of the wartime trumpets echoed through the city at the end of the year. On December 22, 1865, on Forefathers' Day, commemorating the Pilgrims' landing at Plymouth 245 years earlier, a public ceremony was held in Boston to honor the formal return of the flags. In a procession that included infantry, artillery, and cavalry divisions representing every Bay State regiment, each unit's regimental flags were carried through the snowy streets and presented to Governor John Andrew, who stood in front of the State House. The colors were taken from the governor to Doric Hall, and later placed in Memorial Hall, or the Hall of Flags, as a permanent tribute to the part Massachusetts had played in preserving the Union.[45]

But perhaps the last melancholy reminder of the Brothers' War was the tired, dejected, fifty-year-old Confederate prisoner who sat alone in his room in Fort Warren. Soon after the fighting had ended, federal troops arrested Alexander Hamilton Stephens, Vice-President of the Confederate States of America, at his home in Georgia. Sent to Fort Warren by ship, Stephens and his party reached Boston Harbor at night on May 24, 1865, and the next day he was locked in a front room. "For the first time in my life," he wrote in his journal, "I had the full realization of being a prisoner." [46] For the first two months of his confinement, Stephens was allowed out of his room only long enough to walk along the parapet and look out on Boston Harbor. On July 29, however, the lock was taken off his door and he was permitted to walk the grounds anytime between sunrise and sunset. Finally, after being a prisoner for some five months, Stephens was released, and on the evening of October 13 he boarded the ship that would take him back to Georgia. "O God," he wrote as the final entry in his prison journal, "deliver me from all evil." [47] The last Rebel had left Boston; it was all over.

~ ~ ~

THE CIVIL WAR, it is true, was finally over, but what of the larger questions about the conflict's more lasting effects on the elements that made up the greater Boston community? Four years is not a very long time in the enormous sweep of world history, but those four years of war and suffering were enough to significantly change everyday life for the people who made their home in Boston.

Among the members of Boston's highly respected business community, the Civil War changed both political affiliations and social attitudes. For at least a quarter of a century, since William Lloyd Garrison had launched his attack against slavery in 1831, most of the city's "gentlemen of property and standing" had remained aloof from the unsavory controversy. They generally did not approve of the South's peculiar institution, but as long as it was sanctioned by the Constitution, they were willing to allow their Southern brethren to deal with it in their own fashion—especially because a good part of their substantial income derived from Cotton Kingdom products. As Whig party leaders, the so-called Cotton Whigs considered slavery a matter of individual conscience, and refused to allow it to become a political plank in their party's platform. Only in 1854, when Senator Stephen Douglas's Kansas-Nebraska Act allowed slavery to expand north of the 36°30' line, did Boston businessmen finally rise to the bait. Joining their angry colleagues in other Northern states, the Boston men organized Emigrant Aid companies to flood the disputed territory with Free-Soil settlers and turn the tide in favor of freedom. Although they still tried to assure their Southern brethren that they had not become abolitionists, the changing tide of history quickly carried the business community along in a different direction. The Kansas crisis almost immediately collapsed the old Whig party, leaving businessmen such as John Murray Forbes little option but to join the new Republican party. Only a few "old Hunkers" such as Amos A. Lawrence clung to the hope that the middle-of-the-road Constitutional Union Party might still attract a majority of voters in the 1860 election. But when the quixotic gesture failed, the attack on Fort Sumter in the following April swept the last of the old Whig stalwarts into the Republican fold.[48]

Once the war was an accomplished fact, the city's businessmen acknowledged the inevitable, rallied 'round the flag, and supported the Lincoln administration. In the fighting's opening days, they provided the state government with their individual managerial expertise and their collective financial resources. They arranged for military transportation, both by water and by rail; they supported the governor's emergency expenditures until the state legislature could take appropriate action; they recruited soldiers, raised regiments, and trained troops at their own expense. Above all, they brought to the national war effort moral support and civic influence from Boston's highly respected community.

As the Civil War expanded, the status of African Americans was much discussed by the business community. Before the war, conservative Bostonians often sympathized with the plight of African-American slaves in the South, but we find little evidence that these people demonstrated much disquiet for, or knowledge about, the city's free African-American community on the other side of Beacon Hill. With the war on, however, African Americans quickly became a consideration for those who set out to win the war and preserve the Union. Surprisingly, considering their previous lack of interest in African Americans' present status or future prospects, Boston businessmen were quickly reconciled to the idea of emancipating the slaves. By summer 1862, in fact, it seemed that most of the city's businessmen were pressing for some kind of national statement on human freedom. A goal that only a few years earlier would have seemed outlandish now appeared so obvious that many Boston business leaders could not understand what was taking President Lincoln so long to carry it out.

With the Union Club on Park Street as a focal point for Lincoln supporters, the members used the Loyal Publication Society to back the president and also to argue for emancipation, recruiting black troops, and supporting projects designed to help African Americans make the adjustment from slavery to freedom. Drawing upon their earlier experiences in Kansas, several local businessmen proposed that the federal government establish colonies in such Confederate states as Texas, Florida, and the Sea Islands off the South Carolina coast. Here, under Yankee supervision, they would provide free blacks with a "Boston-style" education that would inform their minds, mold their characters, and prepare them for efficiently producing cotton under a free-labor system. Unlike the abolitionist, the typical businessman founded his attitude toward the freed slave not so much on religion or morality as on political equality and sound business practices. "I do not pretend to be philanthropic, or to love the negro, and still less the Irishman, or the Englishman," John Murray Forbes told the abolitionist Wendell Phillips. His approach was based on "a thoroughgoing, hearty belief in the expediency, and justice, and necessity of equal rights, and a thorough disgust of anything like aristocratic or class badges."[49] As soon as President Lincoln's Emancipation Proclamation went into effect in January 1863, making it legal for African Americans to be used in the armed forces, local businessmen also took the lead in creating the all-black 54th and 55th infantry regiments and the elite 5th Cavalry, which made free black Americans part of the nation's military system.

It was precisely this emphasis on the exclusively political basis for racial equality that led Boston business leaders, at war's end, to withhold benefits or opportunities for former slaves beyond those specifically guaranteed to them by constitutional amendment or legislative enactment. Despite emotional pleas by Radicals and abolitionists, who argued that former slaves had "earned" the right to possess their own piece of land—their own "forty acres and a mule,"—by their lifetime of unpaid bondage, the businessmen would not countenance confiscating private property or allocating free land beyond that already permitted under the Homestead Act. Northern proponents of the free-labor ideology greatly emphasized hard work, thrift, sobriety, personal initiative, and the other well-known virtues of the Protestant work ethic. They firmly believed that former slaves would gain much more by eventually purchasing their own piece of land by their own diligence and labor than by receiving a handout from the federal government. African Americans might deserve any educational skills and vocational training needed to help them gain an equal advantage in the competition for upward mobility. Beyond that, however, they did not warrant special economic entitlements or material advantages exceeding those enjoyed by all American citizens.

If Boston businessmen's social attitude changed substantially during the Civil War, their traditional economic philosophy was sturdily reinforced by the remarkable Republican legislative successes in a wartime Congress free of opposition by Southern Democrats. The traditional Whig economic philosophy had been based upon these ideals: a strong central government, a coherent national economic policy, a coordinated national banking system, a protective tariff to promote American manufacturing, and a generous program with federal appropriations for constructing roads, canals, bridges, harbors, and other so-called internal improvements. Ever since the national political success that Andrew Jackson and his Democratic party won in 1828, however, the Whigs had been frustrated in trying to implement these policies. Committed to their own philosophy of states' rights, rural agrarianism, limited spending, and local banking, successive Southern Democrats made certain that any and all Whig legislative proposals met an early death in the U.S. Congress.

The Civil War and abdication of their seats in the House and Senate by Southern senators and representatives opened up the legislative system for the first time to a remarkable stream of Republican economic programs that changed the face of industrial America until well into the twentieth century. Abnormal demands by a wartime economy greatly accelerated an industrial economy that had been slowly taking shape over the past two decades. Factories rapidly proliferated to produce war goods, mechanization spread throughout the factory system, new inventions multiplied, and interchangeable parts were extensively used in production assembly lines, all radically altering the nation's industrial system. And Republican party leaders were making sure that the new national administration would steer these profound changes in the right direction. Without Southern opposition, the Republicans could create a national currency with their system of greenbacks and national banknotes, and organize a national banking structure. The Homestead Act offered free public land to settlers who wanted it; the Morrill Act created land-grant colleges for teaching "agricultural and mechanical arts"; the Pacific Railroad Act gave away thousands of acres of public land that eventually opened up vast regions in the West to transcontinental railroads. The Republican Congress had, in effect, drafted, one historian writes, "a blueprint for modern America" by endorsing an industrialized, capital-intensive, national business structure in which the Republican-dominated federal government would be an active and supportive participant.[50]

Ironically, however, the very industrial system the Boston businessmen so enthusiastically endorsed at war's end was one that would quickly leave a parochial and outmoded Bay State economy in the lurch. By the 1870s, America's "Age of Big Business" was in full sway, with more railroads, larger factories, more sophisticated machinery, greater production, and higher profits than ever before. Before the Civil War, much of the nation had always looked to Boston, the "Hub of the Universe," as a leading center of diversified industrial investment and ingenious capital enterprise. By the time the war had ended, however, the Bay State's financial efforts were rapidly fading into insignificance compared with the gigantic corporate structures and the incredible sums of money being accumulated by such new entrepreneurial giants as Cornelius Vanderbilt, John D. Rockefeller, and Andrew Carnegie. The new fortunes being made in new enterprises dwarfed the incomes derived from old New England shipyards, traditional family businesses, and deteriorating textile mills. It was clear that the old Yankee dollar was no longer what it used to be. "It is time that we perished," confided the historian Brooks Adams gloomily to his older brother, Henry. "The world is tired of us." [51]

Not only had the nation changed industrially and technologically, but the tone and flavor of postwar American society had been transformed. In an age characterized more and more by material forces and secular philosophies, Puritan Christianity's old moral concepts seemed alarmingly out of place. Alexander Hamilton's rational laissez-faire system had become a highly competitive dog-eat-dog jungle where only "the fit" were entitled to survive. The idealistic self-reliance doctrine preached by Ralph Waldo Emerson and Henry David Thoreau was now reduced to mere personal greed and self-satisfaction. Individualism had become "every man for himself"; independence was now interpreted as "the public be damned." Lavish and often vulgar displays of personal wealth, the tasteless scramble to collect mediocre art and to construct sumptuous buildings, and Big Business's all-pervading influence in the nation's corrupt affairs during the scandalous Grant administration convinced many Bostonians that the "new" America was no longer *their* America. [52]

Though long-range prospects for Boston's business community were moving away from the bright outlook they envisioned as the Civil War came to its conclusion, the future seemed much more promising for the city's substantial Irish community. For one thing, the war provided a sudden and quite unexpected opportunity for Irish Catholics to gain a measure of acceptance that would have seemed unthinkable only a few years earlier. The Great Famine of 1846–1847 had produced such an incredible flood of impoverished Irish immigrants that by the mid-1850s a powerful national reaction, the Know-Nothing movement, threatened to cut off all further foreign immigration and reduce immigrants who were already here to a permanent underclass. Most orthodox Protestants of Anglo-Saxon heritage assumed that Irish Catholics were an illiterate, barbarous, and totally unreliable people who would never become assimilated into American culture, and who could never adapt themselves to the nation's democratic political structure.

With the Rebel attack on Fort Sumter, however, and the great conflict in which every able-bodied citizen was regarded as essential, Boston's large Irish-Catholic population became a human resource that could be neither ignored nor neglected. Native Bostonians encouraged the newcomers to enlist, but also vigorously applauded forming separate and distinctive Irish regiments. The loyalty to the Union that the Irish community displayed and the gallantry with which they fought on the battlefields did much to erase, or at least greatly reduce, the troublesome old questions about the Irish ability to assimilate into the American way of life. The honorary degree awarded to the Catholic Bishop of Boston by Harvard College was the city leaders' calculated public demonstration of a new tolerance; this initial gesture of friendship was soon followed by similar concessions. The new instructions to school committees to modify their requirements that Catholic children use the King James Bible or recite unfamiliar versions of Protestant prayers; the agreement to allow Boston City Hospital patients to be attended by a Catholic priest; repeal of the naturalization law requiring a two-year waiting period—these were tangible signs that the Irish were about to enter upon a new and less hostile phase in their lives as Boston residents.

The war not only changed native-born Americans' way of looking at the Irish, but also changed the way in which many of the Irish looked at themselves—especially at their relationship with their country. Irishmen flocked to the colors, signed up with the 9th Regiment, joined the 28th Regiment, for various reasons: to demonstrate their manly courage, to impress their family and friends, to display their loyalty to the Union, to show off for their girlfriends. Peter Welsh of Charlestown got roaring drunk with the boys one night and, rather than return home and face his wife, Margaret, he joined the army next morning. Whatever their individual motives, clearly most of them were also motivated by a desire to fight for the country that had given them shelter in their time of need, and for the Constitution that guaranteed their liberties. Here was a deep sense of gratitude and obligation from an oppressed people to an adopted land that had saved them from oblivion and given them almost everything they owned. During the great struggle, however, when so many men bravely risked life and limb in the inferno of battle, a subtle transformation took place in their own thinking. Many Irishmen began to realize that they were undergoing such great suffering not merely from a sense of obligation to defend someone else's country. No; it was their *own* country they were fighting for. They were truly Americans—their pain and anguish told them so. "This is my country as much as the man that was born on the soil," Peter Welsh wrote to Margaret on February 3, 1863, from an encampment in Virginia. "And so it is with every man who comes to this country and becomes a citizen."[53] This was one Irishman whose experience in the armed services convinced him that he was no longer simply a lodger in someone else's home, but an integral part of the American experiment with a responsibility to the future, even though he realized that he himself might never benefit from it. "It is our duty to do our share for the common wellfare," he told his wife, "not only of the present generation but of future generations."[54]

The four-year conflict was a significant transitional period for Irish social status and also improved their depressed economic circumstances. By joining the Union army and getting a generous bonus, or by gaining employment in nearby armories and shipyards, Irishmen had their first real opportunity to make a little money and gain more acceptance in a community that usually regarded them as little more than lazy loafers. Although many skilled Irish craftsmen are listed on the trade-union rolls of the period as longshoremen, carpenters, tailors, stonecutters, and waiters, most immigrants were still categorized as "labourers"—untrained and unskilled. By the time the war started, however, the newly invented sewing machine, as well as many other new mechanical devices, had made it possible even for "greenhorns" to perform fairly complicated tasks that had once been handled exclusively by highly skilled craftsmen. Many more Irish workers could find employment in garment shops, textile mills, and shoe factories throughout the area by the time the Civil War had begun; and by war's end Irish workers had joined several more trade unions. The Knights of St. Crispin and the Daughters of St. Crispin were then electing Catholic as well as Protestant shoe workers as officers in their associations. As the Union army expanded and battlefield demands increased, employment directly connected with war needs opened up even greater opportunities for work. Irishmen found many well-paying war jobs across the channel at the lower end of the South Boston peninsula, where several large iron foundries turned out guns, cannon, and artillery shells for the Union army, and where shipyards constructed new ironclad monitors for the navy. Many Irish women, too, took their place on assembly lines, some making ammunition at the Watertown arsenal and others working in shops and markets closer to the city.

To jobs in war-related industries was added the extensive construction work that was going on throughout Boston, giving Irish workers chances for jobs that otherwise would not have been available. Such ambitious projects as laying out the South End; constructing the new City Hall, Boston City Hospital, and Church of the Immaculate Conception; the enormous undertaking of filling in the Back Bay, which would continue well into the 1870s and 1880s: all furnished welcome employment for engineers, heavy-equipment operators, truck drivers, and day laborers. The work was hard, the hours long, and the wages low—most women earned less than $1.50 a day—but combined, war work and city construction gave most Irish workers their first real opportunity to bring home a day's pay regularly. They had taken a small but significant step on the first rung of the ladder to eventual economic success. Evidence of definite improvement in Irish Americans' economic fortunes continued immediately after the war as demographic mobility kept pace with material prosperity.

The Irish began moving out of the old, crowded waterfront sections in downtown Boston—the North End, the West End, the South End—into nearby neighborhoods of South Boston, Charlestown, East Boston, Dorchester, and Roxbury. Roxbury was annexed to the City of Boston in 1867; Dorchester in 1869; Charlestown, Brighton, and West Roxbury in 1873, suggesting the speed and numbers with which immigrant families were creating whole new residential districts, which before long would send representatives to serve on the city's Board of Alderman and the Common Council. With new churches, schools, and businesses to be constructed, police and fire departments to be organized, roads and streets to be paved, water mains and sewers to be dug, municipal services had to be developed to accommodate incoming families' needs and provide full-time jobs for many able-bodied Irish-American workers. Such new public utility companies as New England Telephone and Telegraph, Boston Edison Electric, and Boston Gas were especially welcome for opening up badly needed sources of employment which had never before been available in Boston, and which Irish Americans did not have to take away from native Boston workers. With new city neighborhoods in which to live, and with new job opportunities available for first- and second-generation families, the prospects for Irish Catholics looked brighter than anyone might have suspected only a dozen years earlier when the Know-Nothing movement was at its peak.

The one trend that seemed discouraging for the Boston Irish was politics. Before the war, despite stereotypical assumptions, the immigrants had little success in local politics. Their circumstances were desperate; their reception was generally hostile; they had no leadership, no organization, no money, and no support. No Irishmen were to be found in city politics, either on the Board of Aldermen or on the Common Council; only one Irishman was in the police department—"Barney McGinniskin from the bogs of Ireland," he announced to his new comrades on his first day at the station house—and the Know-Nothings ousted him in 1854. Boston may have had two political parties, but the Irish did not achieve prominence in either of them.[55] Even when the Civil War was over, it was by no means clear or inevitable that Irish Democrats would *ever* have a place in Boston political history. After Appomattox, the Commonwealth had only one political party—the Republican party. That was the party of Abraham Lincoln, the Union, victory, and emancipation; the Democrats belonged to the party of Jefferson Davis, the South, secession, and slavery. Massachusetts had very few card-carrying Democrats late in the 1860s and in the 1870s, and there was little evidence that things would change under the stranglehold that Bay State Republicans clamped on the state and local political bureaucracy. Political ascendancy, for the Boston Irish, would come much later.[56]

Even though the war enabled them to achieve tangible social acceptance and economic security, it seems not to have changed the traditional Irish racist attitude toward African Americans residing in the city. Reluctantly forced to acknowledge emancipation as a political reality and conscription as a military necessity during the war, they appear to have found no greater appreciation for the black person's civil rights or social standing once the war had ended. During the fighting, Irish soldiers were sometimes exposed to slavery's harsh reality and shocked by firsthand evidence of its perverse cruelties. The 9th Regiment had encamped on the grounds at General Robert E. Lee's plantation in Arlington, Virginia, where Michael MacNamara and his comrades came across some of Lee's slaves. The young Irish soldier was impressed by one young woman who was "very intelligent" and showed none of the exaggerated and distorted characteristics he had seen "pseudo darkies" display in northern minstrel shows. MacNamara recalled that the men came away with a very bad opinion of Lee's moral character, although they still admired his military ability.[57] Later in the war, MacNamara talked with an elderly black man who had just been freed and told to fend for himself. "We thought, as we stood musing," he wrote afterward, "what a terrible thing to have to pass eighty long years in slavery," and then be turned out "like a broken-down horse" to graze and die. "We felt more than ever, in heart and principle, an uncompromising enmity to human slavery."[58] Apparently some of these sentiments carried over into peacetime. Abolitionist-associated editors at the *Daily Evening Voice,* the only labor publication in the country to support unity for black and white workers as equals, insisted that local African Americans faced a much more "friendly" atmosphere in Boston after white workers returned from the war with changed views about black people.[59] Such changes, undoubtedly genuine enough under wartime pressures, seem to have faded rather quickly during the Reconstruction years. Black and white Bostonians generally resumed their separate everyday lives on opposite sides of Beacon Hill.

Amid the sweeping social changes generated by the war, Boston's active and responsive black community must have had every reason to expect a brighter future. Although Boston had been one of the more progressive northern cities in race relations, the pre–Civil War decades had been difficult and depressing for local African Americans. An old, established, self-contained community never having more than 2,000 individuals, less than 2 percent of the city's population, black residents had been gradually edged out of their dwelling places along the North End waterfront by increasing pressure from Irish immigration. They settled next in a permanent location that ran from the back side of Beacon Hill down to Cambridge Street and the West End's outer fringes, segregated, isolated, and generally ignored by the predominantly white population. Blacks were denied entrance into most apprenticeships and relegated to trades and occupations that furnished services to white residents and provided enough income for a marginal or, for several, a decent mode of living. Boston's black community had, Elizabeth Pleck says, "a rich and varied community life" with active social gatherings, a thriving African church culture, an ambitious literary society, and energetic Masonic lodges.[60]

Black and white Bostonians were completely separate, however, and the antebellum decades tell a story of almost continuous and frustrating struggles by black citizens to achieve racial equality, political legitimacy, and economic opportunity. Repeated attempts during the 1840s and 1850s to desegregate the Boston public schools so that black children could attend the all-white schools were defeated by school committee votes, and the Supreme Judicial Court of Massachusetts rejected arguments in the historic Sarah Roberts case. Only in April 1854 did the state legislature pass a law stating that no child, on account of "race, color, or religious opinions," could be excluded from any public school in the Commonwealth. But still the barriers remained. Several times late in the 1850s, when prominent black citizens sought to form their own military companies and become part of the state militia system, they were informed that admission to the state militia was restricted by law to whites only. As late as 1861, even under sympathetic pressure from the newly elected governor, John Andrew, the state legislature refused to change the clearly racist state militia system.

The Civil War seemed to offer the first tangible signs of substantive change in the traditional depressed status of African Americans. The initial reasons for these changes, it must be admitted, were much more practical and selfish than they were ethical or moral. As the war became more formidable and all-consuming, it was evident that victory would be impossible without eradicating slavery and eventually using African-American manpower. Whatever the reasons, black citizens were amazed to find that in under two years white people were actually agitating for emancipation, and on January 1, 1863, the impossible dream became a historic reality. President Lincoln announced that slavery no longer existed, and that all slaves were "then, thenceforward, and forever free." And as additional assurance that this declaration meant what it said, the president announced that African Americans could be admitted into the armed services to serve their country like all other American citizens. Frustrations, irritations, slights, and insults continued—unequal pay, inadequate weapons, unsuitable uniforms, and so on—but by the war's closing months, as three black regiments from the Bay State fought at the front, freedom's reality began to sink in. And when the conflict's end brought the Thirteenth Amendment to ratify in peacetime the principles of freedom that had been proclaimed in wartime, the postwar future for African Americans must have seemed bright indeed.

And immediately after victory, black citizens, especially those living in Boston, had some reason to look for a brighter tomorrow. Massachusetts Senator Charles Sumner sponsored the abolitionist black lawyer, John Rock, as the first African American to practice law before the U.S. Supreme Court—the same court, ironically, that only eight years earlier had ruled that blacks could not be U.S. citizens. Back home in Massachusetts, Radical Republicans in the state legislature took steps to reward black citizens who had fought for the

Union, arranging to provide Civil War veterans with federal jobs in post offices and customs houses. In 1866, two African Americans were elected to the state House of Representatives and, until the century's end, one or two black men were elected each year to serve in the state legislature, voting solidly Republican in keeping with the spirit of the Great Emancipator. Each ward in the city elected two representatives to sit in the Common Council, and between 1876 and 1895, at least one black resident from the West End (Ward 9) filled one of those seats.

At first glance, these conditions were a far cry from those black Bostonians had faced before the Civil War. Beneath the surface, however, things were by no means as encouraging as they appeared. For one thing, although the number of black residents increased substantially, the traditional African American community's circumscribed boundaries hardly changed. Beginning in 1864, the federally sponsored Freedman's Bureau provided transportation for former slaves who wanted to leave the South and get work in the North. Between 1866 and 1868, 1,083 ex-slaves were shipped to Boston and Cambridge, despite protests by Governor John Andrew, who feared the service would help create a race of "homeless wanderers." Although these new migrants from the South raised the black population from 2,261 in 1860 to 3,496 in 1870, African Americans were still confined to "Nigger Hill," which continued to provide servants' quarters for blacks employed as domestics by Beacon Hill families, and lodgings for those who worked in the food markets near Faneuil Hall and at the docks along the waterfront. Even as many Irish Americans were moving out of the waterfront to other parts of the city and the surrounding neighborhoods, African Americans were still restricted to the one segregated district that had been their home for nearly a century. Before the Civil War, African Americans and Irish Americans in Boston had suffered similarly from poverty, bigotry, and segregation. In the years just after the war, however, the gap between these two oppressed peoples widened as the Irish slowly moved ahead in social acceptance, economic prosperity, and geographic mobility. Black Bostonians enjoyed none of these benefits. Despite the high-sounding phrases in the state's 1854 desegregation law, the public schools reflected the city's segregated housing patterns. Grammar schools in predominantly white neighborhoods such as East Boston, Charlestown, Roxbury, and Dorchester had no black students at all. By contrast, more than a third of the city's black children were enrolled in two grammar schools in the city's West End. Confined to their highly segregated district, black adults were effectively excluded from the modern and commercial parts of Boston where business, banking, and manufacturing required more education and more sophisticated skills and talents. Despite efforts by a small liberal labor group in Boston to integrate free African-American workers into the white labor force during the postwar

Joshua B. Smith operated a thriving catering business in Boston, and in 1851 was one of several black leaders who petitioned the state legislature for a monument to Crispus Attucks, a black man killed during the Boston Massacre. After the Civil War, Smith went into politics and represented Cambridge as a senator in the state legislature during 1873 and 1874. (Massachusetts Historical Society)

years, black people continued to function in their traditional capacities as laborers and stevedores, waiters and caterers, barbers and hairdressers, boot-
blacks and laundresses.[61] Most black Bostonians were able to serve the white
community's needs and bring in enough income to sustain their families in
modest fashion, but they were seldom able to acquire the training, instruction,
or experience that would have enabled them to move up the economic ladder
appreciably. "The Irish, once the most downtrodden group in Boston, had
climbed the social ladder by the turn of the century," observes Elizabeth Pleck
in her work on postwar Boston, "whereas black Bostonians remained at its
bottom rung."[62]

If prospects for black Bostonians promised much but delivered little, prospects for Boston women promised only modest gains but produced much more
than most expected. Well into the nineteenth century, few changes had been
made in American women's legal status or social classification. Denied the
right to vote, control property, bring suit in court, or receive a college education, women were confined to a sphere that encompassed the hearth and the
home. As prospective wives and mothers, they were cautioned to avoid issues
that were "petty, trivial, or unworthy," and advised to focus on domestic arts
that were designed to care for their husbands' needs and their children's welfare. Governed by the strict code of behavior that modern historians label "the
cult of domesticity," the proper Boston lady restricted her outside activities to
modest and voluntary efforts benefiting the church and improving cultural life
for those of her own sex. Some women, chiefly in the lower and lower-middle
classes, were of course forced by economic necessity to work outside the home
for payment. But even in these categories, society tolerated only a reasonable
number of exceptions. During her visit to the United States during the mid-
1830s, the English writer Harriet Martineau listed only four occupations she
found open to women: factory work, domestic service, schoolteaching, and
manufacturing hats and clothing. By the 1850s, that list had expanded—laundresses, stereotypers, cigar makers, workers of gold and silver leaf—but most
of these were not far from the generally accepted skills and trades in which
women's labor was considered appropriate. For Boston women who did not require an outside income to maintain their homes and raise their children, however, the workplace was definitely the exception; the household was the rule.

By late in the 1830s and early in the 1840s, a few women appeared around
New England who were determined to challenge social and legal restrictions
and claim for American women the same civil and political rights long enjoyed
by American men. Motivated by humanitarian ideals, inspired by religious
perfectionism, and stimulated by the rhetoric of Jacksonian democracy, some
prominent women threw themselves into the struggle to free both women and
slaves from servitude. Essentially nonpolitical and nonviolent, these female an-

tebellum reform groups were convinced that their progress would succeed by emotional appeal and rational persuasion. Whether it was Susan B. Anthony in her fight for temperance, Catharine Beecher in the movement for higher education, Lucretia Mott and Elizabeth Cady Stanton in the struggle for women's rights, or Sarah and Angelina Grimké in the crusade to abolish slavery, a group of young, upper-class, well-educated, highly moral women dominated every major reform movement in the mid-nineteenth century. Most of them knew each other well, shared each other's vision of a more nearly equal society, and agreed upon the means and methods for achieving their goals. Coming from comfortable family circumstances, they were able to give freely of their time and energy, received no salary, and devoted themselves morning, noon, and night to their specific reform. Confident and self-assured, they went about their serious business ignoring attacks by critics who labeled them "blue-stockings" and "petticoat rebels," and disregarding mockery from detractors who ridiculed them as "love-starved spinsters." Most of the women felt sure that with enough time their hard work, dogged persistence, fanatical devotion, and tireless energy would eventually, if not inevitably, bring about the changes and reforms to which they devoted their lives.

The Civil War and Abraham Lincoln's eventual announcement of the Emancipation Proclamation convinced women reformers that their work in supporting the abolition movement had borne fruit. The subsequent course of the war, however, also began to make clear that reform, progress, and change could no longer be achieved by the old methods of amateur voluntarism, no matter how idealistically inspired or morally motivated. Indeed, by the time the war was under way, almost all the antebellum reform movements had fizzled out as their leaders became involved in different matters and other issues. Only the abolition movement could be considered a major success, and that was mainly because its objectives had become integral to a war effort whose success would eventually be guaranteed by the kind of organization, management, professionalism, and bureaucracy that ensured total victory in war and thoroughly transformed American society. In his volume *The War for the Union: The Organized War, 1863–1864*, historian Allan Nevins concludes that the Civil War "accentuated and acted as a catalyst" for already-developing local tendencies toward organization, as America shifted from an unorganized society to a well-organized nation.[63]

This phenomenon affected the nation as a whole, and also influenced women's part in American history during the second half of the nineteenth century. When the fighting began, Northern women did all the things that women had always done, and were expected to do, in time of war. In their parlors, in their church basements, and in their classrooms, they rolled bandages, folded blankets, darned socks, knitted sweaters, collected Bibles, wrote letters, and shared the homefront news with the boys on the battlefield. Some Bay State women left their native cities and towns and traveled to the front lines to offer their services more directly and personally. Clara Barton took supplies to the battlefields, where she tended the wounded and comforted the dying. Dorothea Dix, too, offered her professional services to help wherever possible and formed the first organized corps of women nurses. But as the war widened, and as the casualties mounted, it became evident that individual acts of generosity and compassion, no matter how well-intentioned, were neither adequately funded nor sufficiently coordinated to meet the Union war effort's extraordinary demands. In proposing to centralize, professionalize, and streamline the wartime relief work's numerous facets, new organizations such as the U.S. Sanitary Commission, the Women's Central Association of Relief, and the Christian Commission broke with the traditional characteristics of most antebellum reform activities, in which local groups of dedicated and highly motivated women sought to achieve their goals by rational assent and moral suasion. Although the new movements certainly had a strong moral basis, their methods were decidedly practical and definitely political. Success was achieved, not by pious appeals from well-meaning amateurs, but by superior organization, qualified professionals, and sympathetic political supporters. With national associations organized along corporate lines, capable women quickly moved up into middle-management positions, prepared budgets, arranged contracts, handled large sums, and managed transportation facilities. In carrying out these agencies' duties and functions, women traveled far beyond the domestic sphere to all parts of the country, alone and unattended, participated in meetings and conferences, spoke before large public audiences, and learned to deal with men as peers. They held their own in fights with military personnel, disputes with government bureaucrats, conflicts with doctors and nurses, and arguments with congressmen and senators—a far cry from the prewar image of the "subservient female."[64]

At first, much of women's organized activities in war-relief work involved, directly or indirectly, providing Union troops with prompt medical treatment, adequate nursing care, and any supplies that could add to their comfort and convenience. Gradually, however, this experience working as part of a national, professional organization also equipped Northern women with skills and opportunities that went far beyond the duties that many considered the "women's work" of nursing. The Boston women who worked for the Union cause and for abolishing slavery by participating in the Women's Loyal National League must have experienced elation when President Lincoln issued the Emancipation Proclamation in fall 1862. Determined to add emancipation permanently to the law of the land, many of these women moved beyond writing letters and circulating petitions to actually taking part in political lobbying—traveling to Washington, D.C., visiting the White House, meeting with senators, dealing with Congress—seeing at firsthand how politics worked. The political experience gained by Elizabeth Cady Stanton and Susan B. Anthony in working with the Bay State delegation for passage of the Thirteenth Amendment gave these women new insights into the many ways in which political pressure could be used to achieve their long-range goal, woman suffrage.

For the handful of income-producing occupations that Harriet Martineau described thirty years earlier as appropriate for American women, the Civil War had also brought about definite and surprising changes. Nursing, a calling long considered "natural" for the female's compassionate and motherly instincts, had few professional standards, and in the decades before the war women had become "nurses" mostly by "self-proclamation" and had acquired clients mainly by word of mouth.[65] Traumatic experiences in the Civil War, however, together with early experiences in recruiting a nurse corps, made it evident that preliminary screening, standardized training, professional supervision, and authorized accreditation were vital. It was by no means a coincidence that, when in 1863 the first hospital charter was issued to the New England Hospital for Women and Children in Boston, the original by-laws specified that one of the institution's objectives would be "to train nurses for the care of the sick."[66] But women fought to establish their own separate nursing programs free of interference by incompetent hospital administrators and insensitive male physicians. In 1873, they succeeded in establishing three independent nursing schools: the Connecticut Training School in New Haven, the Bellevue Training School in New York City, and the Boston Training School at the Massachusetts General Hospital in Boston. The New York and Boston facilities were achieved by laywomen against doctors' opposition. Professionalism in training nurses was under way.[67]

Schoolteaching, once considered an accepted, natural, but purely temporary occupation in which well-bred women could involve themselves outside their domestic sphere for a beneficial purpose, was already undergoing early stages of professionalization because of reform efforts by Horace Mann of Massachusetts. Using the newly created state board of education, Mann set up standardized curricula, accredited textbooks, graded classrooms, and state-supported "normal schools" for professionally training prospective teachers, rather than relying on devoted but amateurish efforts by needy widows or local ministers' wives. Not long after the Civil War ended, women's access to higher education in the broader sense improved markedly. Before the war, "female seminaries," such as the one Emma Willard founded in Troy, New York, and that Mary Lyon founded in Mount Holyoke, Massachusetts, had offered advanced programs for women emphasizing the social amenities and the fine arts. In 1865, however, Vassar College was the first to teach women by the

Dorothea Lynde Dix was a native of Hamden, Maine, who moved to Boston at the age of thirteen and became famous for her indefatigable crusade for the humane treatment of the mentally ill. During the Civil War, Dix was named Superintendent of Women Nurses for the Union army. Although the assignment proved personally frustrating and unfulfilling, Dix's appointment did much to establish the career of nursing as a recognized profession for American women. (The Bostonian Society)

same standards as those employed by the best of men's colleges, and by the 1870s, Wellesley College and Smith College were providing excellent higher education for women students. The war had accelerated the work of bringing intelligent women out of the shadows cast by benign neglect and into a much brighter future with professional instruction and intellectual fulfillment.

Domestic service, Harriet Martineau pointed out, had long been thought an appropriate, though not always highly regarded, area for which working-class women were naturally suited. By 1850, figures show that Irish servants could claim 70 percent of the Boston situations, and during the war the number of Irish-born domestics continued to increase. American-born daughters of Irish parents found little difficulty in adapting to manners and customs in the well-to-do homes in which they were employed, but more recent arrivals from rural areas in western Ireland took more time adjusting to urban novelties—learning how to use a carpet sweeper, identifying cutlery, distinguishing cuts of meat, and managing a cast-iron stove.[68] Besides Irish women in service, an estimated one-quarter of Boston's black female population between ages ten and thirty-six also resided in white households, where they served as domestics. Very often these African-American women worked as laundresses for the family, washing and ironing clothing and helping to feed the children when the lady of the house was absent.[69]

In the business of making hats, suits, dresses, and other forms of clothing, women's traditional monopoly as milliners, dressmakers, needle workers, and seamstresses was broken—if not directly by the Civil War, at least indirectly by the mechanical inventions and managerial innovations stimulated by the war. Except possibly for skilled tailors who specialized in measuring their male customers for expensive custom-made suits, women had always dominated most other aspects of the needle trade—Carol Lasser describes it as "a distinct female craft structure."[70] Working at home or in small shops or boutiques, women managed a profitable trade in which they worked by appointment, measured precisely to the individual, and turned out superior garments with great skill. According to the historian Wendy Gamber, however, a trio of inventions "wreaked havoc" on this dressmaking craft—the sewing machine, the drafting system, and proportional patterns—so that between 1860 and 1900 the dressmaking shop was overwhelmed by a force Gamber calls "a corporate invasion."[71]

The sewing machine had really made its effective appearance during the 1850s, and over the next five decades, stimulated by lucrative Civil War contracts, sewing-machine production blossomed into a multimillion-dollar industry. Pressured by war demands to produce inexpensive garments and ready-to-wear uniforms, manufacturers came up with a system for cutting cloth and drafting designs that made it possible for unskilled workers, many of them foreigners, to perform tasks that had been done exclusively by highly skilled craftswomen.[72] Standardized male and female "forms," cloth and paper patterns, mechanical cutting techniques, and "pin-on-the-form" tailoring methods completely "de-skilled," traditional millinery and dressmaking work, and greater productivity was achieved at far lower labor cost.[73] Furthermore, women workers now left their homes and shops to work in the new department stores that soon brought together in one location the numerous facets of an industry that had once been greatly decentralized. Customers could now abandon their "little Irish dressmaker" for the dressmaking departments in such fashionable Boston stores as Jordan Marsh, which in 1861 established its first "departmentalized" store to conduct its retail business. Other department stores followed, such as Filene's and Houghton and Dutton, where women customers were able to find in one department the trimmings, accessories, thread, buttons, clasps, and all the other notions for which they usually had to search through dozens of shops and specialty stores. With this innovation, however, a production and retailing system mostly controlled by women was rapidly supplanted by a new system mainly controlled by men. The department store, plus the separation of production from retailing, and the replacement of jobbers with manufacturers together produced changes that Gamber calls "gendered transformations."[74]

After the Civil War, therefore, more and more Boston women found greater independence and financial security by leaving the home and going into the city to take salaried positions in the new department stores. These stores, however, had triumphed over small, female-run shops by replacing individuality in highly skilled labor with the competitive mass-production routine in which most managers and marketers were male. This was one aspect in the postwar economy where greater opportunities for women in a field in which they had always had managerial control failed to meet their expectations for advancement.

~ ~ ~

THE FOUR-YEAR WAR had changed the shape and direction of American history, and had also brought many changes into the life of the Boston community. Some changes were welcome, exciting, and anticipated; others were discouraging, disappointing, and unexpected.

For the Boston business community, the war brought immediate prosperity, new solidarity for the Republican party, and renewed patriotic pride among city leaders whose ancestors had fought at Concord, Lexington, and Bunker Hill. The gallant response by young Brahmins and Harvard graduates as officers in the proud Massachusetts regiments was satisfying proof that the old Boston values were still alive. Before long, however, the new industrial economy generated and accelerated by the war would leave New England far behind, as an antebellum anachronism that could no longer keep pace with giant technology. In the new Age of Big Business, the old Boston values no longer seemed relevant.

For the city's immigrant Irish-Catholic community, the Civil War brought surprising social and religious tolerance, reflecting the city's gratitude for the loyal Irish fight for the Union. That acceptance provided, in turn, the basis for both demographic growth and upward mobility, as members of the immigrant population moved out of their waterfront hovels into working-class neighborhoods of their own choosing. For Irish Democrats, any immediate prospects for political power and influence seemed extremely unlikely, with victorious Republicans dominating national, state, and city governments. The newly acquired social acceptance and financial stability, however, would, by the turn of the century, pave the way for eventual political successes that would allow the Irish to establish their own political base and control city government.

For Boston's African-American population, the Civil War perhaps raised highest expectations but delivered fewest substantial results. The Emancipation Proclamation and subsequent end of slavery guaranteed by the Thirteenth Amendment seemed to offer black Americans a full share in the promise of America. Soon, though, it was clear that inspiring rhetoric would not produce meaningful results. Black Bostonians were still confined to "Nigger Hill," prevented from entering the skilled professions, and denied social acceptance consistent with their political rights. Many generations would pass before the Civil War amendments would bring to America's African-American citizens anything approaching the promised civil rights and racial equality for which the great struggle had been waged.

The many Boston women involved in the Civil War brought back remarkable and stimulating experiences that gave them new skills and proficiencies, dramatically changing their way of seeing themselves as women and their purpose in the world. The ability to travel freely, to speak publicly before mixed audiences, to assume managerial positions in national war-relief organizations, to engage in active politics, to hold their own with military bureaucrats and government officials, gave many women confidence and self-assurance they would carry into professional activities and social-reform movements well into the twentieth century.

For nearly a century and a half, the Civil War has continued to have a fascination in the minds and memories of the American people unlike any other event in the nation's history. This is true not only because of the broad and sweeping changes the war produced in the social, political, and industrial institutions of the United States, but also because of the intimate and personal effects it had upon the everyday lives of so many ordinary people. This was certainly true for Boston. The war lasted only four years, but it brought about a lifetime of changes among the various elements of the city's population. As the unexpected consequences of the war began moving the United States in completely new directions, far beyond what anyone could have imagined, it became clear that things would never again be what they had been. For Boston, as for the rest of the nation, the Civil War marked the end of one era and the beginning of another.

Notes

~~~~~~~

CHAPTER I

1. *Boston Daily Advertiser,* October 12, 14, 1858. Also see Hudson Strode, *Jefferson Davis: American Patriot* (New York, 1955), pp. 309–311.

2. Oscar Handlin, *Boston's Immigrants, 1790–1880* (New York, 1959), p. 56.

3. Walter Muir Whitehill, *Boston: A Topographical History,* 2nd ed. (Cambridge, Mass., 1982), pp. 63, 110–111.

4. Ibid., p. 131.

5. James L. Huston, *The Panic of 1857 and the Coming of the Civil War* (Baton Rouge, La., 1987), emphasizes how the panic helped shape the Republican and Democratic parties' economic policies by the 1860 elections. See also George W. Van Vleck, *The Panic of 1857* (New York, 1943); Samuel Rezneck, "The Influence of Depression upon American Opinion, 1857–1859," *Journal of Economic History* 2 (1942): 1–23.

6. Amos A. Lawrence to Charles Robinson, October 19, 1857, Robinson Papers, Folder III, Archives, University of Kansas, Lawrence, Kansas; Thomas H. O'Connor, *Lords of the Loom: The Cotton Whigs and the Coming of the Civil War* (New York, 1968), pp. 125–126.

7. Charleston *Mercury,* October 14, 1857.

8. *Congressional Globe,* 35th Congress, 1st Session, Appendix: 70–71.

9. See Elizabeth Cutting, *Jefferson Davis: Political Soldier* (New York, 1930), pp. 124–125, for a facsimile of Davis's speech.

10. See Joel H. Silbey, "The Surge of Republican Power," in *Essays on Antebellum Politics,* ed. S. Maizlish and J. Kushma (College Station, Texas, 1982), p. 215, for observations on the South's reaction to New Englanders' radical social views.

11. Ibid.

12. Nancy Woloch, *Women and the American Experience,* 2nd ed. (New York, 1994), p. 115. For work on the woman's sphere, see Nancy Cott, *The Bonds of Womanhood: "Woman's Sphere" in New England, 1778–1835* (New Haven, Conn., 1977); Barbara Welter, "The Cult of True Womanhood, 1820–1860," *American Quarterly* 18 (Summer 1966): 151–175. For studies on women's culture, see Jeanne Boydston, *Home and Work: Housework, Wages, and the Ideology of Labor in the Early Republic* (New

York, 1990); Karen Halttunen, *Confidence Men and Painted Women: A Study of Middle-Class Culture in America, 1830–1870* (New Haven, Conn., 1982).

13. Lawrence Foster, *Religion and Sexuality: Three American Communal Experiments of the Nineteenth Century* (New York, 1981); Ann M. Boylan, *Sunday School: The Formation of an American Institution, 1790–1880* (New Haven, Conn., 1988); Nancy Cott, "Young Women and the Second Great Awakening," *Feminist Studies* 2 (Fall 1975): 15–29; Barbara Welter, "The Feminization of American Religion, 1800–1860," in *Clio's Consciousness Raised*, ed. Mary Hartman and Lois Banner (New York, 1974).

14. Barbara L. Epstein, *The Politics of Domesticity: Women, Evangelism, and Temperance in Nineteenth-Century America* (Middletown, Conn., 1981); Estelle B. Freedman, *Their Sisters' Keepers: Women's Prison Reform in America, 1830–1930* (Ann Arbor, Mich., 1981).

15. Ann Douglas, *The Feminization of American Culture* (New York, 1977); Estelle Entrekin, *Sarah Hale and Godey's Lady's Book* (Philadelphia, 1946); Ruth E. Finley, *The Lady of Godey's* (Philadelphia, 1931); E. Douglas Branch, *The Sentimental Years: 1836–1860* (New York, 1934), pp. 212–213.

16. Ann M. Boylan, "Timid Girls, Venerable Widows, and Dignified Matrons," *American Quarterly* 38 (Winter 1986): 779–797; Lori D. Ginzburg, *Women and the Work of Benevolence: Morality, Politics, and Class in the Nineteenth Century* (New Haven, Conn., 1990); Barbara I. Berg, *The Remembered Gate: Origins of American Feminism, the Woman and the City, 1800–1860* (New York, 1978).

17. Jean Fagan Yellin, *Women and Sisters: Antislavery Feminists in American Culture* (New Haven, Conn., 1990); Gerda Lerner, *The Grimké Sisters from South Carolina: Pioneers for Women's Rights and Abolition* (New York, 1967); Dorothy Sterling, *Ahead of Her Time: Abby Kelley and the Politics of Antislavery* (New York, 1992); Blanche Hersh, *The Slavery of Sex: Feminist Abolitionists in Nineteenth-Century America* (Urbana, Ill., 1978).

18. Ellen DuBois, *Feminism and Suffrage: The Emergence of an Independent Women's Movement, 1848–1869* (Ithaca, N.Y., 1978); Eleanor Flexner, *Century of Struggle: The Woman's Rights Movement in the United States* (Cambridge, Mass., 1959).

19. Paula Blanchard, *Margaret Fuller: From Transcendentalism to Revolution* (Cambridge, Mass., 1978).

20. A modern example of the way in which the label became all-inclusive may be seen in Elizabeth D. Leonard, *Yankee Women: Gender Battles in the Civil War* (New York, 1994). Citing the roles played by Sophronia E. Bucklin of Auburn, New York; Annie Wittenmyer of Keokuk, Iowa; and Mary Walker, M.D., of Oswego, New York, Professor Leonard is perfectly comfortable categorizing these figures as "Yankee Women."

21. O'Connor, *Lords of the Loom*, p. 45.

22. Richard H. Abbott, *Cotton and Capital: Boston Businessmen and Antislavery Reform, 1854–1868* (Amherst, Mass., 1991), pp. 5–8. Also see Robert F. Dalzell, Jr., *Enterprising Elite: The Boston Associates and the World They Made* (Cambridge,

Mass., 1986), for an interesting analysis of social and political attitudes among Boston's financial leaders.

23. O'Connor, *Lords of the Loom,* p. 49.

24. Fletcher Webster, ed., *The Writings and Speeches of Daniel Webster,* 18 vols. (National Edition, 1903), II, pp. 193–230; Robert C. Winthrop, Jr., *A Memoir of Robert C. Winthrop* (Boston, 1897), p. 58.

25. Abbott Lawrence, "Letter to the Whigs of Essex County," August 20, 1844, in *A Memoir of Abbott Lawrence,* ed. Hamilton Hill (Boston, 1884), pp. 76–77.

26. Kinley J. Brauer, *Cotton versus Conscience: Massachusetts Whig Politics and Southwestern Expansion, 1843–1848* (Lexington, Ky., 1967), pp. 128–129.

27. Dale Baum, *The Civil War Party System: The Case of Massachusetts, 1848–1876* (Chapel Hill, N.C., 1984). Baum agrees with the assumption that slavery was a dead issue after the Compromise of 1850. See Michael F. Holt, *The Political Crisis of the 1850s* (New York, 1978), pp. 98–99, for a similar interpretation.

28. William E. Gienapp, *The Origins of the Republican Party, 1852–1856* (New York, 1987), pp. 74–75; Joel H. Silbey, *A Respectable Minority: The Democratic Party in the Civil War Era, 1860–1868* (New York, 1977), pp. 15–16. Both historians agree that Douglas attempted to restore a unified Democratic leadership with his Kansas-Nebraska Act.

29. Eric Foner, *Free Labor, Free Soil, Free Men* (New York, 1970), pp. 55–56; Holt, *Political Crisis of the 1850s,* pp. 147–148, suggests that Douglas miscalculated the depth of the slavery issue and intended the bill to strengthen the party structure. Gienapp, *Republican Party,* p. 78, feels that Foner presents an essentially "static" view of the Republican ideology. Gienapp says it "varied" and shifted with time.

30. The Boston *Times,* May 30, 1854.

31. Amos A. Lawrence to Mr. Andrews, May 26, 1854, Amos A. Lawrence Letterbook (hereafter *AAL Letterbook*), II, p. 335, Massachusetts Historical Society.

32. Eli Thayer, *A History of the Kansas Crusade* (New York, 1889), pp. 25–30; Robert E. Moody, "The First Year of the Emigrant Aid Company," *New England Quarterly* 4 (1931): 148–149; Samuel A. Johnson, "The Genesis of the New England Aid Company," *New England Quarterly* 3 (1930): 90–100.

33. Amos A. Lawrence to Dr. Thomas H. Webb, July 20, 1955, *AAL Letterbook* III, p. 204, MHS.

34. Holt, *Political Crisis of the 1850s,* pp. 151–152, feels that by 1854 many more Northerners were prepared to accept the idea of a "Slave-Power" plot that would crush their liberties.

35. Alice Nichols, *Bleeding Kansas* (New York, 1954), pp. 105–109; James C. Malin, *John Brown and the Legend of Fifty-Six* (Philadelphia, 1942), p. 589; Jay Monaghan, *The Civil War on the Western Border, 1854–1865* (Boston, 1955), pp. 52–56. Holt, *Political Crisis of the 1850s,* pp. 194–196, and Gienapp, *Republican Party,* pp. 297–300, agree that the John Brown and Charles Sumner incidents "electrified the North."

36. Lois E. Horton and James O. Horton, "Power and Social Responsibility: Entrepreneurs and the Black Community in Antebellum Boston," in Conrad Edick Wright

and Katheryn P. Viens, *Entrepreneurs: The Boston Business Community, 1700–1850* (Boston, 1997), pp. 325–328.

37. *The Liberator,* March 16, 1860; Handlin, *Boston's Immigrants,* pp. 60–70.

38. James Horton and Lois E. Horton, *Black Bostonians* (New York, 1979), pp. 55–57.

39. Dr. Rock traveled to Europe for medical treatment during 1858 and 1859. Upon his return to America, he studied law, was admitted to the Massachusetts bar in 1861, and in 1865 became the first black man admitted to practice law before the U.S. Supreme Court. See Horton and Horton, *Black Bostonians,* p. 60.

40. Horton and Horton, *Black Bostonians,* pp. 54–55; Stanley J. Robboy and Anita W. Robboy, "Lewis Hayden: From Fugitive Slave to Statesman," *New England Quarterly* 46 (December 1973): 591–597.

41. Horton and Horton, *Black Bostonians,* pp. 57–58.

42. Ibid., p. 61.

43. Horton and Horton, "Power and Social Responsibility," pp. 330–332. Also see Carol Buchalter Stapp, *Afro-Americans in Antebellum Boston: An Analysis of Probate Records* (New York, 1993), pp. 20–21. Working from probate records in the Suffolk County Courthouse archives, Carol Stapp analyzes the personal property and real estate held by leading black citizens in Boston during the 1840s.

44. Horton and Horton, *Black Bostonians,* pp. 39–45.

45. Ibid., pp. 45–50.

46. Ibid., pp. 50–51; Robert C. A. Hayden, *A History of the Black Church in Boston* (Boston, 1983); Roy E. Finkenbine, "Boston's Black Churches: Institutional Centers of the Anti-Slavery Movement," in *Courage and Conscience,* ed. Donald Jacobs (Bloomington, Ind., 1993), pp. 167–186.

47. Southern slaveholders were infuriated by the violent implications in *Walker's Appeal.* A price was put on Walker's head, and when he was found dead on Boston's Bridge Street in 1830, foul play was immediately suspected. See George A. Levesque, *Black Boston: African American Life and Culture in Urban America, 1750–1860* (New York, 1994), pp. 263–269.

48. Horton and Horton, *Black Bostonians,* pp. 50–57; Stapp, *Afro-Americans,* pp. 30–31; Shirley Yee, *Black Women Abolitionists: A Study in Activism, 1820–1860* (Knoxville, Tenn., 1992), pp. 19–21.

49. Horton and Horton, *Black Bostonians,* pp. 92–93.

50. Carter Godwin Woodson, *The Education of the Negro Prior to 1861* (New York, 1915), pp. 320–321; John Daniels, *In Freedom's Birthplace* (Boston, 1914), pp. 448–449; Thomas H. O'Connor, *Fitzpatrick's Boston, 1846–1866: John Bernard Fitzpatrick, Third Bishop of Boston* (Boston, 1984), pp. 172–173.

51. Handlin, *Boston's Immigrants,* pp. 59–66.

52. O'Connor, *Fitzpatrick's Boston,* pp. 15–16; O'Connor, *The Boston Irish: A Political History* (Boston, 1995), pp. 43–44.

53. Ray Allen Billington, *The Protestant Crusade, 1800–1860* (New York, 1938), pp. 220–234. Also see Jay Dolan, *The Immigrant Church: New York's Irish and Ger-*

man Catholics, 1815–1865 (Baltimore, 1975); Michael Felberg, *The Philadelphia Riots of 1844: A Study in Ethnic Conflict* (Westport, Conn., 1975).

54. The nature and motives of Irish racism in America are treated in Noel Ignatiev's *How the Irish Became White* (New York, 1995). Ignatiev's thesis is that the Irish embraced a vicious form of white supremacy in order to be considered "white" and thus fully accepted into the dominant white society in the nineteenth century. Gilbert Osofsky, "Abolitionists, Irish Immigrants, and Romantic Nationalism," *American Historical Review* 80 (October 1975): 900–925, accentuates Irish immigrants' desire to engage in displays of superpatriotism so as to be accepted into American culture.

55. O'Connor, *Fitzpatrick's Boston,* pp. 161–162. Also see Madeleine Hooker Rice, *American Catholic Opinion in the Slavery Controversy* (Gloucester, Mass., 1964); Robert Leckie, *American and Catholic* (New York, 1970); John Francis Maxwell, *Slavery and the Catholic Church* (London, 1975).

56. *United States Catholic Intelligencer,* October 1, 1831.

57. Ibid., August 20, 1831.

58. Ibid., October 1, 1831.

59. Ibid.

60. This fascinating question—why Irish Catholics appeared so implacably racist when they came to America—is studied by Noel Ignatiev in *How the Irish Became White.* For a scholarly critique of Ignatiev's thesis, see Donald Yacovone's review in *New England Quarterly* 69 (December 1996): 667–669. Yacovone complains that many of Ignatiev's conclusions cannot be reconciled with his findings on antebellum Philadelphia; I have similar problems with antebellum Boston history.

61. Dennis Clark, *Irish Relations: Trials of an Immigrant Tradition* (Rutherford, Va., 1982), p. 143.

62. David Roediger, *The Wages of Whiteness* (New York, 1991), p. 133.

63. Richard N. Le Bow, *White England and Black Ireland* (Philadelphia, 1976), p. 48; Clark, *Irish Relations,* p. 144.

64. Roediger, *Wages of Whiteness,* p. 107.

65. Martin Duberman, *The Anti-Slavery Vanguard* (Princeton, N.J., 1965), p. 171; Roediger, *Wages of Whiteness,* p. 134.

66. *The Boston Pilot,* January 12, 1850.

67. Ibid., June 18, 1853.

68. Ibid., January 30, 1858; February 18, 1860.

69. Ibid., October 24, 1851.

70. Ibid., November 22, 1856.

71. Ibid., April 11, July 11, 1846. A decade later *The Boston Pilot* was still emphasizing the need for obeying the laws. See *The Boston Pilot,* January 17, 1857, and February 13, 1858.

72. Ibid., February 19, 1842.

73. Ibid., February 12, 1842.

74. Francis R. Walsh, *The Boston Pilot: A Newspaper for the Irish Immigrant* (Ann Arbor, Mich., 1969), p. 119. See Ignatiev, *How the Irish Became White,* pp. 6–9, for an analysis of O'Connell's plea and its rejection by the American Irish.

75. *The Boston Pilot,* February 12, 1842.

76. William Gienapp, *Republican Party,* pp. 103, 160–161, warns that the Republican party's origins did not come quickly or easily. Building the party was, he emphasizes, long, complex, and difficult, involving more than the slavery issue.

77. Baum, *Civil War Party System,* p. 93.

78. Holt, *Political Crisis of the 1850s,* pp. 132–133, 158–159, emphasizes political efforts by Know-Nothing members to "oust party hacks" from office and replace them with "new, honest, and more responsive men." Also see Gienapp, *Republican Party,* pp. 92–93, for an analysis of the American party's political basis.

79. John R. Mulkern, *The Know Nothing Party in Massachusetts: The Rise and Fall of a People's Party* (Boston, 1990); Mulkern, "Scandal Behind the Convent Walls: The Know-Nothing Nunnery Committee of 1855," *Historical Journal of Massachusetts* 11 (1983): 22–31. Also see Baum, *Civil War Party System,* pp. 31–32, for a discussion of the Know-Nothing movement's political and religious motives.

80. In *How the Irish Became White,* Noel Ignatiev labels Irish militia companies "the Swiss guards of the slave power" for being part of the large military force that escorted Anthony Burns back to slavery.

81. Walsh, *The Boston Pilot,* p. 140. See Lawrence Lader, *The Bold Brahmins: New England's War Against Slavery, 1830–1863* (New York, 1961), pp. 155–185; Harold Schwartz, "Fugitive Days in Boston," *New England Quarterly* 27 (1954): 191–212; Samuel Shapiro, "The Rendition of Anthony Burns," *Journal of Negro History* 44 (1959): 33–51.

82. See Don Fehrenbacher, *The Dred Scott Case: Its Significance in American Law and Politics* (New York, 1978), for an exhaustive analysis of this case; Stephen F. Maizlish, "The Meaning of Nativism and the Crisis of the Union: The Know-Nothing Movement in the Antebellum North," in *Essays on Antebellum Politics,* pp. 173–175, analyzes the relationship between antislavery and antiforeign thinking, and states that nativism was perfectly compatible with the Republican party's ideals.

83. John Hope Franklin, *From Slavery to Freedom: A History of American Negroes* (New York, 1956), p. 264.

84. *The Liberator,* March 12, 1858. Also see Horton and Horton, *Black Bostonians,* p. 119.

85. William C. Nell, *The Colored Patriots of the American Revolution* (Boston, 1855), pp. 101–102.

86. Horton and Horton, *Black Bostonians,* p. 120.

87. Benjamin Quarles, *Black Abolitionists* (New York, 1969), p. 230.

88. Horton and Horton, *Black Bostonians,* p. 121.

CHAPTER 2

1. Boston *Atlas and Daily Bee,* October 17, 22, 1859. See Betty Mitchell, "Massachusetts Reaction to John Brown's Raid," *Civil War History* 19 (March 1973): 65–79, for a study of Boston newspapers' response to the raid.

2. Richard H. Abbott, "Cobbler in Congress: The Life of Henry Wilson, 1812–1875," Ph.D. diss., University of Wisconsin, 1965.

3. *Worcester Spy,* October 20, 17, 1859, cited in James M. McPherson, *Battle Cry of Freedom: The Civil War Era* (New York, 1988), p. 208.

4. *Springfield Republican,* December 3, 1859. See Mitchell, "Massachusetts Reaction to John Brown's Raid," 66–67.

5. *The Liberator,* October 28, 1859. See Bruce Olds, *Raising Holy Hell* (New York, 1995), for a fictionalized account of John Brown's bitter, brutal life and his sadly defiant end. Mitchell, "Massachusetts Reaction to John Brown's Raid," pp. 71–72.

6. McPherson, *Battle Cry,* p. 210.

7. *Springfield Republican,* November 3, 1849; "Plea for Captain Brown," in *The Writings of Henry David Thoreau,* 20 vols. (Boston, 1906), IV, pp. 409–440. Also see Stephen B. Oates, *To Purge This Land with Blood: A Biography of John Brown* (New York, 1970), pp. 335–336.

8. McPherson, *Battle Cry,* p. 209.

9. Horton and Horton, *Black Bostonians,* p. 124.

10. *Boston Post,* December 3, 1859; *Boston Evening Transcript,* December 2, 1859.

11. Horton and Horton, *Black Bostonians,* p. 124.

12. *Boston Post,* December 3, 1859.

13. *The Liberator,* December 9, 1859. Mitchell, "Massachusetts Reaction to John Brown's Raid," pp. 74–78.

14. *The Boston Pilot,* October 29, 1859.

15. Ibid.

16. Ibid., December 10, 1859.

17. Ibid., November 19, December 3, 1859; January 7, 1860.

18. Ibid., December 10, 24, 1859.

19. Ibid., July 7, 1860.

20. O'Connor, *Fitzpatrick,* p. 187; Walsh, *The Boston Pilot,* p. 150.

21. Foner, *Free Soil, Free Labor,* p. 227.

22. Handlin, *Boston's Immigrants,* p. 208.

23. Roediger, *The Wages of Whiteness,* p. 141.

24. Holt, *Political Crisis of the 1850s,* p. 224, states that the South viewed John Brown's raid not as an isolated incident but as part of a "gigantic conspiracy" fomented by abolitionists and Republicans.

25. McPherson, *Battle Cry,* p. 211.

26. Henry Greenleaf Pearson, *The Life of John A. Andrew, Governor of Massachusetts, 1861–1865,* 2 vols. (Boston, 1904), I, pp. 105–106, 109.

27. Stephen B. Oates, *To Purge This Land with Blood,* pp. 243–247. Also see O'Connor, *Lords of the Loom,* pp. 135–136.

28. O'Connor, *Lords of the Loom,* p. 136.

29. Abbott, *Cotton and Capital,* p. 52. Michael Holt, in *Political Crisis of the 1850s,* argues that the Republicans used Kansas as a convenient issue with which to

wage a much larger struggle against the Slave Power, the "Oligarchs of Slavery" as Charles Sumner called them. Gienapp, *Republican Party,* p. 357, calls the Slave-Power concept a "master symbol" of the Republicans.

30. Abbott, *Cotton and Capital,* p. 52; Gienapp, *Republican Party,* pp. 387–388, 419–424.

31. Pearson, *Andrew,* I, pp. 68–82. Also see William Schouler, *A History of Massachusetts in the Civil War,* 2 vols. (Boston, 1868), I, pp. 11–13.

32. Pearson, *Andrew,* I, pp. 96–97, 100–101.

33. Ibid., p. 116.

34. Hans Trefousse, *The Radical Republicans: Lincoln's Vanguard for Racial Justice* (New York, 1969), p. 134.

35. Foner, *Free Soil, Free Labor,* p. 147.

36. Pearson, *Andrew,* I, p. 128. Dale Baum, *Civil War Party System,* p. 55, sees Andrew and the Radicals as a significant shift from the "old-family" monied interests on Beacon Hill.

37. Abbott, *Cotton and Capital,* p. 53. "Hunker" was the term given in the 1840s to conservative New York Democrats who battled with radical "Barnburners" over the slavery issue. In time the word was applied to any old-fashioned, conservative politician.

38. Ronald P. Formisano, *The Birth of Mass Political Parties: Michigan, 1827–1861* (Princeton, N.J., 1971). Formisano posits that Whig power actually collapsed in 1853, a year before the Kansas-Nebraska Act, by trying to appeal to the immigrant-Catholic vote in the 1852 election.

39. O'Connor, *Lords of the Loom,* p. 137; Baum, *Civil War Party System,* p. 72.

40. O'Connor, *Lords of the Loom,* pp. 137–138; Abbott, *Cotton and Capital,* p. 64.

41. *Springfield Republican,* May 11, 1860; O'Connor, *Lords of the Loom,* p. 40; Abbott, *Cotton and Capital,* p. 65.

42. David Donald, *Abraham Lincoln* (New York, 1995), pp. 255–256; Abbott, *Cotton and Capital,* p. 66; Baum, *Civil War Party System,* pp. 50–51; Silbey, *Respectable Minority,* pp. 18–20.

43. Baum, *Civil War Party System,* p. 75. Baum emphasizes the Democratic party's continued support by old, affluent Brahmins on Beacon Hill.

44. *Boston Post,* December 11, 1860.

45. O'Connor, *Lords of the Loom,* p. 143.

46. Henry Adams, "The Secession Winter, 1860–1861," *Proceedings of the Massachusetts Historical Society* 43 (1910): 660–687. Also see Kenneth Stampp, *And the War Came* (Baton Rouge, La., 1950); Dwight Dumond, *The Secession Movement, 1860–1861* (New York, 1931).

47. James M. McPherson, *Struggle for Equality: Abolitionists and the Negro in the Civil War and Reconstruction* (Princeton, N.J., 1964), pp. 41–42.

48. *Boston Evening Transcript,* December 3, 6, 1860; *Boston Courier,* December 4, 1860; *Boston Post,* December 4, 1860; *The Liberator,* December 7, 1860.

49. Horton and Horton, *Black Bostonians*, p. 125.

50. Ibid., p. 125; McPherson, *Struggle for Equality*, p. 42.

51. Maria Wescott Chapman to Mrs. E. P. Nichol, December 10, 1860, Anti-Slavery Collection, Boston Public Library; McPherson, *Struggle for Equality*, p. 42.

52. *The Liberator*, December 7, 1860; January 4, 1861.

53. Wendell Phillips, *Speeches, Lectures, and Letters*, ed. J. Redpath, (Boston, 1894), p. 344.

54. *Boston Evening Transcript*, December 8, 1859.

55. Pearson, *Andrew*, I, pp. 149–152; McPherson, *Struggle for Equality*, pp. 43–44.

56. *Boston Evening Transcript*, January 24, 25, 26, 1861; *Boston Daily Advertiser*, January 25, 1861; *The Liberator*, February 1, 1861.

57. O'Connor, *Lords of the Loom*, p. 144.

58. *Boston Herald*, February 21, 1861.

59. Letter printed in the *Boston Daily Advertiser*, January 11, 1861.

60. O'Connor, *Lords of the Loom*, p. 145.

61. *Boston Herald*, July 10, 1861.

62. Pearson, *Andrew*, I, pp. 135–136; Abbott, *Cotton and Capital*, p. 68.

63. O'Connor, *Lords of the Loom*, p. 144; Abbott, *Cotton and Capital*, p. 67.

64. O'Connor, *Lords of the Loom*, pp. 145–146; Abbott, *Cotton and Capital*, p. 68.

65. O'Connor, *Lords of the Loom*, pp. 146–147; Abbott, *Cotton and Capital*, pp. 68–69.

66. Pearson, *Andrew*, I, pp. 155–158, 162; Schouler, *Massachusetts*, I, pp. 29–30; Abbott, *Cotton and Capital*, p. 69.

67. Henry Greenleaf Pearson, "Massachusetts to the Front," *Commonwealth History of Massachusetts*, ed. A. B. Hart, 5 vols. (New York, 1920), IV, pp. 506–507.

68. Sarah F. Hughes, ed., *Letters and Recollections of John Murray Forbes*, 2 vols. (Boston, 1899), II, pp. 99–100.

69. O'Connor, *Lords of the Loom*, p. 152.

70. *Boston Post*, February 15, 1861; *The Liberator*, February 22, 1861.

71. Schouler, *Massachusetts*, I, p. 15.

72. Pearson, *Andrew*, I, pp. 139–143; Schouler, *Massachusetts*, I, pp. 17–18.

73. Pearson, *Andrew*, I, pp. 147–148; Schouler, *Massachusetts*, I, pp. 20–21.

74. Pearson, *Andrew*, I, pp. 173–174; Schouler, *Massachusetts*, I, p. 35.

75. Donald, *Abraham Lincoln*, pp. 285–289.

76. Charles Hale to James Amory, April 24, 1861. Miscellaneous Manuscripts, Massachusetts Historical Society.

77. Susan Loring, ed., *Selections from the Diaries of William Appleton, 1786–1862* (Boston, 1922), pp. 236–237.

78. O'Connor, *Lords of the Loom*, p. 155.

79. Loring, ed., *Diaries of William Appleton*, pp. 237–239.

80. Charles Francis Adams Diary, April 15, 18, 1861. Massachusetts Historical Society.

81. Charles Sumner to Henry Wadsworth Longfellow, April 17, 1861. Longfellow Papers, Houghton Library, Harvard University.

82. Sarah Norton and Mark De Wolfe Howe, eds., *Letters of Charles Eliot Norton,* 2 vols. (Boston, 1913), I, p. 234.

83. McPherson, *Struggle for Equality,* p. 55; Edith Ellen Ware, *Political Opinion in Massachusetts During the Civil War and Reconstruction* (New York, 1916), p. 69.

84. McPherson, *Struggle for Equality,* pp. 50–51.

85. Horton and Horton, *Black Bostonians,* pp. 125–126.

86. Richard S. West, Jr., *Lincoln's Scapegoat General: A Life of Benjamin F. Butler, 1818–1893* (Cambridge, Mass., 1965), pp. 35–38.

87. *Boston Post,* November 4, 8, 11, 1859.

88. *Springfield Republican,* October 22, 1850.

89. Francis W. Bird, *Review of Governor Banks' Veto of the Revised Code: An Account of Its Authorizing the Enrollment of Colored Citizens in the Militia* (Boston, 1860). Also see Horton and Horton, *Black Bostonians,* p. 125.

90. Ware, *Political Opinion,* p. 70; O'Connor, *Lords of the Loom,* p. 155.

91. *Boston Post,* June 18, 1861.

92. Thomas R. Navin, *The Whitin Machine Works since 1831* (Cambridge, Mass., 1950), pp. 54–55.

93. Robert C. Winthrop, Diary, April 19, 1861, Winthrop Papers, 36, p. 173. Massachusetts Historical Society.

94. Abbott, *Cotton and Capital,* pp. 72–73.

95. Pearson, *Andrew,* I, pp. 160–162.

96. Sarah Hughes, ed., *Letters and Recollections of John Murray Forbes,* 2 vols. (Boston, 1900), II, pp. 194–196; Pearson, *Andrew,* I, p. 215; Schouler, *Massachusetts,* I, p. 58.

97. O'Connor, *Lords of the Loom,* p. 160.

98. Ibid., pp. 155–156.

99. Abbott, *Cotton and Capital,* 72.

100. Silbey, *Respectable Minority,* p. 41.

101. "The Democrats were caught in one of the most difficult of all political situations," writes Joel Silbey in *Respectable Minority,* pp. 32–35, 90–91. Also see Phillip S. Paludan, *"A People's Contest": The Union and Civil War, 1861–1865* (New York, 1988), p. 86.

102. Thomas G. Frothingham, "Massachusetts in the Civil War," *Commonwealth History,* IV, p. 516.

103. Ware, *Political Opinion,* p. 78.

104. *Boston Post,* September 9, 1861.

105. Ware, *Political Opinion,* p. 69; Silbey, *Respectable Minority,* pp. 39–40.

106. *The Boston Pilot,* December 1, 1860; January 26, 1861. See Francis R. Walsh, "The *Boston Pilot* Reports the Civil War," *Historical Journal of Massachusetts* 9 (June 1981): 5–15.

107. *The Boston Pilot,* April 27, 1861; Brian Kelly, "Ambiguous Loyalties: The

Boston Irish, Slavery, and the Civil War," *Historical Journal of Massachusetts* XXIV (Summer 1996): 165–204.

108. *The Boston Pilot,* April 27, 1861.

109. *Boston Post,* April 27, 1861; *The Boston Pilot,* May 4, 1861; Kelly, "Ambiguous Loyalties," p. 166.

110. Schouler, *Massachusetts,* I, pp. 48–49.

111. Ibid., I, pp. 49–50.

112. Robert F. McGraw, "Minutemen of '61: The Pre-Civil War Massachusetts Militia," *Civil War History* XV (June 1969): 103–107.

113. Ibid., p. 114.

114. Ibid., p. 115.

115. Frothingham, "Massachusetts in the Civil War," pp. 516–517.

116. West, *Lincoln's Scapegoat General,* pp. 46–47.

117. Pearson, *Andrew,* I, pp. 210–211; Schouler, *Massachusetts,* I, pp. 50–51.

118. Pearson, *Andrew,* I, pp. 177–178, 182–183; Schouler, *Massachusetts,* I, pp. 52–53; Pearson, "Massachusetts to the Front," pp. 507–508; Frothingham, "Massachusetts in the Civil War," pp. 516–517.

119. Pearson, *Andrew,* I, p. 180.

120. George Templeton Strong, *Diary of the Civil War, 1860–1865,* ed. Allan Nevins (New York, 1962), p. 124 (April 18, 1861).

121. Pearson, *Andrew,* I, pp. 189–190.

122. Schouler, *Massachusetts,* I, pp. 96–97; Pearson, "Massachusetts to the Front," pp. 508–509; Frothingham, "Massachusetts in the Civil War," pp. 518–519. Also see McPherson, *Battle Cry,* p. 285.

123. Allan Nevins, *The War for the Union,* 4 vols. (New York, 1959–1971), I, pp. 69–71; Margaret Leech, *Reveille in Washington* (New York, 1941), pp. 54–65; Donald, *Abraham Lincoln,* pp. 298–299; McPherson, *Battle Cry,* p. 286.

124. West, *Scapegoat General,* pp. 52–54.

125. Donald, *Abraham Lincoln,* p. 299.

126. Schouler, *Massachusetts,* I, pp. 104–105.

127. *Springfield Republican,* April 25, 1861.

128. Pearson, *Andrew,* I, p. 213.

CHAPTER 3

1. *Boston Post,* April 25, 1861.

2. Charles Francis Adams, *Autobiography* (New York, 1961), p. 117.

3. William J. Reid, *Castle Island and Fort Independence* (Boston, 1995), pp. 95–96.

4. Schouler, *Massachusetts,* I, pp. 123–125.

5. Edward Rowe Snow, *The Islands of Boston Harbor, 1639–1971* (New York, 1936, 1971), pp. 8–10.

6. Ibid., pp. 11–12.

7. Pearson, *Andrew,* I, p. 192.

8. Ibid., pp. 199–200; Schouler, *Massachusetts,* I, p. 53; Frothingham, "Massachusetts in the Civil War," p. 518.

9. Schouler, *Massachusetts,* I, pp. 56–57.

10. Ibid., pp. 176–178, 186–187.

11. Frothingham, "Massachusetts in the Civil War," pp. 520–521. Also see Pearson, *Andrew,* I, pp. 216–217; Schouler, *Massachusetts,* I, pp. 152–154.

12. George W. Adams, *Doctors in Blue* (New York, 1952).

13. William Q. Maxwell, *Lincoln's Fifth Wheel: The Political History of the United States Sanitation Commission* (New York, 1956).

14. *Springfield Republican,* November 11, 1862.

15. Pearson, *Andrew,* I, pp. 225–226.

16. *The Liberator,* April 26, 1861.

17. Horton and Horton, *Black Bostonians,* p. 126.

18. *The Liberator,* May 17, 1861. Also see Schouler, *Massachusetts,* I, pp. 177–178, for a description of the legislation's progress.

19. Pearson, *Andrew,* I, pp. 117–118.

20. Schouler, *Massachusetts,* I, pp. 167–168; Pearson, *Andrew,* I, pp. 231–232. See John T. Morse, "The Cadet Band," *History of the Forty-Fifth Regiment, Massachusetts Volunteer Militia* (Jamaica Plain, Mass., 1908), pp. 193–197, for a description of a band's functions and duties in wartime, including service as an ambulance corps under battle conditions.

21. Jordan D. Fiore, *Massachusetts in the Civil War: The Year of Trial and Testing, 1861–1862* (Boston, 1961), pp. 11–12.

22. Schouler, *Massachusetts,* I, pp. 168–169; Pearson, *Andrew,* I, p. 223.

23. Fiore, *Year of Trial and Testing,* p. 12.

24. Schouler, *Massachusetts,* I, pp. 109–110. Also see Bell Irvin Wiley, *The Life of Billy Yank: The Common Soldier of the Union* (Indianapolis, 1952), pp. 28–33. See James M. McPherson, *For Cause and Comrades: Why Men Fought in the Civil War* (New York, 1997), for a perceptive analysis of the ideals for which Americans fought throughout the conflict.

25. Schouler, *Massachusetts,* I, pp. 111–112.

26. Emerson D. Fite, *Social and Industrial Conditions in the North During the Civil War* (New York, reprint 1963), p. 237.

27. Phillip S. Paludan, *"A People's Contest",* pp. 132–133.

28. Fiore, *Year of Trial and Testing,* p. 13. Also see Wiley, *Billy Yank,* pp. 307–312, for an extensive analysis of the Union army's various ethnic elements.

29. West, *Scapegoat General,* pp. 92–96; Fiore, *Year of Trial and Testing,* p. 21.

30. McPherson, *Battle Cry,* pp. 339–340.

31. Ibid., pp. 340–344.

32. Paludan, *People's Contest,* p. 59.

33. Cited in George M. Fredrickson, *The Inner Civil War: Northern Intellectuals and the Crisis of the Union* (New York, 1965), p. 68.

34. Quoted in Strong, *Diary,* III, p. 185.

35. See Reid Mitchell, *The Vacant Chair: The Northern Soldier Leaves Home* (New York, 1993).

36. Schouler, *Massachusetts*, I, p. 226.

37. Pearson, *Andrew*, I, pp. 106–107; Willis J. Abbott, *Blue Jackets of '61: A History of the Navy in the War of Secession* (New York, 1887), pp. 49–52; Virgil Carrington Jones, *The Civil War at Sea*, 2 vol. (New York, 1961), I, pp. 192–209.

38. West, *Scapegoat General*, pp. 106–107.

39. Schouler, *Massachusetts*, I, p. 67.

40. McGraw, "Minutemen of '61," pp. 109–110.

41. William L. Burton, "Irish Regiments in the Union Army: The Massachusetts Experience," *Historical Journal of Massachusetts* 11 (June 1983): 104–105.

42. Schouler, *Massachusetts*, I, pp. 210–212.

43. A small collection of thirty-six letters from Michael H. Leary, Company B, 9th Massachusetts Volunteer Regiment, is deposited in the Archives of the Burns Research Library at Boston College.

44. Michael H. MacNamara, *The Irish Ninth in Bivouac and Battle* (Boston, 1867); Daniel G. MacNamara, *History of the Ninth Regiment* (Boston, 1899).

45. D. G. MacNamara, *History of the Ninth Regiment*, pp. 6–7.

46. *The Boston Pilot*, July 20, 1861; O'Connor, *Fitzpatrick*, p. 194. Also see Burton, "Irish Regiments," pp. 104–105.

47. D. G. MacNamara, *History of the Ninth Regiment*, pp. 4–5.

48. Ibid., p. 10; M. H. MacNamara, *Irish Ninth*, p. 27.

49. William M. Burton, *Melting Pot Soldiers: The Union's Ethnic Regiments* (Ames, Iowa, 1988), pp. 128–129.

50. *The Boston Pilot*, June 25, 1861.

51. *Boston Herald*, June 12, 1861.

52. D. G. MacNamara, *History*, p. 24.

53. *The Boston Pilot*, June 25, 1861; also see Francis R. Walsh, "Who Spoke for Boston's Irish?" *Journal of Ethnic Studies* 10 (Fall 1982): 21–36.

54. O'Connor, *Fitzpatrick*, p. 195.

55. Ibid.

56. Ibid., p. 196; Burton, "Irish Regiments," pp. 110–111.

57. J. L. Garland, "The Formation of Meagher's Irish Brigade," *Irish Sword* 3 (Summer 1958): 162–165.

58. William J. McLaughlin, "The Fighting Yankees in the Irish Brigade," *North South Trader* (March–April 1979): 15–17, 43.

59. Peter Welsh began regularly corresponding with his wife, Margaret, on September 14, 1862, one day after he joined the regiment. The correspondence ended May 15, 1864, with his last letter from the Carver Hospital in Washington, D.C., where he died from wounds received at Spotsylvania. *Irish Green and Union Blue: The Civil War Letters of Peter Welsh*, ed. Lawrence F. Kohl and Margaret C. Richard (New York, 1986), p. 8.

60. O'Connor, *Fitzpatrick*, p. 197.

61. Ibid., pp. 198–199.

62. The front page of *The Boston Pilot* (September 2, 1862) features an advertisement for "The First Irish Regiment," with a notice that a Roman Catholic chaplain would be appointed to the regiment.

63. O'Connor, *Fitzpatrick,* p. 201.

64. Ibid., p. 202.

65. *Boston Daily Courier,* September 10, 1861. See Ware, *Political Opinion,* p. 77.

66. *Boston Post,* August 17, 1861.

67. *Boston Post,* September 19, 1861; Schouler, *Massachusetts,* I, p. 249. See Silbey, *Respectable Minority,* pp. 49–50, for expressions of Democratic opposition.

68. *Boston Daily Advertiser,* September 28, 1861. Silbey, *Respectable Minority,* pp. 43–44.

69. *Boston Daily Advertiser,* October 2, 1861.

70. Ware, *Political Opinion,* p. 80.

71. Schouler, *Massachusetts,* I, pp. 245–246; Ware, *Political Opinion,* p. 81.

72. Schouler, *Massachusetts,* I, p. 250.

73. Lois Hill, ed., *Poems and Songs of the Civil War* (New York, 1990), pp. 64–65.

74. McPherson, *Battle Cry,* pp. 348–350.

75. T. Harry Williams, *Lincoln and the Radicals* (Madison, Wis., 1965), p. 17.

76. Ibid., p. 110.

77. Paludan, *People's Contest,* p. 63.

78. Charles L. Peirson, *Ball's Bluff* (Boston, 1904); McPherson, *Battle Cry,* p. 362. Also see George A. Bruce, *The Twentieth Regiment Massachusetts Volunteers* (Boston, 1906), pp. 24–53.

79. Schouler, *Massachusetts,* I, pp. 233–234. Also see *History of the Nineteenth Regiment, Massachusetts Volunteer Infantry, 1861–1865* (Salem, Mass., 1906), pp. 22–34; Bruce, *Twentieth Regiment,* pp. 53–58.

80. Fiore, *Year of Trial and Testing,* pp. 25–26.

81. Peirson, *Ball's Bluff.* See Bruce, *Twentieth Regiment,* pp. 59–61, for a detailed listing of casualties.

82. Fiore, *Year of Trial and Testing,* pp. 33–35.

83. James M. Merrill, *The Rebel Shore: The Story of Union Sea Power in the Civil War* (Boston, 1957), pp. 12–13; Jones, *The Civil War at Sea,* pp. 25–26.

84. P. C. Headley, *Massachusetts in the Rebellion: A Record of the Historical Position of the Commonwealth* (Boston, 1866), pp. 552–554.

85. Fiore, *Year of Trial and Testing,* pp. 37–38.

86. Ibid., p. 34.

87. Ibid., pp. 38–39.

88. Schouler, *Massachusetts,* I, p. 203; Pearson, *Andrew,* I, pp. 219–220.

89. Fiore, *Year of Trial and Testing,* p. 36.

90. Samuel Eliot Morison, *The Maritime History of Massachusetts* (Boston, 1941), pp. 369–370.

91. Rowena Reed, *Combined Operations in the Civil War* (Annapolis, 1978), pp. 15, 22, 44–45. Also see Thomas Edmonds, "Operations in North Carolina, 1861–1862," *Military Historical Society of Massachusetts Papers* 9 (1912): 80–82; Hazard Stevens, "Military Operations in South Carolina in 1862," *Military Historical Society of Massachusetts Papers* 9 (1912): 142–227.

92. Jones, *The Civil War at Sea*, I, 324–325.

93. Reed, *Combined Operations,* p. 52; Edmonds, "Operations in North Carolina," p. 82; Stevens, "Operations in South Carolina," p. 227; Jones, *The Civil War at Sea*, I, p. 325.

94. Fiore, *Year of Trial and Testing*, pp. 28–29.

95. West, *Scapegoat General,* pp. 44–47; Fiore, *Year of Trial and Testing,* pp. 29–31. Also see Pearson, *Andrew,* I, pp. 44–47, 183–184, for a summary of Butler's early political career.

96. Pearson, *Andrew,* I, p. 184.

97. Ibid., pp. 185–186; West, *Scapegoat General,* pp. 112–117. Schouler, *Massachusetts,* I, pp. 156–157, contains a copy of a letter from Butler to Andrew, dated May 9, 1861, giving the general's explanation for the slave incident.

98. Schouler, *Massachusetts,* I, pp. 256–257.

99. Pearson, *Andrew,* I, pp. 286–290; Schouler, *Massachusetts,* I, pp. 259–260.

100. Ibid., p. 290.

101. Ibid., pp. 301–302; Schouler, *Massachusetts,* I, pp. 261–266.

102. John A. Andrew and Benjamin F. Butler, *Correspondence Between Gov. Andrew and Maj. Gen. Butler* (Boston, 1862); Pearson, *Andrew,* I, pp. 307–308. Schouler, *Massachusetts,* I, pp. 252–282, presents the entire controversy between the two men.

103. Fiore, *Year of Trial and Testing,* p. 31.

104. Snow, *Boston Harbor,* p. 13.

105. Pearson, *Andrew,* I, p. 318; McPherson, *Battle Cry,* pp. 389–391; Abbott, *Blue Jackets of '61,* pp. 53–55.

106. Donald, *Abraham Lincoln,* pp. 320–323.

107. Charles Sumner, *Charles Sumner: His Complete Works,* 20 vol. (Boston, 1900), VII, p. 78; E. L. Pierce to C. F. Adams, December 31, 1861, Adams Papers; Henry Adams to C. F. Adams, Jr., January 17, 1861, Adams Papers; Charles Francis Adams Diary, December 18, January 6, 13, 1861, Adams Papers, Massachusetts Historical Society.

108. Allan Nevins, *The Emergence of Lincoln: Prologue to Civil War, 1859–1861* (New York, 1950), pp. 438–439.

109. Paul Nagel, *Descent from Glory: Four Generations of the John Adams Family* (New York, 1983); Francis Russell, *Adams: An American Dynasty* (New York, 1976); Jack Shepherd, *The Adams Chronicles: Four Generations of Greatness* (Boston, 1975).

110. Martin Duberman, *The Life of Charles Francis Adams* (Stanford, Calif., 1968), pp. 280–290; Frank J. Merli, *Great Britain and the Confederate Navy, 1861–*

1865 (Bloomington, Ind., 1970), pp. 84–86; Ephraim D. Adams, *Great Britain and the American Civil War,* 2 vols., (New York, 1925), I, pp. 264–266.

111. Fiore, *Year of Trial and Testing,* pp. 39–40; Wiley, *Billy Yank,* pp. 56–58.

112. Fiore, *Year of Trial and Testing,* p. 40.

113. Pearson, *Andrew,* I, pp. 320–324; Fiore, *Year of Trial and Testing,* p. 32.

CHAPTER 4

1. Schouler, *Massachusetts,* I, p. 337.

2. Roy P. Basler, ed., *The Collected Works of Abraham Lincoln,* 8 vols. (New Brunswick, N.J., 1953), V, p. 158.

3. Paludan, *People's Contest,* p. 63; Donald, *Abraham Lincoln,* pp. 338–339.

4. McPherson, *Battle Cry,* pp. 423–441; Donald, *Abraham Lincoln,* pp. 341–342.

5. West, *Scapegoat General,* pp. 121–122.

6. Gerald M. Capers, *Occupied City: New Orleans under the Federals, 1862–1865* (Lexington, 1965), p. 63; Merrill, *The Rebel Shore,* pp. 120–128.

7. West, *Scapegoat General,* pp. 129–131.

8. See Carl Sandburg, *Abraham Lincoln: The War Years* (New York, 1939), I, p. 12, II, pp. 60, 186, III, p. 15, for dramatic portrayals of the pressures upon Lincoln over the cotton question.

9. *Boston Daily Courier,* October 15, 1862. Also see George T. Woolfolk, *The Cotton Regency* (New York, 1958), pp. 14–15.

10. John T. Morse, ed., *The Diary of Gideon Welles* (Boston, 1911), I, pp. 497–498. See also David Donald, *Inside Lincoln's Cabinet: The Civil War Diaries of Salmon P. Chase* (New York, 1954), pp. 143–145, 164–165.

11. U.S. War Department, comp., *The War of the Rebellion: A Compilation of the Official Records of the Union and Confederate Armies* (Washington, D.C., 1880–1901), Ser. I, XV, pp. 582–583.

12. T. Conn Bryan, *Confederate Georgia* (Athens, Ga., 1953), pp. 147–148; John B. Jones, *A Rebel War Clerk's Diary at the Confederate States Capital* (New York, 1866), I, pp. 180–181.

13. Ludwell H. Johnson, *Red River Campaign: Politics and Cotton in the Civil War* (Baltimore, 1958), pp. 52–56; Richard S. West, *Mr. Lincoln's Navy* (New York, 1957), pp. 248–249.

14. Letter from New Orleans, May 13, 1862, Henry Warren Howe, *Diary and Letters Written During the Civil War, 1861–1865* (Lowell, Mass., 1899), pp. 119–120.

15. Capers, *Occupied City,* pp. 67–69; West, *Scapegoat General,* pp. 150–151.

16. West, *Scapegoat General,* pp. 139–140.

17. Letter from New Orleans, December 17, 1862, Howe, *Diary,* p. 130. See also Capers, *Occupied City,* pp. 104–105.

18. *Boston Daily Advertiser,* July 5, 1862.

19. McPherson, *Battle Cry,* pp. 427–428.

20. Nevins, *The War for the Union,* p. 13; McPherson, *Battle Cry,* pp. 454–455.

21. McPherson, *Battle Cry,* pp. 463–468.

22. Ibid., pp. 469–470.

23. M. H. MacNamara, *The Irish Ninth,* p. 102; Burton, "Irish Regiments," pp. 109–110.

24. James B. Cullen, *The Story of the Irish in Boston* (Boston, 1889), pp. 110–111, 245–246. Under Guiney's command, the Boston 9th Regiment went on to fight with great courage at Hanover Court House, Gaines Mills, and Chancellorsville. In May 1864, Guiney was badly wounded in the Battle of the Wilderness and sent back to Boston. See Burton, *Melting Pot Soldiers,* pp. 130–131, for a discussion of the controversies over who should succeed Cass as regimental commander.

25. Schouler, *Massachusetts,* I, pp. 296–297, reports local reaction to the number of casualties returning north from Virginia.

26. Donald, *Abraham Lincoln,* pp. 356–357.

27. Charles Eliot Norton to Elizabeth Gaskell, August 5, 1862, *Letters of Mrs. Gaskell and Charles Eliot Norton, 1855–1865* (London, 1932).

28. *Boston Daily Advertiser,* August 27, 1862.

29. Brian C. Mitchell, *The Paddy Camps: The Irish of Lowell, 1821–1861* (Champaign, Ill., 1988), pp. 6–7.

30. Edward W. Ellsworth, *Massachusetts in the Civil War: A Year of Crisis, 1862–1863* (Boston, 1962), III, p. 12. See Mitchell, *The Paddy Camps,* for a study of the camps that kept the Irish separated from the Yankee residents in the mill town.

31. Donald, *Abraham Lincoln,* p. 361; McPherson, *Battle Cry,* p. 488.

32. McPherson, *Battle Cry,* pp. 523–533; Ellsworth, *Year of Crisis,* pp. 13–14.

33. Donald, *Abraham Lincoln,* pp. 370–371.

34. McPherson, *Battle Cry,* pp. 538–540.

35. Paludan, *People's Contest,* p. 82.

36. McPherson, *Battle Cry,* p. 544.

37. Schouler, *Massachusetts,* I, p. 368.

38. *Boston Daily Evening Traveller,* September 22, 1862.

39. *The Boston Pilot,* September 7, October 4, 1862.

40. For an account of the 20th Regiment's actions during the Battle of Antietam, see Bruce, *Twentieth Regiment,* pp. 159–174.

41. Oliver Wendell Holmes, *My Hunt after the Captain, and Other Papers* (Boston, 1887).

42. Trefousse, *Radical Republicans,* p. 204.

43. Williams, *Lincoln and the Radicals,* p. 10.

44. Peleg Chandler, *Memoir and Reminiscences of Governor Andrew* (Boston, 1881), p. 33. Also see Baum, *Civil War Party System,* p. 60 for a discussion of Sumner's and the Radicals' growing agitation about the slavery issue.

45. Williams, *Lincoln and the Radicals,* p. 40.

46. Ware, *Political Opinion,* p. 92.

47. Ibid., p. 94.

48. "Lincoln would not permit civilian authority to be overruled by the military,"

states David Donald, in his superb biography of the sixteenth president, "and he would not allow sensitive questions concerning slavery and emancipation to be decided by anyone but the President himself." Donald, *Abraham Lincoln*, p. 315.

49. Abbott, *Cotton and Capital*, p. 71.

50. Hughes, ed., *Letters and Recollections of Forbes*, I, p. 202.

51. Abbott, *Cotton and Capital*, pp. 76–77.

52. Ibid., p. 77.

53. Ware, *Political Opinion*, p. 93.

54. Williams, *Lincoln and the Radicals*, p. 104.

55. Ibid.

56. Ibid., p. 164.

57. Ware, *Political Opinion*, p. 97; Williams, *Lincoln and the Radicals*, p. 160.

58. Williams, *Lincoln and the Radicals*, p. 159.

59. Pearson, *Andrew*, II, pp. 4–5.

60. Chandler, *Memoir of Andrew*, p. 55.

61. Ware, *Political Opinion*, p. 99.

62. Quoted in Pearson, *Andrew*, II, p. 9.

63. Ware, *Political Opinion*, p. 101.

64. Walsh, *The Boston Pilot*, p. 167.

65. Ware, *Political Opinion*, p. 104.

66. *The Boston Pilot*, October 4, 1862.

67. Abbott, *Cotton and Capital*, p. 96.

68. Ibid., p. 95; O'Connor, *Lords of the Loom*, p. 97.

69. Abbott, *Cotton and Capital*, p. 95.

70. Ibid., pp. 77–83.

71. Ibid., pp. 84–85.

72. Ibid., pp. 85–86.

73. Ibid., pp. 88–89.

74. McPherson, *Struggle for Equality*, pp. 112–113.

75. McPherson, *Battle Cry of Freedom*, p. 504; Donald, *Abraham Lincoln*, pp. 362–363.

76. McPherson, *Battle Cry*, p. 505.

77. Basler, ed., *Collected Works of Abraham Lincoln*, V, pp. 336–337.

78. McPherson, *Battle Cry*, pp. 508–509. David Donald suggests that Lincoln's floating the idea of colonization was a "shrewd political move" calculated to make eventual emancipation "more palatable" to the border states, as well as to relieve northerners of fears that they would be inundated by freed blacks. See Donald, *Abraham Lincoln*, pp. 367–368.

79. Pearson, *Andrew*, II, pp. 50–51.

80. McPherson, *Struggle for Equality*, pp. 118–119.

81. Trefousse, *Radical Republicans*, p. 228.

82. Williams, *Lincoln and the Radicals*, p. 217.

83. Donald, *Abraham Lincoln*, p. 378.

84. Pearson, *Andrew*, II, pp. 48–49; Donald, *Abraham Lincoln*, p. 373.

85. Silbey, *Respectable Minority,* pp. 56–58.

86. Ibid., pp. 100–109. Also see Donald, *Abraham Lincoln,* p. 313.

87. Fletcher Pratt, *Ordeal by Fire* (New York, 1935), p. 221.

88. Silbey, *Respectable Minority,* pp. 53–55; McPherson, *Battle Cry,* pp. 591–592.

89. Pearson, *Andrew,* II, p. 60; Baum, *Civil War Party System,* p. 65.

90. Schouler, *Massachusetts,* I, p. 373; Silbey, *Respectable Minority,* p. 66. "By the fall of 1862," writes Silbey, "the Democratic party was fully in the field against its political enemy."

91. Pearson, *Andrew,* II, p. 60; Schouler, *Massachusetts,* I, pp. 372–373.

92. Baum, *Civil War Party System,* pp. 67–68.

93. *Boston Daily Advertiser,* December 13, 1862.

94. Paludan, *"People's Contest,"* pp. 101–102; Baum, *Civil War Party System,* pp. 68–69.

95. Donald, *Abraham Lincoln,* pp. 382–383.

96. Ibid., pp. 388–390.

97. *History of the Nineteenth Regiment,* pp. 177–184; Bruce, *Twentieth Regiment,* pp. 182–222.

98. William Corby, *Memoirs of Chaplain Life* (Notre Dame, Ind., 1894), p. 131.

99. Peter Welsh to Margaret Welsh, December 25, 1862, in *Irish Green and Union Blue,* pp. 41–43.

100. Paludan, *"People's Contest,"* pp. 282–283.

101. Donald, *Abraham Lincoln,* p. 399.

102. Boston *Daily Evening Traveller,* December 11, 13, 1862; *Springfield Republican,* December 19, 1862.

103. *Boston Post,* December 15, 1862.

104. *Boston Daily Advertiser,* December 16, 1862.

105. *Boston Post,* December 17, 1862; *Boston Daily Advertiser,* December 17, 1862.

106. *Boston Post,* December 18, 1862.

107. *The Boston Pilot,* December 27, 1862.

108. *Boston Daily Advertiser,* December 16–20, 1862; *Boston Post,* December 18–20, 1862.

109. *Boston Daily Advertiser,* December 16–18, 1862.

110. *Boston Post,* December 30, 1862.

111. *The Boston Pilot,* December 20, 1862. The same editorial was repeated verbatim in the December 27 issue.

112. *Boston Daily Advertiser,* December 25, 1862.

CHAPTER 5

1. Edward F. Reed, "Memories of the Civil War and Camp," *History of the Forty-Fifth Regiment,* pp. 366–367; Ellsworth, *Year of Crisis,* pp. 19–20. Also see Wiley, *Billy Yank,* pp. 59–60 for a description of uniforms and equipment for the enlisted soldier.

2. Ellsworth, *Year of Crisis,* p. 21.

3. Ibid., pp. 18–20.

4. Letter, March 19, 1863, *Irish Green and Union Blue,* pp. 78–79. An account of the festivities was also carried in *The Boston Pilot,* April 4, 1863.

5. W. P. Garrison and F. J. Garrison, *William Lloyd Garrison: The Story of His Life as Told by His Children* (New York, 1885–1889), IV, pp. 69–70. Also see McPherson, *Struggle for Equality,* pp. 120–121; Fredrickson, *The Inner Civil War,* pp. 113–114; Benjamin Quarles, *Lincoln and the Negro* (New York, 1962), p. 143.

6. Ralph Waldo Emerson, *Poems: The Complete Works of Ralph Waldo Emerson* (Boston, 1904), IX, pp. 211–214.

7. Pearson, *Andrew,* II, p. 73; Schouler, *Massachusetts,* I, p. 407. Also see Peter Burchard, *One Gallant Rush: Robert Gould Shaw and His Brave Black Regiment* (New York, 1965), p. 2.

8. Herbert Aptheker, "The Negro in the Union Navy," *Journal of Negro History* 32 (April, 1947). Also see William L. Barney, *Flawed Victory: A New Perspective on the Civil War* (New York, 1975), p. 128.

9. Schouler, *Massachusetts,* I, p. 175.

10. Pauline E. Hopkins, "Famous Men of the Negro Race: Robert Morris," *The Colored American Magazine* 3 (September 1901): 341.

11. Pearson, *Andrew,* II, pp. 73–74, 82–83.

12. Benjamin Quarles, *The Negro in the Civil War* (Boston, 1953), pp. 8–9.

13. Luis F. Emilio, *A Brave Black Regiment: History of the Fifty-Fourth Regiment of Massachusetts Volunteer Infantry, 1863–1865,* 2nd ed. (Boston, 1894), pp. 8–16.

14. Schouler, *Massachusetts,* I, p. 408.

15. Pearson, *Andrew,* II, pp. 74–76.

16. Burchard, *One Gallant Rush,* pp. 71–76; Schouler, *Massachusetts,* I, pp. 408–409.

17. Pearson, *Andrew,* II, p. 78; Burchard, *One Gallant Rush,* pp. 77–79.

18. Edwin G. Walker, *In Memoriam—Robert Walker, Sr., June 8, 1823–December 12, 1882* (Boston, 1883), pp. 39–40. Massachusetts Historical Society.

19. One of the most notorious incidents occurred in April 1864, when the Confederates overran Fort Pillow, a Union outpost on the Mississippi River, and murdered black soldiers after they had surrendered. See Dudley T. Cornish, *The Sable Arm: Negro Troops in the Union Army* (New York, 1956), pp. 173–174.

20. "To Colored Men, 54th Regiment" (Boston, 1863). Broadside, Massachusetts Historical Society.

21. Pearson, *Andrew,* II, p. 84. Also see Horton and Horton, *Black Bostonians,* pp. 127–128.

22. Burchard, *One Gallant Rush,* pp. 83–85.

23. Ibid., pp. 84–85, 86–88.

24. Pearson, *Andrew,* II, pp. 86–87, 89.

25. Quarles, *The Negro in the Civil War,* p. 11.

26. Pearson, *Andrew,* II, pp. 88–89. According to local legend, the conservative members of the prestigious Somerset Club (then on Somerset Street) were so annoyed

by Shaw and his black troops marching by that they drew the curtains shut against the offending sight. This reaction could only have confirmed the earlier decision by John Murray Forbes, Amos A. Lawrence, and the other administration loyalists to establish their own Union Club on Park Street.

27. Pearson, *Andrew,* II, pp. 94–95.

28. Schouler, *Massachusetts,* I, pp. 501–502.

29. Pearson, *Andrew,* II, pp. 98, 108–109, 120.

30. Barney, *Flawed Victory,* p. 146.

31. Ibid., p. 147.

32. For reaction to Colonel Shaw's death and the 54th Regiment's gallantry, see Fredrickson, *The Inner Civil War,* pp. 152–153.

33. Emerson, *Poems,* IX, p. 207.

34. *New York Tribune,* February 11, 1863, cited in McPherson, *Battle Cry,* pp. 564–565.

35. Schouler, *Massachusetts,* I, p. 491.

36. J. A. Andrew to E. M. Stanton, September 5, 1863, John Andrew Papers, Massachusetts State Archives, vol. 36, p. 87. Also see Pearson, *Andrew,* II, pp. 93–94.

37. John T. Morse, Jr., *Sons of the Puritans* (Boston, 1908), p. 158.

38. No history of the 5th Cavalry has been written. I am deeply grateful to John D. Warner, Jr., of Boston College, for sharing with me the results of his research for his doctoral dissertation on the subject. After the war, the 5th Cavalry was sent to the Rio Grande as part of the 25th Army Corps to prevent any possible invasion after Emperor Maximilian's French forces had occupied Mexico. Late in October 1865, the 5th Cavalry was mustered out of federal service and shipped back to Boston. See John D. Warner, Jr., "Crossed Sabres: The History of the 5th Massachusetts Volunteer Cavalry," Ph.D. diss., Boston College, 1997.

39. Donald, *Abraham Lincoln,* p. 429.

40. Schouler, *Massachusetts,* pp. 442–443.

41. Letter, May 7, 1863, *Irish Green and Union Blue,* pp. 90–91.

42. *The Boston Pilot,* May 30, 1863.

43. *Boston Post,* October 8, 1962. See Silbey, *Respectable Minority,* pp. 51–52, 79–80.

44. *Boston Post,* January 3, 1863.

45. Ibid.

46. Silbey, *Respectable Minority,* pp. 81–82, 84.

47. *The Boston Pilot,* January 17, 1863.

48. Fragment, ca. February 1863, *Irish Green and Union Blue,* pp. 62–63. I have used the spelling found in Peter Welsh's original letter. This statement is confirmed by the modern historian Bell Wiley, *Billy Yank,* p. 109, when he states that Irish soldiers' letters and diaries show "an enormous antipathy" toward Negroes.

49. See Warner, "Crossed Sabres," for an account of this exchange in a letter from Charles Douglass to his father dated July 6, 1863, in the Frederick Douglass Papers, Manuscript Division, Library of Congress.

50. *The Boston Pilot,* April 4, 1863.

51. Ibid., May 10, 1862.

52. Ibid., April 4, 1863.

53. Ibid., January 24, 1863. Also see Silbey, *Respectable Minority*, pp. 83-84; O'Connor, *Fitzpatrick*, pp. 208-209.

54. Pearson, *Andrew*, II, pp. 141-142. Schouler, *Massachusetts*, I, pp. 505-506.

55. Iver Bernstein, *The New York City Draft Riots: Their Significance for American Society and Politics in the Age of the Civil War* (New York: 1990). Also see Adrian Cook, *Armies of the Streets: The New York City Draft Riots of 1863* (Lexington, Ky., 1974); Irving Weinstein, *July 1863: The Incredible Story of the Bloody New York Draft Riots* (New York, 1952); Basil Lee, *Discontent in New York City, 1861-1865* (New York, 1943).

56. Schouler, *Massachusetts*, I, p. 476.

57. *Boston Journal*, July 6, 1863; Kelly, "Ambiguous Loyalties," pp. 199-203.

58. Bishop's Journal, vol. V, July 10, July 13, 1863, Archdiocesan Archives, Boston, Massachusetts. James Healy was a member of a large family, his father an Irishman who became a successful Georgia planter, and his mother an African-American slave. Coming north for his education, James graduated from Holy Cross College, became a Catholic priest, was named the first chancellor of Boston, and eventually became bishop of Portland, Maine.

59. Pearson, *Andrew*, II, p. 133.

60. Report of the "Draft Riot" in Boston, July 14, 1863, *The Diary of Major Stephen Cabot, 1st Batt., Massachusetts Volunteer Heavy Artillery* (Boston, 1902). Also see Schouler, *Massachusetts*, I, pp. 479-480; Reid, *Castle Island*, pp. 104-105.

61. *Boston Daily Advertiser*, July 15, 1863. Also see Ware, *Political Opinion*, pp. 129-130; and William Hanna, "The Boston Draft Riot," *Civil War History* 36 (September 1990): 260-262.

62. Schouler, *Massachusetts*, I, p. 480.

63. *Boston Daily Advertiser*, July 15, 1863; Hanna, "Boston Draft Riot," p. 266.

64. O'Connor, *Fitzpatrick*, pp. 210-211.

65. *Boston Daily Advertiser*, July 15, 1863. Also see O'Connor, *Fitzpatrick*, p. 212.

66. *City of Boston Documents: Mayor's Address to the City Council*, July 23, 1863.

67. *Springfield Republican*, February 9, 1863; *Worcester Spy*, February 7, 1863.

68. Abbott, *Cotton and Capital*, p. 100.

69. Forbes, *Letters (Supplementary)*, II, p. 80; Abbott, *Cotton and Capital*, p. 101.

70. Abbott, *Cotton and Capital*, p. 101; Ware, *Political Opinion*, pp. 125-126.

71. Abbott, *Cotton and Capital*, pp. 103-104.

72. McPherson, *Struggle for Equality*, p. 125.

73. Ibid.

74. Ibid., p. 126.

75. *Springfield Republican*, December 2, 1862.

76. Ellsworth, *Year of Crisis*, p. 21.

77. Boston *Daily Evening Traveller,* September 2, 1862.

78. Ellsworth, *Year of Crisis,* p. 21.

79. Gerda Lerner, *The Female Experience: An American Documentary* (Indianapolis, 1977), p. 180. Also see Ann Douglas Wood, "The War within a War: Women Nurses in the Union Army," *Civil War History* 18 (1972): 196–197.

80. David Gollaher, *Voice for the Mad: The Life of Dorothea Dix* (New York, 1995), pp. 19–21, 59–67, 105–113.

81. Helen Marshall, *Dorothea Dix: Forgotten Samaritan* (New York, 1937), p. 202.

82. Gollaher, *Voice for the Mad,* pp. 406–407. Also see Kristie Ross, "Arranging a Doll's House: Refined Women as Union Nurses," in *Divided Houses: Gender and the Civil War,* ed. C. Clinton and N. Silber (New York, 1992), pp. 101–104.

83. Mary A. Livermore, *My Story of the War: A Woman's Narrative of Four Years' Personal Experience* (New York, 1995 ed.).

84. Sister Mary Denis Maher, *To Bind Up the Wounds: Catholic Sister Nurses in the U.S. Civil War* (Westport, Conn., 1989), pp. 128, 131; Jane E. Schultz, "The Inhospitable Hospital: Gender and Professionalism in Civil War Medicine," *Signs* 17 (Winter 1992), pp. 366–367.

85. Adams, *Doctors in Blue,* pp. 178–179; Ginzberg, *Women and the Work of Benevolence,* p. 145.

86. Wood, "War within a War," p. 207.

87. Francis Tiffany, *The Life of Dorothea Dix* (Boston, 1891), pp. 338–339; Livermore, *My Story,* p. 247.

88. In 1881, in failing health, Dorothea Dix moved into a special suite at the New Jersey Hospital at Trenton, where she lived until her death at age eighty-five in 1887.

89. Clara Barton, *The Story of My Childhood* (New York, 1907), pp. 16–20; Stephen Oates, *A Woman of Valor: Clara Barton and the Civil War* (New York, 1994), pp. 7–9; Ishbel Ross, *Angel of the Battlefield: The Life of Clara Barton* (New York, 1956), pp. 9–10.

90. Oates, *Woman of Valor,* p. 11; Elizabeth Massey, *Bonnet Brigades: American Women and the Civil War* (New York, 1966).

91. Oates, *Woman of Valor,* p. 6.

92. Elizabeth Brown Pryor, *Clara Barton: Professional Angel* (Philadelphia, 1987), pp. 3–5; Ross, *Angel of the Battlefield,* pp. 38–40.

93. Paludan, *"People's Contest",* p. 355.

94. Fredrickson, *The Inner Civil War,* pp. 87–89. See Louisa May Alcott, *Hospital Sketches* (Boston, 1863; reprinted, Cambridge, 1960).

95. Livermore, *My Story of the War.* Livermore's war experiences convinced her that only when women got the vote would they be able to defeat the evils of poverty, alcoholism, and prostitution.

96. Ellsworth, *Year of Crisis,* p. 21.

97. Paludan, *"People's Contest,"* pp. 352–353; Nevins, *The Organized War,* p. 321.

98. Fredrickson, *The Inner Civil War*, pp. 89–90.

99. Abbott, *Cotton and Capital*, pp. 74–75; Paludan, *"People's Contest,"* pp. 353–354. See Judith A. Giesberg, "'The Truest Patriots': The United States Sanitary Commission and Women's Reform in Transition," Ph.D. diss., Boston College, 1997.

100. Nevins, *The Organized War*, pp. 318–319.

101. Ibid. For the contrast between the philosophical differences separating the Sanitary Commission from the Christian Commission, see Fredrickson, *The Inner Civil War*, pp. 107–108.

102. Letter, July 17, 1863, *Irish Green and Union Blue*, p. 110.

103. See *Nineteenth Regiment*, pp. 240–243, and Bruce, *Twentieth Regiment*, pp. 294–296, about how the two Massachusetts regiments broke the force of Pickett's charge at Gettysburg.

104. *Boston Daily Evening Traveller*, July 5, 1863.

105. *Boston Daily Advertiser*, July 5, 1863.

106. Adams, *Great Britain and the Civil War*, I, pp. 200–202; David P. Crook, *The North, the South, and the Powers, 1861–1865* (New York, 1974), pp. 9–12; Duberman, *Life of Charles Francis Adams*, pp. 280–285.

107. Adams, *Great Britain and the Civil War*, II, p. 122; Merli, *The Confederate Navy*, pp. 182–183.

108. Hughes, ed., *Letters and Recollections of Forbes*, II, p. 27.

109. Ibid., II, pp. 4–5. Also see Douglas H. Maynard, "The Forbes-Aspinwall Mission," *Mississippi Valley Historical Review* 45 (March 1959), p. 67.

110. Adams Diary, March 31, 1863, Massachusetts Historical Society.

111. Hughes, ed., *Letters and Recollections of Forbes*, II, p. 27.

112. Adams Diary, March 20, 1863, Massachusetts Historical Society.

113. *London Times*, April 7, 1863, cited in Hughes, ed., *Letters (Supplementary) of John Murray Forbes*, 3 vols. (Boston, 1905), II, p. 113, and Maynard, "Forbes-Aspinwall Mission," p. 74.

114. Hughes, ed., *Letters (Supplementary)*, II, p. 116.

115. Maynard, "Forbes-Aspinwall Mission," pp. 76–78.

116. Hughes, ed., *Letters (Supplementary)*, II, pp. 116–117.

117. Hughes, ed., *Letters and Recollections of Forbes*, II, pp. 17–18.

118. Duberman, *Life of Charles Francis Adams*, p. 303; Crook, *The North, the South, and the Powers*, pp. 151–153.

CHAPTER 6

1. Donald, *Abraham Lincoln*, p. 446.

2. Pearson, *Andrew*, II, pp. 126–128.

3. Schouler, *Massachusetts*, I, pp. 419–421, 517–518. See ibid., pp. 493–495, for a detailed listing of cannon and other ordnance in each of the forts.

4. Ibid., p. 486.

5. Pearson, *Andrew*, II, pp. 130–131.

6. Schouler, *Massachusetts*, I, pp. 420–422, 517–520.

7. Ibid., pp. 511, 513, 516–517.

8. Ibid., pp. 497, 505.

9. Cited in Howard T. Oedel, *Massachusetts in the Civil War: A Year of Dedication, 1863–1864* (Boston, 1964), p. 20.

10. Charles Crowley, *History of Lowell* (Boston, 1868), pp. 48–49; Victor S. Clark, *History of Manufacturing in the United States,* 2 vols. (New York, 1929), II, p. 29.

11. Amos A. Lawrence to Mrs. Arnold, May 27, 1861, AA Letterbook, MHS. *Boston Post,* May 8, 1862. Also see Dane Yorke, *The Men and Times of Pepperell* (Boston, 1945), p. 47.

12. *Springfield Republican,* May 12, 1862.

13. William Lawrence, *The Life of Amos A. Lawrence* (Boston, 1888), p. 181.

14. Yorke, *Pepperell,* p. 46. Also see *Charleston Courier,* November 30, December 9, 1861.

15. Fite, *Industrial Conditions,* pp. 83–84.

16. Ibid., p. 85.

17. Ibid., pp. 89–90. Manufacture of men's shirts, which previously had required more than fourteen hours by hand, was reduced to a little less than one hour by machine. Drawers that had taken more than four hours could now be turned out in 28 minutes; nightshirts that had taken more than ten hours could be produced in a little more than one hour.

18. Ibid., p. 91.

19. Schouler, *Massachusetts,* I, pp. 218–220.

20. The only other government armory, at Harpers Ferry, Virginia, was destroyed to prevent it from falling into enemy hands. See Fite, *Industrial Conditions,* pp. 97–98.

21. Reid, *Castle Island,* pp. 106, 110.

22. Thomas H. O'Connor, *South Boston, My Home Town: The History of an Ethnic Neighborhood* (Boston, 1988), p. 62. Also see John Toomey and Edward Rankin, *History of South Boston* (Boston, 1901), pp. 231–234.

23. O'Connor, *South Boston,* pp. 62–63.

24. William C. Darrah, *Cartes de Visite in Nineteenth Century Photography* (Gettysburg, Pa., 1981), pp. 4–7, 19.

25. W. Fletcher Thompson, Jr., *The Image of War: Pictorial Reporting of the American Civil War* (New York, 1959), pp. 17–18. Also see Francis T. Miller, *The Photographic History of the Civil War,* 10 vols. (New York, 1957); Henry W. Elson, *The Civil War through the Camera* (New York, 1912).

26. In May 1864, while fighting in the Wilderness, Ira Pettit was taken prisoner and eventually sent to Andersonville Prison in Georgia, where he died on October 18, 1864. Jean P. Ray, comp., *Diary of a Dead Man: Letters and Diary of Private Ira S. Pettit* (Gettysburg, Pa., 1981).

27. Michael H. Leary to Nellie Desmond, April 29, 1862, Michael H. Leary Letters, Archives, Burns Library, Boston College.

28. Fiore, *Year of Trial and Testing,* pp. 17–18.

29. Boston *Daily Evening Traveller,* 1862.

30. During the war years almost every issue of the *Boston Post* and the *Boston Daily Advertiser* carried elaborate advertisements for investments.

31. Paludan, *"People's Contest"* pp. 177–179.

32. Fite, *Industrial Conditions,* pp. 99–100. See Robert V. Bruce, *Lincoln and the Tools of War* (Indianapolis, 1956), for an outstanding study of the war's technological aspects.

33. Henry M. Schreiber, "The Working People of Boston in the Middle of the Nineteenth Century," Ph.D. diss., Boston University, 1950, pp. 130–135.

34. Paludan, *"People's Contest,"* p. 182; Fite, *Industrial Conditions,* p. 184; Oedel, *Year of Dedication,* pp. 20–21.

35. Fite, *Industrial Conditions,* p. 188.

36. Ibid., p. 187.

37. Ibid., pp. 188–189.

38. Carol S. Lasser, "Mistress, Maid, and Market: The Transformation of the Domestic Service in New England, 1790–1870," Ph.D. diss., Harvard University, 1982, pp. 64–65.

39. Schreiber, "Working People of Boston," pp. 237–238.

40. Douglass Shand-Tucci, *Built in Boston: City and Suburb, 1800–1950* (Amherst, Mass., 1988), p. 35.

41. Constance Burns, "Joseph M. Wightman," "Frederick W. Lincoln, Jr.," *Biographical Dictionary of American Mayors, 1820–1980,* ed. Melvin Holli and Peter Jones (Westport, Conn., 1981), pp. 391–392, 217–218.

42. Shand-Tucci, *Built in Boston,* p. 35.

43. Whitehill, *Boston: A Topographical History,* p. 133.

44. Shand-Tucci, *Built in Boston,* p. 25.

45. Charles F. Donovan, *History of Boston College* (Chestnut Hill, Mass., 1990), p. 19.

46. Whitehill, *Boston: A Topographical History,* pp. 131–132.

47. Allan S. Galper, "Building Boston's Back Bay: Marriage of Money and Hygiene," *Historical Journal of Massachusetts* 23 (Winter 1995): 64–65.

48. Galper, "Back Bay," pp. 66–67.

49. Whitehill, *Boston: A Topographical History,* p. 151.

50. Galper, "Back Bay," p. 62.

51. Ibid., pp. 69–70.

52. Cited in Fredrickson, *The Inner Civil War,* p. 176.

53. *Journals of Ralph Waldo Emerson,* 9 vols. (Boston, 1913), IX, p. 372.

54. John Greenleaf Whittier, *Complete Poems* (Boston, 1892), p. 263.

55. Ibid., pp. 262–263.

56. Ellsworth, *Year of Crisis,* pp. 38–39.

57. *Poems of Oliver Wendell Holmes* (New rev. ed., Boston, 1890), pp. 217–218.

58. Ibid., p. 250.

59. *The Poems of Henry Wadsworth Longfellow,* ed. Louis Untermeyer (Norfolk, Conn., 1971), p. 399.

60. James Russell Lowell, *Works* (Boston, 1892), VII, pp. 297–302.

61. Ralph Waldo Emerson, "The Cumberland," *The Columbia Book of Civil War Poetry: From Whitman to Walcott,* ed. Richard Marius (New York, 1994), pp. 147–149.

62. Julia Ward Howe, *Later Lyrics* (Boston, 1866), pp. 24–25.

63. James Russell Lowell, *The Poetical Works of James Russell Lowell,* 4 vols. (Boston, 1890), II, p. 341.

64. Ellsworth, *Year of Crisis,* pp. 41–42.

65. Norton and Howe, eds., *Letters of Charles Eliot Norton,* I, p. 234.

66. Whittier, *Complete Poems,* pp. 265–266.

67. Ellsworth, *A Year of Crisis,* pp. 43–44.

68. Willis J. Abbott, "Press and Publications, 1889–1929," *Commonwealth History of Massachusetts* (New York, 1920), V, pp. 499–500.

69. Hill, ed., *Poems and Songs of the Civil War.*

70. Ellsworth, *Year of Crisis,* p. 44.

71. Cited in Ware, *Political Opinion,* p. 136.

72. McPherson, *Struggle for Equality,* pp. 123–124.

73. Silbey, *Respectable Minority,* pp. 102–105.

74. Donald, *Lincoln,* p. 455.

75. Ware, *Political Opinion,* p. 120.

76. *Worcester Spy,* January 30, 1863.

77. *Springfield Republican,* February 9, 1863.

78. Cited in Ware, *Political Opinion,* p. 136.

79. Ware, *Political Opinion,* p. 134; Schouler, *Massachusetts,* I, p. 497.

80. *Boston Post,* September 4, 1863; *Boston Daily Courier,* September 4, 1863. See Ware, *Political Opinion,* p. 134; Schouler, *Massachusetts,* I, pp. 498–499.

81. *Boston Post,* September 4, 1863.

82. *Boston Daily Advertiser,* September 25, 1863.

83. Schouler, *Massachusetts,* I, p. 500.

84. Donald, *Lincoln,* p. 455.

85. Ibid., 456.

86. Schouler, *Massachusetts,* I, p. 501; Burns, "Frederick Lincoln," *Biographical Dictionary,* p. 217.

87. Motley to his mother, November 17, 1863. *The Correspondence of John Lothrop Motley,* ed. George William Curtis, 2 vols. (New York, 1889), II, pp. 143–145.

88. Schouler, *Massachusetts,* I, p. 501.

89. Ibid., pp. 474–475.

90. Abbott, *Cotton and Capital,* p. 116.

91. Pearson, *Andrew,* II, pp. 138–139.

92. Schouler, *Massachusetts,* I, pp. 621–622.

93. Abbott, *Cotton and Capital,* pp. 115–116.

94. Donald, *Lincoln,* 459–460.

95. Ibid., p. 460. Also see Abbott, *Cotton and Capital,* pp. 106–107.

96. Donald, *Lincoln,* p. 460.

97. Ibid., pp. 471–472.

98. Williams, *Lincoln and the Radicals,* pp. 301–302.

99. *Boston Daily Courier,* December 29, 1863.

CHAPTER 7

1. James Russell Lowell, *Political Essays: The Writings of James Russell Lowell* (Boston, 1892), V, pp. 185–186; Fredrickson, *The Inner Civil War,* pp. 120–121.

2. William S. McFeely, *Grant: A Biography* (New York, 1981), p. 151; Bruce Catton, *Grant Takes Command* (Boston, 1968), pp. 121–122; Donald, *Lincoln,* pp. 491–492. T. Harry Williams, *Lincoln Finds His General* (New York, 1952), is a masterful survey of Lincoln's search for a winning general.

3. Cited in McFeely, *Grant,* p. 153.

4. Ibid., p. 152.

5. Ibid., pp. 156–158; Catton, *Grant Takes Command,* pp. 129–130.

6. Lowell, *Political Essays,* V, p. 185.

7. Schouler, *Massachusetts,* I, pp. 523–526.

8. Williams, *Lincoln and the Radicals,* pp. 15–16.

9. Ibid., pp. 318–320.

10. Donald, *Lincoln,* pp. 511–512.

11. McPherson, *Struggle for Equality,* p. 260.

12. Fredrickson, *The Inner Civil War,* pp. 127–129.

13. McPherson, *Struggle for Equality,* p. 261.

14. Ibid., p. 263.

15. Donald, *Lincoln,* p. 495.

16. Ibid., p. 307.

17. James G. Randall and Richard N. Current, *Lincoln the President: The Last Full Measure* (New York, 1955), p. 99; Donald, *Lincoln,* pp. 478–479.

18. Thomas G. Belden, *So Fell the Angels* (Boston, 1956), pp. 108–117; Donald, *Lincoln,* pp. 310–311.

19. William F. Zornow, *Lincoln and the Party Divided* (Norman, Okla., 1954), pp. 23–56; Donald, *Lincoln,* p. 483.

20. *Boston Evening Transcript,* March 6, 1864. See Baum, *Civil War Party System,* p. 70.

21. Williams, *Lincoln and the Radicals,* pp. 307–308.

22. McPherson, *Struggle for Equality,* p. 264.

23. *The Liberator,* March 18, 1864.

24. McPherson, *Struggle for Equality,* p. 268.

25. Williams, *Lincoln and the Radicals,* pp. 314–316; Donald, *Lincoln,* pp. 502–503.

26. Schouler, *Massachusetts,* I, p. 586.

27. Silbey, *A Respectable Minority,* pp. 119–122, 167–168; Williams, *Lincoln and the Radicals,* p. 328.

28. Schouler, *Massachusetts,* I, pp. 589–590; Silbey, *Respectable Minority,* pp. 125–130, 132–133.

29. *Boston Post,* August 9, 1864. Silbey, *Respectable Minority,* pp. 116–118, discusses Democratic hopes that party unity would produce victory in 1864.

30. Schouler, *Massachusetts,* I, p. 558.

31. Williams, *Lincoln Finds His General,* pp. 305–307.

32. Bruce Catton, *Never Call Retreat* (Garden City, N.Y., 1965), pp. 35–59; Catton, *Grant Takes Command,* pp. 179–201, 204–205; McFeely, *Grant,* pp. 166–168.

33. Catton, *Never Call Retreat,* pp. 359–361; Catton, *Grant Takes Command,* pp. 217–219, 232–233, 244–245; McFeely, *Grant,* pp. 169–170; Donald, *Lincoln,* pp. 500–501.

34. Catton, *Never Call Retreat,* pp. 363–364; Catton, *Grant Takes Command,* pp. 259–260, 265–271, 276–277; McFeely, *Grant,* pp. 170–173.

35. *Boston Post,* June 3, 1864.

36. Catton, *Never Call Retreat,* pp. 343–347; Catton, *Grant Takes Command,* pp. 290–293, 320–324; McFeely, *Grant,* pp. 175–176.

37. Donald, *Lincoln,* pp. 517–519.

38. *Boston Daily Advertiser,* July 12, 1864.

39. *Boston Post,* July 10–13, July 22, 1864.

40. McPherson, *Battle Cry,* pp. 759–760. Also see *Boston Post,* August 1, 1864 for an early report on the crater explosion, which at first appeared to be a Union victory.

41. *Boston Post,* August 2, 1864. As later reports came in, Boston readers realized just how great the disaster was and how extensive the casualties were.

42. McPherson, *Battle Cry,* p. 759.

43. *The Boston Pilot,* June 25, 1864.

44. *Boston Post,* August 9, 1864.

45. *Boston Journal,* August 24, 1864.

46. *Boston Post,* October–December 1864.

47. Ibid., November 17, 1864.

48. Ibid., November 19, 1864.

49. O'Connor, *South Boston,* p. 63.

50. Cited in the *Boston Post,* November 8, 1864.

51. *Boston Journal,* September 2, 1864.

52. Ibid., September 1, 1864.

53. *Boston Post,* October 25, 1864.

54. Ibid., December 30, 1864.

55. *Boston Journal,* September 1, 1864.

56. Ibid., September 19, 1864.

57. Ibid., September 11, 1864.

58. *Boston Post,* September 23, 1864.

59. *Boston Journal,* September 25, 1864.

60. *Boston Post,* November 4, 1864.

61. *Boston Journal,* September 11, 1864.

62. Ibid., September 23, 1864.

63. Ibid., September 1, 1864.

64. *Boston Post,* November 30, 1864.

65. Ibid., December 1, 1864.

66. Pearson, *Andrew,* II, pp. 149–152; Williams, *Lincoln and the Radicals,* pp. 324–325.

67. *Boston Post,* August 9, 1864.

68. Ibid., August 11, 1864. See Silbey, *Respectable Minority,* pp. 137–138.

69. *The Boston Pilot,* October 22, 1864.

70. *Boston Post,* October 11, 1864.

71. Ibid., October 25, 1864.

72. Ibid., September 21, October 11, 1864.

73. Letter dated December 6, 1864, from near Newtown, Virginia, in Henry Warren Howe, *Diary and Letters Written During the Civil War, 1861–1865* (Lowell, Mass., 1899), pp. 179–180.

74. Donald, *Lincoln,* pp. 530–531.

75. Williams, *Lincoln and the Radicals,* p. 330.

76. Abbott, *Cotton and Capital,* p. 110.

77. Pearson, *Andrew,* II, 164, 167. The Democratic *Boston Post* complained that though this was supposed to be a nonpartisan "patriotic meeting," it was actually an "out-and-out Republican demonstration."

78. Donald, *Lincoln,* p. 544; Ware, *Political Opinion,* pp. 140–142. For an analysis of soldiers' balloting, see Silbey, *Respectable Minority,* pp. 160–161.

79. Williams, *Lincoln and the Radicals,* p. 332; Donald, *Lincoln,* p. 544.

80. Pearson, *Andrew,* II, p. 176; Schouler, *Massachusetts,* I, p. 590.

81. *Boston Post,* November 10, 1864.

82. *The Boston Pilot,* November 12, 1864. See Silbey, *Respectable Minority,* pp. 149–152, 173–176, for an analysis of the 1864 elections from the Democratic point of view.

CHAPTER 8

1. *Boston Daily Advertiser,* January 3, 1865.

2. Ibid., January 27, 1865.

3. Ibid., February 1, 1865.

4. Ibid., February 3, 1865.

5. Ibid., February 6, 1865.

6. Ibid., January 14, 1865, reprints the official reports about General Butler's failure to take Fort Fisher, including Butler's own version of the episode.

7. *Boston Post,* January 18, 1865.

8. Oates, *A Woman of Valor,* pp. 312, 336.

9. *Boston Daily Advertiser,* January 10, 1865.

10. Ibid., February 4, 1865.

11. Ibid., January 14, 1865.

12. Quarles, *Negro in the Civil War,* pp. 326–327.

13. Cited in ibid., p. 326.

14. Ibid., p. 327.

15. *Boston Daily Advertiser*, February 23, 1865.

16. O'Connor, *Fitzpatrick*, p. 224.

17. *Boston Daily Advertiser*, February 5, 1865.

18. Donald, *Lincoln*, pp. 655–667.

19. *Boston Daily Advertiser*, March 6, 1865. Browne's letter to Governor Andrew, dated March 21, 1865, is cited in Pearson, *Andrew*, II, p. 262.

20. *The Boston Pilot*, April 1, 1865.

21. *Boston Daily Advertiser*, March 29, 1865.

22. Ibid., April 3, 1865.

23. Harry Sturgis Russell, the regiment's original commanding officer, had resigned from service in February 1865. Once again I am indebted to John D. Warner, Jr., for sharing with me the results of his doctoral research at Boston College.

24. J. B. Jones, *A Rebel War Clerk's Diary*, II, pp. 89–90.

25. Quarles, *Negro in the Civil War*, p. 332.

26. *Boston Daily Advertiser*, April 6, 1865.

27. Mary N. Stanard, *Richmond: Its People and Its Story* (Philadelphia, 1923), p. 209.

28. Schouler, *Massachusetts*, I, pp. 623–665.

29. *Boston Daily Advertiser*, April 5, 1865.

30. *The Boston Pilot*, April 8, 1865.

31. Schouler, *Massachusetts*, I, pp. 623–624.

32. *Boston Daily Advertiser*, April 10, 1865.

33. *Boston Journal*, April 10, 1865.

34. O'Connor, *Fitzpatrick*, p. 225.

35. *Boston Daily Advertiser*, April 11, 1865.

36. Ibid., December 15, 1863.

37. *Springfield Republican*, April 27, 1864.

38. *Boston Post*, September 4, December 12, 1863.

39. *Boston Daily Advertiser*, April 15, 1865.

40. Schouler, *Massachusetts*, I, p. 627.

41. *Boston Journal*, April 15, 1865.

42. *Boston Daily Advertiser*, April 16, 1865.

43. Pearson, *Andrew*, II, p. 245.

44. *Boston Daily Advertiser*, April 19, 20, 1865.

45. Pearson, *Andrew*, II, pp. 255–256.

46. Snow, *Boston Harbor*, pp. 23–24.

47. Ibid., pp. 25–26.

48. Baum, *Civil War Party System*, p. 55, sees the emergence of Andrew and the Radicals as a major shift from old, conservative money to a younger, more dynamic, and resourceful group of Boston business and political leaders.

49. Cited in Abbott, *Cotton and Capital*, p. 197.

50. According to James L. Huston, *The Panic of 1857*, pp. 265–265, 266–227, the Republicans responded to the Panic of 1857 by gradually supporting tariff protec-

tion, homesteads, agricultural colleges, and internal improvements. The Democrats, by contrast, instituted a retrenchment policy that angered many Northern interests.

51. Cited in Arthur Mann, *Yankee Reformers in the Urban Age* (New York, 1954), p. 8.

52. The spirit of social and cultural disillusionment among Boston's Brahmin class is effectively conveyed by Barbara M. Solomon, *Ancestors and Immigrants: A Changing New England Tradition* (Chicago, 1957), as well as by Mann, *Yankee Reformers.*

53. Peter Welsh to Margaret, February 3, 1863, in *Irish Green and Union Blue,* p. 65.

54. Ibid., p. 67.

55. See O'Connor, *The Boston Irish,* for a survey of the changing Irish political status after the Civil War.

56. See Baum, *Civil War Party System,* pp. 108–109, for a description of the Democratic party's "crippled condition" in Massachusetts in 1866. Joel Silbey, however, in *Respectable Minority,* p. 180, does not feel that the Democrats were particularly weak or crippled during the postwar period. He suggests they may have "appeared" more crippled than they were.

57. M. H. MacNamara, *The Irish Ninth,* p. 59.

58. Ibid., p. 219.

59. Philip Foner, "A Labor Voice for Black Equality: The *Boston Daily Evening Voice,* 1864–1867," *Science and Society* 38 (Fall 1974): 304–325. This view about a modified racism after the war is supported by Donald M. Jacobs, "A History of the Boston Negro from the Revolution to the Civil War," Ph.D. diss., Boston University, 1968, pp. 362, 369–370.

60. Elizabeth Hafkin Pleck, *Black Migration and Poverty: Boston, 1865–1900* (New York, 1979), p. 20. Pleck makes ingenious use of Civil War pension applications by black veterans or their widows to derive valuable evidence, testimony, and life histories.

61. Foner, "A Labor Voice for Black Equality," pp. 310–314, cites efforts by the *Boston Daily Evening Voice* to champion black equality in the American workforce.

62. Pleck, *Black Migration,* p. 41.

63. Nevins, *The War for the Union,* Chapter 8, "The Sweep of Organization," pp. 172 ff.

64. DuBois, *Feminism and Suffrage;* Gerda Lerner, *The Majority Finds Its Past: Placing Women in History* (New York, 1979); Paula Baker, "The Domestication of Politics," *American Historical Review* 89 (1984): 620–647.

65. Lasser, "Mistress, Maid, and Market," pp. 102–103.

66. Josephine Dolan, *A History of Nursing,* 11th ed. (Philadelphia, 1964), pp. 247–248.

67. Ibid., pp. 250–253.

68. Lasser, "Mistress, Maid, and Market," p. 262.

69. Ibid., pp. 216–218. The figure of the "black washerwomen," says Lasser, was common throughout New England at this time.

70. Lasser, "Mistress, Maid, and Market," pp. 88–89.

71. Wendy E. Gamber, "The Female Economy: The Millinery and Dressmaking Trades, 1860–1930," Ph.D. diss., Brandeis University, 1991, p. 288.

72. Ibid., p. 289; Lasser, "Mistress, Maid, and Market," pp. 89–90.

73. Gamber, "Female Economy," p. 297.

74. Ibid., pp. 427–428, 405.

Bibliography

~ ~ ~ ~ ~ ~ ~

Abbott, Richard H. "Cobbler in Congress: The Life of Henry Wilson, 1812–1874." Ph.D. diss., University of Wisconsin, 1965.

———. *Cotton and Capital: Boston Businessmen and Antislavery Reform, 1854–1868.* Amherst, Mass., 1991.

Abbott, Willis J. *Blue Jackets of '61: A History of the Navy in the War of Secession.* New York, 1887.

———. "Press and Publications, 1889–1929," *Commonwealth History of Massachusetts,* vol. 5. New York, 1920.

Adams, Ephraim D. *Great Britain and the American Civil War,* 2 vols. New York, 1925.

Adams, George W. *Doctors in Blue: The Medical History of the Union Army in the Civil War.* New York, 1952.

Adams, Henry. "The Secession Winter, 1860–1861," *Proceedings of the Massachusetts Historical Society* XLIII (1910): 660–87.

Alcott, Louisa May. *Hospital Sketches.* Boston, 1863; reprinted, Cambridge, 1960.

Aptheker, Herbert. "The Negro in the Union Navy," *Journal of Negro History* 32 (April 1947).

Baker, Paula. "The Domestication of Politics," *American Historical Review* 89 (1984): 620–647.

Barney, William L. *Flawed Victory: A New Perspective on the Civil War.* New York, 1975.

Barton, Clara. *The Story of My Childhood.* New York, 1907.

Baum, Dale. *The Civil War Party System: The Case of Massachusetts, 1848–1876.* Chapel Hill, N.C., 1984.

Belden, Thomas G. *So Fell the Angels.* Boston, 1956.

Berg, Barbara I. *The Remembered Gate: Origins of American Feminism, the Woman and the City, 1800–1860.* New York, 1978.

Bernstein, Iver. *The New York Draft Riots: Their Significance for American Society and Politics in the Age of the Civil War.* New York, 1990.

Billington, Ray Allen. *The Protestant Crusade, 1800–1860.* New York, 1938.

Bird, Francis W. *Review of Governor Banks' Veto of the Revised Code: An Account of Its Authorizing the Enrollment of Colored Citizens in the Militia.* Boston, 1860.

Blanchard, Paula. *Margaret Fuller: From Transcendentalism to Revolution.* Cambridge, Mass., 1978.

Boydston, Jeanne. *Home and Work: Housework, Wages, and the Ideology of Labor in the Early Republic.* New York, 1990.

Boylan, Ann M. *Sunday School: The Formation of an American Institution, 1790–1880.* New Haven, Conn., 1988.

———. "Timid Girls, Venerable Widows, and Dignified Matrons," *American Quarterly* 38 (Winter 1986): 779–797.

Branch, E. Douglas. *The Sentimental Years: 1836–1860.* New York, 1934.

Brauer, Kinley J. *Cotton versus Conscience: Massachusetts Whig Politics and Southwestern Expansion, 1843–1848.* Lexington, Ky., 1967.

Bruce, George A. *The Twentieth Regiment Massachusetts Volunteers.* Boston, 1906.

Bruce, Robert V. *Lincoln and the Tools of War.* Indianapolis, 1956.

Bryan, T. Conn. *Confederate Georgia.* Athens, Ga., 1953.

Burchard, Peter. *One Gallant Rush: Robert Gould Shaw and His Brave Black Regiment.* New York, 1965.

Burton, William L. "Irish Regiments in the Union Army: The Massachusetts Experience," *Historical Journal of Massachusetts* 11 (June 1983): 104–119.

———. *Melting Pot Soldiers: The Union Ethnic Regiments.* Ames, Iowa, 1988.

Cabot, Stephen. *The Diary of Major Stephen Cabot, 1st Batt., Massachusetts Volunteer Heavy Artillery.* Boston, 1902.

Capers, Gerald M. *Occupied City: New Orleans under the Federals, 1862–1865.* Lexington, Ky., 1965.

Catton, Bruce. *Grant Takes Command.* Boston, 1968.

———. *Never Call Retreat.* Garden City, N.Y., 1965.

Chandler, Peleg. *Memoir and Reminiscences of Governor Andrew.* Boston, 1881.

Clark, Denis. *Irish Relations: Trials of an Immigrant Tradition.* Rutherford, Vt., 1982.

Clark, Victor S. *History of Manufacturing in the United States,* 2 vols. New York, 1929.

Conyngham, David P. *The Irish Brigade and Its Campaigns.* New York, 1944.

Cook, Adrian. *Armies of the Streets: The New York Coty Draft Riots of 1863.* Lexington, Ky., 1974.

Corby, William. *Memoirs of Chaplain Life.* Notre Dame, Ind., 1894.

Cornish, Dudley. *The Sable Arm: Negro Troops in the Union Army.* New York, 1956.

Cott, Nancy. *The Bonds of Womanhood: "Woman's Sphere" in New England, 1778–1835.* New Haven, Conn., 1977.

———. "Young Women and the Second Great Awakening," *Feminist Studies* 2 (Fall 1975): 15–29.

Crook, David P. *The North, the South, and the Powers, 1861–1865.* New York, 1974.

Crowley, Charles. *History of Lowell.* Boston, 1868.

Cullen, James B. *The Story of the Irish in Boston.* Boston, 1889.

Cutting, Elizabeth. *Jefferson Davis: Political Soldier.* New York, 1930.

Dalzell, Robert F., Jr. *Enterprising Elite: The Boston Associates and the World They Made.* Cambridge, Mass., 1986.

Daniels, John. *In Freedom's Birthplace.* Boston, 1914.

Darrah, William C. *Cartes de Visite in Nineteenth Century Photography.* Gettysburg, Pa., 1981.

Dolan, Jay. *The Immigrant Church: New York's Irish and German Catholics, 1815–1865.* Baltimore, 1975.

Dolan, Josephine. *A History of Nursing,* 11th ed. Philadelphia, 1964.

Donald, David. *Abraham Lincoln.* New York, 1995.

———. *Charles Sumner and the Coming of the Civil War.* New York, 1960.

———. *Inside Lincoln's Cabinet: The Civil War Diaries of Salmon P. Chase.* New York, 1954.

Donovan, Charles F. *History of Boston College.* Chestnut Hill, Mass., 1990.

Douglas, Ann. *The Feminization of American Culture.* New York, 1977.

Duberman, Martin. *The Anti-Slavery Vanguard.* Princeton, N.J., 1965.

———. *The Life of Charles Francis Adams,* Stanford, Calif., 1968.

DuBois, Ellen Carol. *Feminism and Suffrage: The Emergence of an Independent Women's Movement in America, 1848–1869.* Ithaca, N.Y., 1978.

Dumond, Dwight. *The Secession Movement, 1860–1861.* New York, 1931.

Edmonds, Thomas. "Operations in North Carolina, 1861–1862," *Military Historical Society of Massachusetts Papers* 9 (1912): 80–112.

Ellsworth, Edward W. *Massachusetts in the Civil War: A Year of Crisis, 1862–1863.* Boston, 1962.

Elson, Henry W. *The Civil War through the Camera.* New York, 1912.

Emerson, Ralph Waldo. *Poems: The Complete Works of Ralph Waldo Emerson.* Boston, 1904.

Emilio, Luis F. *A Brave Black Regiment: History of the Fifty-Fourth Regiment of Massachusetts Volunteer Infantry, 1863–1865,* 2nd ed. Boston, 1894.

Entrekin, Estelle. *Sarah Hale and Godey's Lady's Book.* Philadelphia, 1946.

Epstein, Barbara L. *The Politics of Domesticity: Women, Evangelists, and Temperance in Nineteenth Century America.* Middletown, Conn., 1981.

Fehrenbacher, Don. *The Dred Scott Case: Its Significance in American Law and Politics.* New York, 1978.

Felberg, Michael. *The Philadelphia Riots of 1844: A Study in Ethnic Conflict.* Westport, Conn., 1975.

Finley, Ruth E. *The Lady of Godey's.* Philadelphia, 1931.

Fiore, Jordan. *Massachusetts in the Civil War: The Year of Trial and Testing, 1861–1862.* Boston, 1961.

Fite, Emerson D. *Social and Industrial Conditions in the North during the Civil War.* New York, reprint 1963.

Flexner, Eleanor. *Century of Struggle: The Woman's Rights Movement in the United States.* Cambridge, Mass., 1959.

Foner, Eric. *Free Labor, Free Soil, Free Men: The Ideology of the Republican Party before the Civil War.* New York: 1970.

Foner, Philip. "A Labor Voice for Black Equality: The *Boston Daily Evening Voice,* 1864–1867," *Science and Society* 38 (Fall 1974): 304–325.

Formisano, Ronald P. *The Birth of Mass Political Parties: Michigan, 1827–1861.* Princeton, N.J., 1971.

Foster, Lawrence. *Religion and Sexuality: Three American Communal Experiments of the Nineteenth Century.* New York, 1981.

Franklin, John Hope. *From Slavery to Freedom: A History of American Negroes.* New York, 1956.

Fredrickson, George M. *The Inner Civil War: Northern Intellectuals and the Crisis of the Union.* New York, 1965.

Freedman, Estelle B. *Their Sisters' Keepers: Women's Prison Reform in America, 1830–1930.* Ann Arbor, Mich., 1981.

Frothingham, Thomas G. "Massachusetts in the Civil War," *Commonwealth History of Massachusetts,* vol. 4. New York, 1920.

Galper, Allan S. "Building Boston's Back Bay: Marriage of Money and Hygiene," *Historical Journal of Massachusetts* 23 (Winter 1995): 61–78.

Gamber, Wendy E. "The Female Economy: The Millinery and Dressmaking Trades, 1860–1930." Ph.D. diss., Brandeis University, 1991.

Garland, J. L. "The Formation of Meagher's Irish Brigade," *Irish Sword* 3 (1958): 162–165.

Garrison, W. P., and F. J. Garrison. *William Lloyd Garrison: The Story of His Life as Told by His Children.* New York, 1885–1889.

Gienapp, William E. *The Origins of the Republican Party, 1852–1856.* New York, 1987.

Giesberg, Judith A. "'The Truest Patriots': The United States Sanitary Commission and Women's Reform in Transition." Ph.D. diss., Boston College, 1997.

Ginzburg, Lori D. *Women and the Work of Benevolence: Morality, Politics, and Class in the Nineteenth Century.* New Haven, Conn., 1990.

Gollaher, David. *Voice for the Mad: The Life of Dorothea Dix.* New York, 1995.

Halttunen, Karen. *Confidence Men and Painted Women: A Study of Middle-Class Culture in America, 1830–1870.* New Haven, Conn., 1982.

Handlin, Oscar. *Boston's Immigrants: 1790–1880.* New York, 1959.

Hanna, William. "The Boston Draft Riot," *Civil War History* 36 (September 1990): 260–275.

Hayden, Robert C. *African-Americans in Boston: More than 350 Years.* Boston, 1991.

———. *A History of the Black Church in Boston.* Boston, 1983.

Headley, P. C. *Massachusetts in the Rebellion: A Record of the Historical Position of the Commonwealth.* Boston, 1866.

Hersh, Blanche. *The Slavery of Sex: Feminist Abolitionists in Nineteenth Century America.* Urbana, Ill., 1978.

Hill, Hamilton, ed. *A Memoir of Abbott Lawrence.* Boston, 1884.

Hill, Lois, ed. *Poems and Songs of the Civil War.* New York, 1990.

History of the Forty-Fifth Regiment, Massachusetts Volunteer Militia. Jamaica Plain, Mass., 1908.

History of the Nineteenth Regiment, Massachusetts Volunteer Infantry, 1861–1865. Salem, Mass., 1906.

Holmes, Oliver Wendell. *My Hunt after the Captain, and Other Papers.* Boston, 1887.

———. *Poems of Oliver Wendell Holmes,* new rev. ed. Boston, 1890.

Holt, Michael F. *The Political Crisis of the 1850s.* New York, 1978.

Hopkins, Pauline E. "Famous Men of the Negro Race: Robert Morris," *The Colored American Magazine* 3 (September 1901): 337–342.

Horton, James, and Lois E. Horton. *Black Bostonians.* New York, 1979.

Horton, Lois E., and James O. Horton. "Power and Social Responsibility: Entrepreneurs and the Black Community in Antebellum Boston," in *Entrepreneurs: The Boston Business Community, 1700–1850.* Ed. Conrad Edick Wright and Katheryn P. Viens. Boston, 1997.

Howe, Henry Warren. *Diary and Letters Written during the Civil War, 1861–1865.* Lowell, Mass., 1899.

Howe, Julia Ward. *Later Lyrics.* Boston, 1866.

Hughes, Sarah, ed. *Letters and Recollections of John Murray Forbes,* 2 vols. Boston, 1900.

Huston, James L. *The Panic of 1857 and the Coming of the Civil War.* Baton Rouge, La., 1987.

Ignatiev, Noel. *How the Irish Became White.* New York, 1995.

Jacobs, Donald, "A History of the Boston Negro from the Revolution to the Civil War." Ph.D. diss., Boston University, 1968.

Jacobs, Donald, ed. *Courage and Conscience.* Bloomington, Ind., 1993.

Johnson, Ludwell H. *The Red River Campaign: Politics and Cotton in the Civil War.* Baltimore, 1958.

Johnson, Samuel A. "The Genesis of the New England Aid Company," *New England Quarterly* 3 (1930): 90–100.

Jones, John B. *A Rebel War Clerk's Diary at the Confederate States Capital.* New York, 1866.

Jones, Virgil C. *The Civil War at Sea,* 2 vols. New York, 1961.

Kelly, Brian. "Ambiguous Loyalties: The Boston Irish, Slaves, and the Civil War," *Historical Journal of Massachusetts* 24 (Summer 1996): 165–204.

Kohl, Lawrence, and Margaret C. Richard, eds. *Irish Green and Union Blue: The Civil War Letters of Peter Welch.* New York, 1986.

Lader, Lawrence. *The Bold Brahmins: New England's War against Slavery, 1830–1863.* New York, 1961.

Lasser, Carol S. "Mistress, Maid, and Market: The Transformation of the Domestic Service in New England, 1790–1870." Ph.D. diss., Harvard University, 1982.

Lawrence, William. *The Life of Amos A. Lawrence: With Extracts from His Diary and Correspondence.* Boston, 1888.

Le Bow, Richard N. *White England and Black Ireland.* Philadelphia, 1976.

Leckie, Robert. *American and Catholic.* New York, 1970.

Lee, Basil. *Discontent in New York City, 1861–1865.* New York, 1943.

Leech, Margaret. *Reveille in Washington.* New York, 1941.

Leonard, Elizabeth D. *Yankee Women: Gender Battles in the Civil War.* New York, 1994.

Lerner, Gerda. *The Female Experience: An American Documentary.* Indianapolis, 1977.

———. *The Grimké Sisters from South Carolina: Pioneers for Women's Rights and Abolition.* New York, 1967.

———. *The Majority Finds Its Past: Placing Women in History.* New York, 1979.

Levesque, George A. *Black Boston: African American Life and Culture in Urban America, 1750–1860.* New York, 1994.

Lincoln, Abraham. *Collected Works,* 7 vols. Ed. Roy Basler. New Brunswick, N.J., 1953.

Livermore, Mary A. *My Story of the War: A Woman's Narrative of Four Years' Personal Experience.* New York, 1995 ed.

Longfellow, Henry Wadsworth. *The Poems of Henry Wadsworth Longfellow.* Ed. Louis Untermeyer. Norfolk, Conn., 1971.

Loring, Susan, ed. *Selections from the Diaries of William Appleton, 1786–1862.* Boston, 1922.

Lowell, James Russell. *Poetical Works,* 4 vols. Boston, 1890.

———. *Works.* Boston, 1892.

McFeely, William S. *Grant: A Biography.* New York, 1981.

McGraw, Robert F. "The Minutemen of '61: The Pre–Civil War Massachusetts Militia," *Civil War History* 15 (1969): 103–107.

McLaughlin, William J. "The Fighting Yankees in the Irish Brigade," *North South Trader* (March–April, 1979): 15–43.

MacNamara, Daniel G. *History of the Ninth Regiment.* Boston, 1899.

MacNamara, Michael H. *The Irish Ninth in Bivouac and Battle.* Boston, 1867.

McPherson, James M. *Battle Cry of Freedom: The Civil War Era.* New York, 1988.

———. *For Cause and Comrades: Why Men Fought in the Civil War.* New York, 1997.

———. *The Negro's Civil War.* New York, 1965.

———. *Struggle for Equality: Abolitionists and the Negro in the Civil War and Reconstruction.* Princeton, N.J., 1964.

Maher, Sister Mary Denis. *To Bind Up the Wounds: Catholic Sister Nurses in the U.S. Civil War.* Westport, Conn., 1989.

Maizlish, Stephen, and John Kushma, eds. *Essays on American Antebellum Politics, 1840–1860.* College Station, Texas, 1982.

Malin, James C. *John Brown and the Legend of Fifty-Six.* Philadelphia, 1942.

Mann, Arthur. *Yankee Reformers in the Urban Age.* New York, 1954.

Marshall, Helen. *Dorothea Dix: Forgotten Samaritan.* New York, 1937.

Massey, Elizabeth. *Bonnet Brigades: American Women and the Civil War.* New York, 1966.

Maxwell, John F. *Slavery and the Catholic Church.* London, 1975.

Maxwell, William Q. *Lincoln's Fifth Wheel: The Political History of the United States Sanitary Commission.* New York, 1956.

Maynard, Douglas H. "The Forbes-Aspinwall Mission," *Mississippi Valley Historical Review* 45 (March 1959).

Merli, Frank J. *Great Britain and the Confederate Navy, 1861–1865.* Bloomington, Ind., 1970.

Merrill, James M. *The Rebel Shore: The Story of Union Sea Power in the Civil War.* Boston, 1957.

Miller, Francis. *The Photographic History of the Civil War,* 10 vols. New York, 1957.

Miller, Kerby. *Emigrants and Exiles: Ireland and the Irish Exodus to North America.* New York, 1985.

Mitchell, Betty. "Massachusetts Reaction to John Brown's Raid," *Civil War History* 19 (March 1973): 65–79.

Mitchell, Brian. *The Paddy Camps: The Irish of Lowell, 1821–1861.* Champaign, Ill., 1988.

Mitchell, Reid. *The Vacant Chair: The Northern Soldier Leaves Home.* New York, 1993.

Monaghan, Jay. *The Civil War on the Western Border, 1854–1865.* Boston, 1955.

Moody, Robert E. "The First Year of the Emigrant Aid Company," *New England Quarterly* 4 (1931): 148–149.

Morison, Samuel Eliot. *The Maritime History of Massachusetts.* Boston, 1941.

Morse, John T. *Sons of the Puritans.* Boston, 1908.

Morse, John T., ed. *The Diary of Gideon Welles.* Boston, 1911.

Motley, John Lothrop, *Correspondence.* 2 vols. Ed. George W. Curtis. New York, 1889.

Mulkern, John R. *The Know-Nothing Party in Massachusetts: The Rise and Fall of a People's Party.* Boston, 1990.

———. "Scandal Behind the Convent Walls: The Know-Nothing Nunnery Committee of 1855," *Historical Journal of Massachusetts* 11 (1983): 22–31.

Nagel, Paul. *Descent from Glory: Four Generations of the John Adams Family.* New York, 1983.

Navin, Thomas R. *The Whitin Machine Works since 1831.* Cambridge, Mass., 1950.

Nell, William C. *The Colored Patriots of the American Revolution.* Boston, 1855.

Nevins, Allan. *The Emergence of Lincoln: Prologue to the Civil War, 1859–1861.* New York, 1950.

———. *The War for the Union: The Organized War, 1863–1864.* New York, 1971.

Nichols, Alice. *Bleeding Kansas.* New York, 1954.

Norton, Charles Eliot. *Letters.* 2 vols. Ed. Sarah Norton and Mark De Wolfe Howe. Boston, 1913.

Oates, Stephen B. *To Purge This Land with Blood: A Biography of John Brown.* New York, 1970.

———. *A Woman of Valor: Clara Barton and the Civil War.* New York, 1994.

O'Connor, Thomas H. *The Boston Irish: A Political History.* Boston, 1995.

——. *Fitzpatrick's Boston, 1846–1866: John Bernard Fitzpatrick, Third Bishop of Boston.* Boston, 1984.

——. *Lords of the Loom: The Cotton Whigs and the Coming of the Civil War.* New York, 1968.

——. *South Boston, My Home Town: The History of an Ethnic Neighborhood.* Boston, 1988.

Oedel, Howard T., *Massachusetts in the Civil War: A Year of Dedication, 1863–1864.* Boston, 1964.

Osofsky, Gilbert. "Abolitionists, Irish Immigrants, and Romantic Nationalism," *American Historical Review* 80 (October 1975): 900–925.

Paludan, Phillip S. *"A People's Contest": The Union and Civil War, 1861–1865.* New York, 1988.

Pearson, Henry Greenleaf. *The Life of John A. Andrew, Governor of Massachusetts, 1861–1865,* 2 vols. Boston, 1904.

——. "Massachusetts to the Front," *Commonwealth History of Massachusetts,* 5 vols. New York, 1920.

Peirson, Charles L. *Ball's Bluff.* Boston, 1904.

Phillips, Wendell. *Speeches, Lectures and Letters.* Ed. J. Redpath. Boston, 1894.

Pleck, Elizabeth Hafkin. *Black Migration and Poverty, Boston, 1865–1900.* New York, 1979.

Pratt, Fletcher. *Ordeal by Fire.* New York, 1935.

Pryor, Elizabeth Brown. *Clara Barton: Professional Angel.* Philadelphia, 1987.

Quarles, Benjamin. *Black Abolitionists.* New York, 1969.

——. *Lincoln and the Negro.* New York, 1962.

——. *The Negro in the Civil War.* Boston, 1953.

Randall, James G., and Richard N. Current. *Lincoln the President: The Last Full Measure.* New York, 1955.

Ray, Jean P., comp. *Diary of a Dead Man: Letters and Diary of Private Ira S. Pettit.* Gettysburg, Pa., 1981.

Reed, Rowena. *Combined Operations in the Civil War.* Annapolis, 1978.

Reid, William J. *Castle Island and Fort Independence.* Boston, 1995.

Rezneck, Samuel. "The Influence of Depression upon American Opinion, 1857–1859," *Journal of Economic History* 2 (1942): 1–23.

Rice, Madeleine H. *American Catholic Opinion in the Slavery Controversy.* Gloucester, Mass., 1964.

Robboy, Stanley J., and Anita W. Robboy. "Lewis Hayden: From Fugitive Slave to Statesman," *New England Quarterly* 46 (December 1973): 591–597.

Roediger, David. *The Wages of Whiteness.* New York, 1991.

Ross, Ishbel. *Angel of the Battlefield: The Life of Clara Barton.* New York, 1956.

Ross, Kristie. "Arranging a Doll's House: Refined Women as Union Nurses," in *Divided Houses: Gender and the Civil War.* Ed. Catherine Clinton and Nina Silber. New York, 1992.

Russell, Francis. *Adams: An American Dynasty.* New York, 1976.

Schouler, William. *A History of Massachusetts in the Civil War*, 2 vols. Boston, 1868.

Schreiber, Henry M. "The Working People of Boston in the Middle of the Nineteenth Century." Ph.D. diss., Boston University, 1950.

Schultz, Jane E. "The Inhospitable Hospital: Gender and Professionalism in Civil War Medicine," *Signs* 17 (Winter 1992): 366–367.

Schwartz, Harold. "Fugitive Days in Boston," *New England Quarterly* 27 (1954): 191–212.

Shand-Tucci, Douglass. *Built in Boston: City and Suburb, 1800–1950*. Amherst, Mass., 1988.

Shannon, William V. *The American Irish*. New York, 1966.

Shapiro, Samuel. "The Rendition of Anthony Burns," *Journal of Negro History* 44 (1959): 33–51.

Shepherd, Jack. *The Adams Chronicles: Four Generations of Greatness*. Boston, 1975.

Silbey, Joel. *A Respectable Minority: The Democratic Party in the Civil War Era*. New York, 1977.

Snow, Edward Rowe. *The Islands of Boston Harbor, 1639–1971*. New York, 1936, 1971.

Solomon, Barbara. *Ancestors and Immigrants: A Changing New England Tradition*. Chicago, 1957.

Stampp, Kenneth. *And the War Came*. Baton Rouge, La., 1950.

Stanard, Mary N. *Richmond: Its People and Its Story*. Philadelphia, 1923.

Stapp, Carol Buchalter. *Afro-Americans in Antebellum Boston: An Analysis of Probate Records*. New York, 1993.

Sterling, Dorothy. *Ahead of Her Time: Abby Kelley and the Politics of Antislavery*. New York, 1992.

Stevens, Hazard. "Military Operations in South Carolina in 1862," *Military Historical Society of Massachusetts Papers* 9 (1912): 142–227.

Strode, Hudson. *Jefferson Davis: American Patriot*. New York, 1955.

Sumner, Charles. *Charles Sumner: His Complete Works*, 20 vols. Boston, 1900.

Thayer, Eli. *A History of the Kansas Crusade*. New York, 1889.

Thompson, W. Fletcher, Jr. *The Image of War: Pictorial Reporting of the American Civil War*. New York, 1959.

Thoreau, Henry David. *Writings*, 20 vols. Boston, 1906.

Tiffany, Frances. *The Life of Dorothea Dix*. Boston, 1891.

Toomey, John, and Edward Rankin. *History of South Boston*. Boston, 1901.

Trefousse, Hans. *The Radical Republicans: Lincoln's Vanguard for Racial Justice*. New York, 1969.

Van Vleck, George. *The Panic of 1857*. New York, 1943.

Walsh, Francis R., *The Boston Pilot: A Newspaper for the Irish Immigrant*. Ann Arbor, Mich., 1969.

———. "The *Boston Pilot* Reports the Civil War," *Historical Journal of Massachusetts* 9 (Winter 1981): 5–16.

————. "Who Spoke for Boston's Irish?" *Journal of Ethnic Studies* 10 (1982): 21–36.

Ware, Edith. *Political Opinion in Massachusetts during the Civil War and Reconstruction.* New York, 1916.

Warner, John D., Jr. "Crossed Sabres: A History of the 5th Massachusetts Volunteer Cavalry Regiment." Ph.D. diss., Boston College, 1997.

Webster, Daniel. *Writings and Speeches of Daniel Webster.* 18 vols. Ed. Fletcher Webster. National Edition, 1903.

Weinstein, Irving. *July 1863: The Incredible Story of the Bloody New York Draft Riots.* New York, 1952.

Welter, Barbara. "The Cult of True Womanhood, 1820–1860," *American Quarterly* 18 (Summer 1966): 151–175.

————. "The Feminization of American Religion, 1800–1860," in *Clio's Consciousness Raised,* ed. Mary Hartman and Lois Banner. New York, 1974.

West, Richard S., Jr. *Lincoln's Scapegoat General: A Life of Benjamin F. Butler, 1818–1893.* Cambridge, Mass., 1965.

————. *Mr. Lincoln's Navy.* New York, 1957.

Whitehill, Walter Muir. *Boston: A Topographical History,* 2nd ed. Cambridge, Mass., 1982.

Whittier, John Greenleaf. *Complete Poems.* Boston, 1892.

Wiley, Bell I. *The Life of Billy Yank: The Common Soldier of the Union.* Indianapolis, 1952.

Williams, T. Harry. *Lincoln and the Radicals.* Madison, Wis., 1965.

————. *Lincoln Finds His General.* New York, 1952.

Winthrop, Robert C., Jr. *A Memoir of Robert C. Winthrop.* Boston, 1897.

Woloch, Nancy. *Women and the American Experience,* 2nd ed. New York, 1994.

Wood, Ann Douglas, "The War within a War: Women Nurses in the Union Army," *Civil War History* 18 (1972): 196–197.

Woodson, Carter G. *The Education of the Negro Prior to 1861.* New York, 1915.

Woolfolk, George T. *The Cotton Regency.* New York, 1958.

Wright, Conrad Edick, and Katheryn P. Viens, eds. *Entrepreneurs: The Boston Business Community, 1700–1850.* Boston, 1997.

Yee, Shirley. *Black Women Abolitionists: A Study in Activism, 1820–1860.* Knoxville, Tenn., 1992.

Yellin, Jean F. *Women and Sisters: Antislavery Feminists in American Culture.* New Haven, Conn., 1990.

Yorke, Dane. *The Men and Times of Pepperell.* Boston, 1945.

Zornow, William F. *Lincoln and the Party Divided.* Norman, Okla., 1954.

Index

~ ~ ~ ~ ~ ~ ~

Manley, John, 18
Mann, Horace, 6, 247
Manning, Jacob, 114
Marblehead, Massachusetts, 158
Marlboro, Massachusetts, 165
Martin, John Sella, 35, 36, 42, 43
Martineau, Harriet, 244, 247, 249
Marye's Heights, 120
Maryland, 64, 80, 86, 92
Mason, James M., 38, 39
Mason-Dixon Line, 33
Massachusetts, Cavalry Regiments: 1st,
 186; 2nd, 134; 5th, 273n38
Massachusetts, Infantry Regiments: 1st,
 67, 70, 104; 2nd, 67, 69, 91, 104,
 105, 129, 159; 3rd, 58; 4th, 58, 63,
 70; 5th, 63, 70, 185; 6th, 58, 59, 60,
 63, 72, 144, 185, 230; 7th, 67, 92;
 8th, 58, 60, 63, 72, 185; 9th (Irish),
 67, 78, 100, 164, 237, 239–240,
 269n24; 10th, 67; 11th, 67, 68, 70,
 104, 164; 12th, 64, 68, 104; 13th, 68,
 106; 14th, 68, 148; 15th, 68, 82, 104,
 203; 16th, 68, 104; 17th, 68; 18th,
 68; 19th, 68, 104, 119–120, 203;
 20th, 68, 82, 103, 104, 106, 119,
 120, 203; 21st, 68; 26th, 88; 28th
 (Irish), 77, 120, 126, 136, 150, 203,
 237; 30th, 88, 214; 31st, 88; 33rd,
 159; 39th, 203; 42nd, 185; 45th, 126;
 54th (black), 129–134, 185, 222, 234;
 55th (black), 130–134, 185, 223, 234;
 60th, 185
Massachusetts Anti-Slavery Society, 20–
 21, 45–46, 219
Massachusetts General Colored Association, 16, 19
Massachusetts General Court, 21, 65,
 118, 157
Massachusetts General Hospital, 66,
 247
Massachusetts Homeopathic Medical Society, 66–67

Massachusetts House of Representa-
 tives, 8, 241–242
Massachusetts Institute of Technology,
 173
Massachusetts School Fund, 172
Massachusetts Soldiers' Fund, 54
Massachusetts Supreme Judicial Court,
 21, 24, 241
Massasoit Guards, 31
Meade, George G., 138, 150, 157, 191,
 192, 193, 199, 202
Meagher, Thomas, 77–78, 120, 122
Medical conditions, wartime, 66–67
Melodeon, 219
Melrose, Massachusetts, 165
Memorial Hall, Boston, 231
Merchants' Exchange, 200, 226
Merrimac, the, 84
Merrimack River, 10, 160, 162, 163
Metropolitan Horse Railroad, 4, 169,
 208
Middlesex Mills, 97
Military Department of New
 England, 88
Militia, Massachusetts, 48, 57
"Mill Girls" of Lowell, 166
Millinery trade, 164, 249–250
Missionary Ridge, Tennessee, 157, 184
Mississippi River, 83, 97, 113, 151, 155
Missouri Compromise. *See* Compromise
 of 1820
Mitchel, William, 77
Mobile, Alabama, 98, 212
Mobile Bay, battle of, 215
Monitor, the, 84, 160, 163
Monitors, building of, 84, 159
Monroe, Timothy, 58
Monroe Doctrine, 90
Monteith, William, 77
Montgomery Guards, 76
Mooney's Juvenile Drum Corps, 74
Morison, Samuel Eliot, 85
Morrill Land Grant Act (1862), 172